Macao and Sino–U.S. Relations

Macao and Sino–U.S. Relations

Edited by
Yufan Hao and Jianwei Wang

LEXINGTON BOOKS
A division of
ROWMAN & LITTLEFIELD PUBLISHERS, INC.
Lanham • Boulder • New York • Toronto • Plymouth, UK

Published by Lexington Books
A division of Rowman & Littlefield Publishers, Inc.
A wholly owned subsidiary of The Rowman & Littlefield Publishing Group, Inc.
4501 Forbes Boulevard, Suite 200, Lanham, Maryland 20706
http://www.lexingtonbooks.com

Estover Road, Plymouth PL6 7PY, United Kingdom

British Library Cataloguing in Publication Information Available

Library of Congress Cataloging-in-Publication Data

Macao and Sino-U.S. relations / edited by Yufan Hao and Jianwei Wang.
p. cm.
Includes bibliographical references and index.
ISBN 978-0-7391-4367-4 (cloth : alk. paper)—ISBN 978-0-7391-4369-8 (electronic)
1. Macao (China)—Economic conditions. 2. United States—Foreign economic relations—China. 3. China—Foreign economic relations—United States. 4. United States—Foreign relations—China. 5. China—Foreign relations—United States.
I. Hao, Yufan. II. Wang, Jianwei, 1954-
HC428.M25M33 2011
337.73051—dc22 2010022268

∞™ The paper used in this publication meets the minimum requirements of American National Standard for Information Sciences—Permanence of Paper for Printed Library Materials, ANSI/NISO Z39.48-1992. Printed in the United States of America

Contents

Introduction

Yufan Hao and Jianwei Wang

Situated at the corner of Southeast China with an area of 28.2 km^2, Macao is a small enclave that seems far away from the world stage of diplomacy. However, in history, Macao was used by Westerners as a major entrance to China and served as a major linkage between China and the outside world. As early as just a few months after the Treaty of Paris in 1784, an American sailing ship named the Empress of China set out from New York for Macao. In August, the ship arrived at Macao, and traded wild ginseng root for tea, cotton cloth, silk, tableware, and spice. The successful trade soon led to a flourishing trade after the Chinese Empress return to New York the next year. In 1844, the first Sino–U.S. treaty was signed at Kun Iam Temple in Wangxia, a village of Macao, on a desk that still exists there now, by the Minister Plenipotentiary of America Caleb Cushing and the Governor General of Guangdong and Guangxi of the Qing Court Qiying, which marked the beginning of diplomatic relations between the two countries. Then Macao, as the sole European settlement on China, had functioned as a nexus between the old empire and the new power across the greatest ocean in the world until Hong Kong was opened as a commercial port under British rule. Thereafter Macao almost had no role to play in Chinese foreign policy, not to mention its relations with the United States, under the Portuguese rule in most of the twentieth century.

That situation, however, has significantly changed since Macao's handover to China in 1999. Macao's international status has visibly risen. With more than sixty countries established consular services in Macao and nearly forty consulates-general accredited to Hong Kong also covering Macao, it maintains extensive relations with various countries and regions in the world. The Macao SAR has signed agreements of visa privileges with seventy-eight countries. It has joined thirteen important intergovernmental international organizations as separate members under the name of "Macao, China" including World Trade Organization, UNESCO, and the World Tourism Organization. Under the same official name Macao has attended more than 400 international conferences. Macao hosted a series of major international events such as the ministerial roundtable of the World Tourism Organization, East Asian Games, Global Consultations Regional Meeting for Asia and the Pacific on International Protection for Refugees, and the Forum for Economic and Trade Cooperation between China and Portuguese-Speaking Countries. International organizations also began to set their headquarters or secretariats in Macao. More than 200 international conventions and treaties apply to Macao.[1] As a result of all these activities and participations, this unique cosmopolitan city has attracted increasing international attention in recent years in its rapid ascendance in the region as well as the world.

Macao's enhanced international profile has been brought about by many factors. First and foremost, Macao has witnessed a spectacular economic development, with its GDP per capita exceeding its neighbor counterpart of Hong Kong in 2006 for the first time in history. The rapid economic growth has enhanced Macao's reputation in East Asia. With its economy further opening to the world market and competition, Macao has become an integral part of the process of globalization and its consequent interdependence and is subject to all its benefits and challenges. Second, as the second SAR (special administrative region) after Hong Kong, Macao is ruled under the formula of "one country, two systems." Under such a system, Macao makes its own policies in regard to its political, economic, and cultural affairs. It also gives it more flexibility and leeway in formulating its economic and functional relations with other countries and regions. Externally Macao can do things other local governments in China or even Hong Kong cannot do. More specifically, Macao began to show its more important role in China–U.S. relations whose agenda has been constantly expending to include more and more low politics and non-traditional security issues.

The Development of China–U.S. Relations Since the George W. Bush Administration

After Macao's return to China in 1999, Sino–American relations have experienced many twists and turns. At the beginning of his administration,

President George W. Bush criticized the Clinton administration for seeking a "strategic partnership" with China. He viewed China instead as a "strategic competitor." In the first year of his term, he even pushed for redefining the relationship in more confrontational terms. The midair collision of a PLA aircraft and a U.S. EP-3 in April 2001 plunged the bilateral relations into crisis and, together with Bush's pro-Taiwan position, chilled bilateral relations. The relations were only stabilized after the 9/11 terrorist attack of 2001, when suddenly Islamic terrorism became the clear and present danger to America. Sino–American relations witnessed a steady improvement since then, although people in both countries remain concerned that the bilateral relations are still on a fragile foundation, as Harry Harding characterized it in the early 1990s.[2]

Yet, after months of costly fumbling, President Bush finally decided to return to the path charted by his predecessors since Nixon, adopted an engaging policy toward China. The deterministic phrase of defining China as "strategic competitor" was abandoned. As Colin Powell, then secretary of state, stated in *Foreign Affairs* in 2004, "Neither we nor the Chinese leadership believe that there is anything inevitable about our relationship—either inevitably bad or inevitably good."[3] The administration adopted a new framework in September 2005, calling China to become a "responsible stakeholder" in international affairs and pledged cooperation toward that end.[4] This policy articulated by then Deputy Secretary of State Robert Zoellick rejected the idea that China should be contained or that China constitutes an inevitable threat posing to the international system. After this policy change, Sino–American relations have remained stable with most issues managed reasonably well and in low profile. Today, although more and more criticism has been heard in America about George Bush's handling of his foreign policy, particularly his policy toward Iraq and Iran, many people view the improvement of Sino–American relations as one of the major diplomatic achievements of the Bush administration.

In this context, the financial turmoil bursting out at the end of 2008 further highlighted the interdependence of the Chinese and American economies as well as China's increasing weight in international affairs, thus the indispensability of China–U.S. cooperation. That reality underlies the Obama administration's determination to avoid a rough start of the relationship after President Obama took office in early 2009. The new policy framework of Obama's administration toward China—"strategic reassurance" articulated by Deputy Secretary of State James Steinberg[5]—also reflects the considerations of Washington in this regard. Behind the new policy framework are still the speculations of Americans on how to respond to a rising China. Although Steinberg says that the United States is eager to continue to work with China to address a variety of global and regional issues, he points out that China's size and importance create "risk of competition and rivalry that can thwart" China–U.S. cooperation. Therefore he advocates that while the two countries should reach a "strategic reassurance" in which the United States and the West are prepared to welcome China's arrival as a prosperous and successful power, China should also reassure the world that its development and growing role will not come at the expense of security and well-being of others. The spirit of this so-called strategic reassurance is reflected in the China–U.S. joint statement issued after President Obama's first visit to China in November 2009.[6]

Within the span of a single generation, China has moved from near isolation to a hub of globalized economy, from an obsolete and bloated military to a much more professional force possessing a certain degree of high-tech excellence, and from hostility to global institutions to active participation in multilateral organizations. While China has become the fastest-growing economy of the world, its diplomacy has also become increasingly sophisticated, expanding its influence both within Asia and in other regions of the world. All this has aroused much concern in the United States and has led many to wonder what kind of international behavior an increasingly powerful China may have in the foreseeable future. Will growing power eventually lead Chinese leadership to challenge the existing international norms, rules, and institutions led by the United States? Or will China's integration with the international economy, its growing middle class, and its increasing participation in international institutions lead to a continuing "status quo" power as China currently appears to be? How should the United States and the world respond to this newly emerged great power? It seems America has started another national debate over China just as it had sixty years ago over Russia at the end of World War II.

Currently there are two views dominating the debates over the subject in the United States. Conservatives with a realist's understanding of international relations believe that China will become assertive and expansive, and may eventually dominate and dictate to the region. Those power theorists focus on China's power and see the need to contain a rising China because they believe that China's desire to alter the rules of the game will grow as China's capabilities increase. Others see China's reform and growing economic integration with the world will make China more open and pluralistic, which may lead to its more predictable and benign international behavior. This view sees the importance of China's growing interdependence with the rest of the world and argues for engaging China further. In fact, there is an increasingly popular belief among observers of China that growing economic interdependence may gradually create a context, both on international and domestic levels, within which constraints will be placed on Chinese foreign behavior and make it more cooperative and less destabilizing. Both views reveal a deep concern about the future role of Chinese foreign policy in world affairs and Chinese policy toward the United States. In this sense, "strategic reassurance" of Obama's administration undoubtedly represents the second kind of view which tries to tie the two countries together with their increasing common interests. In fact, both the common interests and mistrust are in increase between the two countries within either the high politics and traditional security fields or the low politics and non-traditional security ones. The recent issues in bilateral relations can be summarized as follows.

The Taiwan Issue

The Taiwan issue has been the most disputed and disruptive issue in Sino–U.S. relations ever since 1979. Yet the issue seemed to become manageable in George W. Bush's term. After the enactment of the Anti-Secession Law in Beijing in 2005, America has been well aware of the China's bottom line over the issue, and has joined China in maintaining status quo in the Taiwan Straits. With U.S. assistance in this respect, Beijing uses less rhetoric and over-reacts less than before to the irritants initiated by the Taiwanese leaders. Beijing leaders seem to believe that the United States indeed does not support the de jure independence of Taiwan, even though they remain suspicious about the U.S. intention and unhappy over times about Washington providing sophisticated arms to Taiwan. At the end of 2007, the United States publicly opposed Taiwan's "UN Membership Referendum" promoted by the Democratic Progressive Party. The U.S. policy gained positive response from the Chinese government contributing to the stability in the region. However, the Bush administration later approved $6.5 billion in arm sales to Taiwan, which aroused China's fierce criticism and protest. On the other hand, the power handover in Taiwan from DPP to KMT in 2008 and the improvement of the cross-strait relation were beneficial for keeping a relatively harmonious relation between China and the United States. The significant improvement in cross-strait relations after Ma Ying-jeou came to power in May 2008 has largely removed Taiwan as a contentious issue in Sino–American relations. The decision by the Obama administration to sell another package of $6.4 billion of arms to Taiwan in January 2010 rekindled the tension between the two countries on this historical issue.

Economic Issues

China and the United States have become economically interdependent to each other. The overall trade between the two countries was $409.25 billion in 2008, an increase of 5.8 percent compared to the previous year. U.S. exports to China were $71.46 billion, an increase of 9.5 percent; and imports from China were $337.79 billion, an increase of 5.1 percent. As a result, the trade deficit suffered by the United States was $266.33 billion, an increase of 4.0 percent, which has become a major concern in Washington. China is the second trade partner, third export destination, and first import origin for the United States. In 2008, the foreign direct investment from the United States to China was $2.944 billion, and the outward foreign direct investment from China to the United States $0.462 billion.[7]

Meanwhile, the close economic ties did not prevent trade wars between the two countries. From 1995 to 2008, the United States initiated anti-dumping against China in the WTO regime eighty-seven times, and China initiated twenty-two times against the United States. And the United States adopted anti-dumping actual measures against China sixty-six times, and China adopted sixteen times against the United States. During the same era, the United States complained against China in the WTO regime for eight cases, while China complained against the United States for four cases.[8]

In this context, from the end of 2006 to December 2008, China and the United States held five biannual Strategic Economic Dialogues. The discussions on the dialogues included macroeconomic cooperation and financial services, cooperation on energy and environment, trade and investment, product quality and food safety, international economic cooperation, which led to a number of results in areas of strategic importance that strengthened and deepened the bilateral economic relationship.

Some special interest groups allege that China engages in unfair commercial practices such as policies affecting exchange rate level, intellectual property rights, subsidies, and accumulation of foreign exchanges reserves. Some believe that the U.S. trade sanctions against China are inevitable as the support is deep and bipartisan. Under the Obama administration, because of the protectionist instinct of the Democratic Party and domestic economic difficulties, trade and other economic frictions between the two countries have the tendency to intensify. Avoiding a trade war that will be damaging to both sides has become a constant task for the governments of both sides.

Changing Perception of China in America

People have long realized the significance of perceptions in the U.S.–China relations as the source of this fragility, and the study of mutual perceptions has achieved a prominent place in the scholarly literature on Sino–American relations.[9] Indeed, what is perceived, though not necessarily a reflection of reality, has important impacts in determining a particular policy action. It is widely believed that the United States and China held ambivalent and contradictory mutual perceptions, and these perceptions, along with numerous stereotypes, have contributed considerably to the volatility of Sino–American relations for the last 100 years. However, some recent public opinion surveys seems to suggest that there has been a notable shift in Sino–American imagery in recent years toward the hardening of negative and demonized images. Due to this shift, a rise of anti-American nationalism in China and anti-Chinese sentiments in America has become noticeable.

Despite the terrorist attacks that occurred in America on September 11, 2001, China is still hesitant to trust America regarding its intentions toward China. While some Chinese saw 9/11 as an opportunity for the two countries to build trust, many Chinese remained suspicious that the United States would continue its pursuit of world domination, under the new flag of anti-terrorism and to contain China. A report[10] in 2008 by the Pew Global Attitudes Project released that 48 percent of Chinese hold an unfavorable view of the United States, while 41 percent view America favorably. At the same time, 42 percent of Americans hold an unfavorable view of China, while 39 percent view China favorably, and 62 percent of Americans see China as neither partner nor enemy.

Although 47 percent of Chinese in the Pew Global Report viewed the United States favorably, the Chicago Council on Foreign Relations found that a large majority of Americans (75 percent) see a significant increase in China's military might as "mainly negative." In 2006, a total of 53.4 percent of U.S. residents taking part in a Zogby interactive poll said China represents a competitor to the United States while 38.2 percent say the country is a threat. Only 2.9 percent said China is a partner with the United States, a figure less than the 5.5 percent who gave "not sure" as their answer in 2007.

Fifty-three percent of the Chinese believe China will someday replace the United States as the world's leading superpower, while 54 percent of Americans doubt that. Eighty-two percent of Americans consider China's growing military power as a bad thing, and 53 percent even say China's growing economy is a bad thing.

According to the Chicago Council on Global Affairs,[11] Americans tend to believe that China will catch up with the United States economically, but they are unconcerned about this even though most do not trust China to act responsibly in the world. The Chinese public rejects the idea that the United States should continue to be the preeminent world leader but few want the United States to disengage from world affairs. Most would like the United States to reduce its overseas military presence. In 2007, 75 percent of U.S.

residents taking part in a Zogby interactive poll[12] said China is the top U.S. economic rival, and 71 percent said they are concerned about China's increased consumption of fossil fuels and other non-renewable energy.

More interesting, a survey conducted in September 2007 by the Zogby Poll shows that 61 percent of American respondents believe the U.S. government should support Taiwan's petition to gain membership in the international body just as it did for Kosovo. This is in sharp contrast with the Chinese perception on American policy toward Taiwan. The Bush and Obama administrations' decisions to sell arms to Taiwan have caused very negative reactions among the Chinese public in general and Chinese netizens in particular.

The Special Role of Macao in the China–U.S. Relationship

All these major issues in Sino–American relations discussed earlier have significance and implications for Macao. In addition, although the traditional security issues remain salient between the two countries, China–U.S. relations are increasingly occupied and shadowed by non-traditional security and low politics issues such as financial stability, international terrorism, climate change, and transnational crimes. In both traditional and non-traditional and high-political and low-political issues, Macao plays a special role in the China–U.S. relationship.

First, American economic and other influences have entered Macao in a swift pace unimagined only a decade ago after Macao's handover. In 2002, the Macao SAR government ended the local monopoly on the casino business. As a result, American capital (Wynn Resorts, Las Vegas Sands) entered the Macao gambling industry rapidly, starting a new page in Macao–American relations. Since the gambling industry plays a pivotal role in Macao's economy, the increase of American influence in Macao has impact not just on Macao's well-being, but also on its relations with the central Chinese government. With fast inflow of American money also came American ideas, values, cultures, and ways of life and doing things, as well as new problems facing the Macao society.

Second, with Macao's further exposure to international economics and politics, its function in other salient international issues that might affect U.S–China relations such as anti-terrorism, nuclear non-proliferation, drug-trafficking, and money laundering has also caught headlines in rent years. The Bank of Delta Asia incident involving North Korea is a typical example in this regard.

Third, Macao's unique role in solving another key issue affecting China–U.S relations—Taiwan—is also worth mentioning. Since the handover,

Macao managed to take a more pragmatic and flexible approach to deal with sensitive cross-strait relations. Very often Macao served as a good office for officials and semi-officials from both sides of the Taiwan Strait to meet and discuss issues of common concerns. The so-called Macao model became the synonym of goodwill and reconciliation across the Taiwan Strait.

In this sense, the academic and policy significance of this book is multifold. First of all, the traditional study of Sino–American relations has almost exclusively focused on the relationships between the two central governments: how Washington and Beijing react to each other. The relationship has seldom been looked upon from a local perspective. Yet with the intensification of economic globalization and overall decentralization of Chinese foreign policymaking, the dynamics of Sino–U.S. relations cannot be fully understood just from the two capitals. Localities could be important new variables in explaining this pivotal relationship.

Also, from the vantage point of Macao studies, there have been numerous studies on Macao's economic, social, and political development as well as its relationship with Europe, particularly with Portuguese-speaking countries. But there are very few studies about Macao's relations with other major countries in the world. As discussed above, under new circumstances, major powers, particularly the United States, have increased their presence and influence in Macao. But very few systematic studies of Macao's non-European major power relations have been done. This book will fill the gap in a timely fashion.

Finally, this book can also make academic contributions to China study in general. China's "one country, two system" formula to govern Hong Kong and Macao after handover has been carefully scrutinized by Western scholars. However, most studies focus on the implication of this formula on domestic politics within Hong Kong and Macao and their respective relations with the central government. Its impact on Hong Kong and Macao's external relations has not been fully investigated. As Macao's external relations is becoming complex and multifaceted, especially with the United States and other regional players, the subject deserves more thorough and in-depth research and analysis. This book is one big step toward that direction.

Book Content

This book is based on an international conference on "Macao and Sino–U.S. Relations" held at the University of Macao during December 13–15, 2007. Many well-known American and Chinese scholars and researchers on U.S.–China relations attended the conference and participated in the project.

Most of them presented papers which analyzed various aspects of Macao's relations and ties with the United States. After the conference, the editors went through all the papers and selected a group of them pertinent to the book theme for further revision and resubmission.

The book is divided into five parts. The first part gives an overview of Sino–American relations in general. A number of American and Chinese veteran scholars of this relationship have offered their insights. Harry Harding, a leading China scholar in the United State and the author of *A Fragile Relationship*, offered some reevaluation of his two main conclusions in his 1992 book: the U.S–China relationship was "fragile," and the two countries were "neither friends nor foes." He seems to be dissatisfied with both characterizations. After seventeen years of the publication of his book, he finds that the relationship has become far less fragile and far more resilient due to the significant increase of mutual interdependence, sustainable policies, and concern with other more immediate issues. Although the American public still sees China as neither friend nor foe, he would rather see China as both a challenge and an opportunity. According to him, the two countries more likely tend to become "economic competitors, but strategic partners" with an ever-increasing breadth of the relationship.

Zhang Shuguang, a historian by training, looks at the current U.S.–China relationship from the historical experience of the Cold War. The broad theme of his chapter is whether the two countries can avert another Cold War. He argued that both sides learned some bitter lessons from the Cold War period. There is a consensus on the Chinese side that China can no longer afford another Cold War with the United States largely because of its irreversible course of economic modernization and integration into the world system. Just like Harding, Zhang also emphasizes the importance of China's ever-increasing economic interdependence, political, military, social, and cultural contact and exchanges with the United States in maintaining U.S.–China cooperation instead of confrontation. Nevertheless he argues that the relationship is still facing serious challenges, including China's rapid rise, ideological and value differences, and international crises. If not managed well, a Cold War–style confrontation between the two giants is still possible. Thus, according to him, the jury is still out.

Relatively speaking, Ding Xinghao, a veteran observer of China–U.S. relations for decades, sounds more optimistic in his assessment of the relationship. His chapter focuses on the impact of economic globalization on Sino–American relations. According to him, economic globalization has been transforming the ties between the two countries, and they are economically so interdependent that differences between them can only be resolved by dialogues, not conflicts. According to him, the 9/11 terrorist attack, a tragic event resulting from globalization, fundamentally changed the strategic environment under which the two countries interact with each other. The United States started changing its views of major power relations and developing a new conceptual framework for China and U.S.–China relations. The global financial crisis, another landmark event related to globalization, has been changing the balance of power and influence between the United States and China as well as other emerging new powers. U.S. power and influence has declined and it needs more help from countries like China in managing world problems. As a reflection of this important change, the new Obama administration began to talk about "partnership" more than "leadership" in dealing with other power centers in the world. That also led President Obama's "new thinking" on American policy toward China. Ding concludes that the Obama administration has decisively shifted the U.S. policy from containment to engagement although the idea of hedging has yet to be abandoned. It is time for the two countries to further build strategic mutual trust to avoid the mentality of zero-sum game in their relations.

The second part of the book is devoted to Macao–U.S. relations in general from both historical and current perspectives. Paul Van Dyke provides a very interesting narrative of Macao's role in Sino–American relations prior to the signing of the Wanghsia Treaty in 1844, which is not well-known to people. Starting from the late seventeenth and early eighteenth centuries, Macao began to play an important role in China's trade with Western countries through Canton. The successful voyage of the *Empress of China* in 1784 indicated that the United States joined other Western powers to conduct trade with China and to explore the Chinese market. Since then U.S.–China trade expanded rapidly. Just like other Westerners, the United States was involved in both legal and illegal trade with China. Van Dyke's fascinating description indicates that Macao's role in Sino–American relations is more complicated than previously thought. He introduced one seldom told part of the story that involved Hawaii. Hawaii was gradually pulled into the international trading networks involving Americans who were heading to China to do business. Hawaii established substantial trade and human relations with Macao and Canton. Both Macao and Hawaii became bases for American missionaries. Hawaii was drawn closer to events in Macao when more American missionaries and traders went to Macao and China. Those American missionaries won good reputations for their medical and educational work in Macao and Canton. Overall in the late eighteenth and early nineteenth centuries, Macao was the gateway for all Americans going to China to trade and became the center for agents to arrange American trade with China. And both Macao and Hawaii were pulled into larger Sino–American relations.

Liu Bolong's chapter, on the other hand, focuses on the development of Macao–U.S. relations after Macao's handover to China in 1999. Overall the American influence in Macao has significantly increased in recent years, not just economically, but also culturally. With the opening of the gambling franchise, foreign investment has poured into Macao with the bulk from the United States. Most American gaming companies have been doing very well in Macao irrespective of the short-term setbacks of the world financial tsunami. The United States remains the most important trade partner to Macao. Besides increasing economic presence, the American government has also promoted cultural and academic exchanges with Macao with a growing number of American musicians, artists, athletes, professionals, and students coming to Macao to visit or reside. The author largely takes the increasing American influence and interest as positive and welcoming. He argues that the United States could help Macao to modernize in many ways such improving its gambling regulations and management, fighting corruptions and even building a civil society and making progress in democratization. On the other hand, he also recognizes the inflow of American capital and influences did cause some debates and controversies among the local population regarding foreign competition and intervention. Therefore he suggests that the American government and companies should do more to promote mutual understanding and to improve their images in Macao.

Indeed Chinese images of the United States in Macao are the subject of C. X. George Wei's chapter. He discusses American images in Macao from three vantage points: Chinese images of early Americans who arrived in Macao in the late eighteenth and early nineteenth centuries, the images of Americans and America of Chinese reformers and revolutionaries in Macao, and the image of Americans in modern Macao. According to Wei, the perceptions of Americans and the United States among the Chinese in Macao are mostly positive at most times. The early Americans, particularly those American missionaries, left good impressions on those Chinese who had contact with them. Americans were perceived as more honest and trustful than other Westerners. Even some Chinese government officials such as Lin Zexu and Chi Ying obtained favorable perceptions of American missionaries largely because of their medical achievements. Famous Chinese reformers and revolutionaries from Macao such as Yung Wing and Sun Yatsen all had highly positive and admiring views of Americans as people and the United States as a democratic, powerful, and prosperous country. The United States became a source of their inspiration and progressive ideas.

Macao's image of the United States has remained positive since World War II. People's interests in things American soared after the establishment of China–U.S. diplomatic relations in 1979. Many believe that the U.S. legislations and policies on Macao, as well as American business presence in Macao, helped elevate Macao's international status and brought economic benefits to the enclave. Nevertheless not all is positive about the United States. People in Macao had a very negative view about the American war in Iraq. They also worried about the possible negative political, economic, and cultural ramifications of some American foreign policies and American business operations in Macao.

The four chapters in part II focus on the most important aspect of Macao's ties with the United States—economic relations. Zhang Lili gives an overview of Macao's role in Sino–U.S. economic and trade relationship. He argues that because Macao's unique geographical location, special historical background, high degree of autonomy in running its capitalist economy with free port and separate custom, Macao possesses a special status in Sino–U.S. economic and trade relations. With the rapid development of China in recent decades, foreign economic and trade relations have become more and more important for China. As the biggest economy in the world, the United States is one of the most important trading partners of China. Macao has benefited greatly from the overall robust U.S.–China economic and trade relations. After the turnover, with support of the central government, the Macao SAR government has improved its investment climate in key areas. The decision to open the lottery industry to foreign investment in 2002 proved to be a crucial step to dramatically enhance Macao's economic relations with the United States. Macao has quickly become the largest direct investment location in China for American capital, especially in the gambling and entertainment industries. It also serves as a hinge point in promoting U.S. trade with the Pearl River Delta in China. Moreover, Zhang asserts that Macao also plays a role as a showing window of China's peaceful development, facilitating the enhancement of trust and reduction of misgivings between China and the United States.

Following this general survey, T. J. Cheng and Sixin Sheng's and Wuyi Wang's chapters concentrate or the key component of Macao's economy: the gambling industry, which has the largest U.S. imprint. Cheng and Sheng's chapter presents a detailed analysis of Macao's gambling industry with a special reference to American investment. The authors first give a general picture of Macao's gambling industry, especially after the gambling market was open for international competition in 2002. The liberalization of the gambling industry and U.S. investments played crucial roles in Macao's soaring economic growth. They define the past decade as the golden age of Macao's economy with the gambling industry as the largest contributor, which in turn largely benefited from U.S. investment. The introduction of American competition has not only improved the service quality of the local gaming business, but also exerted a positive influence over Macao's tourism industry. However the gambling industry, as the pillar of Macao's economy, is also facing a series of challenges and problems. First, the industry was hit hard by the global financial crisis. Second, the American investment in Macao tends to be controversial: some perceive it as a savior and others a threat. People debated about the political motivations and implications of American economic activities in Macao. Third the author questioned the long-term sustainability of the economic model that overly relies on the gambling industry, particularly on Chinese VIP gamblers. Finally, Cheng and Sheng made some policy recommendations to address these issues.

This line of making policy suggestions to improve Macao's gaming industry is followed by Wuyi Wang's chapter. He points out that after initial success of the gambling liberalization which let to changes in market size, market structure, and casino operating patterns, Macao's casino regulation system seems to run into an "institutional bottle neck." According to him, gambling is a policy-driven industry and the government needs to take measures to standardize and modernize Macao's gaming regulation regimes. In this respect, he suggests that the Nevada model of casino regulations could be used in Macao to carry out these reforms. Among other things that Macao can learn from the Nevada model, he suggests that the regulations should change from a system of counting tax to reporting tax as the former is no long suitable because of the growing number of license holders, casinos, and game tables. The system of license issuing should be changed from one company, one license to one casino, one license because it is easier for the government to tax the licenses, to differentiate and discipline the responsible entity in terms of obligation, and for the regulator to deal with casino property transactions. Following the Nevada model, the licenses should not be issued to casino institutions, but to individuals who own and manage casinos and therefore subject these personnel for rigorous background checks and investigation, which is seldom done in Macao. Wang also proposes that Macao's gaming industry should be regulated by one single regulatory body instead of four separate ones. It could help information and responsibility sharing and facilitate communication, enhance specialization and professionalization, and unify prosecution and other judicial matters. Finally, the author also makes a case to regulate the junket rollers who recruit and usher VIP gamblers. He concludes that "the freer a is gaming market, the stricter it should be governed and regulated."

Part IV goes beyond the bilateral Macao–U.S. and China–U.S. relations to deal with some regional issues that nevertheless have important implications for Macao's role in a broadly defined U.S.–China relationship. Hou Ying's chapter includes a case study of Banco Delta Asia's involvement in North Korea's money-laundering business to demonstrate Macao's subtle role in critical regional issues that might affect Sino–American relations. She made a point that the role of Macao in Sino–U.S. relations did not seem significant until the BDA issue which put Macao under the world spotlight. BDA is a Chinese family-owned bank in Macao. In 2005, the U. S. Treasury Department designated BDA as a "primary money laundering concern" and described it a "willing pawn" of North Korea engaging in illicit activities, imposing financial sanctions against BDA. Under U.S. pressure the Macao monetary authority froze the $25 million related to North Korean accounts and suspended all commercial ties with North Korean companies. Eventually the United States agreed to release the funds for North Korea to return to the six-party talk. According to Hou, the interaction between China and the United States on the BDA affair reflects common, as well as divergent, interests on the North Korea issue between the two countries. The difference provides ground for Kim Jong Il to maneuver and gain. However the "one country, two systems" policy gives Beijing more flexibility in dealing with diplomatic issues taking place in Macao, minimizing some contradictions in various Chinese foreign policy objectives. The author concludes that the BDA case indicates that Macao can play a special role as an intermediate or buffer in China–U.S. relations.

Jianwei Wang's chapter deals with allegedly the most important and sensitive issue in U.S.–China relations—Taiwan. He attempts to identify conceptually and empirically some unique and even indispensible role Macao has played in cross-strait relations. Also comparing Macao with Hong Kong, he contends that unlike Hong Kong, which often ran into difficulties in its relations with Taiwan after the handover, Macao's function in cross-strait relations actually has been enhanced since 1999. Using phrases like "Macao connection," "Macao formula," "Macao model," and "Macao approach," the author has articulated and proved that this small and quiet enclave has provided a valuable channel of communication and negotiations between Beijing and Taipei, particularly when overall cross-strait relations were frozen because of political difficulties. Many factors contributed to Macao's instrumentality in cross-strait relations including its closer historical ties with Taiwan, less political sensitivity and world recognition compared to Hong Kong, both Beijing and Taipei's more flexible and tolerant attitudes toward Macao–Taiwan relations, and the Macao government's sensible and pragmatic approaches in dealing with Taiwan-related issues. As a result, the Macao government was able to achieve a smooth transition of its relations with Taiwan after the turnover, to solve a number of practical issues in the relationship, to maintain official relations with the Taiwan authorities, and to create a model for semi-official consultations and negotiations in managing cross-strait functional issues. Looking ahead, the author holds that although Macao is facing new challenges in its relations with Taiwan after overall cross-strait relations have significantly improved, thus reducing Macao's role as a "third place," Beijing still wants Macao to continue to serve useful and special functions in cross-strait relations in terms of pioneering and exploring new ways to move cross-strait relations to a higher level. In that sense, Macao can make positive contributions to overall U.S.–China relations.

Keelian Huang explores the future of Macao's gaming industry from a unique regional perspective. He defines gambling as an important part of Chinese social activities. He traces back the development of Macao's gaming institutions, the core of its economy, to the 1840s, taking three different formats over the years. Gaming became a means of survival after Hong Kong's rise as an alternative international platform in the 1840s. But it only became an "institutionalized industry" after the 1999 handover and under the practice of "one country, two systems." The MSAR Basic Law gave gambling legal and political endorsement. American gaming giants are the biggest beneficiary of the MSAR's new development strategy. The huge success of the paradigm shift in gaming industry was accompanied by scandals which caused some social instability. People also worried about possible U.S. domination of the gaming industry and consequent intervention in Macao's domestic affairs. Some even raised the possibility that Macao may become a center for the United States to build up a ring of commercial gambling hubs surrounding China. Huang suggested some measures to address and correct some of these apprehensions and negative fallouts of the booming gambling industry in Macao. He argues that Macao could draw experience from the Las Vegas model by diversifying and internationalizing its gambling industry and by moving away from the model of "gambling only" to that of "gambling plus." In an even broader sense, with Singapore's entry in the gaming industry in East Asia, Huang considers that the diversification and internationalization of Macao's gaming industry should bring Las Vegas and Sentosa into the operational scheme in which Macao can be a key player. He predicts that a ring of gaming hubs will emerge around mainland China. A Las Vegas–Macao–Sentosa triangle incorporated into the 10 + 1 and 10 + 3 FTA will be a promising paradigm not just for the United States, Macao, and Singapore, but also for other

East Asian countries. Such a tripartite complex, he argues, will also be conducive to the development of Sino–U.S. relations.

Iong Hoi Sun expands Macao's role in Chinese foreign policy even further. Her chapter discusses the function of Macao as a potential platform for China's relations with Portuguese-speaking countries (PSCs) in Africa and Latin America. In recent years, Chinese foreign policy has given more preferences to PSCs for economic, energy, diplomatic, and strategic reasons. Macao is in a special position to serve as a positive platform in China's new diplomatic initiatives with PSCs. Among other things, as a SAR, Macao has more freedom and favorable political conditions in interacting with PACs, such as visa-free entry to some PSCs. By the same token Macao has some advantages in trading with these countries such as the entreport of sea trade, low property and labor cost, and similar legal frameworks to the European market. Moreover, Macao has long-standing historical and cultural connection with the Portugal world, which will greatly facilitate its relations with PSCs. Finally, after Macao opened its gaming industry and attracted big U.S. investment, Macao's international profile has visibly increased, strengthening its potential to serve as a platform for convention and meeting opportunities. For these reasons, Macao can well serve as platforms for bilateral trade and economic cooperation with PSCs and for liaison and organization of international events. However, Sun also points out that to accomplish this mission, Macao still faces some challenges and constraints. For example, Macao lacks sufficient and high quality human resources particularly those who can speak both Chinese and Portuguese. The scale of the existing transportation network in Macao is still too small to meet the demand of future development, putting limitations to its logistic capacity. Another challenge for Macao to become a service platform is its small territory, which makes it unable to support large manufacturing companies to reduce the vulnerability of an economy too much dependent upon the gambling industry.

The last section intends to put Macao's role in U.S.–China relations into comparison with Hong Kong. Both of them are SARs which are supposed to enjoy high degree of autonomy in internal and, to a lesser degree, external affairs under the formula of "one country, two systems." Historically both Macao and Hong Kong played unique roles in China's relations with Western countries including the United States. Both of them are facing new opportunities and challenges in their relations with external major powers such as the United States in the post-colonial period.

Ming Chan did a lengthy and rich study of American relations with Macao and Hong Kong covering the 1840s to present, with emphasis on the post-1949 era. During the pre-1949 period, although Hong Kong was dominated by Great Britain, the United States gradually established its economic, cultural, and religious presence on the island. During the Cold War, with tacit British support, the United States utilized Hong Kong as a strategic asset in its containment of Communist China, turning the colony into an intelligence and subversion base against China, although the United States never committed itself to defending Hong Kong in face of possible Chinese military actions. Unlike Hong Kong, Macao, under Portuguese rule, drew very little U.S. interest. While Hong Kong suffered the brutal Japanese rule during World War II, Macao escaped the war as a neutral haven. Due to its far less strategic prominence, the United States did not spend much effort to cultivate Macao as an anti-China base during the Cold War. Although Portugal complied with the U.S.-led anti-PRC embargo, Macao thrived as a major hub for smuggling vital supplies to the mainland. American attention to both Hong Kong and Macao significantly increased before their handover back to China, as exemplified by the passages of the U.S.–Hong Kong Policy Act (USHKPA) and U.S.–Macao Policy Act (USMPA). But in comparison, Americans worried much more about Hong Kong's return, taking proactive measures to influence the political development there. In the post-1997 and 1999 period, America's economic and cultural ties with both Hong Kong and Macao intensified. However the exercise of its influence has taken different forms in these two cities. The United States replaced the United Kingdom to become the most important foreign power trying to influence the political process of democratization in Hong Kong with little success while the American economic clouts of gaming businesses, in Chan's opinion, have been literally transforming the Macao SAR, much more than in Hong Kong. In the final analysis, Chan argues that American relations with Hong Kong and Macao are still conditioned and constrained by the overall Sino–American relations, as illustrated by cases such as the Macao Banco Delta Asia and U.S. Navy visits to Hong Kong. Beijing constantly worries about the "political internationalization" of Hong Kong and "Havanization" of Macao. How much influence the United States can have in Hong Kong and Macao depends on whether Beijing perceives it as in its interest.

Hu Weixing's chapter largely compared Hong Kong and Macao's post-handover experience in both domestic and external development. He made the point that Hong Kong has never viewed Macao as a serious competitor in the region as well as in greater China. People in Hong Kong even look down upon Macao, considering it a backward and poorly governed place. Hong Kong always placed itself on a par with places like Singapore and Shanghai, not Macao, although they are close neighbors. The developments in Macao and Hong Kong since the handover, however, is shaking this traditional thinking regarding Macao as Hong Kong begins to feel the heat from this small city. In some aspects, Macao has outperformed Hong Kong. Among other things, Macao's post-colonial transformation has been more smooth than Hong Kong. Macao's economy has developed much faster than Hong Kong with its annual GDP growth rate and GDP per capital surpassing Hong Kong by big margins. The practice of "one country, two systems" also has turned out to be more successful in Macao with much less intervention from the central government. He analyzes various factors to explain Macao's and Hong Kong's different post-colonial experience including colonial legacy, political leadership, state-society relationship, and institutionalization. Regarding U.S policy toward Hong Kong and Macao, while its policy objectives toward the two SARs are more or less similar, Washington has much more substantial economic interest and stronger interests in promoting human rights and democratization in Hong Kong than in Macao. But interestingly the U.S. government tends to have more positive evaluation of the development in Macao than in Hong Kong.

Finally, Morton Holbrook presents an analysis of American perspective on Macao and Hong Kong. He starts with an observation that there is no single American perspective on the role Macao and Hong Kong play in U.S.–China relations. Rather the American government, U.S. business communities, and other Americans such as tourists, sports figures, and NGOs tend to have their own vantage point of evaluating Macao and Hong Kong. For the U.S. government, as a global power, Macao and Hong Kong do not have a high priority in the U.S. overall foreign policy. Its views on Macao and Hong Kong are most directly reflected by the U.S. Consulate General in Hong Kong, which also has jurisdiction over Macao as well as the State Department's annual reports on the two former colonies to the Congress. He characterized these perspectives as "measured praise and criticism." On the one hand, the U.S. government recognizes the success in implementing "one country, two systems" in both Macao and Hong Kong with rule of law, free market, human rights, and civil liberties largely guaranteed and respected. On the other hand, Washington is not satisfied with the degree of democracy and progress in democratization in the two SARs. For the American business community, it is generally upbeat about business conditions and environment in Hong Kong and Macao. Hong Kong has ranked number 1 on every index of economic freedom. Although U.S. business does have some complaints about Macao's regulatory system, it nevertheless continues to expand its investment there. The author, a former government official, also discusses his own views on Hong Kong and Macao. For him, although both cities are still unique, they are becoming more integrated, particularly economically, with the mainland. Overall he thinks the two SARS have been successful since the handover, in no small part owing to their own post-colonial leadership and China's realistic and practical approach. The political and economic support from the United States, in Holbrook's view, also played a positive role.

Acknowledgement

The editors of this book want to take this opportunity to express their heatfelt appreciation for Lexington Books for its valuable support for and confidence in this project. Editors Michael Sisskin, Lindsey Schauer, and Patricia Stevenson are highly professional and competent. They are a great pleasure to work with. It has been a long and assiduous process to put the manuscript together because of the various circumstances, but all the editors involved have shown great understanding and patience, for which we are very grateful. Without their hard work, the book could not have seen the light of day.

Notes

1. "Macao's participation in international conference and activities," Office of the Commissioner of the Ministry of Foreign Affairs of the People's Republic of China in the Macao Special Administrative Region," www.fmcoprc.gov.mo/eng/xnyfgk/t53574.htm; *Xinhua*, "Lu Shumin: Macao compatriots share the lofty international reputation of the great motherland," December 17, 2009.
2. Harry Harding, *A Fragile Relationship: the United States and China since 1972* (Brookings Institution Press, 1992).
3. Colin Powell, "A strategy of partnership," *Foreign Affairs*, January/February, 2004, pp. 22–34.
4. Robert Zoellick, "Whither China: from membership to responsibility," remarks to National Committee on U.S.–China Relations, September 21, 2005.
5. James Steinberg, "Obama administration's vision of the U.S.–China relationship," the Center for a New American Security, September 24, 2009
6. "U.S.–China Joint Statement," White House, November 17, 2009.
7. Ministry of Commerce of People's Republic of China: www.mofcom.gov.cn.
8. World Trade Organization: www.wto.com.
9. David Shambaugh, *Beautiful Imperialist: China Perceives America, 1972–1990* (Princeton, N.J.: Princeton University Press, 1991); Steven Mosher, *China Misperceived: American Illusions and Chinese Reality* (New York: Basic Books, 1990); Richard Madsen, *China and the American Dream* (Berkeley: University of California Press, 1994); Jianwei Wang, *Limited Adversaries: Post-Cold War Sino–American Mutual Images* (Oxford: Oxford University Press, 2000), to name a few.

10. Pew Global Attitudes Project: Global Economic Gloom—China and India Global Exceptions, June 2008.

11. The Chicago Council of Global Affairs: World Public Opinion 2007.

12. Zogby International: www.zogby.com.

PART I

U.S.–CHINA RELATIONS: PAST AND PRESENT

CHAPTER ONE

Do China and America Still Have a "Fragile Relationship?" Are They Still "Neither Friend nor Foe?"

Harry Harding

Back in 1992, when I was a senior fellow in the Foreign Policy Studies Program at the Brookings Institution, I published a book on U.S.–China relations that was titled *A Fragile Relationship: The United States and China Since 1972*.[1] The book attained some modest notoriety for two reasons: my characterization of the U.S.–China relationship as "fragile," and my forecast that the future relationship would be one in which the two countries were "neither friends nor foes."[2]

Over the eighteen years since that book appeared, I have often been asked whether I thought those two conclusions—that the Sino–American relationship was fragile, and that the relations between the two countries were unlikely to be either friendly or antagonistic—were still valid. From today's perspective, I believe that the second conclusion is still correct but incomplete, but that the first conclusion no longer holds. One reason for this change is that the U.S.–China relationship has also evolved along a third dimension: it is far more complex and comprehensive now than it was in 1992, when the historical narrative in *A Fragile Relationship* ended, let alone in 1972, when that narrative began.[3] Because of this, the relationship between the two countries contains even more elements of both cooperation and competition than it did in 1992, but it has become far less fragile and far more resilient.

A Fragile Relationship?

In retrospect, it was appropriate to have characterized the relationship between China and the United States between 1972 and 1992 as a fragile one.

When the rapprochement between the two countries began with the Nixon visit, the United States and China had virtually no ties between them: no diplomatic relations, virtually no trade, no investment, no tourists, no student exchanges. In fact, in the comparison made famous by the late Michel Oksenberg, before the U.S. ping-pong team visited China in 1971, more Americans had set foot on the moon than had visited the People's Republic of China with the consent of both governments.[4]

Although bilateral ties grew rapidly after the normalization of relations in 1978, the relationship remained fragile. The original strategic rationale for the rapprochement—the common threat posed by the Soviet Union—began to weaken, and then disappeared altogether along with the Soviet Union itself in 1991. Each country was disappointed by how the relationship had evolved from its Cold War origins: Americans were discouraged by slow progress on political reform; Chinese were dismayed by the refusal of the United States to abandon its commitments to the security of Taiwan. Although commercial relations expanded rapidly, the terms of trade and investment between the two countries had become controversial by the mid-1980s, particularly as the American trade deficit with China emerged and increased. Above all, the June 4, 1989, crisis sorely tested the relationship. American public approval of China collapsed overnight, and many Chinese concluded that the United States wanted a weak and unstable China, rather than a strong and successful one.

But the relationship survived that trying period. The Clinton administration drew back from its initial threat to withdraw China's most-favored-nation trade status unless there was "overall significant improvement" in the country's human rights record. Nor did a subsequent crisis in the Taiwan Strait in 1995–1996 cause the relationship to rupture. Instead, the two sides exchanged summit meetings in 1997 and 1998, tried to identify common interests, and announced that they wanted to "build toward a constructive strategic partnership" in the twenty-first century. Beijing and Washington agreed on the terms of China's membership in the World Trade Organization, as the result of which China obtained permanent most-favored nation status—relabeled as "permanent normal trade relations," or PNTR—with the United States. Trade and investment between the two countries, as well as various kinds of societal exchanges, grew rapidly, particularly after Deng Xiaoping's recommitment to his policy of "reform and opening" in the early 1990s. So by 1998 the relationship had developed to the point that it was far less fragile than it had been before.

Although the ties between China and the United States were becoming increasingly robust, their relationship remained highly turbulent, sometimes experiencing dramatic ups and downs The mistaken American bombing of China's embassy in Belgrade in 1999, and the subsequent collision between a Chinese fighter and an American EP-3 reconnaissance aircraft in early 2001, produced serious strains in the relationship. In both the 2000 election campaign and in its early months in office, the new Bush administration began calling China a "strategic competitor" rather than a prospective "strategic partner," and China began talking again about opposing hegemonism on the part of the United States. The increasing debate over the value of the *renminbi* relative to the dollar, and the threats from some members of Congress to impose sanctions against China unless it revalued its currency, also revealed the risk of continued volatility in the relationship.

But despite the turbulence in their relationship, the two countries have become more interdependent than ever before. Each nation's economy depends to an increasing degree on the health of the other: China depends on the United States to buy its goods; the United States depends on China to fund its debt and to keep inflation low.[5] Each country needs the other's cooperation on key international issues, such as the situation on the Korean peninsula. Moreover, each country has defined its policy toward the other in ways that make it more sustainable. Each is committed to engagement and cooperation, although each also seeks strong relations with other powers as a way of hedging against a possible downturn in the U.S.–China relationship. In addition, both governments face challenging problems at home and abroad, particularly the sustainability of economic growth and political stability in China and the conduct of the global war on terrorism in the United States. Neither seeks trouble with the other.

This combination of mutual interdependence, sustainable policies, and concern with other more immediate issues makes major changes in either country's approach to the other less likely, and the relationship between them less fragile and less volatile, than had been the case in the past. In this regard, it is extremely significant that the 2008 U.S. presidential election campaign did not produce calls from any major candidate for fundamental changes in American policy toward China. In fact, the degree of attention paid to China was far less than what might have been expected, given the size of the American trade deficit with China at a time of severe economic recession. Although he differed with George W. Bush on many issues domestic and foreign, Barack Obama neither promised nor made any significant departures from his predecessor's China policy. On the contrary, he described the U.S.–China relationship in virtually identical language, he continued the Bush administration's most important strategic initiative toward China (what is now called the Strategic and Economic Dialogue), and he appointed a major Republican politician, Jon Huntsman, to be his ambassador to Beijing. All this conforms with what I have called the "revised mainstream policy" toward China: a combination of engagement, integration, and hedging.[6]

So does this mean that the U.S.–China relationship has been transformed from fragility to durability and from volatility to stability? Unfortunately, such a conclusion would be too optimistic. There are several "long-tail" risks in the relationship—developments that have low probability, but would have great negative impact if they occurred.[7] The possibility of eventual conflict in the Taiwan Strait, either because of a movement toward independence by Taiwan or because of an attempt to compel unification by the mainland, is unlikely now, but cannot be completely ruled out for the future. The collapse of North Korea, even if not desired by either side, might prove difficult to manage, especially in the absence of prior consultations on how to respond. And it is possible that disputes over trade, human rights, or climate change could lead to the imposition of sweeping and severe economic sanctions and counter-sanctions by both sides. Although the relationship is no longer fragile, and although its volatility has declined, the risk of a more competitive, or even conflictual, relationship is still conceivable. The relationship is far more stable than it once was, but it remains vulnerable to a particularly strong shock.

Neither Friend nor Foe?

As I predicted back in 1992, the American public today sees China as neither friend nor foe. For example, in a Harris poll conducted in July 2007, the plurality of those surveyed (40 percent) put China in a middle category, as "not friendly" but not an adversary. A smaller percentage viewed it as a "close ally" or "friendly" (30 percent), and an even smaller percentage viewed China as an "enemy" (23 percent).[8] But, although even today the public opinion polls still support my characterization of China as "neither friend nor foe," I am increasingly as dissatisfied with this description as with my portrayal of the bilateral relationship as "fragile." Describing American perceptions of China as "neither friend nor foe" may tell us what the U.S.–China relationship is not, but it does not say what it is.

Like many other analysts, I increasingly see China as both a challenge and an opportunity for the United States, and the U.S.–China relationship as containing, simultaneously, both cooperative and competitive aspects.[9] This is because the two countries increasingly acknowledge that they have common interests. They share a common concern about transnational issues, such as communicable disease, transborder crime, international terrorism, proliferation of weapons of mass destruction, and climate change. They have a common interest in peace in the Asia–Pacific region, in stability in those developing countries in which they do business, and in the prosperity of the other as a major trade and investment partner. Both China and the United States are highly integrated into a global economic system, and they therefore share a common interest in the vitality and stability of that system.

Moreover, the two countries have also shown an increasing ability to work together to advance those common interests. Beijing and Washington cooperate in several aspects of counterterrorism, not only sharing intelligence, but also participating in the Container Security Initiative (CSI). They have worked well together in the Six-Party Talks, aimed at promoting the complete dismantling of the North Korean nuclear program. After hard bargaining, the two countries agreed on the terms of China's membership in the World Trade Organization. They have come to a better understanding of each other's "red line" in the Taiwan Strait, and appear committed to honoring it.

Nonetheless, the two countries have differing perspectives on key issues and institutions. Although both sides oppose proliferation, the United States is far more willing to impose sanctions on countries that proliferate weapons of mass destruction than is China, and China is reluctant to participate in such intrusive verification measures as the Proliferation Security Initiative. Although they both seek to promote economic growth in the Third World, the United States and China offer different models of development, which some have labeled the "Washington Consensus" and the "Beijing Consensus," respectively. China and the United States both take advantage of globalization, but they have different views on the Doha Round in the WTO. Although they share a concern about climate change, they differ over which countries have the greatest responsibility for controlling carbon emissions. And while both Washington and Beijing support key international institutions, they have different views about the future of the IMF, the United Nations, and various economic and security structures in the Asia–Pacific region.

And, of course, the two countries still differ on two long-standing issues—Taiwan and human rights—that raise strong emotions on both sides. The United States would support any relationship between Taiwan and the mainland that was peacefully arrived at and genuinely acceptable to both sides, but opposes the attempt of either side to impose its will on the other unilaterally. China regards this position—and some of the more specific policies that flow from it, such as continued sales of American arms to Taiwan—as an intervention in its internal affairs, and suspects that it may reflect an American desire to perpetuate the separation of Taiwan and the mainland. On human rights, the United States wishes to see an evolution toward a more pluralistic political system in China and better protection of the civil and political rights of the Chinese people. Beijing believes that this again constitutes intervention in China's internal affairs, and believes that the United States should acknowledge the progress China has made in promoting social and economic rights and should respect China's desire to reach its own definition of what constitutes a democratic political system

Not only do the interests of the two countries diverge, but they are often competitive. The Chinese and American militaries are planning for contingencies, however unlikely, in which they may have to confront each other. This is leading the PLA to develop asymmetrical strategies and weapons systems (cyber warfare, anti-satellite weapons, anti-ship missiles, etc.) that can negate America's advantages in military technology, and the United States to develop measures to counter China's plans for asymmetrical warfare. The two countries are advancing competing—although not diametrically opposed—norms on human rights, development, and sanctions.[10] Chinese firms, as they seek a bigger share of the value chain, and particularly as they "go global," are competing for market share, brand recognition, and royalties with American firms both inside and outside China. Some believe that China and the United States are competing for access to energy and other natural resources in parts of the Third World.

Partly as a result of this combination of convergent and divergent interests, the U.S.–China relationship remains controversial in both countries. Skeptics question the motives of the other side. Alarmists view the military capabilities of the other as a threat. Nationalists call for tougher action against the other. Those who defend present policies, or who are more optimistic about the relationship, are sometimes maligned as "panda-huggers" in the United States, or as members of the *qinmei pai* (the "pro-United States faction") in China. And yet, as noted above, the critics of the relationship do not appear able to offer alternative policies that would differ significantly from the approach each side is presently taking toward the other.

In short, the relationship is one in which the two countries are both colleagues and competitors, with both common and divergent interests. The key is which sectors of the relationship are competitive, and which are collaborative. Here, I do not agree with former U.S. Secretary of State Colin Powell, who once implied that China and the United States were "strategic competitors" but "economic partners."[11] In fact, the situation is more likely to be just the opposite: the two countries will increasingly become economic competitors, but strategic partners. But if Powell's characterization ever became true, the situation could become very dangerous. Competition is normal in the commercial marketplace—in fact, in many countries there are penalties against those who engage in collusion to limit competition. Conversely, competition is dangerous in the strategic realm: it can lead to costly arms races, increase the chances of war by accident, and produce considerable suspicion about each other's long-term intentions.

Moreover, it is also important which element of the relationship dominates. If the relationship becomes primarily cooperative, then the competitive elements are secondary, their impact is limited, and the competition can even be healthy. If, in contrast, the relationship becomes primarily competitive, then the cooperative elements may become increasingly marginalized if not eliminated altogether.

The Increasing Breadth of the Relationship

In short, my earlier characterizations of U.S.–China relations are not the best way to describe the relationship today. It is better to see the relationship as resilient than as fragile, and as a blend of competition and cooperation than as "neither friend nor foe." But there is a third dimension along which the relationship has changed that can contribute to a better understanding of the transformations of the other two: the increasing breadth of the relationship, as reflected in the increasing number of items on the bilateral agenda.

When *A Fragile Relationship* was published in 1992, the U.S.–China relationship was dominated by a small number of issues: Taiwan and human rights at the top of the agenda, with increasing concerns about the bilateral trade imbalance and about China's alleged role in exporting technology related to missiles and weapons of mass destruction. Those issues are still on the agenda, although there is somewhat more confidence now that China accepts and abides by international non-proliferation regimes.

But the agenda today is crowded with additional issues. It includes not only the familiar bilateral issues (Taiwan, trade, and human rights), but also newer ones (such as China's direct investments in the United States and the activities of Beijing's sovereign wealth fund). The agenda also comprises a long list of transnational issues, including energy security, climate change, terrorism, global health, transborder crime, the military balance, Third World development, regional and global economic architecture, regional security architecture, and global governance. And of course the two countries exchange views, and sometimes cooperate, on issues involving third countries, such as North Korea, Burma, Iran, Afghanistan, Somalia, and Sudan.

The expansion of the bilateral agenda helps explain why the relationship has evolved in the ways that it has. In addressing these issues, the two countries find that they have both common and divergent interests. That's why they are both colleagues and competitors. And the growing number of bilateral and transnational issues—issues that can be addressed successfully only through cooperation—increases the level of mutual interdependence. That is why the relationship is less fragile and more robust than it was before.

But why has the relationship become so much broader now than it was, say, in 1992? The answer essentially lies in China's success in a globalizing world. Globalization—and the associated increases in financial flows, demands for energy, emissions of greenhouse gases, proposals for new economic and security institutions, and the like—has introduced a multitude of new issues on the international agenda. And the rise of China's comprehensive national power and the increasingly global scope of its national interests and its foreign policy mean that China is more important to managing those issues than ever before. The U.S. request that China become a "responsible stakeholder" in international affairs reflects the American acknowledgement of China's increasingly important role in dealing with a wider range of international issues.[12]

As a result, the would-be specialist on U.S.–China relations now has to understand not just the history of the Taiwan issue and the different definitions that Beijing and Washington bring to their discussions of human rights. He or she also has to understand something about international financial flows, the implications of appreciation and depreciation of foreign currencies, the nature of the international energy market, the various approaches to dealing with global warming, the alternative strategies for promoting development, competing views of regional economic architecture, and so forth. In other words, the "specialist" on U.S.–China relations must actually be a generalist, if he or she is to be able to comment knowledgeably and insightfully on the U.S.–China relationship.

Even worse, those who study U.S.–China relations must know more about each country than ever before. One of the most valuable contributions to the ongoing discussions of U.S.–China relations in the United States is a book produced jointly by the Center for Strategic and International Studies and the Peterson Institute for International Economics, called *China: The Balance Sheet*.[13] The book provides an overview of various features of Chinese domestic politics, economics, and society that shape China's foreign policy. It deals comprehensively with such topics as the challenges to continued economic growth, social unrest, corruption, demographic trends, the social safety net, environmental challenges, the nature of the CCP, current ideological trends, the rule of law, the contours of Chinese foreign policy, Chinese foreign economic relations, and so on. All of these topics are necessary to understand how Beijing acts toward the rest of the world, including the United States.

But a "balance sheet" that focuses exclusively on China examines only half of the U.S.–China relationship. There is also a need for a book called *The United States: The Balance Sheet* that raises similar questions on the American side. If Americans must understand why China has surplus savings, and how that affects the trade deficit with the United States, then they also need to understand why their own country has a savings deficit, and how that contributes to the same problem. If Americans should appreciate why Chinese resist what they describe as international "hegemony," they also need to consider the desire in some quarters in the United States to create and maintain a unipolar world, centered on Washington. If Americans are well advised to understand the so-called Beijing Consensus on Third World development, they also need to grasp the origins and content of the so-called Washington Consensus with which it competes.

Conclusion

In short, over the fifteen years since the publication of *A Fragile Relationship*, China and the United States have become more interdependent, have developed an increasing stake in the successful management of major international issues, and are therefore acknowledging a greater need for cooperation. As a result, the U.S.–China relationship is no longer as fragile as it was in the 1970s and 1980s, or even as turbulent as it was in the 1990s and early 2000s. It has become increasingly resilient, able to ride out all but the most severe shocks.

But China and America still have different interests and values, have not yet established high levels of mutual trust or mutual understanding, and may well be experiencing a significant shift in their relative power. They hold different views on many international issues, even where they share common interests. They are competing for advantage, bilaterally, globally, and regionally. Their relationship should not be assumed to be completely invulnerable to a very serious shock, nor should such a shock—such as a crisis in the Taiwan Strait or on the Korean Peninsula—be completely ruled out. Even a series of smaller events could exacerbate the mistrust and suspicion that already exists, thereby increasing the vulnerability of the relationship.

So: a fragile relationship, no. A resilient relationship, yes. A complex relationship, certainly. But the United States and China have not yet forged a relationship that we can declare, with confidence, to be entirely stable or completely positive.

Notes

This essay is based on my remarks to the conference on "Macao and Sino–U.S. Relations," sponsored by the University of Macao, on December 11, 2007.

1. Harry Harding, *A Fragile Relationship: The United States and China Since 1972* (Washington: Brookings Institution, 1992). My first conclusion has been mischaracterized as implying that I thought the United States should refrain from doing anything that might offend China, but that was not my intention. My characterization of the relationship as "fragile" was descriptive, not prescriptive.

2. This phrase was not prominently featured in the book itself, but was the title of a companion essay published at the same time: "Neither Friend Nor Foe: A China Policy for the Nineties," *Brookings Review* 10, no. 2 (Spring 1992), pp. 6–11.

3. As President Barack Obama put it in July 2009, in his opening remarks to the U.S.–China Strategic and Economic Dialogue in Washington, "[when President Nixon visited China in 1972] our dialogue was guided by a narrow focus on our shared rivalry with the Soviet Union. Today, we have a comprehensive relationship that reflects the deepening ties among our people."

4. Michel Oksenberg, "The Strategies of Peking," *Foreign Affairs*, 50, no. 1 (October 1971), pp. 15–29.

5. The economic historian Niall Ferguson has used the term "Chimerica" to describe the growing economic interdependence between the United States and China. See "From Empire to Chimerica," in his *The Ascent of Money: A Financial History of the World* (New York: Penguin, 2008), ch. 6.

6. See Harry Harding, "China Policy for the Next U.S. Administration," in *America's Role in Asia: Asian and American Views* (San Francisco: The Asia Foundation, 2008), pp. 183–94.

7. On long-tail risks—that is, risks that have low probability but very high impact—see Ian Bremmer and Preston Keat, *Fat Tail: The Power of Political Knowledge for Strategic Investing* (New York: Oxford University Press, 2009); and Nassim Nicholas Taleb, *Black Swan: The Impact of the Highly Improbable* (New York: Random House, 2007).

8. I cite the Harris poll because it is one of the few that explicitly offers a middle option. Most other polls do not. And when forced to choose, Americans will make the choice depending on the way the question is posed. If it is between "ally" and "adversary," the majority will say "adversary"; but if the choices of "friendly" and "unfriendly" are added, the plurality will say "friendly."

9. This assessment is reflected in the title of one recent book on China: C. Fred Bergsten, Charles Freeman, Nicholas R. Lardy, and Derek J. Mitchell, *China's Rise: Challenges and Opportunities* (Washington, D.C.: Peterson Institute for International Economics, 2008).

10. See Harry Harding, "China's Views of International Norms and Institutions," in David Shambaugh and Gudrun Wacker (eds.), *American and European Relations with China: Advancing Common Agendas* (Berlin: Stiftung für Wissenschaft und Politik, June 2008), pp. 109–22.

11. More precisely, he said, "China is a competitor and a potential regional rival, but also a trading partner willing to cooperate in the areas, such as Korea, where our strategic interests overlap." Quoted in the testimony of Assistant Secretary of State James Kelly before the Senate Subcommittee on East Asian and Pacific Affairs, May 1, 2001.

12. The concept of "responsible stakeholder" was introduced by then-Deputy Secretary of State Robert Zoellick in "Whither China? From Membership to Responsibility," speech to the National Committee on U.S.–China Relations, September 21, 2005.

13. C. Fred Bergsten, Bates Gill, Nicholas R. Lardy, and Derek J. Mitchell, *China: The Balance Sheet—What the World Needs to Know Now About the Emerging Superpower* (New York: Public Affairs, 2006). See also the sequel, already cited above: Bergsten, Freeman, Lardy, and Mitchell, *China's Rise: Challenges and Opportunities*.

CHAPTER TWO

Averting Another Cold War in Asia: A Chinese Perspective on U.S.–China Relations

Zhang Shuguang

Chinese–American relations have been undergoing immense fluctuations since the early 1970s. For pessimists, the relationship has been mostly characterized by asymmetrical interactions, limited cooperation, and sustained confrontation.[1] For optimists, the relationship has seen subtle but fundamental changes from, for example, limited contacts to comprehensive relations, from cooperation in restricted areas to that in all aspects of the relationship, and from asymmetrical interactions to more symmetrical ones.[2]

Pessimistic or optimistic, it is important to remember that the current Chinese–American relationship has grown out of the decades-long Cold War confrontation, and as fragile as it has been,[3] it might nevertheless go both ways. It seems hardly possible or rational even to think that the Cold War experience would repeat in the future, *but we probably should.*

Lessons from the Cold War

History, indeed, is what we learn about what has happened in the past. No matter how diligently we historians labor, our learning about the Cold War history—if it has become a history—remains, however, preliminary.[4] Our limited learning about the past will, no doubt, affect our present behavior and future attitude.

Although serious scholarly probe into the insights of the Cold War saw a late start and slow progress in China,[5] commentators, analysts, strategists, and even out-spoken decision makers seem to have firmly formed and vocally expressed their understanding of this decade-long but rather recent event in international politics. Interestingly, though, many in China tend to see the Cold War from the vantage point of Chinese–American relations, which, they believe, entail two cold wars: one "hot" (1949–1972) and one "cold" (since 1989). And these cold wars have their own dynamics, but going through a common cycle with a beginning, a middle, and an end. Thus, referring to Washington's sanctions against Beijing in the aftermath of Tiananmen, Deng Xiaoping pointed out in late 1989: "With one cold war ended not so long ago has another cold war just started."[6]

Ever since, Chinese public criticism on America's insisting on the "cold war logic" or cold war thinking in dealing with China has gained a great deal of currency. From Clinton's "engagement" to G. W. Bush's "congagement," from the call for China to be a "stakeholder" to the proposed "hedging strategy" against China, from the tightening of the U.S.–Japan–Korea defense arrangements to the discussions on an alliance to link the Pacific Ocean with India, from the allegedly U.S. sponsored "colored revolutions" in central Asia to the talks on the needs for the West to utilize the 2008 Olympic Games as a leverage against Beijing, and from the worries about the "Beijing consensus" to even recent Franco–German legal actions against piracy by Chinese state-owned enterprises (the so-called patent-gate), the Chinese officials found little evidence of U.S. "vicious intentions" for another cold war against China.[7] It has become a popular claim that Washington, in its efforts to maintain U.S. global power without an equal, needs "an archenemy" to define its global purpose, national interests, and political coherence; and the rise of a Communist China fits the profile very well.[8]

Whether or not there exists a second cold war between China and America is subject to further debate. Although few Chinese, if any, would like to go back to the hot confrontation period in Chinese–American relations, many harbor the belief that if the two countries wind up in another cold war, China might not lose, or at least not as badly as the former Soviet Union.[9] One thing is for sure: the potential cost for Chinese–American mutual containment might be greater than the last time. Although the United States is the initiator of globalization and China the late partner, both are the biggest beneficiaries of all. Should China be compelled to withdraw and isolate itself, it might not be an exaggeration to contend that the current international economic system from which the United States derives much of its strength might be severely hurt.

However, there seems to be a consensus that China can no longer afford another cold war with the United States. Reasons often cited would go as the following.

First, China has already been set on the path toward modern development and there's no turning around. Finding fatal flaws in the Soviet model, the Chinese people are proud of being able to catch up with and benefit from globalization before too late. Already being penalized for riding on the wrong bus during the earlier years of the Cold War, China would have to conform to the trends of the future, not to go against them.

Second, it would be more difficult than ever before for any central leadership to galvanize popular support for another Cold War grand strategy or foreign and defense policy. Having clearly learned that Mao's theories on "world revolution" or "third worlds" were largely invalidated, the Chinese people have embraced Deng Xiaoping's line of "reform and opening." Any challenge to or change of such a "base line" would warrant a political legitimacy crisis in which no political leader could expect to survive.

Third, China has already come to realize that it surely is in the best interests of China if the country faces no definitive enemy, or take a lead in power struggle, nor does it have to ally with any other great powers, regional or global. All of these principles are derived mainly from the lessons China learned from the Cold War in a hard and sometime bloody way. Thus, to retain a stable external environment and construct a sustainable "harmony" in world politics has become a long-term foreign-policy objective that few Chinese would object.

Fourth, although committed to military modernization, no well-informed Chinese would like China to slip into a Cold War arms race, especially with the United States, Japan, Russia, and/or India. Believing that it was the uncontrollable arms race that finally collapsed the Soviet Union, few Chinese would want to fall into a military buildup trap which the United States seems to have deliberately set for China this time. Such a concern seems to have underlined China's revolution in military affairs (RMA), which was initiated under the Jiang Zemin leadership and has yet to aim for a comprehensive military buildup, even when Beijing has the resources to spare and know-how to employ and even when a call for building military muscles gains increasing popularity in China.

Fifth, another round of U.S.–China Cold War may very well lead to a hot and disastrous war. With still vivid memory of how misperception and miscalculation caused China to take part in a series of armed conflicts involving the United States (Korea, Taiwan, Indochina, and Vietnam), Chinese foreign and defense policy analysts seem convinced that it would be more difficult to manage any type of security dilemma which is bound to rise in a

U.S.–China confrontation. Although knowing one another more than ever before, the profound divergence in values, beliefs, and historical consciousness that are deeply embedded in the past U.S.–China Cold War experiences would invariably affect, if not frame, the strategic mindsets in both Beijing and Washington.

Convincing or not, it is no accident that the current Chinese leadership under Hu Jintao has tried to do everything possible to avoid being dragged into another cold war with the United States. It is also no surprise that Hu proclaimed at the recent seventeenth party congress China's commitment to peace, development, and cooperation in order to construct "a harmonious world."

Unimagined Opportunities

All things considered, opportunities to avert a U.S.–China cold war seem better than even. There can be little doubt that after thirty-five years of slow but steady normalization, the two countries have more or less reached extensive commonalities, especially in some critical areas. Each adds to the motives for cooperation, not confrontation.

First, the drastically growing U.S.–China economic relations have invariably forged a pattern of economic interdependence. According to the U.S. Commerce Department, the bilateral trade in 2006 had amounted to $343 billion, representing 20.2 percent growth over the previous year, rendering the United States as China's second-largest trading partner and China as the United States' third largest.[10] By the end of July 2007, direct U.S. investment in China, which is represented by 53,754 projects, has a total value of $55.42 billion. Catching up quickly, direct Chinese investment in the United States increased to $3 billion by the end of June 2007.[11] Also, having already held $256.7 billion worth of U.S. government bonds by the end of 2005, the rate of Chinese holdings is surely going up.[12]

The fast-growing stakes in U.S.–China economic relations seem to have moved both increasingly and invariably into bilateral and multilateral cooperation in promoting regional and global prosperity. Both, for example, offered the same degree of support for such regional dialogues as ASEAN Regional Forum (ARF), the Council for Security Cooperation in the Asia Pacific (CSCAP), and more recently the Shangri-La Dialogue.[13] As beneficiaries of the existing international economic system, both also support multilateral institutions including the UN, the World Bank, International Monetary Fund, and even the World Trade Organization (WTO); and both desire international cooperation to meet global challenges ranging from environmental protection to containing the spread of bird flu virus.[14] To institutionalize high-level collaboration in addressing bilateral economic concerns, both agreed to a U.S.–China Strategic Economic Dialogue in September 2006 and have since held two meetings with "constructive" outcomes.[15]

Second, close political contacts between the two have largely reduced probability for misunderstanding and miscalculation. Now leaders of the two countries regularly meet and talk over the phone. Lower-level officials also meet and talk with one another rather regularly. Various mechanisms have been put into effect to facilitate such contacts. Most prominent of all have been the strategic dialogues between the two governments at the ministerial level. Numerous Chinese and American official delegations travel across the Pacific. As a result, official communication has become increasingly two-way symmetrical.

Intensive contacts at increasing depth have facilitated mutual learning and appreciation in the two countries. To ease up cultural-bound difficulties, both governments put people who know the other side well in key positions. The appointments of "new China hands" in the U.S. government (Henry Paulson, Susan Schwab, and Thomas Christiansen, to name just a few) in 2006 were much welcomed in Beijing. And when announced to head Chinese foreign ministry in April 2007, "Tiger" Yang Jiechi, a long-time friend of the Bush family, received positive coverage in the United States. Enthusiasm was also aroused when two Western-educated, internationally renowned scientists received ministerial posts in China: Wan Gang to lead the ministry of science and technology and Chen Zhu as public health minister. As people involved in the policymaking process get to know one another, they find it increasingly easier to engage in direct, candid, and sophisticated negotiations. The previous problem of misunderstanding at policy levels is no longer serious.

Third, although still in a limited fashion, China and the United States resumed military contacts after a long suspension since the EP-3 collision in April 2001. Among the recent exchanges, U.S. Chairman of the Joint Chiefs of Staff General Richard Myers came to Beijing in January 2004. Later the same year, Chinese Defense Minister General Cao Gangchuan returned him a visit in Washington. After the allegedly "hard-liner" U.S. Secretary of Defense Donald Rumsfeld visited China in the fall of 2005, senior U.S. military commanders have become frequent and high-profile visitors to Beijing. They include Commander-in-Chief of the Pacific Fleet General Gary Roughead in November 2006, Chairman of the U.S. Joint Chiefs of Staff General Peter Pace in March 2007, and Roughhead's successor General Timothy J. Keating in May 2007.

In addition, the two countries have been engaging in military and defense dialogues more frequently than ever before. Along with a series of defense consultative talks between senior officials from both defense departments, Consultation Mechanism to Strengthen Military Maritime Safety was initiated and, as part of the arrangement, both navies exchanged naval port calls in May 2007.[16] More recently, the two even conducted a joint military exercise to meet unconventional threats in the Asia–Pacific.[17]

Fourth, the level of social and cultural exchanges between the two has reached an unprecedented height. Student exchange has been going strong after the slowdown during the immediate years of 9/11. In the fiscal year of 2006–2007, U.S. Embassy to Beijing revealed, a total of 51,546 student visas were issued, amounting to 80 percent of all the applicants.[18] Media organizations have been collaborating with one another in promptly bringing home news of the other. Tourism has been on a record high. Business people and government officials find it a routine trip to fly across the Pacific. Although already 54 per week in 2005, the number of flights between China and the United States is projected to reach 249 per week by 2010.[19]

The liberalization of people-to-people exchange has contributed to the closing up of value discrepancies between China and the United States. For one thing, China's social system and public policies have changed a great deal. The Chinese government has increasingly attached importance to rule of law, good governance, and social justice. It has publicly advocated protection of human rights: the National People's Congress, China's legislative body, passed an amendment to the Constitution in March 2004, stipulating that the state must respect and protect human rights. It has also—cautiously, though—continued the experiment on democratic reforms: modeled after nationwide village-level elections, several provincial governments are permitted to try out with township election. Speaking to the Japanese legislators in April 2007, Chinese Premier Wen Jiabao proclaimed that China wants "democratic politics" and will push for "socialist" democracy to spread incrementally.[20] These and other changes on the Chinese side have narrowed the value differences between the two countries, thereby expanding the political basis for U.S.–China cooperation.

Fifth, the two countries are more and more on the same page in combating common global problems. Either through international institutions or regimes or via bilateral agreements, the two saw cooperation on an increasing range of areas including global climate change, illegal immigration, anti-smuggling, anti-cross border crimes, intellectual property protection, AIDS prevention, and maritime safety. The two countries are also cooperating on an increasing number of high-profile issues including UN peacekeeping, humanitarian relief, nonproliferation of weapons of mass destruction, and the war against transnational terrorism.

Sixth, U.S.–China collaboration on resolving international disputes and maintaining regional stability becomes more of a norm. The Chinese government has expressed its welcome to constructive U.S. presence in the region.[21] The U.S. government has encouraged China to play a positive role in regional cooperation through its participation in the ARF and APEC as well as other governmental or non-governmental dialogues. A frequently celebrated example is their joint effort to curtail and manage the Korean nuclear crisis. Sharing the same goal of maintaining a nuclear-free Korean peninsula, both worked in dissuading Pyongyang from going any further with its nuclear weapon program. It is also noteworthy that Beijing's foreign ministry and Washington's State Department seemed to have coordinated each other's moves in responding to Taiwan's recent push for "*de jure* independence" through a UN referendum.

Seventh, the weight of immediate strategic priorities might be potent to persuade leaders in both capitals to be more tolerant with potential threats. The United States, for example, is expected not to be able to reorient its strategic focus from other regions onto China any time soon. The United States is believed to be still sunk in a strategic stalemate since 9/11, evident in no victory of the war on terror, no peace in sight from the Iraqi war, no settlement with the Iranian nuclear challenge, and no hope in resolving the Israeli–Palestine dispute. Elections already held (in Australia) and soon to be held (Russia, Pakistan, etc.) are projected to add more global challenges to Washington than to Beijing. Even a democratic administration in the United States in 2009 might still be compelled to forego China, as domestic economy and external crisis might force the new president to focus just on how to survive his first term. This prospect may avail Beijing a breathing time till its next party congress (the eighteenth).

Serious Challenges

Along with really good opportunities, Chinese–American relations are still faced with really serious challenges. If not effectively managed, a U.S.–China cold war might still be more than a possibility.

The first serious challenge is perceptive. That is, how exactly both perceive the scope and nature of China on the rise.

The sustained economic growth in China has increased China's weight in regional and world affairs. Some economists believe that China would become the third-largest economy in 2007.[22] According to a recent World

Bank estimate, China's contribution to global economic growth would sooner than later exceed that of the United States.[23] China's economic growth is, however, perceived to have enabled the government not only to improve its people's living standards, but also modernize its defense facilities and enhance its diplomatic capabilities, thus facilitating China's desire to project its might regionally and globally.

More important, the rise of China is believed to warrant an almost inevitable confrontation between the United States, an established power, and China, the "new kid on the block." As the interests of the established powers and those of the rising ones would ultimately collide, China has been consistently perceived as the most serious potential threat to the United States. "Over time," John Mearsheimer wrote in 2001, "China could become the most powerful rival the United States has ever faced."[24] This sentiment also finds expression in the Pentagon's *Quadrennial Defense Review Report* and *Report on the Military Capabilities of the People's Liberation Army* since the end of last century. Although facing no "peer competitor," these reports have repeatedly claimed, the United States would have to be prepared for the potential challenge from China, Russia, and/or India.[25]

The perceived U.S.–China rivalry is thus projected as a zero-sum game: what is good for China is bad for the United States, and vice versa. Thus, those in the United States who hold this view see China's economic growth as a threat to the United States, not as new opportunities for U.S. economy and welfare; they regard China's efforts to improve its relations with its neighbors as the latter's attempt to expand its influence at the expense of the United States; and they find China's desire to improve military-to-military relations with the United States as attempts to steal U.S. military secrets instead of efforts to build mutual confidence. And in short, they find the rise of China as a dangerous challenge to U.S. supremacy.[26]

It is interesting and important to note that many in China have been echoing and in effect reinforcing such perception. To them, the United States as the established power would never allow China to rise. U.S. intentions toward and efforts at enhancing its military alliance with Japan, developing military ties with Chinese neighbors (India, Singapore, Vietnam), prolonging its military operations in central Asia, selling weapons to Taiwan, upgrading military capabilities in Guam are aimed to resurrect the strategic encirclement of and containment against China of the Cold War period. In response, China should and must get prepared militarily to meet such a challenge, once and for all.[27]

The second serious challenge stems largely from concerns over differences in values and political orientation and thus structural uncertainties. Differences in values and political priorities between the two countries generate mutual suspicion. Despite significant political, economic, and social changes over the past decades, China remains different from the United States in terms of core values, ideology, and political priorities. As a socialist country led by a communist party, China's official ideology is still Marxism although with Chinese characteristics according to the Chinese government. As an Asian country attaching relatively more importance to communal interests and less to individual rights, China will be less willing to protect individual interests if it comes at the expense of sacrificing communal ones. And as a developing country undergoing rapid economic and social transformations, China will assign priority to economic development and political stability instead of protection of political freedom and civil rights.

To most Americans, the Chinese political system is not democratic: no multiparty competition, no free elections, no free press, and no free association. Since most Americans subscribe to the theory of democratic peace, that is, democratic countries do not fight with one another, they are worried that as long as China remains authoritarian, its rise would pose a threat to the interests of the United States.[28]

Therefore, they are likely to support and even push their government to exert pressure on China to adopt a real "democracy." This in turn restrains the U.S. government to take a more positive approach toward China than now, and further complicates interactions between the two countries.

More closely related to the Cold War experiences, the Chinese leadership's understanding of and assessment on U.S. policy intentions toward China vary by which party, Democratic or Republican, is in the White House and has majority seats on Capitol Hill. Beijing's experiences in dealing with Washington over the past sixty years have formulated a notion that, leaning more toward liberal and idealist underpinnings, a Democratic government tends to be more hostile toward China than a more realist-oriented Republican leadership. The U.S.–China confrontation saw more intensity and hostility during the Truman, Kennedy, Johnson, Carter, and Clinton administrations than those of Eisenhower, Nixon, Reagan, and Bush. Even a new-conservative George W. Bush administration proved tough, largely vocally, on Beijing. An anticipated Obama victory in the ongoing U.S. presidential election and possibly eight years of a Democratic government that has vowed to change the political course back onto the liberal track caused concerns in Beijing. If to invoke its historical consciousness, the Chinese leadership would have to get prepared for a possibly intensified ideological challenge from the United States and subsequently U.S. allies.

The third serious challenge is more of immediate urgency. That is: exactly how the United States and China, independently or interactively, meet external challenges and manage possible international crises from now through the year of 2012.

Both China and the United States would be forced to face and manage at least ten different contingencies entailing strategic implications as to whether or not a U.S.–China cold war could be delayed or averted.

(1) Taiwan's presidential election in May 2008 and post–Chen Shui-bian cross-strait relationship
(2) Unfolding crisis in Pakistan and gradual and complex involvement by the great powers, regional or global alike
(3) Possible Western boycotting against the Beijing Olympics Games of August 2008 and Shanghai Expo of May 2010 and their aftermath effects
(4) Uncertainties in the Shanghai Organization arrangements as a result of Russia's presidential election in January 2008
(5) A unification process in the Korean peninsula probably without China's participation
(6) A possible U.S.–Japan–Australia–New Zealand–India alliance system or possible across-Pacific/Indian international security arrangements
(7) Negative effects of economic globalization—WTO's five-year performance report, especially over intellectual property theft (it is estimated that more than 60 percent of China's high technology would continue to depend on overseas transfer in the next ten years)
(8) Changes in the international institutions with, in particular, UN reforms and the issue of permanent membership at the Security Council
(9) External and internal pressure on democratization in Hong Kong, Macao, and even on the mainland
(10) A better than even chance of China's economic slowdown and crisis after the Shanghai Expo in 2010, which might instigate political demands from the unfortunate

It's virtually unpredictable how Beijing and Washington would handle those issues and manage their potential risks. Although foreign and defense policy deliberation and formulation remains a highly centralized process in China, it's getting increasingly easier for scholars and outsiders to probe into the insights of decision making on foreign policies. New changes have nevertheless taken place since 2001. For better or worse, the most noteworthy ones are bureaucratic competition is becoming real, think tanks are mushrooming, scholarly views are valued more, special interest groups are exerting more and more pressure, and top leaders are occasionally seeking advice outside the box.

Looking Ahead

Looking to the near future, how China and the United States manage their relations will be more and more important not only for the two countries but also for the region and the world as a whole. Both would benefit tremendously if they could attain a constructive and cooperative relationship. Only by doing so would it be highly likely that a U.S.–China cold war be delayed and eventually averted.

Within the framework of "harmonious world," the Hu leadership seems very cautious in its U.S. policy. This is evident in its persistence in pursuing a firm but flexible policy: wider application of China's soft power will go along with firmer projection of China's hard power (ruan de geng ruan, ying de geng ying in Chinese). Translated into policy terms, it entails, at least, China intensifying its efforts to shape and build an image of "peaceful rising" in the world's public opinions through public diplomacy, but at the same time, it will protect and advance its national interests via prudent manipulation of power politics.

Given its profound suspicion of and distrust in Chinese motives, the Bush administration has not yet come around to treat China as a cooperative partner, rather than a strategic competitor. Whoever succeeds Bush in 2009—even Democratic hopeful Obama—may highly unlikely change the course and would probably stay on the track of "con-gaging China" for at least the first four years.

Under the circumstances, it seems unlikely for U.S.–China relations to move closer in a significant way. Neither is it likely that the relationship would see a sudden downturn. Cooperation between the two countries, however, is more likely to remain cautious and limited.

Finally, China and the United States still need to pass the "litmus test" which Nixon and Kissinger tried to run in 1972.[29] That is, will the rise of China create stability and prosperity or just a cluster of power and power reconfiguration?

A Mid-Term Report[30]

Almost two years have passed since this author first presented these possible challenges. Indeed, it has been rather dramatic and eventful for both the United States and China, particularly as the world was plunged in October 2008 into the gravest economic crisis since the Great Depression of 1929. The worldwide economic crisis has in effect garnered unprecedented risks and opportunities for U.S.–China relations to survive over the past twenty months.

First, there are dangerous risk-opportunity calculations in both Washington and Beijing. When the crisis was radioactive, speculations as well as assessments on its potential implications on U.S.–China relations began to fly. From the American perspective, some believed that the risks (ranging from an increase of Chinese global influence to a trade war leading to armed conflicts) outweighed the opportunities (from China acting as a "responsible stakeholder" to a U.S.–China strategic partnership).[31] From a Chinese perspective, the opportunities might outweigh the risks. Some in China would go so far by calling for extreme measures including selling out China's share of U.S. government bonds or buying out American bankrupted business. Although showing caution on both sides, such a risk–opportunity projection seems to linger, rendering the relationship vulnerable.

Second, U.S.–China cooperation appears to have by far been on an emergency basis. Convinced that the United States and China would need each other in time of economic crisis, Washington and Beijing have been leaning toward limited and short-term cooperation in rescuing the disastrous economy. The Obama administration has, however, been walking on a delicate line of "co-gagement": encouraging China to spend more, it exercised tougher anti-dumping measures against Chinese products; disengaging from Taiwan, it "accidentally" approved an arms-sale deal to the nationalist regime; and keeping its pressure on China to raise its currency's value, it has recently claimed that China was found "not manipulating" its currency. Chinese leaders remain "cautiously optimistic" about U.S.–China cooperation, which is bound to have surprises and require relentless "struggle." It is no surprise that the Chinese premier cautioned his American guests Kissinger, Shultz, Perry, and Rubin on October 12, 2009, that the past thirty-odd years of U.S.–China relations revealed one lesson, namely, "cooperation leads to mutual benefit, confrontation produces mutual detriments, mutual trust warrants progress, and mutual skepticism moves [us] backward."[32]

Third, committed to its international responsibilities, the PRC is becoming more and more assertive in constructing its cluster of powers, consequently alarming the United States. Rejecting the "G-2" (U.S.–China) proposal in reshaping international political economy, Beijing becomes more inclined than before toward alliance politics. Its tacit acceptance of the G-4 (or the BRICs), vigorous push for the launching of a China-ASEAN Free

Trade Area in January 2010, positive reaction to the newly elected Prime Minister Hatoyama's proposal to build an East Asian community,[33] and even Premier Wen Jiabao's high-profiled visit of Pyongyang and equally celebrated summit with Russia's Prime Minister Putin in October 2009 have invariably given rise to serious concerns in Washington over China's regional policies, which may prove detrimental to U.S. interests in Asia.

Fourth, becoming increasingly confident in going its own way, Beijing cautiously but surely reorients its domestic priorities. Although enlarging public spending to halt the drastic drop of China's economic growth rate, Beijing is determined to transform its economy from export-dependent to domestic consumption–oriented. Aware of its economic leverages over the United States and West Europe, it appears less restrained in tightening up political control in the name of retaining social stability (evident in its management of the ethnic riot in Xinjiang in July 2009) and insisting in one-party rule (voiced in the 2009 National parade).

To realists, liberals, or constructivists, there is no denying that it continues to be gravely difficult in characterizing current U.S.–China relations. Whether or not the unexpected economic crisis would prove a critical turning point in the relationship remains to be a contentious topic. Thus, the litmus test is still in effect.

Notes

1. Zhou Jianming, "Relative Security and U.S. Strategy of Containment," *Guoji Guancha* (*International Review*) 6 (2007), 69–77.

2. Jia Qingguo, "Sino–American Relations: Beyond Engagement and Containment," paper presented at the conference on "The End of the Cold War: The Making of the U.S. Grand Strategy," November 19–21, 2007, Peking University.

3. Harry Harding, *A Fragile Relationship: The United States and China Since 1972* (Washington, D.C.: The Brookings Institution Press, 1992).

4. John Lewis Gaddis, *We Now Know: Rethinking Cold War History* (New York: Oxford University Press, 1997), 281–95.

5. The one with the most serious studies comes from the recently established Center for Cold War International History Studies at East China Normal University, led by Shen Zhihua, Li danhui, Yang Kuisong, Yu Weimin, Dai Chaowu, and Cui Pi, among others.

6. Cited from Wang Jisi, "What Lessons Have Chinese Learned from the Cold War History," paper presented at the conference on "The End of the Cold War: The Making of the U.S. Grand Strategy," November 19–21, 2007, Peking University.

7. See, for example, Zhang Liping, "The Basic Logic underneath U.S. Strategic Thinking toward China," *Guoji wenti yanjiu (International Affairs Studies)* 3 (2005);

Wang Linxia, "U.S. Engagement Strategy toward China Aims for Peaceful Evolution," *Dangdai shijie yu shehuizhuyi (Contemporary World and Socialism)* 6 (2005); Yuan Peng, "U.S.–China Relations into the Third Phase," *Huanqiu shibao* (*Transworld Times*), May 26, 2006, 4.

8. Wang Jisi, "What Lessons Have Chinese Learned from the Cold War History."

9. Zhou Jianming, *Meiguo guofang zhuanxing jiqi dui woguo de yingxiang (U.S. Defense Transformation and Its Impact on China)* (Shangdong People's Press, 2006), conclusion.

10. www.uschina.org/statistics/tradetable.html.

11. "U.S. investment in China hits $55.5 billion," September 26, 2007, finance.people.com.cn/GB/71364/6316169.html.

12. "China still holds the largest share of U.S. government bonds," February 17, 2006, news.xinhuanet.com/fortune/2006-02/17/content_4191335.htm.

13. Shanghai Institute for International Affairs, *2007 Guoji xingshi nianjian (A Survey of International Affairs in 2007)*, Shanghai Cishu Press, 2007, 194–206.

14. Xu Jian, "International Situation in 2006 and China's Diplomacy," *ibid.*, 209.

15. *Ibid.*, 207–8.

16. "U.S. Navy vessel pays port call to Qingdao," China Military Online, May 23, 2007, english.pladaily.com.cn/site2/news-channels/2007-05/23/content_824047.htm; "China Takes Positive Attitude Towards Military Co-op with U.S.," Xinhua, September 14, 2006, english.cri.cn/2946/2006/09/14/167@139430.htm.

17. "U.S.–China Navies will hold a joint exercise," September 6, 2007, news.xinhuanet.com/mil/2006-09/07/content_5062192.htm.

18. "U.S. Consular-General says a total of 51,546 students visas are issued this year," *China Daily*, November 21, 2007, p. 4.

19. news.xinhuanet.com/fortune/2005-05/12/content_2947950.htm.

20. Premier Wen Jiabao's Speech to the Japanese Diet, April 12, 2007, news.xinhuanet.com/world/2007-04/12/content_5968135.htm.

21. See Ambassador to the United States Zhou Wenzhong's speech at the Asia Society, September 22, 2005, www.china-embassy.org/chn/zmgx/t213523.htm.

22. business.sohu.com/20070717/n251099606.shtml.

23. business.sohu.com/20070913/n252117130.shtml.

24. John Mearsheimer, "The Future of the American Pacific," *Foreign Affairs*, September/October 2001.

25. See, for example, Department of Defense, "The Report of the Quadrennial Defense Review," May 1997; "Quadrennial Defense Review," February 3, 2002; National Foreign Intelligence Board, "Global Trend 2015: A Dialogue About the Future with Nongovernment Experts," NIC 2000–02 December 2000; The White House, "A National Security Strategy for A New Century," December 1999; "National Security Strategy," September 17, 2002.

26. Jason D. Ellis, and Todd M. Koca, "China's Rising: New Challenges to the U.S. Security Posture," *Strategic Forum*, No. 175. October 2000, Institute for National Strategic Studies, National Defense University.

27. For example, see Zhou Jianming, *Woguo ershiyishiji guojia anquan zhanlue (Our National Security Strategy toward the Twenty-First Century)* (Shangdong People's Press, 2005), chapter 1.

28. Daniel Twining, "Asia's challenge to China," 209.200.80.89/publications/article.cfm?id=343.

29. Kissinger to Nixon, "Mao, Chou and the Chinese Litmus Test," February 19, 1972, U.S. Department of State, *Foreign Relations of the United States*, China, 1969–1972, Vol. 17 (Washington, D.C.: Government Printing Office, 2006), p. 673.

30. The above remarks were drafted in August 2007 and delivered at the conference on U.S.–China relations and Macao in December. Upon an agreement on publishing the proceedings of the conference papers in August 2009, the editors requested to attach a "mid-term report" on the assessments presented almost two years ago.

31. Winny Chen and Nina Hachigian, "The Importance of U.S.–China relations," Center for American Progress, January 28, 2009, www.americanprogress.org/issues/2009/01/importance_china.html; Simon Tisdall, "Will U.S.–China relations sink or swim?" March 10, 2009, www.guardian.co.uk/commentisfree/cifamerica/2009/mar/10/china-usa.

32. Wen Jiabao's remarks at a meeting with Kissinger, Shultz, Perry and Rubin, October 12, 2009, news.sina.com.cn/c/2009-10-13/030716425343s.shtml.

33. See, Liang Yunxiang, "Potential of Sino–Japanese ties," October 10, 2009, www.chinadaily.com.cn/cndy/2009-10/10/content_8773448.htm.

CHAPTER THREE

Common Interests, Conceptual Framework, and Strategic Opportunity: Sino–U.S. Relations in the Context of Globalization

Ding Xinghao

A Lens From Macao

It is truly special and even unique to discuss Sino–U.S. relations in Macao, especially with the background of globalization.

Macao witnessed America's open door policy toward China, when the Treaty of Wangxia (Wang-hsia) was signed between the U.S. government and Qing Dynasty in its suburb in 1844. With this treaty, China was then forced to open its door and to be involved in globalization.[1]

Now China, for the first time, and in a real sense in its history has initiated by itself an open policy toward the rest of the world for more than three decades. Three decades are not at all long by China's long history, but the changes of the world, America, and China are indeed dramatic. It is economic globalization which has transformed the world, America, and China, and Sino–U.S. relations transformed too.

Today, Macao has a totally different symbolic meaning in Sino–U.S. relations. America's Las Vegas is acknowledged worldwide as a symbol of American power. However, Macao will soon or has almost overtaken Las Vegas as the largest gambling city in the world. Why is America transferring some of its power from being based at home to being based in China? People cannot but acknowledge the magic strength of globalization.

Another historical event related to Macao was the Opium War. Why was there not a second opium war between America and China? China now enjoys a surplus of about $230 billion with the United States, which amounts more than one-fourth of the U.S. total trade deficit. But in 1840 when Chinese trade surplus with the Great Britain was less than one-fourth of British's total trade amount, the Opium War happened and China suffered from it.[2] This was indeed a big difference. People cannot understand this phenomenon without a perspective of Sino–U.S. relations against the background of globalization. China and the United States are already economically interdependent to such an extent that differences or conflicts can only be solved by dialogue, not head-on. This is also why we need to focus on common interests, consensus, and opportunities when we discuss this most important bilateral relationship in the world.

Common Interest and Evolving Conceptual Framework

There is little doubt among the international community that the Sino–U.S. relationship is one of the most important bilateral relationships in the world. Even though this relationship is far from being harmonious, it has nonetheless developed to a state that few could have ever envisioned thirty-seven years ago when the Sino–U.S. *Shanghai Communiqué* was released in Shanghai. The Sino–U.S. relationship has, in the current context of economic globalization, evolved from a largely one-dimensional relationship based on security interest only to a comprehensive relationship of in-depth cooperation involving a broad range of fields and featuring a great interdependence of interests.

To be clear about today, study yesterday. Historically speaking, for the Sino–U.S. relationship to be stable, there must be two preconditions. The first one is, needless to say, the existence of common interests; and the second one is the recognition of a conceptual framework that is largely acceptable to both sides, without which the bilateral relationship is easy to fluctuate.

When President Nixon visited China in 1972 there was between China and America broad and serious political, economic, and cultural, as well as ideological, disagreements. What brought the two countries together was a need to contain the Soviet expansion, particularly in the Asia–Pacific region. This common security interest, as an adhesive gluing the two parties, functioned to overcome their differences in other fields.[3] After the 1970s, China took the initiative in building a conceptual framework for the bilateral relationship, which was termed "anti-hegemony." Despite its initial reluctance to endorse the concept, especially during the Reagan administration when issues like human rights and Taiwan raised their heads, the United States, on the whole, accepted the conceptual framework, and this basic consensus proved highly significant to maintaining the stability of Sino–U.S. relations.

However, the conceptual framework of the bilateral relationship began swaying following the end of the Cold War. The flurry of events in the late 1980s and early 1990s, such as the disintegration of the Soviet Union, the vast change in Eastern Europe, and the Tiananmen incident in China, highlighted in a dramatic way the previously somewhat neglected Sino–U.S. divergence in political systems, diplomatic strategy, and various other areas, thus destroying altogether the adhesive of common strategic interests. Thereafter, leaders of both countries attempted to identify some new strategic commonality so as to find a new base for their bilateral relationship. The Clinton administration conceived its framework of "human rights," but it did not become any key note of the bilateral relationship. It was only during the second term of President Clinton, when his administration gradually accepted the Chinese-sponsored "strategic partnership," that the Sino–U.S. relationship stabilized. Yet it should be noted that, failing to win endorsement by the broad American society and the U.S. Congress in particular, the conceptual framework of "strategic partnership" came to be dropped toward the end of the Clinton era.

The United States gained its initiative in defining the conceptual framework shortly after the Bush administration took power. Wolfowitz, Cheney, and others proposed a wholly new conceptual framework of "strategic competitor." Although the common interests of the two countries by no means changed, the new concept changed the China policy of the United States. Fortunately, the Chinese government, keeping a low profile, did not make aggressive response to the new positioning of the United States, and the 9/11 terrorist attack put an immediate stop to the framework. As a matter of fact, even before 9/11, some moderates in the Bush government were already realizing the danger of the radical conceptual framework, as indeed demonstrated by the EP-3 incident, since this framework lost touch with the reality of bilateral relations. Before the dramatic change of 9/11, the U.S. *QDR* in 2001 pointed out, though without mentioning the name of China, that an emerging military power in the Asia–Pacific region would challenge American interests. These words reflected the new realist strategic orientation of the Bush administration to contain any potential adversary. With 9/11, President Bush's view of the world changed, and together with it, the American way of engaging China. The change in the China policy of the United States is clearly evident when comparing as follows the above-mentioned *QDR* of 2001 and the *NSS* (national security strategy) report that came out after the terrorist attack.

First, as already pointed out, whereas *QDR* implied that China was a strategic competitor, *NSS* viewed China as one of the major powers that the

United States could cooperate with, and probed the possibility of establishing a "constructive relationship" with "a changing China." Besides, while recognizing the "profound disagreements" with China on human rights, Taiwan, and so forth, *NSS* noted that the United States would "narrow [those] differences" so that they would not erode the consensus already reached.[4]

Secondly, as *QDR* continued to view the world in the traditional perspective of contention among powers, the American strategy as a logical consequence would be preventing the emergence of China from posing a threat to U.S. predominance. In contrast, *NSS*, in viewing the cross-border terrorism and the "rogue states" that support terrorism as the foremost enemy of the United States, proposed that strategic cooperation should be developed with powers, including China, under the banner of fighting terrorism.

China also made its own major strategic choice in the wake of 9/11. It arrived at an agreement with the United States on the anti-terror issue, which enabled President Bush to believe that China and the United States should not be adversaries at least in the short run. President Bush deserted the framework of "strategic competitor" at the APEC summit meeting in 2001, and remarked that "the United States is China's friend."[5] Following that, he put forward the "3C framework" of "candid, constructive cooperation." On the whole, since most countries expressed their support for the anti-terror strategy, the United States adjusted its views on relations among powers after the end of the Cold War, so much as that President Bush stated in his report on national security strategy that the major powers were witnessing the best opportunity for constructing their good relations since the emergence of nation-states in the seventeenth century.[6] Clearly, with neither "strategic partnership" nor "strategic competitor" widely endorsed in the United States, the conceptual framework of the Sino–U.S. relationship was still in a process of transition.

In comparison with the primary feature of the American China policy changing with the situation during the first Bush term, the second Bush term saw a more deliberate conceptual definition of the Sino–U.S. relationship by moderates. A case in point is the concept of "stakeholder" proposed by Zoellick in response to the Chinese concept of "peaceful rise." Zoellick's speech was made on the basis of tripartite coordination among the Department of Defense, the State Council, and the National Intelligence Committee. It is noted that there is little change of the U.S. China policy in essence, as the key note is still "engagement and hedging." What has aroused interest is not just the term "stakeholder," but more the adjective "responsible" before it. Obviously, to be "responsible" in the United States perspective is not only to have China integrated into the U.S.–dominated international system, but to have China being responsible to the U.S.–dominated regime as defined by the United States. Although it was a new attempt to define the Sino–U.S. relationship in the desired American way, Zoellick's speech was welcomed by many Chinese, taking it as a step forward in U.S.–China relations. With "stakeholder," this relationship would hopefully raise to a new level, departing from a narrow consensus based on security concerns only to a broader one, which was in accordance with the context of economic globalization.

It is still uncertain whether Zoellick's concept can survive his departure from the Department of State. What did happen is that, although Colin Powell once remarked that the Sino–U.S. relationship was in its best state in more than three decades, Condoleezza Rice avoided her predecessor's characterization of the relationship. President Bush himself said that the bilateral relationship is "complex," showing that he neither believed that the current relationship was in its best state, nor conceived that it should become a strategic competition. With the proposition of "stakeholder," some justification can be made for certain China policies of the United States, in the sense that some contradictions between the two sides can be viewed as contradictions within the system, allowing for discussions or claim-making. President Bush agreed that on the economic level, China and the United States were strategic partners, while on other levels, there might not be a similar partnership. It was thus difficult to say "stakeholder" had truly become a conceptual framework facilitating the strategic stability of the bilateral Sino–U.S. relationship.

In terms of conceptual framework, China expected a more or less positive expression, while the United States favored a somewhat neutral expression. The assumption of "China threat" had a fairly deep social foundation in the United States, and the Chinese theory of "peaceful rise" needed to downplay these negative voices. The good news was that intellectual interactions were increasing between the two countries, which was followed by a number of official dialogues at levels from the top down to the governmental working level in different areas. Unexpectedly, China and the U.S.–China relations turned out not an issue in the U.S. 2008 presidential campaign, and then was seen a smooth transition of Sino–U.S. relations from the Bush administration to the Obama administration.

Strategic Turning Point

A key reason for the improvement of the Sino–U.S. relationship has been the strategic opportunity emerging since the 9/11 terrorist attack, which has led to the shift in the American strategic focus. Previously engaged in seeking new enemies, with China targeted as a potential enemy, the United States after 9/11 turned to al-Qaeda, international terrorism, and states sponsoring terrorism. Such a strategic turnabout gave rise to a radical change in the overall international pattern, and "China threat" came to be shelved to some extent.

Second, the United States has changed its strategic view of relations among powers. The Bush administration began to depart its historical determinism in favor of a belief that there do not necessarily have to be conflicts among powers. Believing that there is possibility or even inevitability of cooperation among major powers, the Bush administration has made adjustments in handling its relations with other major countries.

Third, as the United States sees it, China has also modified its diplomatic strategy. Besides, as widely recognized, China has a massive domestic agenda to focus on, ranging from ensuring social equity, promoting balanced development, facilitating social stability, protecting the environment, fulfilling its WTO membership commitment, guaranteeing smooth leadership succession, not to mention overcoming resistance to further reform and opening up. The vast challenges that China faces in all these fields mean that there is a limit to its participation in external affairs. Furthermore, the United States knows that with its relatively hard-line China policy and the predominant position of the United States, China is confined in its maneuvering, so that China's opting for cooperation is more in the interest of China. This understanding on the part of the United States contributed to the adjustments in the China policy of the Bush administration, as symbolized by the change from the "strategic competitor" concept to the de facto relationship of constructive cooperation.

Finally, the United States has come to realize the necessity of a healthy Sino–U.S. relationship after experiencing the upturn and downturn of its China policy. On the positive side, China, after 9/11, for example, has proven its worth as a cooperative partner in sharing anti-terror intelligence, persuading Pakistan to support the American anti-terror policy, and so forth. On the negative side, the EP-3 incident demonstrated fully the danger of conflict and antagonism between the two countries. The Bush administration has certainly drawn lessons from both sides.

If one is to view 9/11 as a watershed, security cooperation, though not absent before, has definitely acquired new significance since then. On issues formerly not directly related with China, and not just restricted to the Iraq question, China has rendered understanding and cooperation not unimportant to the United States. On those issues more directly related with mainland China, from Taiwan to the Korean peninsula, Chinese cooperation and facilitation have proven indispensable for preventing uncertainties from getting out of control. There is no doubt that in the era of globalization, and following 9/11 in particular, the space and urgency for Sino–U.S. security cooperation have both increased, with especially nonconventional security issues moving to the center of the stage.

It is right to say that 9/11 has fundamentally changed the strategic environment for Sino–U.S. interactions, as confirmed by the American official statement that there is now a greater opportunity of cooperation among major powers. On numerous occasions, American officials have termed China a "friend," not a "strategic competitor." Of course, the transformation in the wake of 9/11 also contains certain negative factors. The impact of the Bush administration's "preemptive strike" or "preventive strategic defense" is still to be watched in the long run. Besides, the American tendency to put into the basket of anti-terrorism all such things as fighting al-Kaeda, preventing the proliferation of weapons of mass destruction, seeking regime change in "rogue states," and promoting democracy in the whole Middle East also is difficult to win China's whole-hearted support.

Specifically on the Iraq and North Korea issues that offer opportunities of security cooperation, the Sino–U.S. bilateral security relationship may also be strained if they are handled inappropriately. In the runup to the Iraq war, China was obviously taking a position different from the United States, even though China took a low profile in comparison with American allies like France and Germany. Despite the fact that it has been modifying its diplomatic position and international behavior, China does not wish to lose its anti-hegemony image, just as it does not wish to lose its own independent judgment on global issues. On the North Korea issue, while sharing a considerable common ground in keeping the Korean peninsula nuclear-free and in safeguarding peace and stability there, China is also wary of certain backlashes of the Korean crisis, such as refocus of the American attention on China; deployment by the Pentagon of medium-range missiles in Northeast Asia, more frequent visits of the U.S. aircraft carriers to the region, and organization of the Northeast Asian Command of U.S. forces; and initiation of another round of arms race in China's neighbors, Japan in particular, including Japan's participation in the American anti-missile test and its launch of spying satellites.

A healthy development of the Sino–U.S. relationship is conducive to the stability of the cross-Taiwan–strait relations. With the increasing recognition of China's valuable role on various regional and global issues like North Korea, South Asia, Iraq, and anti-terrorism, and also with the growth of high-level coordination between the two countries, Washington has not only expressed its disappointment at Chen Shuibian's lack of cooperation in areas of economy and security and otherwise, but also warned Taiwan not to take any petty opportunistic actions. To a certain extent, Taipei authorities are also aware that undermining Sino–U.S. relations can boomerang at the end of the day. Having said this, the United States will not in any significant way change its Taiwan policy, just as it will not make any concessions on arms sales to Taiwan.

Time to Build Up Mutual Strategic Confidence

For China–U.S. relations, 2009 has been seen by many both in China and the United States as a good year. Since President Obama came to power in the White House in January 2009, Sino–U.S. relations have been moving forward steadily and rapidly. Dialogue at different levels between the two governments increased significantly including the first China–U.S. strategic and economic dialogue; exchanges in various areas expanded including military to military one, and cooperation furthered on economic and trade interactions, energy, climate change, and environment, even in the area of anti-terrorists. It is noteworthy that the frequency of high-level dialogue and consultation reached a record high, with the Beijing Summit of President Hu Jintao and President Obama, which highlighted the bilateral relations between the two countries in the year 2009. It is encouraging that the two countries have now agreed to identify the Sino–U.S. relationship as positive, cooperative, and comprehensive. The two leaders also determined to work in joint efforts to meet with the challenges of the world at present and in the rest of twenty-first century.[7] With these inspiring steps taken by the two governments, growth of the Sino–U.S. relationship will hopefully keep its momentum and be carried on into the next decade.

The Current International Landscape

The year 2009 was when the international situation was undergoing dramatic and profound changes. It was against this backdrop that the Sino–U.S. relationship achieved noticeable developments.

First and foremost, the global financial crisis was a grand background that we can't avoid talking about in terms of China–U.S. relations. This serious crisis exposed the world to the negative side of globalization, to the malady of the international financial system, and loopholes or even lack of superintendence mechanism on financial institutions. People felt called upon to transform the global financial system from chaos to management. The international order too underwent deep changes that never took place before. It is smart to say the word "crisis" has two faces; that is, danger is always accompanied by opportunities. So it means financial crisis has turned out to be an opportunity for China and the United States to cooperate rather than compete as both countries suffered and were influenced by the crisis, and needed to tackle the financial setbacks and bring the world economy out of the bottom of the valley.

Second, international terrorism is still one of the major threats to world stability. It is a challenge to most countries in the world and the United States in particular. Presently, the United States needs China's cooperation, and China, for its own interest, would provide necessary assistance to bring about stability and peace in South Asia, particularly Afghanistan and Pakistan.

Third, there are emerging powers represented by India, Russia, Brazil, and China on the global and regional scene who will play an important role in world affairs and cannot be ignored. However, it is still too early to identify the world pattern as a multipolar one.

Last, there are evolving domestic trends in the United States, and China as well, though in different context and to different extent.

The general public mood in both countries is to get past the influence the financial crises brought to their lives. Most Americans demanding changes expected much of the Obama administration, such as three grand reform programs on clean energy, Medicare, and a control mechanism over financial institutions. There might be a tendency of inward looking, which would bring about a mood of trade protectionism.

On the part of China, the big issue is how to go on with macro management of China's economy. Hopefully, there will be steady and sustainable economic growth in the new decade. It also demands reform on economic systems and mechanisms. Furthermore, with a rapid economic developments, Chinese society has gradually moved toward the pluralistic. Public opinion has been paid greater attention with regard to not only domestic, especially economic, policies but also foreign policies.

President Obama's New Strategic Thinking

The financial crisis, which stemmed from Wall Street in August 2008, weakened U.S. strength and position of leadership in the world, and U.S. reputation and credibility in the international community was reduced. It is perceived, however, the United States is by all means still the only superpower in the world. Its overall decline of power has not yet come into being, neither is it seen in the foreseeable future. But it is only one side of the story. Today, people have already seen that with some emerging powers, including China, on the rise, the United States is going downhill gradually. Therefore, the Obama administration has to review and readjust its foreign policies both in the regional and global levels while putting economic recovery at home as the first priority, and by so doing it aims to maintain U.S. leadership in the international financial system.

With evolving domestic politics and changing international situation, President Obama has to be realistic, though some American elites would rather call him a practitioner. If one looks at his performance in the first ten months at the White House, Obama is less ideological than his predecessors and more pragmatic, in particular quite resolute and timely in making adjustment to American foreign policies.

With some powers rising and gaining weight in the international arena, the United States has come to realize that it can no longer solve problems in the world by itself; it needs help from other countries, from not only its allies but also developing countries. So the Obama administration, as many observers put it, has inclined to take a multilateral approach instead of unilateral attitude in its relations with other nations.

In diplomatic areas the Obama administration uses more of its soft power than its hard power, which is so-called smart power as necessary in dealing with other nations.

President Obama also has a kind of new thinking with regard to the relationship between the concepts of "leadership" and "partnership." For decades since the end of the Cold War, when Americans talk about "leadership and partnership," they actually focus on "leadership," leadership in deed and partnership in name. Now Obama has chosen to partnership in handling global issues and global management. But to many people, Obama's idea is essentially to have partnership either global, regional, or bilateral under U.S. leadership.

Obama's China Policy and Sino–U.S. Relations

President Obama has stated on different occasions and more recently in his statements at the press conference with President Hu Jintao in Beijing in November 2009 that "the United States welcomes China as a strong, prosperous and successful member of the community of nations."[8] He set the tone for his administration to identify China as a common member of the international community, if not a friend of the United States. Political analysts in China commented that the adjusted U.S. China policies reflect certain new ideas of President Obama.

First, in the past two decades or so, U.S.–China policy had been swinging between containment and engagement. It looks as if the Obama administration has fundamentally shifted from the concept of containment to engagement. But it is also noted the United States has so far not yet dropped the idea of hedging against China. It demonstrates lack of strategic trust with China.

Second, President Obama obviously looks at China's rise with a new eye. He seems to believe the era of zero-sum game is over. If Robert Zoellick's stakeholder concept was somewhat to stress that China needed to assume more responsibility, today the United States not only welcomes China's rise but also is adapting to China's rise. From the Chinese point of view, the United States and China are in the same boat, especially as both are living in a time when cooperation is extremely needed to reduce as much as possible the impacts of the financial crisis upon the world economy, and to realize economic recovery of the world as soon as possible.

Third, in line with U.S. emphasis on soft power and smart power, the Obama administration has taken a new look in its diplomacy with other countries. Americans are less arrogant and more modest, talking more of partnership and a little less of leadership. China understands that as a long-time superpower, the United States has its difficulty. The Chinese also think the United States and China need each other. It is not gracious to stress China needs more from the United States or vice versa.

Last but not least, Obama together with Hu Jintao have agreed that the two countries must respect each other's national core interest; the two nations should not intervene in each other's road to development or model of development.

The Beijing summit highlights Sino–U.S. relations in 2009, making the bilateral relationship turn a new page, achieve a new level. It can be said now the relationship between the United States and China indeed goes far beyond any single issue. As U.S. Deputy Secretary James Steinberg recently put it, "In this world, and under those circumstances, the logic of international cooperation is overwhelming, . . . we need to work with China to meet global challenges."[9] China welcomes such an optimistic statement. But to leave some room, we can only be cautious. There are nevertheless a number of issues facing the two countries:

1. The so-called theory of rebalance the world economy. To Chinese political elites, the purpose of such rhetorics by some American think tanks and scholars is to shove responsibility of financial crisis onto other countries.
2. Trade conflict between the United States and China is already a reality and will soon become a big headache. Trade protectionism on the U.S.

end will be a challenge to further improve the bilateral relations. If the top leaders follow the agreement they reached at the Beijing summit, acknowledge the other's difficulties at home, and observe the role of give and take, the two nations will compromise on the negotiation table for their mutual interests. In final analysis, the United States and China are such economically interdependent that they can't separate from each other in years ahead.

3. Appreciation of RMB demanded by the United States and protection of equity capital of China in the United States are two, among others, important disputed areas. If both countries want to see a stable and sustainable development of world economy, and most important, if both could take an objective and long-term point of view, these problems could be settled.
4. Arms sales to Taiwan is an issue that needs immediate attention. In terms of national core interest, it is at the top of the Chinese government's list. The Obama administration is expected to understand the desires of the Chinese government and to take the public mood of China into account before it takes steps.

It is only natural that there are disagreement and difficulties between the United States and China, and there are going to be even more ahead. They can be solved if both will make joint efforts to build mutual trust and mutual strategic confidence between the two nations. Leaders Obama and Hu Jintao possessed new ideas and new concepts in handling the most important and delicate bilateral relationship in the world and further progress of Sino–U.S. relations is hopeful. If they should be more creative, this relationship can be brought into the new decade, even the young century in a healthy, normal, and sustainable shape.

Globalization: The Genuine Opportunity

Economic globalization is restructuring the world economy, increasing interdependence and integration among countries, and also giving the Sino–U.S. relationship a global connotation.

At the end of the Cold War, only about one billion people were living under the market economic system. Nearly twenty years later, this figure has grown to four billion, encompassing peoples in China, India, Russia, and Eastern and Central European states. Massive marketization has definitely brought about serious restructuring of the global economic landscape, engulfing many more countries than ever into the worldwide flow of all elements of production factors. While globalization is, on the whole, delivering positive results in improving the welfare of peoples, it is also known for causing certain negative effects, and distributing unevenly its consequences both positive and negative.[10] Obviously, both China and the United States have largely benefited from globalization in the past thirty years or so. But other countries, even including certain Middle East states, have also reshaped their mindset amid globalization. All this points to the trend that global interdependence and common interests will further develop against any possible odds. It is against this background that we should rebuild the basis of the Sino–U.S. relationship. As it has been said sometimes, that if this bilateral relationship was defined by what both countries were against when the *Shanghai Communiqué* was released thirty-seven years ago, today it should be defined by what both are supportive of.

There are at present three big forces and their processes of development that have a strong bearing on China, the United States, their relationship, and the rest of world as well.

The first is the emergence of China. Beijing realizes how it gets integrated into the world and to what extent it interacts harmoniously with the world matter a lot for the international community. Meanwhile, Beijing knows well that it has got an even tougher domestic agenda. From its part, the United States should understand that many challenges lie ahead of China, such as, say in the social field, creating a big number of jobs, coping with ageing before getting rich, providing a basic healthcare system, reforming its education system, and so on. Economically, problems are even more daunting, like a highly weak banking sector, a still degrading environment, a growing gap between the rich and poor, an increasing need for energy imports, and others. Of course, it is more clear than ever that in this globalization era, China cannot possibly sort out its domestic issues well without giving due regard to the external environment.

The second is the influence of the United States. The American public has, since the turning point of 9/11, radically reshaped their perception of the U.S. position in the world. Americans used to perceive no major security threat to their country, but in one day, they began to feel a wholly complex situation of a real and palpable threat targeted squarely at Americans. On the one hand, the United States can hardly understand the Muslim world and its fanatics, even though it is also a religious nation. On the other hand, the Iraq war has torn apart American society. On top of it, Americans, and people in the rest of the world as well, are currently living in the shadow created by the financial crisis. The general public mood of the United States might turn to an inward-looking attitude, which may have significant impact upon U.S. foreign and economic policies.

The third is the emergence of other countries and regions like India, Brazil, and Africa. Interactions with these new players call for a new thinking and a new pattern for the United States and China. The atmosphere between the two countries is also increasingly influenced by so-called third party issues. The most salient example in this regard is interaction of the countries on the Darfur issue. Although this issue has no direct effect on bilateral U.S.–China relations, it has also become a hot subject for domestic and international discussion and debate. Many Americans use this issue to measure China's international behavior and to condition American policy and attitude toward China. Another case in point is China's policy toward Iran nuclear issue. Such growing "internationalization" of the relationship is more reflected in the competition and cooperation of the two countries in international bodies such as the United Nations.

Although it is generally believed to have promoted and benefited from globalization, the United States has got a very diverse domestic scenario as well. Many Americans have lots of worries about their ecological environment, their security environment, their job safety, continued wave of immigration, increasingly recalcitrant technology, hallowing out of their manufacturing, a soaring trade deficit, overstretching of American capabilities overseas, rising anti-Americanism abroad, a massive pandemic like the avian flu, and so on, not to say a new round of terrorist attacks. These domestic forces may restrict the American will and power to engage the world. So, both China and the United States need to balance well between internal and external sectors, and between active participation in international affairs and intervention with other countries' internal affairs.

On the other hand, America has been keen on carrying out its diplomacy with its values, such as freedom, democracy, human rights, the rule of law, and so forth. Quite invariably, this raises concerns or doubts of not a few countries including China. The Sino–U.S. relationship, though much improved recently, still harbors elements of mistrust. America is wary of China's rise, while China is concerned that the United States might once again target China after resolving problems in Afghanistan, Iraq, North Korea, and Iran. For the moment, debates in the United States about China's future are far from over. Therefore, it is urgent that mutual strategic confidence is built between China and the United States, which is the core of strategic reassurance. It is believed that mutual understanding between Hu Jintao and Obama was reached at the Beijing summit in November 2009. President Obama has stated that the U.S.–China relations will determine the future of the rest of twenty-first century, while President Hu Jintao reiterated that China and the United States need to build joint efforts toward a positive, cooperative, and comprehensive relationship. With these statements by the two leaders, it is assured that the two countries will be able to meet the challenges at the regional and global level, and bilateral as well, in the future.

Looking into the future, people have reason to be cautiously optimistic. Although China and the United States have experienced numerous crises, tensions, and strategic mistrust over the last thirty-five years, they have always managed to pull back from confrontation and sought to maintain and strengthen their bilateral relationship despite seemingly intractable differences on many issues. Today in the era of globalization, the Sino–U.S. relationship is entering a period of significant transformation due to ever-changing domestic and global environments and, therefore, needs a fresh look at new ideas and new concepts. Then a healthy and sustainable U.S.–China relationship will be hopeful.

Notes

1. Yang Shengmao, *A History of American Foreign Policy* (Beijing: People's Publishing House, 1991).
2. Ibid.
3. Ding Xinghao, *Thomas Robinson: New Ideas and New Concepts of Sino U.S. Relations* (Shanghai Education Publishing House, May 1995).
4. George W. Bush, "The National Security Strategy of the United States of America," White House, September 17, 2002.
5. *Survey of International Affairs* (Shanghai Education Publishing House, January 2002).
6. "National Security Strategy of the United States of America," 2001.
7. China–U.S. Joint Statement, Beijing, November 17, 2009.
8. President Barack Obama, "Joint Press Statement by President Obama and President Hu of China," Beijing, November 17, 2009, america.gov/st/texttrans-english/2009/november.
9. James Steinberg, "Administration's vision of the U.S.–China Relationship, Keynote Address at the Center for a New American Security," Washington, D.C., September 24, 2009, www.state.gov/s/d/2009/129686.htm.
10. George C. Lodge, *Managing Globalization in the Age of Interdependence* (San Diego: Pfeiffer & Company, 1995).

PART II

MACAO AND THE UNITED STATES: AN OVERVIEW

CHAPTER FOUR

Macao, Hawaii, and Sino–American Trade: Some Historical Observations, Interactions, and Consequences

Paul A. Van Dyke

It is well known that Macao is the place where the first U.S. treaty with China was signed in 1844 at Wanghsia (Mongha). From this time forward, Americans continued to be intricately tied to China's future, which has been the subject of many articles and books. Much less is known, however, about Macao's role in Sino–American interactions prior to the signing of the Wanghsia Treaty. This study will briefly retrace American activities in the Pearl River Delta before 1844 to gain a better understanding of where Macao and Hawaii fit into the broader context of Sino–American relations. We begin with an introduction of the establishment of foreign trade at Guangzhou (Canton), and Macao's role as the gatekeeper of that commerce.

Introduction

The capture of Taiwan in 1683 by the Qing government and subsequent opening of foreign trade in the following year are well-known events in Chinese history. Four ports were allowed to conduct foreign trade, including Ningbo, Quanzhou, Xiamen, and Canton. The Portuguese in Macao, of course, had been actively trading with China since 1557, and the Spanish carried on a regularly trade with China from Manila and also sent ships to Macao. Other foreigners, however, were not allowed to trade at Macao so the opening of these new ports was an important event in Chinese foreign trade and relations.

Once the word was out that trade was welcomed in China, foreign ships began going there to try out the market. Private traders, such as Armenians and Muslims from India, were among the first of the new arrivals to establish a regular commerce with Canton and other ports. These private traders had been expanding their operations between India and Manila since at least the 1660s, and from there they created direct trade connections with China's ports. By the 1690s, they had established agents in Macao, who managed the trade and ordered goods for the ships to arrive in the next season.[1]

East India companies' ships, such as those of the French and English, also began arriving in the newly opened ports. By 1700, these two nations had discovered that the best terms and most lucrative business could be negotiated at Canton, and within a few years other foreigners were going there as well.[2] By 1720, Canton had become the center of China's foreign commerce. The East India companies continued to try out the other three ports, to see if better terms could be found, but always returned to Canton. In 1757, the Qing government issued a decree closing the other three ports to foreigners, which secured Canton's monopoly on the commerce.

Macao and the Canton Trade

Macao played a major role in these exchanges with foreigners from the start. Chinese who learned some Portuguese served as linguists and compradors (provision purveyors) and Chinese fisherman based in Macao earned extra income guiding foreign ships into the delta. A small group of Chinese professionals called "Macao pilots" were licensed to guide ships from the lower delta to Whampoa (Huangpu), where all foreign ships were required to anchor. These licensed pilots lived in Macao and were the only persons allowed to guide ships up and down the Pearl River.[3]

No ships were allowed past the military forts at Humen (the entrance to the Pearl River known to foreigners as Bocca Tigris), on the inward or outward passages, without a Macao pilot aboard. This requirement gave administrators in Canton control over who came to trade and when they would be allowed to leave. For most of the large companies' ships, it was unthinkable to traverse the river without a pilot and his dozens of helpers. Because their drafts ranged from eighteen to twenty-four feet and the shallowest parts of the river were eighteen feet at low tide, it was mandatory for them to have pilots so the vessels remained in the deepest parts of the channels. They could only move with the ebb and flow of the tides. For small private ships such as those of most Americans a pilot was not always necessary, because their drafts were much shallower (often less than eighteen feet). Chinese regulations, however, required all ships to have a pilot whether they needed one or not, which was a point of contention to some Americans.

Macao was administered by Portugal, but the city was under the supervision of the governor-general of Guangdong and Guangxi Provinces, who was based in Guangzhou. Officially, foreigners were not allowed to stay year-round in Canton, and only Portuguese citizens and their households were permitted to stay year-round in Macao. Foreigners who went to Canton to trade were required to leave when their ships departed or moved downriver to Macao. When the next ships arrived in the following season, they could apply for permission to return to Canton. If their ships did not show up, then they were expected to leave China.

Foreign women were not allowed upriver so if they were onboard, they needed to disembark at Macao. They could stay in that city continuously so long as their husbands or family members were still involved in commerce upriver. Women reunited with their men folk each year when the latter returned from Canton after their ships departed.

City officials in Macao were sometimes asked to mediate when problems arose between Chinese and other foreigners. Trade disputes, accidents, injuries, thefts, and murders happened on occasion in Macao and the lower delta, which might require Portuguese assistance. If the incidents took place in the upper delta, however, then Macao officials were not usually involved.

On the whole the area south of Humen was administered more liberally than the area north of Humen. Officials in the lower delta, including Macao, regularly engaged in connivances with foreigners such as allowing merchandise to be unloaded and smuggled into China in exchange for a fee. Portuguese merchants in Macao had been making use of these contraband channels since the city's beginning so by the eighteenth century the procedures and connivance fees were well established. Americans were quick to learn how to channel goods through these contraband networks.[4]

Foreign ships were monitored by government as soon as they arrived in Chinese waters, but the reporting of their arrivals might be delayed until local officials had received their connivance fees and the contraband they were carrying safely unloaded. Ships were able to move about fairly freely in the lower delta, with little interference from authorities. If ships stayed lingering too long in the delta, however, a government patrol would be sent to investigate and order them to leave. The movement of vessels north of Humen, however, was strictly controlled, and a permit was required every time a ship wanted to move from one location to another.

Two Chinese tidewaiters boarded each foreign ship at Humen on their inward passage. From that moment to the time they returned to Humen on their return trip, these officers stayed with the ships. Thus the stop gate, as far as trade was concerned, was Humen. Portuguese, Americans and numerous other foreigners exploited this gap in administrative control by carrying on extensive smuggling activities in the delta.

After 1700, when East India companies' ships began arriving at Canton on a more regular basis, companies' officers regularly engaged in illicit activities. The contraband trade of these employees, however, was usually limited to personal items they sold and purchased in Canton. The companies were also regularly involved in illegal trade, such as exporting gold and the forbidden silks of yellow and red (colors reserved exclusively for the emperor's use). These illicit exchanges were normally carried out upriver between Whampoa and Canton. It was thus not the case that all smuggling was done in the lower delta. All other merchandise, including other foreign imports, and Chinese exports of tea, porcelain, and silk were traded through legal channels.

With the rise of opium smuggling in China in the second half of the eighteenth century came an increase in the smuggling of other commodities. Foreigners secretly unloaded their contraband near Macao, before proceeding upriver to obtain a return cargo of legal cargo. They needed to have some trade goods in order to obtain permission to go upriver, because a cargo of silver coin alone was not sufficient to qualify as a "merchant ship" (which were the only vessels allowed upriver). The quantity of the imports did not need to be large; a few chests of foreign fabrics or a quantity of sandalwood, tin, or animal skins, combined with chests of silver coins, were generally sufficient.

The freedom of being able to move about the delta undisturbed combined with the ease of engaging Chinese in illegal trade and the loosely defined import requirements gave foreigners considerable leeway in selling some of their imports illicitly downriver. The majority of their imports could be channeled through the contraband networks and thereby avoid import duties at Canton. Customs superintendents (Hoppos) and governor-generals in Canton were usually aware that some smuggling was going on in the delta, which is probably one of the reasons why they continually brought up the idea of taxing import silver. If silver was taxed at a rate equal or higher to what foreigners would have paid in duties on imports, then there was nothing to be gained by smuggling downriver. Companies rarely engaged in these activities downriver, but private traders from India, and private Europeans and Americans, used these networks regularly.[5]

By the 1760s, some vessels began arriving with their hulls filled entirely with opium.[6] Prior to this happening, the drug generally made up a small portion of import cargos. It was treated more as a speculative commodity that traders brought to try out the market. By the time Americans arrived in

1784, however, the opium market had matured with some ships carrying nothing but the drug. After unloading the opium in the delta, smugglers could purchase a small amount of cargo from other foreigners to qualify as a merchant ship and apply for permission to trade at Whampoa. The silver that was obtained from opium sales was used to purchase tea and other exports so ships could leave with their hulls full of saleable merchandise.[7]

Before 1820, most of the contraband was either unloaded downriver and channeled through Macao, or brought to Whampoa and smuggled into Canton. The latter option involved the two Chinese tidewaiters that were assigned to each foreign ship. They lived with their families and servants in two sampans chained one to each side of the ships. Tidewaiters' jobs were to watch that no merchandise was loaded or unloaded without permission, but in practice, they abused their authority regularly. For a fee of six to seven dollars per picul, tidewaiters would permit opium chests to be unloaded from the ships. In fact, tidewaiters even attended the weighing of the opium to ensure they received their proper payments, and sometimes transported the drug themselves from Whampoa to Canton in exchange for another fee.[8] Tidewaiters' boats were not inspected at the tollhouses in the river so this was the perfect cover for smuggling.

In other cases, Chinese buyers arranged for boats to pick up the contraband at Whampoa, and then paid the tidewaiters to keep quiet. Chinese compradors were very active in this smuggling, because they could hide contraband easily in their boats among the many other items they carried, and compradors' boats did not have to stop at the tollhouses. Many products were smuggled into China using these methods, and each item had well-established connivance fees attached to it. In 1817, an American merchant observed that the connivance fees to smuggle goods from Whampoa to Canton were, on the whole, 40 percent less than if the merchandise had been traded legally, so this was a considerable saving.[9]

As numerous studies have shown, the silver that was received from opium sales was an essential component in the growth of the export tea trade. Without that silver, it would have certainly hindered growth, which was not a good outcome for the reputations and future careers of governor-generals and Hoppos. Consequently, there were strong personal incentives for these top officials to turn a blind eye to these illegal exchanges and hope that the smuggling would not create problems during their stint in Canton. Officials were usually assigned to their posts for about three years, but it could be more or less according to the circumstances at the time.[10]

As long as the legitimate trade did not suffer decline, and continued to grow, it was better for the sake of officials' careers not to expend human and financial resources on the quashing of smuggling. If there was a drop in the volume of legal trade, it would likely trigger a crackdown on contraband in order to bring the quantities back to former levels. Beijing, of course, kept hearing reports of opium smuggling in the delta and put pressure on local officials in Canton to do something about it. These pressures gave rise to periodic crackdowns on contraband, but these efforts were often done more as a sign to superiors that their orders were being followed than as sincere efforts to end smuggling. Hoppos and governor-generals needed to be careful that crackdowns on smuggling did not bring about a reduction of the legal export trade, or they would have to answer to the emperor. Such an outcome could easily lead to demotion and a less desirable post in the future.

By about 1800, the opium trade had become so visible at Whampoa that top officials decided it needed to be suppressed. A couple foreign ships had tried anchoring there year-round with the specific intention of operating as an opium warehouse.[11] When too much of the drug arrived, prices plummeted and these warehouse ships (called "hulks") provided a means of keeping the product in China until the market recovered. These hulks had been anchoring in the lower delta since at least 1780, but piracy became such a threat in the late 1790s that they moved upriver to Whampoa. When the Hoppo found out about these activities, however, he ordered the hulks to leave.[12]

These periodic crackdowns were usually short lived and not effective in the long term. Smugglers simply moved to other locations during the disturbances, and then returned to Whampoa when the crackdowns subsided or when the next Hoppo or governor-general took up their posts. New officials needed some time to get to know the trade, and while they were busy doing that, smugglers went about their businesses.

The suppression of the opium trade in the delta has received much coverage in previous studies, but a couple of those events are key to this discussion so we will briefly summarize them here. In 1814 and 1815, attempts were made to quash the contraband trade in Macao and Whampoa, and orders were issued to inspect all ships for opium. On January 1, 1815, the Xiangshan magistrate arrested eighteen opium dealers in Macao, and in the following August, Chinese officials demanded that Portuguese vessels there be examined to ensure they had none of the drug aboard.[13]

On June 20, 1815, another edict from Xiangshan County seat was sent to Macao forbidding the propagating of Christianity. The suppression of religion is important to note because, as will be shown below, Qing officials often saw the propogation of Christianity and opium trafficking to go hand in hand.[14] On September 10, the Dutch reported that the opium dealers who were incarcerated in January were still in prison. On December 21, four of the eighteen dealers were banished to Yili (Kulja, present city of Yining).[15] The trafficking of contraband in China, however, was little affected by these localized crackdowns.

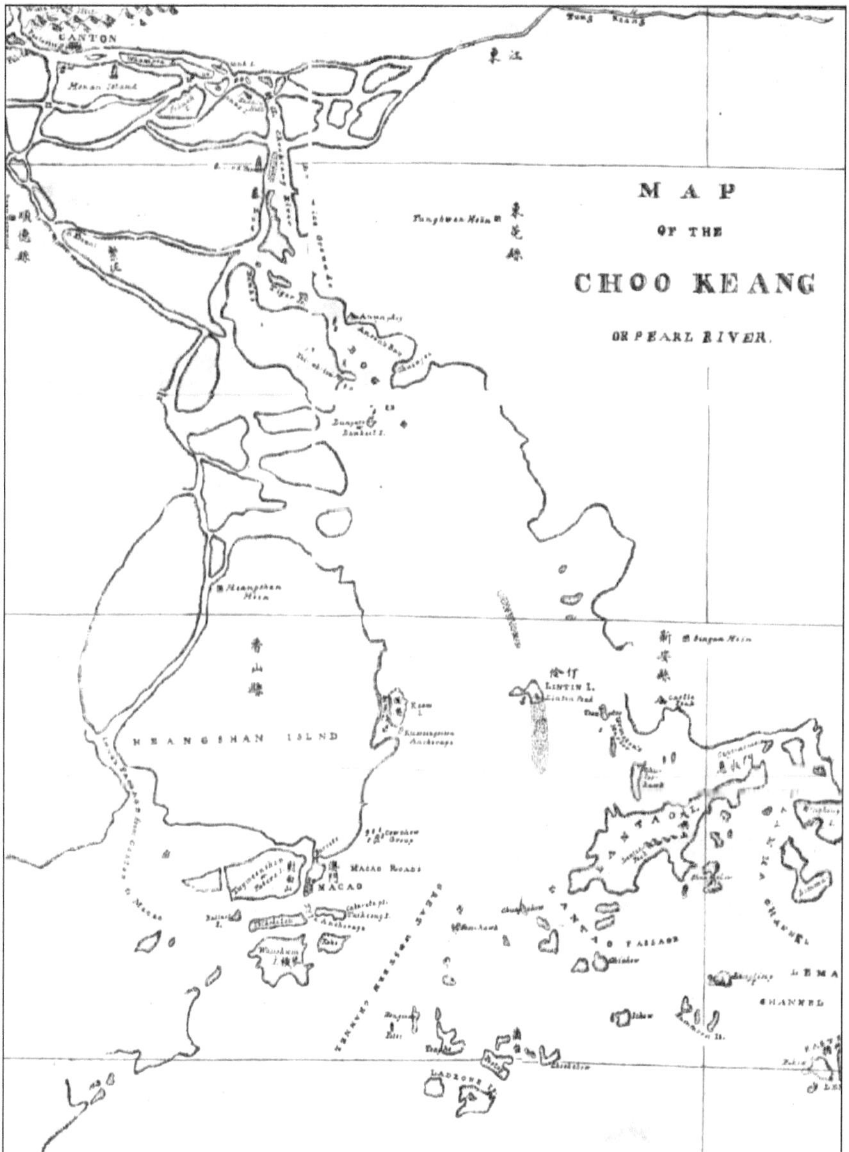

Map 1: Pearl River Delta
***Source: Chinese Repository*, vol. 3, no. 2 (June 1834), p. 88**

In 1819 and 1820 initiatives were launched again to quash the opium trade at Whampoa, and this time saw some success. Smugglers were discouraged from operating at Whampoa, but then moved their operations downriver to Lintin Island, where they had more freedom to carry out their activities. At the same time, Macao became a less desirable place to sell the drug because of high transaction fees so some Portuguese began sending their ships to Lintin as well. From 1820 to the outbreak of the first Opium War in 1839, Lintin Island and the adjacent ports of Kumsingmoon (Qi'ao Island) and Capsingmoon (near Hong Kong) became the center of the contraband trade (see map 1). Together they formed the Lintin network.[16]

Now that we have laid the background of how legal and illegal trade operated, we can understand better the early American interactions with China.

Beginnings of Sino–American Trade

Major Samuel Shaw and his friend and comrade in arms, Captain Randall, were commissioned to serve as commercial agents aboard the American ship *Empress of China* in 1784.[17] These were much different assignments from what these two military men had been trained for. The signing of the Treaty of Paris in 1783 ended the American War of Independence and cut short many military careers, such as those of Shaw and Randall. The opportunity to go to China provided the two men with not only an income but also a way to continue serving national interests, albeit in peacetime fashion. Shaw would later become instrumental in helping the young nation establish itself in international politics and commerce.[18]

Americans were welcomed when they arrived at Macao and Canton by other foreigners operating there, including the Portuguese, French, Dutch, Danes, Austrians, Swedes, and British. In their small ship and small numbers Shaw and Randall must have felt very much out of place, and overwhelmed by what they saw and heard around them. The *Empress of China* was one of forty ships trading at Whampoa in 1784. It was a relatively small ship compared to the large East Indiamen so it would have appeared very insignificant when anchored next to all the other ships.

As far as commerce was concerned, the *Empress of China* made up only a tiny fraction of total trade at Canton, perhaps no more than 1 percent. With 100 to 150 men aboard the East India companies' ships and about 30 to 80 men aboard the ten or so private vessels in port there were upward of 4,000 foreigners in China (without including the thousands of Portuguese at Macao). The *Empress of China* had a crew of 42 men so the Americans were outnumbered by about 100 to 1. European ships, cargos, and people continued to dominate the China trade into the nineteenth century, but Americans gradually came to play a significant role that influenced the outcome of history.[19]

The successful voyage of the *Empress of China* was seen by many Americans as a sign that their young nation was coming of age. The prestige of being involved in the China trade alongside other powerful nations of the world was a boost to national pride, morale, and confidence.[20] Americans did not see themselves as 1 percent of the foreigners in Canton, or 1 percent of the trade with China, but rather as one nation among equals in a very prestigious commerce. Entrepreneurs in increasing numbers began to speculate in financing voyages to Asia, and as a result, the trade expanded to twenty-one American ships in 1800, twenty-five in 1815, to around sixty ships each year in the early 1830s.[21]

By 1800, Sino–American trade had expanded to about one-third that of the total British trade so in a very short time Americans had expanded the numbers of their ships and voyages dramatically. In terms of overall exports, the American trade by 1800 was quite substantial making up perhaps 10 to 15 percent of overall volume, which, except for the British Company, equaled or surpassed what each of the other East India companies handled annually in the eighteenth century.[22]

As briefly discussed above, there were two types of American trade in China, legal and illegal. In order to understand American operations more clearly, and at the same time bring out Macao's role in these operations, a brief explanation is provided here of each type.

Sino–American Legal Trade

American ships that came to trade legitimately with China had to first stop at Macao. In the early nineteenth century, an Englishman by the name of John Budwell established an inn called the Macao Tavern to accommodate small private traders. Budwell's inn was conveniently located on Macao's Praya Grande and became a favorite stop for many Americans. Table 4.1 shows the costs to stay and eat at the Macao Tavern in 1819.

Budwell brought the new arrivals up-to-date on the procedures to gain permission to go upriver to Whampoa. The first thing to do was send a letter to the Portuguese governor announcing their arrival and asking permission to enter Macao, which they (or Budwell) did immediately upon arrival. Then, a pilot had to be obtained who requested permission from the Junminfu 軍民府 military garrison in Qianshan for permission to guide the ship upriver. Budwell helped Americans arrange these matters, while they sat in

Table 4.1 Expenses Incurred at Macao Tavern on November 20, 1819

American Ship *General Hamilton* to John Budwell	Spanish Dollars (Patacas)
Nov. 18, 1819: To Bed Room	1.00
Nov. 19: To Breakfast	0.50
ditto: To Dinner	1.50
Nov. 20: To Bed Room	1.00
Total	4.00

These prices were copied from a receipt in the Rhode Island Historical Society (RIHS)
Source: Ship Papers, Box 157, Ship General Hamilton Papers 1818-1820

his pub, enjoyed a meal and a bed, and caught up on the latest gossip and news about trade.

After receiving their permission chop (license) and a pilot, the ship left Macao for Humen, where the entry permit and pilot's papers were inspected. After clearing customs, the pilot engaged several tow- and buoy-sampans to help the ship through the deep channels of the river. A day or two later, the tides carried the piloting procession to Whampoa, where all foreign ships were required to anchor (twenty kilometers downriver from Canton).

At Whampoa, Americans engaged a licensed comprador to supply them with provisions and Chinese servants and laborers while they were in China, and a licensed linguist to take care of obtaining all of the necessary chops and to mediate the terms of trade with Chinese officials. The ship was then measured by customs officers so the port fees could be determined. At this time, a Chinese merchant was appointed to stand security for the ship, and then trade could commence.

The ships remained at Whampoa until they had unloaded all of their imports and filled their hulls with Chinese exports. Depending upon the size of the ship, the time Americans spent in port could vary from a couple weeks to several months. American officers went to Canton to arrange the trade with Chinese merchants, where they rented apartments in foreign buildings known as "factories." In addition to each ship having a comprador to supply the crew with provisions, officers in Canton were also required to hire a licensed factory comprador to attend to their needs.

The crews remained aboard the ships at Whampoa, but were usually allowed shore leave to visit Canton at least once before leaving China. Most of the crews were paid their wages a week or two prior to departure, which gave them money to purchase small items. They could bring back as many items as would fit into their sea chests.[23]

Figures in table 4.2 show an increase of American imports and exports, from 1804 to 1818, with a growth of about 250 percent. These figures were copied from the American consular office in Canton so they should be fairly reliable. The figures represent only legal trade and do not include contraband that Americans smuggled in and out of China. That commerce grew in unison with the legal trade.

Sino–American Illegal Trade

In the early years, American commercial ventures in China tended to be highly speculative, which if not conducted with care could lead to the ruin of everyone involved. After arriving in China, some traders were greatly disappointed to learn of the depressed market for their furs, and other goods, and surprised at the high port fees they were required to pay if they took their ships upriver to Whampoa. These and other disappointing factors led to many Americans seeking alternative ways to do business with China.[24]

For small ships of less than 500 tons (which included most American ships), the port fees amounted to seven to ten taels per ton capacity, which calculated to about 3 to 7 percent of the value of their export cargos. The port fees for large company ships of 1,200 to 1,600 tons, in comparison, only amounted to about 1 to 1.5 percent of the export cargos so, in this respect, larger ships had a significant advantage over the smaller ships. As a result of these high fees, many Americans tried to avoid going upriver and sold their goods illegally in the lower delta.[25]

Before 1836, Americans were not permitted to trade directly at Macao, but they could hire a Chinese fisherman to guide them into one of the smuggling harbors in the delta to unload their merchandise. The contraband would then be unloaded into small vessels, channeled through and taxed in Macao, and then smuggled upriver. After the contraband trade moved to Lintin Island in 1820, many American ships went there to sell their goods.[26]

American smugglers avoided taking their ships to Macao Roads so they would not be pressured into hiring a Macao pilot and then be required to go upriver to Whampoa. The first thing to do upon arrival in Chinese waters was to hire a local fisherman from one of the fishing vessels in the delta, to

Table 4.2 American Imports and Exports for 1804 and 1818 (in millions of Spanish dollars).

Year	Imports	Exports	Spanish dollars (in millions)
1804	3.5	3.8	7.3
1818	10.2	9.1	19.3

"Total value of imports & exports in the port of Canton in American vessels from the year 1804 to 1819 inclusive, with the amount of shipping each year, and the quantities of teas, silks, and Nankeens exported; compiled from office documents procured at the Consular office in Canton."
Source: HSP: 687 Waln Family Papers, vol. 2, fol. 52

guide the ship to Lintin harbor (or adjacent Kumsingmoon or Capsingmoon). Some Americans managed to traverse the route without a pilot. After arriving at the island, captains and merchants could go ashore to Macao without a problem and catch up on the latest news.

At Lintin and Macao, smugglers could take care of all the necessary arrangements to sell their merchandise on the black market. The contraband at Lintin was smuggled into China on Chinese boats called "fast crabs" or "scrambling dragons," which bypassed Macao and went directly to Chinese agents upriver. These vessels were built specially for this purpose, with upwards of forty to sixty oarsmen in each of them. They could outrun any government patrol boats, and carried contraband in both directions, up and down river.

Just like legitimate ships going upriver to Whampoa, smugglers operating in the lower delta also needed backhauls to cover the costs of their return passages. There were three ways of obtaining these exports: the goods could be purchased illegally from the crab boats at inflated prices; smugglers could arrange for goods to be purchased at Canton and shipped downriver aboard other foreign vessels; or smugglers could go upriver themselves to get what they wanted.

The most effective way to get a return cargo was to purchase a cargo of rice at Lintin, and then apply for permission to go upriver as a "rice ship." Ships carrying rice paid reduced port fees at Whampoa, and after unloading the product, they could purchase a return cargo. This alternative was much preferred because it allowed smugglers to pick the products they wanted at the prices they felt acceptable. With the other two options (purchasing from the crab boats or from other foreigners), there was little selection and prices were inflated to compensate for carrying the goods downriver. Some American firms such as Russell and Company and Perkins and Company sent ships to Batavia, Manila, and/or Singapore specifically to obtain rice to supply to the opium ships at Lintin. After the rice was taken out of the ships at Whampoa, they could pile as many Chinese exports in their holds and on their decks as they could carry without falling into the water (depending on the weather). The excess merchandise was then sold or transferred to other ships at Lintin Island so they would have a backhaul.[27]

By the 1830s, there were thirty-five to forty fast crabs servicing smugglers. The contraband trade had now expanded to the point that in some years, there were more foreign ships trading illegally in the lower delta than there were going upriver to Whampoa. On November 1, 1837, for example, the English-language newspaper, *Canton Press*, recorded twenty-four ships (not including the hospital ship) anchored at Whampoa (trading legally), and thirty-three ships anchored at Lintin (trading illegally). Included in those numbers are four American ships at Whampoa and seven at Lintin.

During inclement weather or when Chinese patrols came to Lintin, American ships and other small vessels moved to Kumsingmoon. The American Baptist missionary Rev. Lewis Shuck spent much of the year of 1836 in Macao, and visted Kumsingmoon in September. He reported that it was "an excellent place of anchorage, where there are about thirty vessels now at anchor, and among the number many from the United States."[28] There were many Americans involved in both types of commerce each year and it is important to understand this in order to see more clearly the effects their activities were having on Macao.[29]

Macao and the Contraband Trade

The contraband trade had adverse effects on Macao's economy, which was partially the result of American activities in the lower delta. By the 1820s, some of the trade that had been going through Macao was now diverted to the Lintin network, owing to the more advantageous terms that could be obtained there.[30] Numerous attempts were made to introduce ways to bring the contraband trade, especially opium, back to Macao, but none saw much success.

In a change of policy, Macao officials decided in 1836 to invite all foreigners back to the city, with special emphasis on opium traffickers. Figure 4.1 shows the advertisement the Macao government placed in the *Canton Register*. Prior to this happening, only Portuguese-owned cargos were admitted into the city, but now all foreigners were encouraged to bring their contraband there. The scheme, however, did not bear fruit, because foreigners still found it more advantageous to trade in other ports in the delta.

This advertisement was, of course, contrary to Chinese law and policy, which required all non-Portuguese to trade at Canton. And the open invitation to smugglers, including Americans and other opium traffickers, was a blatant disregard for the Chinese prohibition of the drug. Macao officials' bold attempts to reinvigorate the city's economy, in a way that completely ignored the administration in Guangzhou and Beijing, is an example of how desperate they had become to increase revenues, by whatever means possible.

The events that followed the opium wars and the effects they had on Macao have been treated extensively in other studies so we will not elaborate on them here. The 1840s were equally troubling for Macao, as were the 1830s, with most foreigners escaping to Hong Kong in 1844. The city did not recover from the effects these other harbors were having on its commerce until it began to issue monopolies on certain industries, such as gambling, tobacco and opium processing, and fireworks and match manufacturing. By the 1850s, gambling was especially successful, which took advantage of the

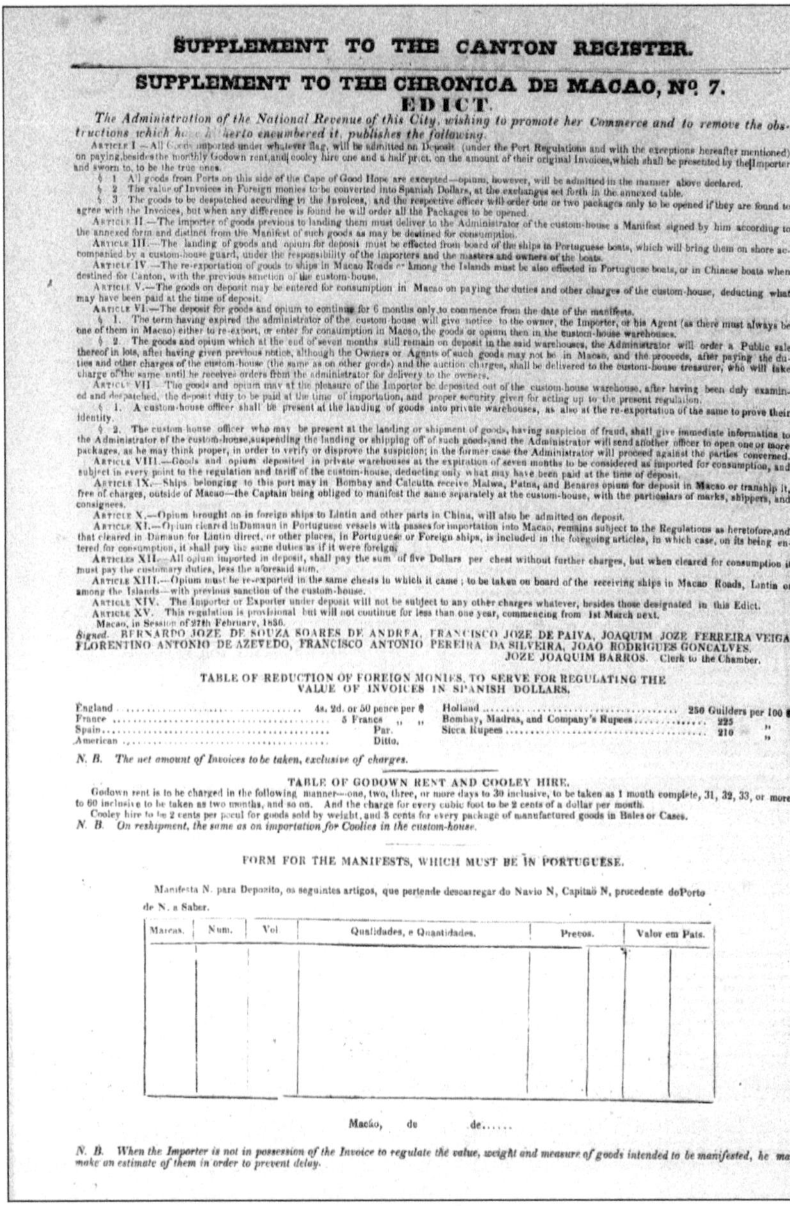

SUPPLEMENT TO THE CANTON REGISTER.

SUPPLEMENT TO THE CHRONICA DE MACAO, Nº. 7.

EDICT.

The Administration of the National Revenue of this City, wishing to promote her Commerce and to remove the obstructions which [illegible] hitherto encumbered it, publishes the following.

ARTICLE I.—All Goods imported under whatever flag, will be admitted on Deposit (under the Port Regulations and with the exceptions hereafter mentioned) on paying, besides the monthly Godown rent, and cooley hire one and a half pr. ct. on the amount of their original Invoices, which shall be presented by the Importer and sworn to, to be the true ones.

§ 1 All goods from Ports on this side of the Cape of Good Hope are excepted—opium, however, will be admitted in the manner above declared.

§ 2 The value of Invoices in Foreign monies to be converted into Spanish Dollars, at the exchanges set forth in the annexed table.

§ 3 The goods to be despatched according to the Invoices, and the respective officer will order one or two packages only to be opened if they are found to agree with the Invoices, but when any difference is found he will order all the Packages to be opened.

ARTICLE II.—The importer of goods previous to landing them must deliver to the Administrator of the custom-house a Manifest signed by him according to the annexed form and distinct from the Manifest of such goods as may be destined for consumption.

ARTICLE III.—The landing of goods and opium for deposit must be effected from board of the ships to Portuguese boats, which will bring them on shore accompanied by a custom-house guard, under the responsibility of the importers and the masters and owners of the boats.

ARTICLE IV.—The re-exportation of goods to ships in Macao Roads or among the Islands must be also effected in Portuguese boats, or in Chinese boats when destined for Canton, with the previous sanction of the custom-house.

ARTICLE V.—The goods on deposit may be entered for consumption in Macao on paying the duties and other charges of the custom-house, deducting what may have been paid at the time of deposit.

ARTICLE VI.—The deposit for goods and opium to continue for 6 months only, to commence from the date of the manifests.

§ 1. The term having expired the administrator of the custom-house will give notice to the owner, the Importer, or his Agent (as there must always be one of them in Macao) either to re-export, or enter for consumption in Macao, the goods or opium then in the custom-house warehouses.

§ 2. The goods and opium which at the end of seven months still remain on deposit in the said warehouses, the Administrator will order a Public sale thereof in lots, after having given previous notice, although the Owners or Agents of such goods may not be in Macao, and the proceeds, after paying the duties and other charges of the custom-house (the same as on other goods) and the auction charges, shall be delivered to the custom-house treasurer, who will take charge of the same until he receives orders from the administrator for delivery to the owners.

ARTICLE VII.—The goods and opium may at the pleasure of the Importer be deposited out of the custom-house warehouse, after having been duly examined and despatched, the deposit duty to be paid at the time of importation, and proper security given for acting up to the present regulation.

§ 1. A custom-house officer shall be present at the landing of goods into private warehouses, as also at the re-exportation of the same to prove their identity.

§ 2. The custom-house officer who may be present at the landing or shipment of goods, having suspicion of fraud, shall give immediate information to the Administrator of the custom-house, suspending the landing or shipping off of such goods, and the Administrator will send another officer to open one or more packages, as he may think proper, in order to verify or disprove the suspicion; in the former case the Administrator will proceed against the parties concerned.

ARTICLE VIII.—Goods and opium deposited in private warehouses at the expiration of seven months to be considered as imported for consumption, and subject in every point to the regulation and tariff of the custom-house, deducting only what may have been paid at the time of deposit.

ARTICLE IX.—Ships belonging to this port may in Bombay and Calcutta receive Malwa, Patna, and Benares opium for deposit in Macao or tranship it, free of charges, outside of Macao—the Captain being obliged to manifest the same separately at the custom-house, with the particulars of marks, shippers, and consignees.

ARTICLE X.—Opium brought on in foreign ships to Lintin and other parts in China, will also be admitted on deposit.

ARTICLE XI.—Opium cleared in Damaun in Portuguese vessels with passes for importation into Macao, remains subject to the Regulations as heretofore, and that cleared in Damaun for Lintin direct, or other places, in Portuguese or Foreign ships, is included in the foregoing articles, in which case, on its being entered for consumption, it shall pay the same duties as if it were foreign.

ARTICLES XII.—All opium imported in deposit, shall pay the sum of five Dollars per chest without further charges, but when cleared for consumption it must pay the customary duties, less the aforesaid sum.

ARTICLE XIII.—Opium must be re-exported in the same chests in which it came; to be taken on board of the receiving ships in Macao Roads, Lintin or among the Islands—with previous sanction of the custom-house.

ARTICLE XIV. The Importer or Exporter under deposit will not be subject to any other charges whatever, besides those designated in this Edict.

ARTICLE XV. This regulation is provisional but will not continue for less than one year, commencing from 1st March next.

Macao, in Session of 27th February, 1836.

Signed. BERNARDO JOZE DE SOUZA SOARES DE ANDREA, FRANCISCO JOZE DE PAIVA, JOAQUIM JOZE FERREIRA VEIGA, FLORENTINO ANTONIO DE AZEVEDO, FRANCISCO ANTONIO PEREIRA DA SILVEIRA, JOAO RODRIGUES GONCALVES.

JOZE JOAQUIM BARROS. Clerk to the Chamber.

TABLE OF REDUCTION OF FOREIGN MONIES, TO SERVE FOR REGULATING THE VALUE OF INVOICES IN SPANISH DOLLARS.

England	4s. 2d. or 50 pence per $	Holland	250 Guilders per 100 $
France	5 Francs " "	Bombay, Madras, and Company's Rupees	225
Spain	Par.	Sicca Rupees	210 "
American	Ditto.		"

N. B. The net amount of Invoices to be taken, exclusive of charges.

TABLE OF GODOWN RENT AND COOLEY HIRE.

Godown rent is to be charged in the following manner—one, two, three, or more days to 30 inclusive, to be taken as 1 month complete, 31, 32, 33, or more to 60 inclusive to be taken as two months, and so on. And the charge for every cubic foot to be 2 cents of a dollar per month.

Cooley hire to be 2 cents per pecul for goods sold by weight, and 3 cents for every package of manufactured goods in Bales or Cases.

N. B. On reshipment, the same as on importation for Coolies in the custom-house.

FORM FOR THE MANIFESTS, WHICH MUST BE IN PORTUGUESE.

Manifesta N. para Deposito, os seguintes artigos, que pertende descarregar do Navio N, Capitaõ N, procedente do Porto de N. a Saber.

Marcas.	Num.	Vol	Qualidades, e Quantidades.	Preços.	Valor em Pats.

Macão, de de......

N. B. When the Importer is not in possession of the Invoice to regulate the value, weight and measure of goods intended to be manifested, he may make an estimate of them in order to prevent delay.

Figure 4.1. Invitation for Smugglers to come to Macao
***Source:* Canton Register, March 15, 1836 (supplement)**

rapid rise and success of Hong Kong and the many Chinese there who were now eager to try their luck at the gaming tables in Macao.[31] In a small but significant way, Americans were partially responsible for that outcome, by contributing to the success of other depots in the delta.

As shown above and below, the history of Macao and connections to Sino–American relations is more complicated than previously thought, with various intermingled, interconnected, and interrelated consequences. But there is yet one more part of the story that still needs to be told, which involved Hawaii.

Macao, Hawaii, and Sino–American Trade

Three products gave Americans an advantage in the Chinese market: furs from the Northwest Coast, ginseng from Canada, and sandalwood from Hawaii. By the time Americans arrived in China, these items were already being traded extensively. As Americans gained more control over these resources they gained an edge in the market. Ginseng was grown in several countries in Asia, and Russians had been trading Northwest furs to the Chinese at Kamchatka for many years. French, Spanish, Portuguese, and British private traders based in India, Manila, and Macao were also experimenting in marketing American furs in the later half of the eighteenth century, and sandalwood from India and Timor had been going to China for centuries.

French ships had been carrying ginseng to China since the early eighteenth century, which they obtained from the French-owned Northwest Fur Company in Canada. Ginseng was collected and then forwarded to France, where it was put onto ships bound for China. In the early eighteenth century, Jesuit missionaries had suggested that ginseng might be a good item to market in China, but it was not until later that substantial amounts were carried there.[32] By the time Americans became involved in the trade all of the products were fairly well established.

In the 1790s, most of the trade in ginseng from Canada and furs from the Northwest Coast were taken over by New England merchants. Canadian ginseng was sometimes shipped to Canton across the Atlantic Ocean, but most of the furs went via the Pacific. After procuring their cargos on the Northwest Coast, Americans sailed for the Sandwich Islands where they replenished their provisions and supplies before heading to China. Hawaii was gradually pulled into the international trading networks, and it was not long before it was discovered that sandalwood there sold well in China. Large quantities of that wood were consumed in China each year for the making of incense. All of these products were traded by Americans in China both legally and illegally.[33]

Hawaiian chieftains proved to be very enterprising individuals and quick to pick up on the importance their islands were becoming in Sino–American trade. They gained control over sandalwood areas, monopolized some of the provisioning depots that were established, and invested directly in shipping Hawaiian cargos to China themselves. The Hawaiian chief Tiana (also spelled "Kaiana") even traveled to Macao and Canton in 1787 aboard a private British ship, and became a great spectacle and favorite among foreigners there. He had his portrait painted by the famous Chinese artist Spoilum (Shi Bei Lin 士卑林) in Canton and purchased many Chinese products to carry back to his homeland. Tiana also helped to repatriate another Hawaiian, by the name of Wainee, who had remained in China from a previous Northwest voyage owing to her extended illness. Wainee unfortunately died on the return passage home.[34]

From this time forward, Hawaii began to play an intricate role in Sino–American trade and relations. Animals and plants, including cattle, goats, turkeys, rabbits, pigeons, and lime and orange trees, were purchased in Canton and transported to Hawaii, transforming it into a major provisioning depot for ships sailing the Pacific. Over time, these interactions continued to pull more Hawaiian and American traders and investors into international commerce. The Hawaiian King Kamehameha gained control of some of the sandalwood producing areas, and had it shipped to Canton. He also sold sandalwood to other traders bound for China. Later sugarcane became a major Hawaiian export. By the 1870s, the provisioning trade had grown into a substantial industry for many Hawaiians, and extended to all of the islands.[35]

The interactions went in the other direction as well with Chinese sailors and laborers sailing from Macao to the Sandwich Islands aboard American and private European ships. Before the signing of the Nanking Treaty in 1842, it was illegal for Chinese to seek employment aboard foreign ships. However, there were ways to get around the restrictions, by engaging the foreigners in the lower delta where the control and movements of ships were less restrictive. Hiring Chinese could be done fairly easily in Macao, and then the men were picked up at a remote location in the delta such as Lintin Island.

Disease and illness also traveled along the trade networks. Foreigners involved in the China trade brought a disease to Hawaii not unlike typhoid, which quickly spread throughout the local population claiming many victims. King Kamehameha also contracted the fever. The early Chinese arrivals were blamed for bringing leprosy to the islands, which infected not only the migrants but some of the local inhabitants. Canton and Macao both had leprosy colonies, and visitors to the Hawaiian Islands commented how they had seen people in those two cities who were infected with this disease. They drew parallels with the leprosy communities they saw in Hawaii, which infected Chinese as well.[36]

From the 1780s to the 1810s, private British, French, Portuguese, and Spanish traders from India, Pondicherry, Macao, and Manila were also venturing to the northwest coast of North America. Many of these ships stopped in Hawaii, and everyone was trying to lay claim to the islands. Many of these entrepreneurs had connections to Portuguese and other agents in Macao, who helped finance voyages and arrange sales and purchases in China. In many ways, Macao was closely involved in these interactions with Hawaii and North America, either directly through merchants based there or indirectly through commission agents who lived there and helped arrange the sales of the cargos.[37]

Russians were also involved in these Sino–Hawaiian–American interactions, which had connections back to Macao. Russia had long claimed rights to the American Northwest Coast and to the Sandwich Islands. In 1814 and 1815, Russians made a concerted effort to regain control of some of this territory. In the latter year, the medical practitioner Georg Anton Schäffer was commissioned by the Russian American Company to promote Russian interests in the Hawaiian Islands, which of course involved China. Schäffer went to Hawaii to set up trading alliances with King Kamehameha, which was a disappointment to the king's American trading partners. Kamehameha's extensive involvement in the China trade made him the preferred ruler with whom to form such alliances so he was the obvious target of Schäffer's attention.

As fate would have it Kamehameha fell ill again, and his favorite wife, Queen Kaahumanu, contracted yellow fever. Being a medical doctor by practice, Schäffer was able to treat both of them, which brought him immediate favors. But suspicions of what the Russian was up to continued to trouble Kamehameha, and in the end Schäffer failed to convince the king to side with him. The persons responsible for many of these new diseases and illnesses in Hawaii, of course, were the China traders who were going to and from Macao.

In the meantime, Kamehameha's adversary, King Kaumualii, fell ill with dropsy, and Schäffer ran to his aid. He was able to cure Kaumualii and his wife, who had also contracted a fever. Kaumualii embraced the Russians and signed an agreement with Schäffer. This new alliance was a great setback for both Kamehameha and the Americans because the year before, Kaumualii had obtained a significant supply of armaments from the American captain, James Bennett, which included fifty muskets and forty-two rifles. Kaumualii was now in a position to negotiate armaments from the Russians as well, which could threaten both Kamehameha and American interests on the islands, and more important, their trade with China.[38] Besides the transmission of diseases, however, what does all of this have to do with Macao?

In early November 1814, the Russian ship *Henry*, Captain Alles, arrived at Macao. The vessel was flying a Russian flag and Alles requested permission to trade upriver at Canton. The Qing government, however, had a separate agreement with Russia to trade at Kamchatka so Alles was forbidden entry. He left China with his ship on November 25. On December 7, however, the *Henry* showed up again at Macao but this time flying a Danish flag. Chinese officials caught onto the deception and would not allow the ship past Bocca Tigris. The *Henry* finally departed for Europe on February 27. Schäffer would later learn from Alles' mistakes and take a different approach.[39]

With the Hawaiian side of things now in place—at least as best as could be arranged, Schäffer set off for Macao in 1815 to get the China side of the trade into shape.[40] He met with the Swede, Sir Anders Ljungstedt, who arrived at Macao a few weeks after Schäffer. Ljungstedt was an influencial figure and later become Sweden's first Consul General to China.[41] He was skilled in diplomacy and spoke several languages including Russian, English, and Swedish and he had taught in Russia for ten years. Ljungstedt had also served as Russian translator for the Swedish king Gustaf IV Adolf during his journey to Russia so he was a logical choice for Schäffer to befriend.

After several weeks of friendly correspondences, Schäffer granted Ljungstedt power of attorney to represent the Russian American Company in Macao and Canton. This event was witnessed by the Macao official, Miguel Arriaga, who also acknowledged Russian claims to the Sandwich Islands. These exchanges brought Macao into another complicated angle in Sino–American relations. As more Americans began going to China to trade and for religious motives, Macao became increasingly more involved in and affected by Sino–American interactions.[42]

Christianity and Opium

Religious propagation often followed in the wake of commerce, and the opium trade was no different. In August 1814, the Dutch in Macao learned that the Jiaqing emperor had issued a new decree forbidding the sale of opium and the propagation of new Christians.[43] On the surface, it might seem strange to ban opium and Christianity in the same edict, but there were good reasons for these two topics to be connected. A Chinese Christian in Macao by the name of José Xavier dos Santos (many Macao converts adopted Portuguese names) had done much to advance the opium trade in that city in the 1770s and 1780s. Portuguese, Armenians, Swedes, English, and numerous others, who were also Christians, were regularly bringing opium to China, and this was the case from the very beginning of that trade.[44]

It is thus not surprising to find Qing officials seeing opium and Christianity going hand in hand. In order to find out who was doing the smuggling in Macao, for example, one just needed to ask a Christian (they all seemed to know what was happening).[45] On September 1, 1814, "18 Chinese Christian men" were arrested by Chinese officials and taken out of Macao through the gate at Fort St. Francisco so they could be interrogated about the opium trade. The information gleaned from these and other informants led to the arrests in 1815 of the opium smugglers mentioned above (who may have been the same persons as were interrogated). The connections made between Christians and opium included Americans, of course, so these Chinese views and attitudes were as much a part of Sino–American relations as they were a part of Sino–Portuguese and Sino–British relations.[46]

By the 1830s, both Macao and Hawaii had become bases for American Protestant missionaries. In 1821, on the other side of the Pacific, the first American missionaries arrived in Hawaii and began allying with anyone who would have them. The first American missionary in China was Elijah Coleman Bridgman who arrived in 1830. Other American missionaries, such as Mr. Shuck (mentioned above), soon followed him.

As American intercourse with China increased, initiatives were launched to discover new sources of trade commodities in the Pacific that could be marketed in Canton.[47] While all of this was happening, Hawaii was drawn closer to events happening in Macao, as more American missionaries and traders set their course across the pacific. Hawaii and Macao were caught between these sojourners, with China on one end of their journey and the United States on the other end.

There were of course many positive results that arose from these encounters. American missionaries, such as Peter Parker, were enormously influential and effective in their medical work in Macao and Canton, and became widely known and respected throughout China. And American missionaries were much involved with the promoting and advancing of education to all classes of Chinese society, especially women. Unfortunately, many of these worthy and sincere efforts did not have lasting effects in Macao or China. In order to understand the forces behind the signing of the Wangshia Treaty and the development of Sino–American relations in the late eighteenth century, all of these factors need to be taken into consideration.

Conclusion

Macao was the gateway for all Americans going to China to trade legally. It was the first stop upon arriving in China and the last stop before returning home. Macao became the center for agents arranging American trade, legal and illegal. As outside smuggling depots diverted trade away from Macao, the city suffered in paralled, and over time, China developed a very severe opium problem that had dramatic effects on the Chinese people and society. Sino–American interactions were central to both outcomes.

The diverting of trade and revenues away from Macao continued after foreigners moved to Hong Kong in 1844. The events that followed this move are complicated and complex, but basically, Macao was unable to compete with these other ports in the delta. Finally, in the 1850s, a partial solution was found in issuing monopolies, especially in gambling, which saw immediate success.

Macao's and Hawaii's historical developments were also, to some extent, linked together. Some of the furs from the North American coast and sandalwood from Hawaii that arrived in China were sold on the black market in the delta. Hawaiians went to Macao and Canton, and Chinese went to Hawaii and the United States from Macao, which impacted both places. Hawaii became a major provisioning depot for ships sailing the Pacific, as well as a source of sandalwood to market in China. The fight for trade and influence in Hawaii had links to Macao, with the Portuguese, Spanish, French, English, Russians, and others attempting to extend their influences through agents living there, and Hawaiians seeking to gain more control over the Chinese cargos. In addition to these exchanges came new illnesses and diseases to Hawaii, which affected and threatened everyone on the islands. Chinese migrants were blamed for bringing some of the illnesses, which were beginnings of anti-Chinese sentiments that later emerged in San Francisco.

By the 1830s, American missionaries were active in both Hawaii and Macao, which brought religion into play. American religious encounters affected the two places, as missionaries traveled along the trade routes. Whether they wanted it or not, Macao and Hawaii were pulled into the spheres of Sino–American influence in the late eighteenth and early nineteenth centuries, which, in various ways, affected the courses their histories were to take. Macao, Hawaii, and Sino–American trade were so intertwined to each other that a change in one could have a corresponding affect on the others.

Notes

1. Pierre Chaunu, *Les Philippines et le Pacifique des Ibériques (XVIe, XVIIe, XVIIIe siècles)* (Paris: S.E.V.P.E.N., 1960), 208–19. For a discussion of the Armenians and Muslims trading in China, see Carl T. Smith and Paul A. Van Dyke, "Four Armenian Families," *Review of Culture*, International Edition no. 8 (October 2003): 40–50; Carl T. Smith and Paul A. Van Dyke, "Armenian Footprints in Macao," *Review of Culture*,

International Edition no. 8 (October 2003): 20–39; and Carl T. Smith and Paul A. Van Dyke, "Muslims in the Pearl River Delta, 1700 to 1930," *Review of Culture*, International Edition no. 10 (April 2004): 6–15.

2. C. Madrolle, *Les Premiers Voyages Français a la Chine: La Compagnie de la Chine 1698–1719* (Paris: Augustin Challamel, 1901); and British Library (BL): India Office Records (IOR) G/12/4-7.

3. This summary of how to enter the Pearl River and the procedures to engage in trade at Canton are taken from Paul A. Van Dyke, *The Canton Trade: Life and Enterprise on the China Coast, 1700–1845* (Hong Kong: Hong Kong University Press, 2005), passim.

4. Paul A. Van Dyke, "Rise of the Lintin Smuggling Network in the 1820s: Implications for Macao and the American China Trade," paper presented at international conference titled "Americans, Macao and China 1784–1950: Historical Relations, Interactions and Connections," University of Macao, December 2008.

5. For a brief discussion of the rationale behind the taxing of import silver at Canton in the eighteenth century, see Van Dyke, *The Canton Trade*, 118–19.

6. In 1767, there is a clear reference to a Portuguese ship carrying a cargo to China consisting of "nothing but opium." Many ships carried opium to China at this time, but it was usually a small part of their cargos. As the opium market in China grew, more ships were commissioned to carry nothing but the drug. Van Dyke, *The Canton Trade*, 120–34.

7. The opium trade in China now has a huge body of literature. For a more recent study of how it developed, see Carl A. Trocki, *Opium, Empire and the Global Political Economy: A Study of the Asian Opium Trade 1750–1950* (London: Routledge, 1999).

8. James Holman, *Travels in China, New Zealand, New South Wales, Van Diemen's Land, Cape Horn, etc. etc.* (London: George Routledge, 1840), 116–17.

9. Historical Society of Pennsylvania (HSP), 687 Waln Family Papers, vol. 1, J. F. Leaming, "Notes on the Chinese Trade," 34, 38; and BL: IOR G/12/148 p. 129. For a list of some of connivance fees in 1834, see John Robert Morrison, *A Chinese Commercial Guide* (Canton: Albion Press, 1834), 30.

10. The opium-silver-tea exchanges have been studied by numerous scholars, of which a couple are listed here. Trocki, *Opium, Empire and the Global Political Economy*; David Edward Owen, *British Opium Policy in China and India* (New Haven, Conn.: Yale University Press, 1934; reprint, Hamden: Archon Books, 1968).

11. For a examples of the small Danish ship *Fredriks Nagor* and the private ship *Nancy* operating as opium hulks at Whampoa at this time, and the Chinese governments' suppression of the same, see National Archives, The Hague (NAH): Canton 97, 1797.08.17; and BL: IOR G/12/118, 1797.07.14 p. 58, G/12/122 p. 174, G/12/126 p. 236, and G/12/134 pp. 48–51.

12. Van Dyke, "Rise of the Lintin Smuggling Network in the 1820s."

13. Lau Fong 劉芳 and Zhang Wenqin 章文欽 (eds.), *Qingdai Aomen Zhongwen Dang'an Hui bian* 清代澳門中文檔案匯編 (A Collection of Ming Chinese Documents Concerning Macao) 2 vols. (Macao: Aomen Jijinhui Chuban 澳門基金會, 1999)

1:242–47; and Hosea Ballou Morse, *The Chronicles of the East India Company Trading to China, 1635–1834*, 5 vols. (Cambridge, Mass.: Harvard University Press, 1926; reprint, Taipei: Ch'eng-wen Publishing Co., 1966), 3:236–39; and NAH: Canton 101.

14. Jin Guo Ping 金 國 平 and Wu Zhiliang 吳 志 良 (comps), *Correspondência Oficial Trocada Entre As Autoridades de Cantão e Os Procuradores do Senado. Fundo das Chapas Sínicas em Português (1749–1847)*, 8 vols. (Macao: Macao Foundation, 2000), 5:no. 129.

15. NAH: Canton 101.

16. Van Dyke, "Rise of the Lintin Smuggling Network in the 1820s."

17. There continues to be misunderstandings that surface in the historical literature of a second American ship in China in 1784. During a visit to the Historical Society of Pennsylvania (HSP) in August 2007, for example, one of the staff referred me to the journal of the *United States* as one of the earliest ships to sail to China. A search on the Internet will produce other such claims. These rumors originate from a ship's logbook titled "Log and Journal of the Ship *United States* on a Voyage from Philadelphia to China in 1784." The title is a misnomer because the ship did not go to China, but rather India, the French colony of Pondicherry, and then returned from there to Philadelphia. The journal was published by the *Pennsylvania Magazine of History and Biography* in 1931, and later reprinted by the Historical Society of Pennsylvania. As a result, the title continues to show up in library catalogs and on the Internet, which keeps the rumors alive that there were two American ships in China this year. Samuel W. Woodhouse, "Log and Journal of the Ship *United States on* a Voyage from Philadelphia to China in 1784," *Pennsylvania Magazine of History and Biography* (1931), 225–26.

18. Information about Shaw and Randall was taken from Shaw's published journal. Josiah Quincy (ed.), *The Journals of Major Samuel Shaw: the First American Consul at Canton* (Boston: Wm. Crosby and H. P. Nichols, 1847; reprint, Documentary Publications, 1970).

19. Philip Chadwick Foster Smith, *The Empress of China* (Philadelphia: Philadelphia Maritime Museum, 1984), 25–26.

20. For a discussion of the effects the China trade had on the American public, see John Haddad, *The Romance of China: Excursions to China in U.S. Culture: 1776–1876* (New York: Columbia University Press, 2000), available online at www.gutenberg-e.org.

21. For the number of ships in China each year, see Louis Dermigny, *La Chine et l'Occident: Le Commerce a Canton au XVIII Siècle 1719–1833*, 3 vols. and Album (Paris: S.E.V.P.E.N., 1964), vol. 2, "Trafic a Wampou."

22. For the three years from 1799 to 1801, the total exports from Canton and Macao (including Chinese junk cargos) amounted to approximately 155,000 tons (average 51,666 tons per year). About 39 percent of those cargos were handled by the English East India Company, 11 percent by the other East India companies, 13 percent by non-American private ships, 10 percent by Portuguese ships in Macao, 14 percent by Chinese junks (estimated to be thirty junks at 250 tons each), and the

remaining 13 percent by American ships. Paul A. Van Dyke, "Port Canton and the Pearl River Delta, 1690–1845" (Ph.D. diss., Dept. of History, University of Southern California, 2002), 88–92. The Canton junks and Portuguese tonnages are based on estimates in Van Dyke, *The Canton Trade*, 146–47.

23. This summary of the American legal trade was taken from Van Dyke, *The Canton Trade*, passim.

24. For a nice summary of the fur trade and some of the smuggling in the delta that was connected to that commerce, see Dick A. Wilson, "King George's Men: British Ships and Sailors in the Pacific Northwest-China Trade, 1785–1821" (Ph.D. diss., Dept. of History, University of Idaho, 2004), passim.

25. Van Dyke, *The Canton Trade*, 106–7.

26. Some Americans died in China and are now buried in the Old Protestant Cemetery in Macao. For a list of Americans and others interred in the Old Protestant Cemetery in Macao, see Lindsay Ride and May Ride, *An East India Company Cemetery: Protestant Burials in Macao* (Hong Kong: Hong Kong University Press, 1996). Americans died at Cumsingmoon as well. Three Americans from the ship *Macedonian*, were buried there on Qi'ao Island in September 1853 (exact day of death unknown), as follows: John C. Logan, John Smith, and Otho Sullivan. Capt. William Cole died at Cumsingmoon on July 2, 1836, and was also interred at the foreign graveyard on Qi-ao Island. The location of this graveyard is not known, but the names are preserved in the preceeding document

27. Van Dyke, *The Canton Trade*, 135. In 1830, James Holman mentioned that his ship carried an excess cargo of 2,000 chests of tea, which was to be loaded on the *Merope* anchored at Lintin: "By shipping her cargo outside the Bogue [Bocca Tigris], she avoided the heavy duties to which all vessels render themselves liable that enter the river, though ships are permitted to take on board what they please for others outside, not only without subjecting themselves to the exaction of duty, but gaining a small freightage for the trouble of the transport." Holman, *Travels in China*, 143. An American aboard a ship at Whampoa in 1836 reported the following in a letter: "If you could get a peep of our Cabin I am sure you would not know it again. I have nearly filled it up with goods, leaving scarcely room to turn round and completely blocked up the Cabin Windows. Our deck is piled up with goods so as to shut up the Skylight and the light is entirely excluded. When we get to Lintin this will be remedied. That is all the goods which are now on deck will be left there." These goods were carried downriver to load on the smuggling ships anchored at Lintin. HSP: Sword Family Papers, box 1, letter to Miss Mary Parry dated February 19, 1836. Another example of the transferring of goods from Whampoa to Lintin can be found in *Quarterly Review* (January–March 1830), 156–57.

28. Rev. J. Lewis Shuck, "Journal of Mr. Shuck," *Baptist Missionary Magazine*, vol. 17 (1837), 226.

29. *Canton* Press, November 4, 1837. The summary in the previous paragraphs of how Americans carried on their trade in China is taken from Van Dyke, *The Canton Trade*, passim.

30. Van Dyke, "Rise of the Lintin Smuggling Network in the 1820s."

31. The rapid rise and success of gambling in Macao is a subject discussed in many history books. For examples, see Deng Kaisong邓 开 颂. Aomen Lishi 澳門歷史 (1840–1949年). (History of Macao 1840–1949) 澳門 (Macao):澳門歷史學會, 1995; Huang Qichen 黄启臣, Aomen tong shi 澳门通史 (General History of Macao). Guangzhou 广州: Guangdong jiao yu 广东教育, 1999.

32. Jonathan Goldstein, *Philadelphia and the China Trade 1682–1846* (University Park: Pennsylvania State University Press, 1978), 17.

33. For a more detailed discussion and examples of Americans smuggling furs, sandalwood, and other products into China, see Van Dyke, "Port Canton," chapter six: "The 'Contraband' Trade."

34. This summary of the American–Hawaii–Canton trade was taken from the following sources: Edward Joesting, *Kauai: The Separate Kingdom* (Kauai: University of Hawaii Press and Kauai Museum Association, Ltd., 1987), 44–45; Robert Kingery Buell and Charlotte Northcote Skladal, *Sea Otters and the China Trade* (New York: David McKay Co., 1968), 43–69; Gibson, *Otter Skins, Boston Ships, and China Goods*, 22–61; John Meares, *Voyages made in the years 1788 and 1789, from China to the North West Coast of America. To which are prefixed, and Introductory Narrative of a Voyage performed in 1786, from Bengal, in the ship Nootka; Observations on the probable Existence of a North West Passage; and some account of the Trade Between the North West Coast of America and China; and the latter Country and Great Britain* (London: Logographic Press, 1790; reprint, Amsterdam: Da Capo Press, 1967), 10; Carl L. Crossman, *The Decorative Arts of the China Trade: Paintings, Furnishings and Exotic Curiosities* (Woodbridge, Suffolk: Antique Collectors' Club, 1988), 36–37. For references to foreigners capitalizing on the provisions trade in Canton, and to Hawaii's becoming a provisions depot, see Meares, *Voyages*, 10; Bancroft Library, University of California, Berkeley (BC): G161 P55 v. 6 x. Otto Von Kotzebue, *Voyage of Discovery in the South Sea, and to Behring's Straits, in search of a Northeast Passage; undertaken in the years 1815, 16, 17, and 18, in the Ship Rurick*, part I (London: Bride Court, 1821); and Wilson, "King George's Men," passim.

35. Meares, *Voyages*, 10; Charles Nordhoff, *Northern California, Oregon, and the Sandwich Islands* (1874; reprint, Berkeley: Ten Speed Press, 1974), 60–84; and Joesting, *Kauai: The Separate Kingdom*, 45–46. See also Frederic W. Howay (ed.), *The Voyage of the New Hazard* (Fairfield, Wash.: Ye Galleon Press, 1970); Charles H. Hammatt, *Ships, Furs, and Sandalwood: A Yankee Trader in Hawai'i, 1823–1825* (Honolulu: University of Hawai'i Press, 1999); Auguste Duhaut-Cilly, *A Voyage to California, the Sandwich Islands, & Around the World in the Years 1826–1829*, trans. and eds. August and Neal Harlow Frugé (Berkeley: University of California Press, 1999); Peter Corney, *Voyages in the Nothern Pacific: Narrative of Several Trading Voyages from 1813 to 1818, between the Northwest Coast of American, the Hawaiian Islands and China, with a Description of the Russian Establishments on the Northwest Coast. Intersting Early Account of Kamehameha's realm; Manners and Customs of the People, etc. And Sketch of a Cruise in the Service of the Independents of South America in 1819* (Honolulu: Thos. G. Thrum, 1896).

36. Joesting, *Kauai: The Separate Kingdom*, 44–45, 61–64; Buell and Skladal, *Sea Otters and the China Trade*; Gibson, *Otter Skins, Boston Ships, and China Goods*, 22–61; Nordhoff, *Northern California, Oregon, and the Sandwich Islands*, 103–6.

37. For examples of these foreigners being active in the Northwest Coast and Hawaii, see Wilson, "King George's Men," passim.

38. This narrative of Russians in Hawaii and Macao was taken from the following sources: Joesting, *Kauai: The Separate Kingdom*, 70–78; and Richard A. Pierce, *Russia's Hawaiian Adventure, 1815–1817* (Berkeley: University of California Press, 1965), 212–13.

39. The narrative of the *Henry* and Captain Alles was taken from Dutch records. NAH: Canton 101, entries under November 2 and 25 and December 7, 1814, and January 1 and February 27, 1815.

40. According to the British East India Company's lists of ships in China in 1815, the ship that arrived that year from Kamchatka was the *Brutus*, Captain Dior. The *Brutus* arrived in China on May 13 and departed on October 15, but the entry makes no mention of whether the ship had stopped at Hawaii. A couple other ships also arrived in China that year from the northwest coast, the *Pedlar* and the *Beaver*. BL: IOR G/12/199 p. 134.

41. In 1820, Ljungstedt was appointed first Swedish Consul General in China. According to Dutch records, the private Swedish ship, *Drotningen*, Captain Hanson, arrived in China on June 2, 1815, from Gothenburg, Rio de Janerio, and Batavia. Another private Swedish ship *Grave Rosen*, Captain E. Nisse, arrived on July 14, 1815, from Batavia and Manila. There is no mention of passengers. NAH: Canton 101, entries dated June 2, 1815 and July 14, 1815. The English East India Company's (EIC) diary does not show either of these Swedish ships in the list of arrivals this year. EIC consultations confirm that the *Drotningen* arrived on June 2, but show it having originated from Stockholm with a stop at Batavia. BL: IOR G/12/101, June 6, 1818, p. 35. Ljungstedt died in Macao; his grave is in the Old Protestant Cemetery, and he has a street named after him in Macao.

42. Joesting, *Kauai: The Separate Kingdom*, 70–78; Richard A. Pierce, *Russia's Hawaiian Adventure, 1815–1817* (Berkeley: University of California Press, 1965), 212–13. The latter source contains Ljungstedt's agreement with the Russians in Macao, which was signed by Arriaga as witness.

43. NAH: Canton 101, entry dated August 20, 1814.

44. The Portuguese citizen Thomé Francisco de Oliveira and the Chinese Christian José Xavier dos Santos were much involved in the opium trade in Macao in the 1770s and 1780s. Van Dyke, *The Canton Trade*, 126. In the 1830s, Christian missionary Charles Gützlaff also helped advance the opium trade in China. For a summary of the development of the opium trade in China, see Van Dyke, *The Canton Trade*, 120–34.

45. In 1777, Catholic Bishop D. Alexandre da Silva Pedrosa Guimarães expressed concerns about the competiton that Macao merchants were now facing from other foreigners in their opium trade, which threatened their monopoly of that product. He recommended expelling the foreigners (especially Armenians) so Macao merchants

could retain their advantages in opium. And if the bishop was supporting this commerce then priests were most likely promoting it as well. Thus, it was not just laymen who were advancing the opium trade in China, but Christians on all levels, and Catholics and Protestants alike. Smith and Van Dyke, "Armenian Footprints in Macao," 34.

46. This information was taken from NAH: Canton 101. It is unclear whether the eighteen men interrogated and the eighteen men who were later arrested were the same persons.

47. Michael Block, "The Importance of the China Trade in American Exploration and Conquest in the Pacific, 1830–1850," paper presented at international conference titled, "Americans, Macao and China 1784–1950: Historical Relations, Interactions and Connections," University of Macao, December 2008.

CHAPTER FIVE

The Stories of David and Goliath: An Analysis of the U.S.–Macao Relations

Liu Bolong

In December 2009, Macao celebrated its tenth anniversary of reversion back to China under the "one country, two systems" framework. The opening of Macao's gambling franchise has brought an enormous amount of foreign investment into Macao, ushering in a new period of economic prosperity of Macao. Among the six gambling licenses granted by the Macao SAR government, two and half licenses belong to American capital.[1] American casinos have invested heavily in this small enclave, pledging to transform Macao into another Las Vegas on Chinese territory. In fact, Macao gambling income surpassed that of Las Vegas in 2009 by a large margin. Although Macao is small in area and population, U.S.–Macao relations have reached the point of extreme importance for Macao in the future. Out of six gambling franchises in Macao, the American casinos, especially Wynn, Venetian, and MGM, are flagship casinos which attract huge number of visitors to the enclave and earn more than 50 percent of gambling revenues in Macao. Therefore, the study of the status and future relations will be essential to the stability and future development of Macao.

Macao develops its external relations on the basis of the "one country, two systems" framework which serves as a mini-constitution for Macao government and its society. According to the Basic Law of Macao, the SAR government has the right to establish economic and cultural relations with other countries in the world, except in the fields of diplomacy and defense where the central government holds negotiations and signs agreements with other countries. Under the Basic Law, Macao has joined international economic organizations as an independent member and carries out all related activities in defense of its commercial interests and working toward a common goal of trade and financial and cultural prosperity globally.[2] Hence, Macao has been granted full autonomy to develop its economic, financial, and cultural relations with the United States, one of the most important trade partners for Macao.

The United States promulgated its "United States–Macao Policy Act" in 2001 which serves as the legal base for the United States to develop its relations with Macao.[3] The law acknowledges the special status of the Macao Special Administrative Region in U.S. law and recognizes Macao's high degree of autonomy in the fields of social, cultural, legal, and economic development. "The new law specifies that the United States should play an active role in maintaining Macao's confidence, prosperity and unique cultural heritage and that the United States should maintain the mutually beneficial ties between the people of the United States and the people of Macao."[4] Under the law, the U.S. government has the responsibility to support continued economic prosperity and U.S. commercial interests in Macao, encourage the process of democratization and human rights in Macao. Based on the above principles, economic, social, and cultural exchanges between the two will win full support of the U.S. government.

Since the opening of the gambling franchise, both sides have made serious efforts to expand commercial and cultural relations. Before the handover, a small number of American companies operated in Macao but now, if you go to one Macao supermarket, you will find it no difference if you are shopping in the United States. You will find many American expatriates in the streets and supermarkets of Macao. What is the status of Macao–U.S. relations? What's the potential for bilateral relations in the future? From a globalization point of view, we could also analyze the pros and cons of large-scale American interests in Macao.

Expanding U.S.–Macao Relations

The United States remains the most important trade partner of Macao's history. In recent years, although due to low-cost labor and improved investment environment, many Macao manufacturing companies have moved their production bases to Pearl River Delta. Since the end of the worldwide textile agreement, Macao lost its competitive advantage as it can no longer receive large amounts of textile quotas from the United States and the EU. However, thanks to the strong export momentum in mainland China, Macao retains its entrepot status and some companies in Macao are doing well in re-exportation and logistical services. Table 5.1 shows Macao's bilateral trade with the United States over the last five years.

As far as the Macao exports are concerned, in 2007, Macao exported nearly 8.2 billion MOP to the United States, equal to 50 percent of Macao's export total (nearly 20 billion MOP). The United States remains the most important Macao export market.[5]

Since the opening of the gambling franchise, Macao has witnessed the exponetial growth of foreign investment into Macao, the bulk of which are from the United States. Among them the Venetian Sands was the quickest to take action. In 2004, it invested $240 million to open the first Las Vegas–style hotel in Macao and was rewarded satisfactorily. In nine months, it got its investment back and began to earn profits. In the first half of 2007, the Sands Casino in Macao achieved profits of $592 million, a figure much higher than the group's flagship in the United States, the Venetian in Las Vegas.

In September 2006, another Macao franchise holder, Stephen Wynn, the Las Vegas gambling magnate, opened Wynn Macao Hotel and Casino right next door to local gambling flagship Hotel Lisbon, with investment of $1.2 billion.[6] According to media reports, the Wynn adopts a restrained aesthetic, with mild lighting even on the gaming floor and décor in beige and brown with occasional splashes of red.[7] Macao people never experienced such a high degree of luxury before and the hotel is packed with mainland and Hong Kong visitors during the holidays. The hotel has 600 luxury rooms, 200 gambling tables, and 380 tiger slot machines. The small lobbies lead to a shopping promenade dotted with the names of Tiffany's, Louis Vuitton, and Prada.[8] Steven Wynn received windfall profits by selling half of his gambling franchise to another conglomerate, MGM Las Vegas, and he pocketed $900 million out of this deal. With this extra money, he plan to invest in another two casinos on the island of Taipa in the next few years.[9]

The main American company, Las Vegas Sands, has increased its investment through another flagship hotel, Macao Venetian, along the reclaimed land between the two islands in Macao, the Cotai Strip. The Americans

Table 5.1 U.S.-Macao Bilateral Trade (MOP 1,000)

Year	2003	2004	2005	2006	2007
Imports from the U.S.	871,921	1,130,601	1,276,302	1,997,370	2,428,990
Exports to the U.S.	10,320,232	10,990,030	9,646,803	9,021,310	8,291,780

Source: Government Information Bureau, Macao Year Book 2008, pp. 592-93.

have realized their grand scheme: the Venetian Macao opened on August 28, 2007. The hotel boasts an investment amount of $2 billion with 3,000 suites, 110,000 square meters of exhibition center, a performing arena which can contain 15,000 viewers, and a Venetian Canal shopping center.[10] This is the first phase of a grandiose plan initiated by Sands and its chairman, Sheldon Adelson. The group plans to invest up to $12 billion on the Cotai Strip and build the area into a golden strip with more than ten international brand hotels and a total room number of 20,000. The Cotai Strip will be fully financed by the Las Vegas Sands alone and ten top-end international hotels will be invited to join.[11] The Venetian Macao would transform Macao from a tourist destination attractive only to Hong Kong and Pearl River Delta residents to a tourist center in Asia, a destination which will attract new visitors from Southeast Asia, Japan, Europe, and the United States. The Venetian strategy seems to succeed. Since its opening in August, Macao's total gambling revenues will surpass the historical height of 7.32 billion PTC in May 2007, one month before China began to restrict its individual visitors to Macao once in a month.[12] The opening of Venetian Macao gives people high hope for the growth of conference and exhibition industries in Macao. According to the conference participants in Macao Venetian, Macao will no longer be restricted to only the gaming and gambling industry, and it will have opportunities to become a tourist hub with tourism, conferences, exhibitions, and entertainment.[13]

No one could have predicted the sudden deterioration of the economic climate worldwide in 2008. Since the financial tsunami hit the capital market in October 2008, the American entertainment giants experienced harsh reality in Macao. Adelson had to suspend the construction of his new hotels in Cotai indefinitely and he has to repay his astronomical amount of debt in the near future. The rumors were spreading in Hong Kong and Macao that Sands Macao could go bankrupt in 2009.[14] The rapid recovery of Asian economies in the second half of 2009 saved the life of Macao Sands. Macao Wynn had successfully collected $1.6 billion in the Hong Kong stock market and Sands Macao will also get listed on the Hong Kong stock market soon. The crisis is over. In the year 2009, Macao again experienced double-digit growth of its gambling income. The international investment banks predict bullish scenarios for Macao gambling companies in the future.

As seen in table 5.2, among six concessions, two are total U.S. capital, one is half U.S. (MGM) and half local. In this configuration, U.S. capital and local casinos are the two main camps in the Macao casino market.

Along with the expansion of the gaming industry in Macao, many American companies are coming to Macao to explore the opportunities in other areas of the Macao economy. According to *Macao Daily*, many Wall Street consulting companies began to recommend stocks related to Macao development. Apart from the two American gaming conglomerates, some American property companies which invested in Macao property were promoted by these consulting firms. One report indicated that Macao is now entering a period of precious opportunities not seen in a thousand years. As Las Vegas Venetian Chairman Anderson said, even ten Macaos will never saturate the enormous market because Macao has too many visitors. His words was very convincing to the Wall Street analysts as Macao Sands returned its investment in nine months' time and Anderson's company saw its stock skyrocketing three times since its investment in Macao.[15] After a difficult year in 2008, the Macao gambling industry witnessed a strong and quick comeback in 2009. In 2008, American gambling companies occupied over 40 percent of the total gambling income in Macao, a benevolent balance between the American, Hong Kong, and local capitals (see figure 5.1).

The gross gambling income rose by over 40 percent in 2009. Influenced by positive income figures in 2009, the shares of Macao casino operators rose

Table 5.2 Macao's Casino Concession Holders

1	Sociedade de Jogos de Macao (SJM)
2	Wynn Cooperation
3	Galaxy Entertainment
4	Las Vegas Sands
5	MGM and SJM
6	Melco PBL Entertainment

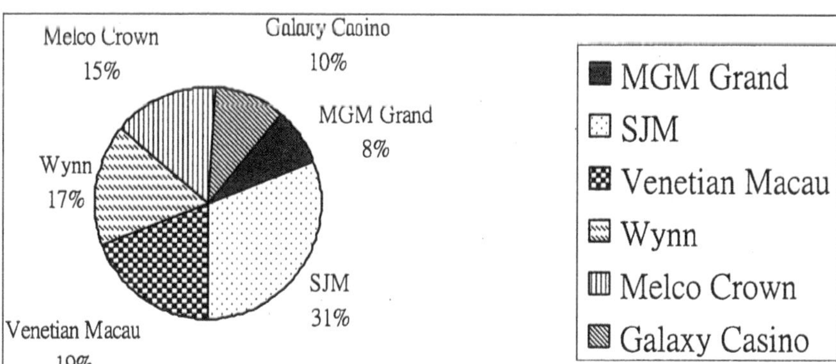

Figure 5.1. Gambling Market Share in Macao (2008)
Source: **Tang Anqi and Lian Xinsen (eds), *Investigation on Macao Gambling and Entertainment Studies* (Macao: Macao Economic Society), 15–16, table 2.1.**

in the Hong Kong stock market, which signals that Macao gambling operators will enjoy quick and healthy growth in the years to come. Many international investment banks predicted that Macao will see its gambling momentum maintain in the year 2010 and beyond.[16]

On the Macao Peninsula, another American conglomerate, U.S. MGM, is building its hotel and casinos in partnership with the daughter of Stanly Ho, the Macao casino guru. The MGM hotel opened in the beginning of 2009.

Apart from investment, the U.S. government is promoting its cultural and academic exchanges with Macao. More Fulbright Scholars have been sent to teach and research at University of Macao. At the Macao Musical Festival, U.S. performing troops from Broadway take up the main performing tasks at the closing ceremony and are welcomed by Macao citizens. For example, one Broadway musical show, *West Side Story*, had to add two more nights to entertain enthusiastic Macao music lovers during the Macao Music Festival in 2005; some of them still complained that they could not get tickets. In October 2009, Venetian Macao organized a friendly match between two American tennis giants: Sampras and Agassi, which had full-house effect. Venetian Macao granted scholarships to students in Macao University and Macao Institute of Tourism.[17] The American Olympic basketball team engaged in two friendly matches in Macao before going to Beijing to participate in the Olympics.[18] Audiences in Hong Kong and Macao are extremely receptive to frequent visits by American and worldwide iconic singers to the territory.

Analysis of Future U.S.–Macao Relations

Macao SAR government is determined to introduce world-class entertainment groups to the local gambling market with the hope that the new arrivals will help Macao upgrade its gambling environment and qualities. Macao will embrace the momentum of globalization whole-heartedly, following the excellent example of Mainland China under its helmsman Deng Xiaoping, who led China into a period of openness and reform, which has brought dazzling achievements for the Chinese people over two decades. I would analyze U.S.–China relations based on the theory of globalization.

As we all know, in the world of high development of communication and transportation, globalization is a unstoppable process embracing all countries in the world. Concerning the effects of globalization, there are three theoretical schools: one school sees it as a trend which will help the host country to develop its economy and increase welfare for its citizens. The second school believes that globalization will serve as an obstacle for its national economy and lead to a road of self-destruction for its national industries. The third school goes the middle road with a strong belief that globalization is a trend to follow and the country will benefit enormously through international trade and foreign investment. However, we must pay attention to the negative impact of the globalization and take some measures to protect national industries with vital strategic impact to the country.[19] China has taken the middle road and realized the objectives of using foreign investment to boost its exports and domestic structural reforms. Normally, the countries which insist on self-reliance and refuse international investment will lose in international competition and result in a much lower living standard for its citizens.

In Macao's case, most of the people in Macao take a positive attitude concerning large-scale American investment in Macao. First, the investment could help upgrade the Macao gaming industry and improve management quality in Macao. Before the opening of the gambling franchise, Macao was notoriously known for its low quality management in all its casinos, which were poorly decorated, crowded, and full of smoke. The guests were forced to hand in a certain percentage of their profits (if they were lucky) as rewards to the casino employees whether they agreed or not. The Chinese-style management depended on personal relations which could arouse a great degree of dissatisfaction among the casino employees.[20] Gradually Macao lost its competitive edge and the gaming profits decreased year by year. Since the opening of the gambling franchise, the Macao SAR government witnessed the soaring of its gambling taxes by a large margin each year. After all, in tourism and the entertainment business the foundation for competitive edge is quality of management and profession service. For management expertise, the Las Vegas casinos meet the highest quality internationally and have boosted Macao's image and reputation in this respect.

As seen in table 5.3, the opening of the gambling franchise and the introduction of world-class entertainment companies have resulted in the tremendous improvement of Macao government income. From 2004 to 2008,

Table 5.3 Gambling Taxes for Macao (million MOP)

Year	Gambling Taxes	Total Taxes	Percentage of Gambling Taxes in Total Government Revenue
2004	15236.6	23863.5	63.8
2005	17318.6	28200.8	61.4
2006	20747.6	37188.5	55.8
2007	30948.0	35079.4	88.22
2008	41896.5	44874.3	93.36

Source: Macao Census and Statistics Department, www.dsec.gov.mo/index.asp?src=1/chinese/indicator/c_piem_indicator_html.

Macao gambling taxes increased from 15.2 billion MOP to 44 billion MOP, an increase of 220 percent.[21] In the first nine months of 2009, Macao received gambling revenues of $10.6 billion, a steady increase compared with the figures a few years before despite the grave influence of the financial crisis.[22] It was reported that in the whole year of 2009, Macao's gambling revenues reached a historical high. China decided to loosen its traveling visa limits to its Chinese citizens to Macao with the hope of boosting Macao's economy and set a good example of political harmony and economic prosperity for big brother Hong Kong to follow in the future.

The opening of top-class U.S. hotels in Macao will add momentum to the much needed versatile development of Macao economy. As a mini-economy, Macao depends on gaming as its dragon-head industry. More than 60 percent of its government taxes come from the gaming industry. In the year 2009, gambling taxes reached an astonishing 98 percent of total government revenue. As society understands, such a heavily tilted economic structure will pose potential threat to the Macao economy in the future if structural changes occur in the external environment. Young people also feel the pressure when they can only find decent jobs in casinos. It is an urgent need for the Macao society to nurture other sectors of its economy and seek multiple development of its economic structure. For this, the opening of the Venetian Macao Hotel provides some hope in real sense. This giant program, which costs $2 billion, will bring to Macao top-class hotels, entertainment, exhibitions, fine food, boutique shops, sports, and world-class performances, which are aimed at not only the gamblers, but also businessmen who attend exhibitions, families who come to enjoy food and shopping, and fans who come to enjoy world-class concerts. "What concerns people here most is the opening of the Macao Venetian, which will bring charm of versatile development of Macao."[23] Since its opening, many successful world-class conferences and exhibitions at Venetian Macao have proved the case.

Before the financial crisis occurred in 2008, there were strong criticisms of American capital influx in the Macao society, especially the Macao local casino operators whose businesses faced strong competition from international conglomerates. The typical criticism is exemplified by an article authored by a Macao legislator, Chow Kam Fai, in *Macao Daily*. In his article, Chow claimed that American conglomerates take advantage of large amounts of borrowed money from the stock market, and try to manipulate the local economy. Furthermore, Americans influence Macao politics and sovereignty, and control Macao resources, which will result in intervention in the Macao free market economy and local legislation, even against the principles of "one country, two systems." He blamed many local bottleneck economic problems, like human resource shortage and higher property prices on American involvement in Macao, and appealed to the Macao SAR government to legislate on anti-monopoly law to support the healthy development of Macao economy.[24]

In fact, Macao society has long discussed the issue of foreign capital, especially American capital, and how it could influence Macao's political development by controlling the Macao gambling industry. Quite a number of Chinese scholars have raised the issue many times and influenced thinking of central government on this issue. According to their judgment, the political system based on "one country, two systems" framework will face serious challenges. Many analyses are exaggerated with the purpose of adding pressure on the Macao government to grant local businesses more privileges in the competition. Local media have also pointed out the groundlessness of such reasoning: "It is not a good thing to put business competition into political framework and handle the issue by ideological means. It is unfavorable to the development of Macao under the situation of globalization. Macao should make double efforts to promote itself in a healthy way. In fact, Macao could no long adopt a policy of self-reliance. If we cannot create comparative advantages by ourselves, we shall have the possibility of being marginalized in world economic development. If Chinese capital gambling companies cannot raise their own level of quality management and cooperate governance and they have to use political framework to promote their business interests, this will add no benefit to the benevolent competition in the Macao gambling market."[25] As an internationalized city, Macao should take an open attitude in its economic development and embrace competition. The introduction of foreign capital will bring benefits to the development of the city and its international image. The dazzling achievement over the last decade in its economic development reflects the success of the Macao policy of opening its gambling franchise. It will be considered as the most important policy decision for the Macao government over the last decade.

The Macao media also raised some questions about one local bank: Banco Delta Asia. In 2005, the American Treasury accused it of laundering money for North Korea. The Macao SAR government had to take over the management of the bank and calm nervous investors who lined up before the bank, scrambling to withdraw their deposits: "In September last year, the Golden Boulevoud program of the Macao Venetian appeared to have some problems, then all of a sudden, the American Treasury sent out unconfirmed accusation that Banco of Delta Asia is laundering money for North Korea, which almost turned Macao into financial crisis."[26]

Before the financial tsunami, there was a heated debate between Macao Sands and a Macao local gambling guru, Stanley Ho, over whom to blame for the vicious competition owing to labor shortage as a result of the opening of new casinos. However, since the financial tsunami, as Venetian Macao faced a debt crisis and the majority of Macao casinos agreed to unify commission policies for casino middlemen, the dispute has apparently calmed down. Some scholars in China raised the issue of American capital, demanding law changes to accommodate their business practices in Macao. They voiced the opinion that these American companies endeavored not only to change the legal system in Macao, but also imposed their influence on regulations as far as casino management is concerned. "Despite the facts that people hold different opinions on this, the American companies want to change the regulations on casino credit-lending and reduce gambling taxes as preconditions of their large-scale investment in Macao."[27] The American capital Wynn Company did raise the demand in this respect; however, we should consider this demand legitimate and contributing to the Macao casino regulations. In general, Macao still practices loose supervision and regulation of Macao casinos, which will be considered detrimental to the future healthy development of Macao gambling industries, especially when Macao has to face competition from new and well-regulated Singapore casinos. The author tends to argue that American demand meets the regulation trend in the future. Some comments from the local media also support this argument: "Apparently, Macao gambling industry has to face the issue of how to better supervise and regulate itself. This is one issue which must be solved in the process of development and should not be connected and dealt with through the angles of political argument or ideological consideration."[28] Since 2004, the Macao government has established the system of issuing middlemen licenses. These middlemen in casinos must register and pay taxes for their business activities. However, a few companies still use loopholes in the system by using the names of VIP departments in the casinos, or they establish relations with registered middlemen companies to attract Mainland businessmen from state enterprises, financial institutions, and senior civil servants to come to Macao and gamble with astronomical amounts of public money, which have resulted in corruption cases in China. The Chinese authorities have since carried out strict control on free travelers to Macao either for public or for private reasons. So it is absolutely necessary to establish and supervise the middlemen system in casinos.[29]

From the American perspective, the Macao Policy Act stipulates that support for democratization is a fundamental principle of U.S. foreign policy, around the world and in Macao.[30] With this purpose in mind, American officials and citizens will feel the need to quicken the speed of democratization in Hong Kong and Macao. In view of the situation leading officials are conservative businessmen who do not believe that it is feasible to promote a universal franchise in Macao. The discrepancy in values and perspectives could cause some problems concerning the official relations of the two.

Besides, apart from the often-occurred trade skirmishes, the American government has the perspective that Macao could turn into a transit spot for drug trafficking and prostitute trafficking. The CIA classifies Macao on the Tier 2 Watch List for women trafficking and drug trafficking. "Macao is a transit and destination territory for women trafficked for the purpose of commercial sexual exploitation."[31] The U.S. government is helping Macao in training anti-smuggling officers in Macao customs.

In general, both sides hold positive perspectives on bilateral relations, but some degree of misunderstanding and misjudgment exist that, if dealt with incorrectly, could damage bilateral relations to some extent in the future. In the author's view, the American government should pay more attention to carry out cultural and academic exchanges to enhance the mutual understanding of its peoples, especially young people. University of Macao has sent dozens of students each year to serve as exchange students in American universities and when they return they will pass the correct message about the real picture of a Macao society. With the heavy amount of American investment and so many American citizens in Macao, the American Consulate should organize such activities with intense frequency. American companies should be able to sponsor more local activities to give society an image that they do care about local issues. The issuing of scholarships to students at the University of Macao and Macao Institute of Tourism is one step in right direction. The efforts by the U.S. government and companies in this respect will greatly change the image of the United States among Macao citizens.

From Macao's perspective, a more comprehensive knowledge of American investment in Macao should be expressed to indicate that American investment boosts the reputation of Macao and sends Macao to high-class quality management, which serves as a core value for a tourist city as Macao. We should try to avoid extreme nationalism at the time of globalization today. The financial tsunami proved that even American conglomerates had to calculate financial risks and could lose in such a business world of high competition. Some accusations against American companies are invalid and do not fit with today's world trend. It is the opening of the gambling franchise without prejudice which brought economic prosperity of today. As one local businessman, Tseng Ruiguan, expressed in a journal interview, the introduction of large-scale high-end hotels produced enormous positive results to Macao without a trace of shortcoming.[32] International hotels enhance the reputation of Macao as a small city and raise its competitiveness in the international traveling industry.

The addition of top-quality international hotels has imposed heavy pressure on medium- and small-sized local hotels in a short period. However, long-term impact will be positive because the influx of large number of international hotels and casinos brings about profitable business opportunities for Macao in the future, in consideration of the facts that Macao has become a metropolitan city and more visitors visit Macao. As statistics indicate, Macao has witnessed a steady increase of its visitors since the opening of gambling franchise (see the table 5.4 and figure 5.2).

Meanwhile, as competition intensifies in the Macao gambling market, local gambling companies have to dig deep into their wallets and think of modernizing their casino decoration and management to face the challenge. When feeling the pressure, the local casino king, Stanley Ho, has to begin the process of listing his company on the Hong Kong stock market. In this way, his company could collect more capital in the stock market for the purpose of initiating more new projects and programs to keep his largest share in

Table 5.4 2003-2008 Macao Visitor Arrivals (by thousand)

2003	11,887.9
2006	21,998.1
2007	26,993.0
2008	22,933.2

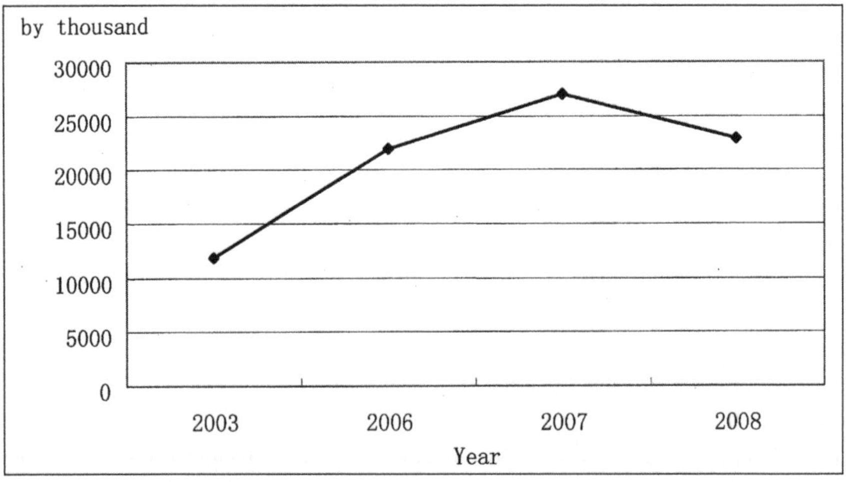

Figure 5.2. 2003-2008 Macao Visitor Arrivals*
***There were no statistics of 2004-2005 from Macao Census and Statistics Department.**
***Source:* "The Statistics and Census Service of Macao, Macao Statistics 2008, page 239."**

the Macao gambling market. His company will become more transparent and efficient as requested by the Hong Kong stock market.[33] As Macao manifested that, in the past, corruption was a serious problem in the Macao government, it is correct for the SAR government to send its anti-drug customs officers to study in the United States. All in all, 50 percent of Macao exports go to the United States, a major partner in Macao foreign trade.

Macao should also strengthen its governance and establish a civil society to accommodate the future development in democratic reforms and open society in the future. For the moment, as the education level is still quite low and the majority of Macao populace are not composed of middle-class citizens, it is not the right time for universal franchise as far as the democratic process is concerned. From a larger point of view, Macao should be able to prepare itself for a democratic future and nurture a civic society. As far as per capita GDP is concerned, Macao ranks at the top of Asian countries, even higher than that of Japan. However, the income gap is still quite high and the per capita income of working people in Macao still lags behind Hong Kong and Japan (see figure 5.3).

The main task of the future Macao government will be to develop its economy and formulate sound and systematic social welfare policies, so that middle-class citizens can form the bulk of Macao society in the next decade. For this, U.S. help should not be considered as a conspiracy, rather, it should be considered as genuine help.

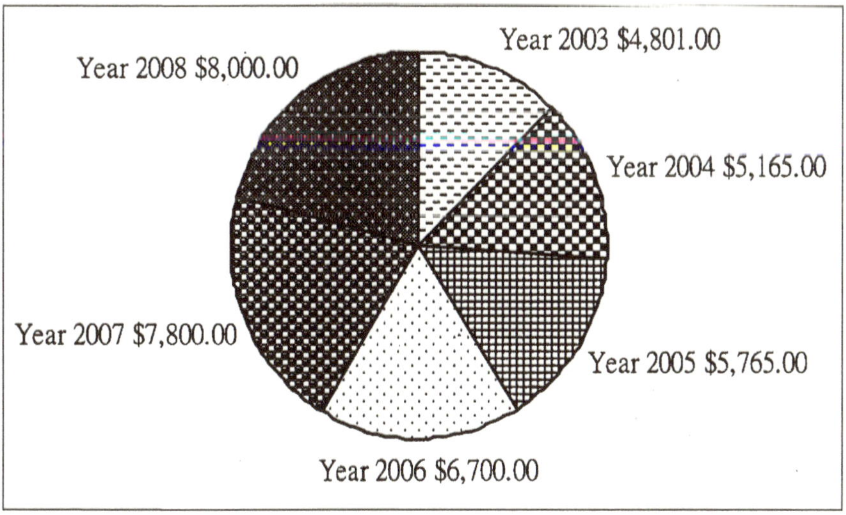

Figure 5.3. Average Monthly Income of Macao Citizens
Source: **"Macao Statistics 2005, page 168; Macao Statistics 2008, page 97."**

Conclusion

Since the opening of the gambling franchise in Macao, U.S.–Macao relations have experienced exponential growth. Traditionally, Macao has a large percentage of exports destined for the American market. With the extermination of the textile agreement, the trade becomes less important as many Macao manufacturing companies have moved to Pearl River Delta. However, the mammoth amount of investment brought over by the Las Vegas giant entertainment groups has exposed the potential significance of bilateral relations in the future. This time, the Macao SAR government gives close attention to the development of this relationship. Even the American government and American public pay much more attention to development in Macao. Much of Macao news receives close attention by the main media in the United States, like CNN or the *New York Times*.

Bilateral relations develop in a direction beneficial to both sides. Macao gains a lot from new hotels and investment from the Las Vegas groups, especially in aspects of upgrading its service qualities and waging a breakthrough in its essential efforts to enrich its economic structure. The modern economy suffices the local government with means to support social reforms in society and transform Macao into a modern area. The per capita income of Macao citizens now has surpassed those in Hong Kong, and even Japan in 2009, and Macao has become number 1 in Asia as far as the per capita GDP is concerned. This development also supports U.S. interest in Asia and enables Las Vegas companies to triple their stock prices on Wall Street. American interest in Macao is no longer minimal among the U.S. government and the public.

To develop a healthy mutual relationship, both sides must strive to overcome some negative aspects. Americans should enhance cultural and academic exchanges with Macao counterparts to show to the Macao people the real picture of U.S. society. They should put Macao citizens on an equal footing and help Macao in its modernization processes. From the Macao point of view, we must understand globalization has its pros and cons; in general, it will hasten economic development and boost the welfare of the local citizens. Isolationism is no longer the universal value of the world today and Macao should recognize the normal process of globalization. China, through its open-door policy, has achieved dazzling results in economic terms and becoming a respected force in international arena. Although at present, it is premature to develop a universal franchise in Macao society, Macao should prepare itself for a society which will develop directly to democracy and openness. This is an international trend which will be accepted by the local youth in the future. On this basis, the author believes that future Macao–U.S. relations will develop healthily.

Notes

1. Among the six license holders, two of them belong to Wynn Resort and Venetian Sands, the biggest casino operators in Las Vegas. Half of one license was bought by MGM Casino, which intends to establish its brand name in Macao in partnership with SJM.

2. Macao has joined thirteen international governmental organizations; UNESCO and World Tourist Organizations are the most important for Macao.

3. "United States Congress Passes Law recognizing Macao SAR's Special Status," Consulate General of the United States, hongkong.usconsulate.gov/pas_pr_2001010301.html.

4. Ibid., p. 2.

5. Government Information Bureau, *Macao Yearbook 2006*, pp. 592–93.

6. Ibid., p. 1.

7. "Macao: Where Developers Are Gambling on Gambling," *New York Times*, travel.nytimes.com/2006/12/31/travel/31next.html.

8. Ibid., p. 3.

9. "United States Congress Passes Law recognizing Macao SAR's Special Status," p. 2.

10. Ibid., p. 1.

11. *Macao Daily*, September 7, 2007.

12. *Macao Daily*, September 17, 2007.

13. *Macao Daily*, September 12, 2007.

14. *Macao Times*, January 21, 2009.

15. *Macao Times*, September 7, 2007.

16. "Casino Stocks Soar on Strong Macao Gambling Revenues," uomacao.com, January 29, 2010.

17. *Macao Daily*, October 31, 2009, p. 2.

18. *Macao Daily*, July 28, 2008, p. 1.

19. For details, see Joshua S. Goldstein, *International Relations*, 6th edition (Beijing: Peking University Press, 2005), pp. 305–6.

20. One employee working in a casino-related hotel told me that they even had to pay for their division head, who went to the nightclub for entertainment.

21. Macao Census and Statistics Bureau, www.dsec.gov.mo/index.asp?SRC/indicator.html.

22. Macao Business Intelligence, no. 50, October 2009, p. 20.

23. He Yuemin, "The Charm of Versatile Development," *Business Information*, August 2007, no. 24.

24. Chow Kam Fai, "Behind Macao prosperity," *Macao Daily*, October 26, 2007, p. 12.

25. *Macao Overseas Daily*, May 4, 2008, p. 1.

26. "The Strategy and Impact of American Companies in Macao," *Citizen Daily*, August 14, 2006, news.veryeast.cn.

27. Hou Ying, "Macao's Cooperation and Association with U.S. and EU," in *Annual Report on Economy and Society of Macao (2008–2009)*, eds. Hao Yufan, Wu Zhiliang (Beijing: Social Sciences Academic Press, 2009), p. 469.

28. "Some Comments on Mainland Scholars' Opinion towards Casino Industry in Macao," *Macao Overseas Chinese Daily*, May 4, 2008, p. 1.

29. *Macao Daily*, April 13, 2008, p. A11.

30. See note 3 on page 98.

31. Central Intelligence Agency, *The World Factbook*, www.cia.ov/library/publications/the-world-factbook/geos/mc.html.

32. See *Business Intelligence*, December 2009, no. 5, pp. 42–45.

33. *New China Macao Daily*, March 10, 2008, p. 2.

CHAPTER SIX

Past and Present Images of Americans in Macao

C. X. George Wei

It is well known that before the First Opium War and Hong Kong was taken over by the British, Macao served as the bridge for economic and cultural exchanges between China and the rest of the world, mostly Western countries, including Portugal, Netherlands, France, Great Britain, and others, as well as India, Japan, Southeast Asia, Africa, Latin America, and the United States. The study of Macao's role in Sino–European relations has attracted many Chinese and Western scholars, giving rise to extensive research on the subject. The United States was a latecomer among the imperialist powers in maritime history and much less influential in Sino–Western relations, and as a result, scholars have paid little attention to the impact the United States had on China through Macao and Chinese images of Americans. This situation, however, has changed significantly since the handover of Macao from Portugal to China. As giant American enterprises such as Wynn Resorts, Las Vegas Sands, and Venetian Macao joined the race to enter the casino business and establish footholds in Macao, there has been much renewed interest in understanding the impact Americans are having on Macao's economy, social and political developments, as well the role Macao would play in future Sino–American relations. We now want to understand past and present images of Americans in Macao and the role they will play in shaping U.S.–China–Macao relations in the future. How did/do Chinese in Macao view resident Americans? Did/do Macao's perceptions of Americans reflect the reality and change of Sino–U.S. relations in general? Did/do Macao's perceptions of Americans imply other scenarios or trends in Sino–U.S. relations? With these questions in mind, this study will retrace and highlight Chinese perceptions of Americans, past and present, to shed light on this understudied subject.

Early Encounters and Images of Americans in Macao

The earliest Chinese encounter with Americans occurred when John Green, the captain of an American ship called *The Empress of China* set out from New York on February 22, 1784, and dropped anchor at Macao on August 23, 1784. "The Chinese were intrigued by the strange combination of stars and red and white stripes" on "the newly made American flag."[1] One of the passengers on board was Major Samuel Shaw, who carried a commission signed by President George Washington to serve as commercial agent for the United States of America in Canton. In October 1790, Major Shaw sold his own vessel, the *Massachusetts* to the Danish Asiatic Company in Canton for $65,000. This ship was one of the largest Americans had built and represents their rapidly advancing power of the seas and technological development. They would later develop the "China Clippers," which were not only small, handsome, and maneuverable, but also fast.[2]

Indeed, the number of American ships with cargos of cotton and ginseng coming to China to trade for tea and Nankeens, passing Macao, quickly increased to five in 1786, fifteen in 1789, and forty-two in 1821.[3] In 1796, U.S. dollars were introduced into U.S.–China trade. By the early nineteenth century, the United States became an important competitive rival of the British in China.[4] While exchanging their cargos with Americans and counting the American payment in U.S. dollars, the Chinese businessmen could not help but study the American national coin stamped with the head of General Washington with fifteen stars and the motto of "liberty" and an eagle surrounded with laurels on the reverse. How these Chinese merchants were thinking about this American motto of liberty we cannot know, but the image of Americans among the Chinese merchants in the Pearl River Delta was certainly associated with the American coins with the "liberty" motto.

The increase of the Sino–American trade at Canton brought American people and missionaries to Macao as well. In 1802, only two American citizens resided at Macao, but this number increased to twenty in 1826, in addition to a large number of American citizens at Canton who often visited Macao at the height of the trading season.[5] On September 7, 1807, the American ship *Trident* that left New York on May 12 arrived in Macao with Robert Morrison (馬禮遜), the first Western Protestant missionary to China. The first American Protestant missionary Elijah Coleman Bridgman (卑治

文), however, did not arrive in China until 1830; the first American medical missionary Peter Parker (伯駕) arrived in February 1834; and the first American Presbyterian missionary, Thomas McBryde (麥克布萊德), landed in Macao in December 1841. McBryde left Macao the next year owing to health problems and was replaced by Walter M. Lowrie (婁禮華). The latter was later joined by seven other American Presbyterian missionaries, who arrived between 1843 and 1846.[6]

Elijah Coleman Bridgman began a small, informal school in Canton in the fall of 1830, and took his students with him to travel downriver. They spent four months in Macao from June to September 1831. Bridgman was quite pleased as his students "had behaved well" and "had made progress."[7] In February 1844, David B. McCartee (麥嘉諦) and Richard Cole (谷立) brought a printing machine and a Chinese character–English letter matrix to Macao, and began to print reading materials for missionaries. They printed 13,000 copies of the Gospel in one single day (September 7, 1844). In May 1845, a school for boys was established by the Presbyterian missionaries at Macao, with an enrollment of about thirty students. The Chinese students were very interested in religious and science courses.[8]

These American missionaries and their activities in Macao had a significant impact on society and helped to establish a favorable image of Americans (described below). These positive images, however, were tarnished by the materialistic Americans who were involved in the opium trade. In 1816, the crew of the American ship *Wabash*, which was carrying a cargo of that drug, was murdered by a boat full of Chinese men pretending to offer their services, but then plundered the ship of its cargo.[9]

Chinese views of Americans at the time, especially before the First Opium War, were partially evolved from their comparisons of Americans with other foreigners. In dealing with the case of Terranova, an Italian sailor on the American ship *Emily* who "accidentally" killed a boatwoman in a sampan on Whampoa River in October 1821, Captain Copeland initially refused to surrender his sailor to the Chinese authorities unless they promised the man would be returned after the trial. However, after Chinese war boats surrounded the ship and 1,000 Chinese soldiers were placed aboard the *Emily*, Terranova finally surrendered himself. The Americans allowed the Chinese judge to have the trial on the *Emily*. In the end, Terranova was retried in Canton and sentenced to death by strangulation, which was carried out immediately.

In a similar case, the British Superintendent Charles Elliott not only refused to meet the demands of Lin Zexu to hand over the British sailors who destroyed a temple near Kowloon in July 1839 and killed a Chinese man, Lin

Weixi, but also seized Hong Kong Island in the following August, which eventually led to the outbreak of the First Opium War. The Qing government realized that among foreign powers the British were the most dangerous and cunning, the French the next, and the Americans were "respectful and obedient."[10] Lin Zexu believed that the Americans were honest and trustful.[11] The report from the Grand Council for Military Affairs stated on March 22, 1844, that "Americans have since ever traded quietly, and have never challenged China, who never caused any trouble."[12] Even the Emperor Jiaqing knew that American businessmen in Guangdong knew "the law of imperial China was strict so they treat it with respect and have been well-behaved."[13]

The Chinese view of Americans could be influenced by other foreigners' view of Americans as well. In the early nineteenth century, the British were fierce rivals of the Portuguese and American newcomers so the Portuguese in Macao tended to side with the Americans. During the American War of 1812 and the Embargo Act of England, the Portuguese did not only allow at least one American ship to trade under the Portuguese national flag, but also vigorously protested against the British seizing the American ship *Hunter* in April 1814 near Macao, which carried cargos under the Portuguese flag.[14] It seems that the local Portuguese at Macao took the Americans as the power of the time that could resist Great Britain. Indeed, it was the Americans that attempted to fight against the monopoly of the East India Company over trade.

In defiance against the Co-hong and the East India Company, who were anxious to confine all foreign trade to themselves, American merchants tended to trade more extensively with small Chinese merchants, who were outside of the Co-hong.[15] We could imagine that small Chinese merchants would welcome the opportunity to conduct business with American merchants and viewed them as friendly, flexible, and courageous people and that some Co-hong merchants resented Americans for their violation of the exclusive privilege of the Co-hong. Howqua, who favored the Americans over the British, was an exception, and there were others. These Chinese merchants would have undoubtedly been impressed with the Americans' shrewdness, persistence, and sense of adventure, in their business dealings.

Historical records have not preserved much information on the Chinese view of Americans during these early encounters, but there are a few records that give us an idea of what their perceptions might have been of America. For instance, similar to the Portuguese positive view of Americans, some Chinese officials concluded that in comparison with other foreign traders the Americans "had quietly conducted their trade ever since, and had no conflict with or intension to challenge China."[16] *The Canton Register* (1827–1844), the first English-language publication in China, was published half of the year in Canton and the other half in Macao. It was established by a young American, William W. Wood (伍德), and published every week with commercial and social information on foreigners in China. William Wood often criticized the East India Company, but *The Canton Register* was financed by Jardine and Matheson, the largest private British company. As a result, William Wood soon lost his job at *The Canton Register*. Then, after working for Russell and Company for some time, Wood started his own publication *The Chinese Courier and Canton Gazette* on July 28, 1831 (the title was changed to *The Chinese Courier* in April 1832). But it could not compete with the other periodicals, and ceased on September 23, 1833.[17]

The above-mentioned publications, along with two other important journals related to Macao, *The Canton Press* (called *The Macao Press* in Chinese 澳門新聞紙) and *The Chinese Repository* (澳門月報 or 中國叢報), played an important role in importing Western and American ideas into China. Wei Yuan's (魏源) *Illustrated Treatise on the Maritime Kingdoms* (海國圖志) included much informaton from *The Chinese Repository*, which was edited primarily by American missionary Elijah Coleman Bridgman (卑治文). *The Canton Press* was established by Edmund Moller (慕勒) in 1835, and printed in Macao from July 1839. Lin Zexu paid great attention to this journal and ordered his assistants to collect and translate all the information on current affairs from *The Canton Press* and *The Chinese Repository*, such as opium production, international response to China's ban on opium trade and smoking, Western activities in China's neighboring states, and so forth. The effort to collect information from *The Canton Press* continued from July 1838 to November 1840, which resulted in six handwritten volumes, and stopped only when Lin was removed from his official position.[18] Among those translators was a young man from Macao and American merchant and Sinologist William C. Hunter.[19] Lin's keen interest in the information on the West, especially America, was attested by his decision to order Liang Jinde (梁進德) to translate Hugh Murray's *Cyclopedia of Geography*, which allocated one-fifth of its total space for information about the United States. Learning from all these publications, Lin discovered that "among foreign countries is England the strongest which only America and France still could compete against. . . . It seems that the way to deal with the situation is to use foreigners to balance against foreigners."[20]

Lin's positive view of Americans might also come from the fact that he was much impressed by the medical achievements of American missionary Peter Parker (伯駕). Peter Parker arrived in Macao in 1834, and opened a clinic in the "Thirteen Factories" in Canton the next year. More than two thousand patients, including Lin himself, were treated by him. From July to October 1838, Parker opened a clinic in Macao and treated seven hundred patients. Lin had been troubled by hernia disease and secretly sought help from Parker. Parker not only successfully cured Lin's hernia, but he also provided Lin with a piece of good advice on how to ease opium smokers' withdrawal from opium addiction. As a result, Lin appraised Parker at many public occasions.[21]

During the First Opium War, Lin's trust in Americans was further tested. On April 26, 1840, the Americans at the "Thirteen Factories" sent Lin a warning message that a large British fleet would come to China in June to blockade Canton. Upon reviewing this message, Lin and his assistants discussed whether American words could be trusted and they concluded that the Americans were honest, because they had fought against England with their blood seventy-five years previously to gain their independence.[22]

Peter Parker's medical activities in Canton and Macao also resulted in the development of a positive view of Americans among Chinese officials, including Chi Ying (耆英), chief negotiator of the Treaty of Wanghsia, and High Commissioner and Governor of Guangdong and Guangxi; Huang Entong (黃恩彤), assistant to Chi Ying for negotiation; and Pan Shicheng (潘仕成), the representative of China for the negotiation, who stayed in Macao to negotiate the Treaty of Wanghsia. It was signed at the Kun Iam Temple in Macao on July 3, 1844.

The parents of both Chi Ying and Pan Shicheng were once the patients of Parker and cured by him. Grateful to Parker, Chi Ying gave him two pieces of inscribed boards with his own handwriting: "Miraculous Hands to Bring the Dying Back to Life" and "Bring Longevity to the Earth and Heal the Patients." Huang Entong also knew Parker well owing to his medical success. He was so impressed by the American missionary that he initiated a clause (item 17) during the negotiation of the Treaty of Wanghsia that Americans would have the right to build churches in China's treaty ports, which was eventually included in the final version.[23]

Thus, although Macao's contact with Americans in the early stage was confined to a few government officials, businessmen, and literati, the image of the United States in Macao was, in general, positive in comparison with that of other foreigners. This Chinese view in favor of America shaped in Macao, though limited, would have a profound impact and felt later, not only in Macao but also throughout China, after it entered the stage of reform and revolution.

Americans through the Eyes of Reformers and Revolutionaries in Macao

To trace the image of Americans in Macao, one cannot ignore some Macao students' views of America, among whom the most influential were

Yung Wing (容閎) and Wong Shing (黃勝). Yung Wing was born at Nam Ping (South Screen) of Pedro Island, about four miles to the west of Macao, on November 17, 1828. At the age of seven, Yung Wing went to the school established by a British woman, Mrs. Gutzlaff, wife of Rev. Charles Gutzlaff in Macao. On February 23, 1839, Rev. Samuel Robbins Brown (塞繆爾・布朗), so-called a Maker of the New Orient and a graduate of Yale University in 1838. He established the Morrison School in Macao in November 1839.

Brown took Yung Wing, Wong Shing, and Wong Foon (黃寬) to America for education. They boarded Captain Gillespie's *Huntress*, departed from Whampoa on January 4, 1847, and arrived at New York on April 12, 1847.[24] At first, these Chinese boys stayed at the home of Brown's wife, Mrs. Elizabeth Brown, but then later moved to the residence of Rev. Shubael Bartlett and his wife, who were the parents of Mrs. Brown. At Monson Academy, Miss Rebekah Brown taught Yung Wing courses on physiology and psychological philosophy. Miss Brown was a kind, peaceful, and meek lady with a great heart.

Rebekah Brown, who later became the wife of Dr. A. S. McClean of Springfield, Massachusetts, gave him much help when Yung Wing studied at Yale. Mrs. Phoebe H. Brown, mother of Rebekah Brown, took good care of the Chinese boys. She was an optimistic woman and possessed great moral strength and merit though she went through many difficult days in her own life. For that, she won great respect from Yung Wing. That is why Yung Wing chose Springfield as the headquarters for the first group of 120 Chinese students studying in America under his supervision.[25]

Yung Wing had high regard for Americans. He appreciated their kindness and was so grateful to the Brown family that he named his first son Morrison Brown Yung and his second son Bartlett G. Yung in honor of Robert Morrison, Samuel Brown, and the Bartlett family. During the Civil War, Yung Wing demonstrated his love for his second homeland America by voluntarily offering his service to Brigadier-General Barnes of Springfield, the father of his Yale schoolmate.[26] In 1875, Yung Wing married Mary Kellogg (1851–1886) from Avon, Massachusetts, which was one of the two dreams that he "wished to become true."[27]

The young Yung Wing regarded American missionaries as open-minded and greatly relied upon them during his academic pursuits in the United States. On April 15, 1849, he wrote to American missionary Samuel Wells Williams (衛三畏), asking him to find a job for his brother Yung Asum and to persuade his father, Yung Ming Cheong, to let him stay in America longer in order to finish his liberal education. "They could not observe things as you and other open-minded people do," Yung Wing said.[28] On December 25, 1850, he wrote Samuel W. Williams another long letter, saying that "the old Yale campus is surrounded by an atmosphere of inspiration. . . . My mind has never been so shocked and I am really enjoying being influenced."[29]

Inspired and influenced by his own educational experience in American, Yung Wing was determined to reform China, by encouraging more Chinese students to study in the United States. He was determined and said "that through western education Chinese might be regenerated, become enlightened and powerful. To accomplish that objective became the guiding star of my ambition."[30] Partially owing to his effort, 120 Chinese students went to the United States in the summer of 1872 to pursue higher education, many of whom later became important statesmen, industrial leaders, top economic managers, and military officers. Moreover, Yung Wing advocated learning the banking business from the United States and using the capital and talent of American businessmen to build railroads.[31] In the 1870s, Yung Wing played a critical role in investigating the exploitation and torturing of Chinese coolies in Peru and negotiating with Spain and Peru to stop the coolie trade. By the 1840s, Macao had became a notorious place for exporting Chinese coolies to Latin American countries. Living in Macao then, Zheng Guanying (鄭觀應) wrote many articles criticizing the coolie business.[32] Interestingly enough, although the United States was one of the countries that had imported Chinese coolies, the U.S. government was viewed by many Chinese as a reliable international force against the abuse of Chinese coolies and for human rights. From 1859 to 1868, Chinese coolies repeatedly wrote to American officials in charge of business or the U.S. minister in Peru to complain about their sufferings and ask for help.[33]

The U.S. government responded to these requests through Frederick Low, U.S. Minister to China, who sent the Qing government serious memorandums on June 15, 1872, concerning the stoppage of the coolie trade.[34] In the ensuing negotiations with the representative of the Peru government in 1873, Li Hongzhang (李鴻章), the Chinese chief negotiator, called Yung Wing to participate in the negotiations to solve the coolie issue. Familiar with American and international laws, Yung Wing used American cases to turn down the Peruvian request for continuing the coolie trade and confiscating the contracts signed by Chinese coolies.[35] The American actions against the coolie trade at Macao and Yung Wing's reliance on American laws to fight against the coolie trade would no doubt leave a profound and positive image of the United States among the people in Macao.

Another student from Macao who went to the United States with Samuel Robbins Brown was Wong Shing. Wong Shing returned to China in 1848 because of illness. Nonetheless, his short stay in American had influenced his views of the world. In 1871, he and Wang Tao moved the printing office of the London Missionary Association to China, and established the Chinese General Printing Office (中华印务总局) there. This was the beginning of a modern press in China. In 1873, Wong Shing took the second group of Chinese students to study in America. Next year, he supported Wang Tao to transform the Chinese General Printing Office into *Daily Circulation* (循环日报), the first newspaper for reform in modern China, with a political commentary. It was the most successful newspaper since Chinese-published newspapers began. He translated many Western books and wrote several articles together with Wang Tao on military technology for reformers.[36] Obviously, Wong Shing shared much of Yung Wing's view of America.

If Yung Wing's and Wong Shing's views of America only reflected Macao's individual perception of the United States and their actions influenced by American values were mostly done outside Macao, *Learning the New* (知新報) established by Kang Youwei (康有爲) and Liang Qichao (梁啟超) was an indigent product of Macao and became a popular newspaper, both locally and nationally. *Learning the New* was financially supported by a Macao businessman and Kang's student He Huitian (何惠田) and also He Tingguang (何廷光). Under Xu Qin's (徐勤) editorship, the newspaper started its first issue on February 22, 1897. One issue was published every five days, but then extended to every ten days beginning with the twentieth issue. It ceased publication on January 20, 1901.[37]

In the first issues of *Learning the New*, readers could see the image of the United States in Macao as well as in the minds of the reformers. "Within only more than one hundred years since its independence," a newspaper editorial article once pointed out, "America has become such a prosperous and powerful nation." "A dozen small countries in South America," the article described, "have had no wars because of the American leadership. . . . The United States ruled with no admonition." "In about one hundred years, good knowledge competitively developed. From various and remote nations, came out Washington who established democracy. Napoleon arose but monarchism declined. . . . From the era of monarchism to the time of democracy is the third change." "Thus," the article concluded, "Asia contains the old habits of the world; Europe started the new path of the earth, and America achieved the great law of the universe."[38] Clearly, in the view of the editor and reformers of Macao, the United States was a powerful democratic nation and presented the great path for the rest of the world to follow.

Among all the reformers in Macao the most important is Sun Yat-sen. Sun was not born in Macao, but he was once a Macao resident. Sun's father was a shoemaker who lived in Macao during his early years and it was from Macao that Sun departed for America at the age twelve. In his five years of studying and living in Honolulu, Sun was enormously influenced by American and European cultures, education, and democratic ideas. In 1883, it was again from Macao that Sun departed for Hong Kong to continue his college education. During his college time, Sun frequently traveled between Hong Kong and Macao. In 1892, Sun graduated from the College of Medicine for Chinese at Hong Kong, headed by the famous American Dr. John Kerr, and moved to Macao, where he stayed for several periods until 1897.

Initially, Sun worked at the *Kiang Wu* hospital in Macao, and later he opened his own private clinic and pharmacy there. He cooperated with a Macanese, Francisco Hermenegildo Fernandes, for the publication of the first Macao bilingual weekly newspaper, the *Echo Macanese* (*Ching-Hai Ts'ung Bao* or *Shing-hai Tsung Pao* in Chinese section, 1893–1895), which published several articles that introduced Sun's ideas and political actions.[39] It was believed that it was during this period of time and at Macao that Sun developed his republican ideals and goals, which were undoubtedly influenced by his education and life in America, his supporters from the United States, and his living in the house of an American Protestant minister at Canton after his political failure in 1895. Thus, the political ideals of Sun as a Macao resident reflected the most notable image of the United States in the enclave in the late nineteenth century as a democratic, prosperous, progressive, and powerful nation, which would continue to exercise its influence in China in the twentieth century, especially during and after the Second World War.

The Image of Americans in Modern Macao

By the time when the Second World War broke up, owing to the fact that the United States was allied with China and the most powerful force fighting against China's enemy Japan, the positive perception of the United States among Chinese in Macao dominated their outlook. The local newspaper of Macao often used enlarged bold headlines to report the policy of the United States toward China.[40] Although newspaper reports tried to be neutral and value-free, the tone and format of many newspaper headlines related to the United States, such as "Governors of Forty Two States of America Will Host the Celebration of the Independent Days of China," "The Independent Days of China Is Wildly Celebrated Everywhere in the United States," "The American Ambassador to China Will Send a Delegate to Macao to Discuss How to Evacuate Chinese," "The Anti-American Aid Movement Aborted,"[41] overtly revealed the great appreciation and gratitude of Macao people for the American support to the city and of China.

Some reports and commentaries on American political and economic systems were much less neutral, and expressed authors' admiration and passion for American democracy, which was believed to be central to the stability and prosperity of the United States. For instance, *Residents' Daily* (*Shimin ribao*, 市民日報) used much space to systematically introduce to its readers the constitutional government of the United States, its House of Representatives, past and current presidents, and so on.[42] It was believed that "due to the nature of the American political structure there has been little chaos and turmoil in America since the era of Washington and Jefferson . . . the security of the United States mostly resulted from this kind of political system,"[43] and that a farmer's right to owing a piece of land "is the necessary dignity that the citizen of a free and democratic country deserves."[44] Yet, while greatly appreciating American democracy and power, the people of Macao never forgot to point out some weaknesses of Americans, such as the phenomenon that "Americans love gambling" (which Macao residents could easily identify with).[45]

The admiration for the United States among Macao people has been strong since World War II. By the 1960s, the textile industry of Macao began to rely upon the U.S. market,[46] which no doubt drew Macao closer to the United States. Many youths in Macao went to the United States for a better education, opportunity, and life.[47] When the news was announced in 1978 that the United States and the People's Republic of China would soon establish a formal diplomatic relationship, which became true in 1979, many people in Macao were ecstatic and believed this would promote U.S.–Macao relations.[48] From then on, Macao's interests in American culture increased significantly. Macao's newspaper began reporting all kinds of things about America, such as the beggar king of Washington, the ideal husband in the mind of an American wife, American women's craze for cosmetic surgery, and popular dance in America.[49]

Macao–U.S. relations also passed a serious test after the Beijing incident in 1989. The U.S. government put economic sanctions on China (section 902 of P. L. 101-246), but carefully and skillfully excluded Macao from, which ensured Macao–U.S. relations remained intact. Ten years later, when Macao was about to be returned to China, U.S.–Macao relations faced another uncertainty. But again it was well managed to meet the challenge. After some serious discussions, both the Houses of Representatives and Senate of the United States respectively passed H.R.825: United States–Macao Policy Act of 1999, February 24, 1999, and S 1430: United States–Macao Policy Act of 1999, on July 26, 1999,[50] which eventually became the "U.S.–

Macao Policy (Title II of the Malaria Control Act of 2000)" in 2000. "U.S.–Macao Policy of 2000" declared that "the United States should play an active role in maintaining Macao's confidence and prosperity, Macao's unique cultural heritage, and the mutually beneficial ties between the people of the United States and the people of Macao."[51] Many Macao residents and scholars acclaimed the passage of this act, which they believed showed the United States had gained confidence in the independence of Macao and "one country, two systems." This law would elevate the international status of Macao and promote U.S.–Macao trade, foreign investment in the city, business opportunities for Macao businessmen, and educational opportunities for Macao students.[52] They thought, "Americans pay great attention to the contractual spirit, trust and honor, and like to do everything through legal papers."[53]

Meanwhile, the Macao government followed the practice of most European countries to confer American citizens a special treatment of visa-free entry into Macao for fewer than thirty days. In response, the U.S. government issued "Macao Policy Act of 2001," which declared, "In recognition of this treatment and the highly secure new Macao SAR travel documents . . . the United States grants ten-year multiple entry visas to eligible Macao residents coming to the United States as tourists or for short-term business purposes."[54] As a result of this act, Macao residents are also eligible to "participate in future lotteries under the Diversity Visa Program," to win a lucky lottery visa to the United States. This kind of reciprocal treatment between Macao and the United States has certainly promoted the economic and cultural interaction between the two sides. By the end of the last century and the beginning of this century, the number of Americans who visited Macao reached an average of 85,000 per year.[55]

Based on the above economic and cultural relations between Macao and the United States, it is no wonder that many Macao people hold positive views of American people and American culture and products. They have welcomed and appreciate American culture, which is represented by the recent performance of *Chicago* in the city. Many people were enormously touched and enlightened by American arts and this theatrical performance. As another sign, the American model of "general education" has also been promoted in Macao. Macao's youth have been eager to study and learn English in America with the belief that it will help them find a better job at American casinos. Some scholars of Macao have pointed out that the city was not well known in the world before American casino operators arrived, and that many people had the misconception that Macao was just a small territory belonging to Hong Kong. American casinos and their family-oriented enterprises are renowned worldwide, and have helped make Macao a global city in its own right. As a result, there is now increasingly more interest in foreigners investing in Macao.[56]

Thus, two centuries after the first Chinese encounters with Americans, the historical images of the United States in Macao have not only continued, but remain stronger. But there are downsides as well. After the Iraq War broke out and American casinos became very competitive, some local Chinese became very negative toward the United States, which has split Macao's perceptions of the United States. Many people of Macao believed that the purpose of the United States to launch the Iraq War and to forcefully transplant the American model of "democratic freedom" on Iraq under the name of anti-terrorism was actually to control the natural resources in the Middle East.[57]

A few Macao people even began to worry that American activities of anti-terrorism might result in the penetration of terrorist actions in Macao and terrorist attacks on American businesses there. It was feared that this would lead to the introduction of American imperialistic ideals into Macao. These apprehensions were combined with fears that once Macao conferred its gambling right to American corporations and opened its gate to the inflow of American capital and investments, American influence in Macao would increase significantly and affect Macao's laidback lifestyle, and in its place, be supplanted by the strange and powerful American culture.[58] These are reasons why some people have opposed the idea of copying a Las Vegas model for Macao. They believe that the United States was attempting to use Christian culture and values to reform the culture of the rest world and unity the world culturally.[59]

Indeed, the Macao people were much shocked by the decisions that 160 Chinese employees of Las Vegas Sands were fired and that the U.S. government put Banco Delta Asia SARL on the list of money laundering. These actions were seen by many Macao people as American hegemonism, which judged everything according to American perspective and interests.[60] Macao people began to fear that the globalization of Macao would turn the city into a fairytale land like Las Vegas or Disney World and that the Macao Venetian Hotel would become the new cultural symbol of Macao, overshadowing the long-lasting world heritage cites.[61]

Moreover, the earlier positive views of "U.S.–Macao Policy of 2000" among Macao people began to change for the worse. Some people pointed out that owing to one of the clauses in "U.S.–Macao Policy of 2000" that authorized that if the president of the United States "determines that Macao is not sufficiently autonomous to justify treatment under a particular law of the United States," the president "may issue an Executive order suspending the application of such law."[62] The White House has been constantly monitoring events in Macao. [63] Many people in Macao were very unhappy that the U.S. government's accusation that Banco Delta Asia SARL helped North Korea launder money, which almost led to a financial crisis in Macao and which resulted in the fact that the U.S. government put its hands not only in Macao's finance and casino business, but also in the airport and customs service.[64]

More seriously, some people worried, as Americans invested more into casinos, they would hire more than thirty thousand employees and pay a large proportion of Macao taxes. If this happened, then it was feared that one senior manager of a giant American business could possess power to influence local politics, and turn Macao into a bridgehead for a "color revolution" in mainland China.[65] One of the Macao legislators blamed American capital for causing the shortage of human resources and the rising costs of housing in Macao.[66]

Interestingly, after the global financial storm occurred in 2008, the negative views of Americans among the Chinese in Macao began to change. People of Macao worried that the possible withdraw of American business from Macao would cause economic disaster and recession. What a taxi driver expresses below very much revealed Macao people's sympathy with American firms: "The government of Macao or China should try to help Sands and Wynn get back to its sound footing when it is in trouble now because they have greatly contributed to the prosperity of Macao!"[67] This time, even when American casino enterprises have a massive layoff, people in Macao did not complain about that at all. Those who have lost their jobs or who are afraid of losing their jobs simply try to find a new one, become more competitive in their search, and also look for a more stable employment. All of this raises many questions. How long will this sympathetic and collaborative mood among Macao people toward Americans last? Will it reverse again when the larger economic and political environment or U.S.–China–Macao relations change? Answers to these and other questions and their outcomes are dependent on the economic interactions between American firms and their Chinese counterparts as well as the development of the economy in Macao in the near future.

In brief, the above retraces and analyses the images of Americans in Macao from their beginnings to the present, and have shown that although in general the Chinese perception in Macao of Americans has not been in conflict with mainland Chinese perceptions. Images of the United States among Chinese under different regimes have differed from time to time. While most Chinese had no contact with Americans and had no idea who they were in the late eighteenth and the early nineteenth centuries, many Chinese in Macao had encounters with them and knowledge of America.

They have had positive opinions about Americans, which, at times, influenced perceptions in mainland China. By the time of China's Civil War, owing to the propaganda against American imperialism launched by the Chinese Communist Party and the bad behaviors of some American marines who allegedly committed various crimes, including shootings of alleged Chinese thieves, stabbing a Chinese rickshaw driver to death, and raping Chinese civilians,[68] the image of the United States among the Chinese on mainland China began to become more negative.

After 1949, the governments of Macao and Communist China pursued different policies toward the United States, and the U.S. government also implemented different policies toward them. As a result, the dominant image of the United States in mainland China became very negative. This difference demonstrated that the image of the United States among Chinese is an "imaged community" very much conditioned by the political and economic relations between the two parties, which has little to do with their different races, cultures, and religions and much to do with politics. The image of the United States in Macao often paralleled that of mainland China and somewhat dependent on the present status of U.S.–China relations. But it was mostly determined by U.S.–Macao relations, politically and economically, since Macao has been an independent political entity and treated as such. Moreover, owing to the unique position of Macao standing between China, the United States, and the West, Macao often served as the window and gauge of U.S.–China relations. The continuity or discontinuity shown in the image of the United States in Macao and a comparison of the images of the United States in Macao and mainland China could reveal and reflect the true nature of Sino–American relations and signify a trend or change in U.S.–China–Macao relations. The importance of Macao's role in China's past and present foreign relations with the United States and the West should not be underestimated.

Notes

A different, shorter version of this article was published by *Review of Culture*, Macao, in the spring of 2010.

1. Jose Maria Braga, *With the Flowery Banner: Some Comments on the Americans in Macao and South China* (Macao, 1940) open page and page 12.

2. Tereza Sena, "Historical Background of Macao with Particular Focus on the First Americans in China," in *Macao—Cultural Dialogue Towards A New Millennium, Proceedings of A Symposium*, eds. Iêda Siqueira Wiarda and Lucy M. Cohen (Washington, D.C.: Catholic University of America Press, 2004), 61–63; Jose Maria Braga, *With the Flowery Banner*, 12–14, 19–20.

3. Jose Maria Braga, *With the Flowery Banner*, 14–15, 37; Tereza Sena, "Historical Background of Macao with Particular Focus on the First Americans in China," 37–38.

4. Kenneth S. Latourette, *History of Early Relations Between the United States and China (1784–1844)* (New Haven, Conn.: Yale University Press, 1919), 11.

5. Jose Maria Braga, *With the Flowery Banner*, 17, 44.

6. These seven American Presbyterian missionaries are James C. Hepburn (1843), Richard Cole (1844), Davie B. McCartee (1844), Robert Q. Way (1844), Andrew P. Happer (1844), John Lloyd (1844), M. S. Culbertson (1844), A. Ward Loomis (1844), J. B. French (1846), W. M. Speer (1846), and John W. Quarterman (1846). See Tang Kaijian and Yan Xiaohua, "A Brief Count of the Early Activities of American Presbyterian Missionaries in Macao," *Research on Macao History*, no. 3 (December 2004): 99–101; Tereza Sena, "Historical Background of Macao with Particular Focus on the First Americans in China," 66–73.

7. Murray A. Rubinstein, *The Origins of the Anglo-American Missionary Enterprise in China, 1807–1840* (Lanham, Md.: Scarecrow Press, 1996), 290–91.

8. Tang Kaijian and Yan Xiaohua, "A Brief Count of the Early Activities of American Presbyterian Missionaries in Macao," 106–7.

9. Jose Maria Braga, *With the Flowery Banner*, 23–24; *Yue haiguan zhi* (*The History of Custom Services at Guangdong*), vol. 24, *Shibo* (*The Port Trade*), 476.

10. *Chouban yiwu shimo* (*The Whole Story of Planning to Deal with the Barbarians-Related Business*) (Beijing: Zhonghua Press, 1964), vol. 6, *Daoguang Period*, 3119.

11. Dominie Shi Fong Lee, *The American Missionaries, The Mandarins, and the Opium War: Canton, China* (Shanghai: Shanghai renmin chubanshe, 2004), 64–65.

12. Zhongshan Archives and the First Historical Archives of China (eds.), *The Selected Archives on Xiangshan from Ming and Qing* (Shanghai: Shanghai Ancient Books Press, 2006), 518–19.

13. "Trade Ports," *The History of Custom Services at Guangdong*, vol. 24, 476.

14. Jose Maria Braga, *With the Flowery Banner*, 22–23.

15. Jose Maria Braga, *With the Flowery Banner*, 43–45.

16. The Defensive and Administrative Governor of Guangdong and Guangxi Cheng Juecai, "Memo on the Process in Stopping through Persuasion the Demand from the American Minister for Visiting Beijing," March 22, 1844. *The Compilation of the Archives and Literature Related to Macao Issues from Ming and Qing*, vol. 2, edited by the First National Archive of China, Macao Foundation and the Institute of Classical Studies of Jinan University (Beijing: Renmin chubanshe, 1999), 514.

17. Tereza Sena, "Historical Background of Macao with Particular Focus on the First Americans in China," 74.

18. Chen Shurong and Huang Hanqian (eds.), *Lin Zexu and Macao* (Macao: Macao Huahui Printing Company, 1990), 177.

19. Ibid., 129, 150.

20. Zhao Deyu, *Western Knowledge Coming to the East and the Responses from China and Japan—A Comparative Study of the Western Learning in China and Japan* (Beijing: Zhishi chubanshe, 2001), 220–22.

21. Dominie Shi Fong Lee, *The American Missionaries, The Mandarins, and the Opium War)*, 34–35; *The Chinese Repository*, vol. 13, pp. 302–3; Edward V. Gulick, *Peter Parker and the Opening of China* (Cambridge, Mass.: Harvard University Press, 1973), 117–18; Zhang Wenqin, *Macao and Chinese History and Culture* (Macao: Macao Foundation, 1995), 38.

22. Dominie Shi Fong Lee, *The American Missionaries, The Mandarins, and the Opium War*, 64–65.

23. Zhang Wenqin, *Macao and Chinese History and Culture*, 38, 46.

24. Yung Wing, My *Life in China and America*, trans. Xu Fengshi and Hui Tiejiao (Shanghai: Hunan Renmin Chubanshe, 1981), 1–2, 23–25.

25. Wing, My *Life in China and America*, 13–18, 94.

26. Wing, My *Life in China and America*, 79–80.

27. Wing, My *Life in China and America*, 12.

28. April 15, 1849; December 25, 1850, Yung Wing to S. W. William, Unpublished Missionary English Correspondence, Yale Sterling Memorial Library (YSML), Yale University; Gao Zonglu, "Yung Wing and Chinese Young Students in America," in *Yung Wing and China's Modernization*, eds. Wu Wencai, Gao Demin, and Liang Zhenxing (Zhuhai: Zhuhai chubanshe, 1999), 424–66.

29. Liang Baihua, "Yung Wing's 'Western Learning' and China's Modernization," in *Yung Wing and China's Modernization*, eds. Wu Wencai, Gao Demin, and Liang Zhenxing, 312.

30. Wing, My *Life in China and America*, 20.

31. Wing, My *Life in China and America*, 119–21; Gao Zonglu, "Yung Wing and Chinese Young Students in America"; Xiao Yiting, "Yung Wing's Activities to Reform China," *Yung Wing and China's Modernization*, 409.

32. First National Archive of China, Macao Foundation, and the Institute of Classical Studies of Jinan University (eds.), *The Compilation of the Archives and Literature Related to Macao Issues from Ming and Qing*, vol. 6 (Beijing: Renmin chubanshe, 1999), 698–710.

33. Wei Qingyuan, A *Commentarial History of Macao* (Canton: Guangdong renmin chubanshe, 2005), 238; *The Compilation of the Archives and Literature Related to Macao Issues from Ming and Qing*, vol. 3, 25–26; vol. 5, 651.

34. *The Compilation of the Archives and Literature Related to Macao Issues from Ming and Qing*, vol. 3, 37–40.

35. Wei Qingyuan, A *Commentarial History of Macao* (Canton: Guangdong renmin chubanshe, 2005), 247–58.

36. Liu Shengyi, "The Contribution from Yung Win and His Schoolmates to the Cause for China's Modernization," *Yung Wing and China's Modernization*, 343–56.

37. Jin Shulun, *Anecdotes of Macao* (Beijing: Zhongyang wenxian chubanshe, 1999), 150–54; Lu Juan, "The Establishment of *Learn the New* at Macao in Late Qing," *Research on Macao History*, no. 5, November 2006.

38. "A Public and Comprehensive View of the Global Trend," *Learning the New*, no. 2 and no. 4, January 26 and February 6 (lunar month), 1897.

39. Jin Shulun, *Anecdotes of Macao*, 167–72; Tereza Sena, "Historical Background of Macao with Particular Focus on the First Americans in China," 88–90.

40. *Residents' Daily* (*Shimin ribao*), November 19–23, 25, 27–30, December 1, 3, 8–9, 12–13, 17–22, 26, 1948; January 1, 7–8, 17, May 27, June 14, August 22, September 22, December 7, 9, 13, 26, 1949; January 18, February 9, 14, May 16, 1950.

41. *Residents' Daily* (*Shimin ribao*, 市民日報), October 1 and 9, 1944; February 9, 1949; March 16, 1949.

42. *Residents' Daily* (*Shimin ribao*, 市民日報), September 25, October 12, 1944; February 21, April 15–18, 1945; April 23–27, June 8, 10, and 28, 1946.

43. *Residents' Daily*, January 27, 1949.

44. *Residents' Daily*, March 13, 1949.

45. *Residents' Daily*, May 22, 1949.

46. *Residents' Daily*, August 18, 1965.

47. *Residents' Daily*, October 6, November 23, 1965.

48. *Residents' Daily*, December 17, 1978; January 1, 1979.

49. *Residents' Daily*, March 5, 9, 22, April 6, 23, 1979.

50. H.R.825: United States–Macao Policy Act of 1999 (February 24, 1999), Consulate General of the United States in Hong Kong, hongkong.usconsulate.gov/usmo_pa_1999022401.html; S 1430: United States–Macao Policy Act of 1999 (July 26, 1999), Consulate General of the United States in Hong Kong, hongkong.usconsulate.gov/usmo_pa_1999072601.html.

51. U.S.–Macao Policy (Title II of the Malaria Control Act of 2000), Consulate General of the United States in Hong Kong, hongkong.usconsulate.gov/usmo_pa_2000121401.html.

52. Macao News, "The Fact that the United States Recognizes the Macao Status Shows Its Increased Confidence in Macao," *Macao Daily News*, January 4, 2001.

53. Macao News, "Whose Hand Will the Flower of the Gold Area Fall into?," *Macao Daily News*, May 31, 2002.

54. "United States–Macao Policy Act Report as of March 27, 2001," Consulate General of the United States in Hong Kong, hongkong.usconsulate.gov/usmo_pa.html.

55. "U.S.–Macao Policy Act Report 2001," Released by the Bureau of East Asian and Pacific Affairs.

56. Yin Hongwei, "The Number One Gambling City in the World?," *The Window of South Wind* (*Nanfengchuang*), the First Issue of December, 2006.

57. Chen Yuan, "The Feeling and Recognition of Nowadays—After Watching the Music Drama 'Chicago,'" *Macao Daily News*, November 8, 2004; Macao News by Yi Lin, *Macao Daily News*, December 20, 2004; Macao News, "Improve English Capacity and Competitive Strength for Future: The Number of Students Who Plan to Study in America and Work in American Firms Increased," *Macao Daily News*, February 20, 2006; "People of Macao Are Calmly Anti-War," *Cheng Pao*, April 12, 2003; Bi Yu, "Quote Out of Text," *Macao Daily News*, July 13, 2004.

58. Wu Wen, "Quote Out of Text," *Macao Daily News*, June 27, 2004; Bi Yu, "Quote Out of Text," *Macao Daily News*, July 13, 2004.

59. Li Yan, "Meaningful Words on Lotus Mountain," *Jornal Informacao*, November 12, 2004; "Economy," *Macao Daily News*, December 12, 2004; Huang Hongzhao, "A Simply Analysis of Macao Culture," *Macao Daily News*, June 18, 2006.

60. Yong Yi, "Words from Chinese People of Macao," *Jornal San Wa Ou*, November 8, 2006; Yu Ding, "Commentarial Points from Macao," *Jornal Do Cidadao*, March 21, 2007.

61. Song Weixiong, "Behind Macao's Success: The Super Casino City vs. Social Development," *Jornal San Wa Ou*, September 27, 2007.

62. U.S.–Macao Policy (Title II of the Malaria Control Act of 2000), Consulate General of the United States in Hong Kong, hongkong.usconsulate.gov/usmo_pa_2000121401.html.

63. "Forum on Finance and Economy: The Strategy of American Enterprises for Entering Macao and Their Impact," *Journal Do Cidadao*, August 14, 2006.

64. Ibid.

65. Yong Yi, "Words from Chinese People of Macao," *Jornal San Wa Ou*, October 27, 2007.

66. Zhou Jinhui, "Behind Macao's Prosperity," *Macao Daily*, October 26, 2007, 12.

67. The author's conversation with a taxi driver on November 18, 2008, Macao.

68. Zhiguo Yang, "U.S. Marines in Qingdao: History, Public Memory, and Chinese Nationalism," in *Exploring Nationalisms of China: Themes and Conflicts*, eds. C. X. George Wei and Xiaoyuan Liu (Westport, Conn.: Greenwood Press, 2002), 57–75.

PART III

MACAO AND THE UNITED STATES: ECONOMIC DIMENSIONS

CHAPTER SEVEN

Analysis on the Special Role of Macao in Sino–U.S. Economic and Trade Relationships at the Very Beginning of the Twenty-First Century

Zhang Lili

Since the establishment of the Macao Special Administrative Region, under the strict implementation of the central government's general principles—"one country, two systems," "Macao people governing Macao," Macao entered a phase of rapid development in the first nine years of the twenty-first century. With its economic prosperity, the significant improvement of living standards of the people, and its international economic status, Macao attracted enormous attention from the world. Many factors resulted in Macao's significant achievement, one of which is that Sino–U.S. relations have developed comprehensively in the twenty-first century and thus led to the rapid improvement of Sino–U.S. economic and trade relations. Owing to its special location and policy advantage, Macao benefits from it and also plays a special role in it.

The Special Status of Macao in Sino–U.S. Relations

Macao, a special region with only thirty kilometers and a population of about 500,000 at present, is to west of the estuary of Peal River in Gang dong Province. This place has always been the intersection between the East and the West since the time of "Western influence extending to the East." Portugal first occupied Macao and continued its colonized administration there for several centuries.

Since the early establishment of the People's Republic of China ("New China" for short), New China had suffered severe blockade, embargo, isolation, and strikes from Western countries following the United States. Taking into account tough conditions of Cold War and proceeding from national interest, the central government of the PRC kept a "window" open as the channel of international communication and exchanges with capitalized countries and national countries, with the aim of breaking down the severe blockade of imperialist America. The central government adopted the policy of "planning for long and displaying the best use"[1] toward Hong Kong and Macao. In so doing, the two capitalist "windows," which played a special role, were kept open at the marginal area of New China among the bloc of socialist countries. Despite that both China and Portugal adopted the policy of "the maintenance of status quo" on the issue of Macao administration, Portugal did not establish diplomatic ties with New China during a period of almost thirty years after the founding of PRC. On February 8, 1979, the ambassador-level diplomatic tie was established between the two countries

By the 1980s, the major impediment between China and Portugal relations was the Macao Question. As for Macao, which had been colonized for more than four hundred years, the fundamental policy of Chinese government in the settlement of Macao Question follows: Macao was and is one part of Chinese territory, and Chinese government must take back Macao and resume the exercise of sovereignty over Macao before the year of 2000, and Macao's stability and development should be maintained before its return. At the end of June 1986, both Chinese and Portuguese governments began diplomatic negotiations on the issue of Macao, and conducted altogether three rounds of negotiations by late July. With the common and concerted effort by both parties, the whole process of negotiations went smoothly. Noticeably, there once emerged the argument of delaying the date of Macao's return to China until the twenty-first century. However, on December 31, 1986, the spokesman of Chinese Ministry of Foreign Affairs seriously pointed out that "the attempt to return Macao after the year of 2000 will never be accepted."

In March 1987, the China–Portuguese Joint Declaration was reached fully and completely. On the date of January 15, 1988, China and Portugal held the ceremony of exchanging agreements at Beijing, which then came into force officially.

The main body of China–Portuguese Joint Declaration is as follows:

1. The PRC decided to exercise its sovereignty on Macao on December 20, 1999.
2. The fundamental policy would be under the guide of the principle of "one country, two systems," proposed by the Chinese government in the settlement of the Macao Question.

3. The Portuguese government, together with Chinese cooperation, would be responsible for Macao's administration during the transition.
4. The land contract and its concerning items in the transitional period would be made into rules, and the land working group would be erected in charge of the negotiation on the details.[2]

The main content of the fundamental policy put forward by the Chinese government in the China–Portuguese Joint Declaration was as follows:

1. The Macao Special Administrative Region (SAR) would be established in accordance with the provisions of Article 31 of the Constitution of the PRC.
2. Macao's present social system, economic structures, lifestyles and basic laws would remain unchanged after the establishment of the Macao SAR.
3. The Macao Special Administrative Region would be directly under the authority of the Central People's Government of the PRC, and would enjoy a high degree of autonomy, except in foreign and defense affairs which are the responsibilities of the Central People's Government. The Macao Special Administrative Region would be vested with executive, legislative, and independent judicial power, including that of final adjudication and independent finance.
4. Macao would continue to serve as the free port and separate customs region, and also keep and develop the economic and cultural relations with all different countries and regions as well as concerning international organizations.
5. Due regard would be given to the economic interests of Portugal and other countries in Macao.
6. China's special policy toward Macao would be ruled by the National People's Congress and the Basic Law of Macao SAR, and will be kept unchanged for fifty years.

The successful settlement of the Macao Question proves again the practical significance of "one country, two systems," and demonstrates the promotion and sample effect for the cause of Chinese reunification. The settlement of the Macao Question accords with the common aspiration of all the Macao and Chinese people, and finally materializes Macao's return to the motherland after its leave of more than four hundred years.[3]

On the night of December 19, 1999, Chinese National Chairman Jiang Zemin and his counterpart of Portugal, together with other high officials of the two countries, attended the glorious turn-over ceremony in Macao. At midnight the national flag of Portugal was lowered and the Chinese national flag rose up at 00:00 on the 20th, which symbolized the return of Macao after being ruled by Portugal for more than four hundred years, and the end of Western colonization on China's last land. Following was the inauguration ceremony of the first chief executive officer of Macao SAR and other high officials. The SAR government of Macao has been established since then.

Ever since its return, Macao SAR has undertaken effective administration under the support from the central government. With social stability and a thriving economy, Macao, whose people share the common mind, is faced with an unprecedented opportunity to embark on the path of rapid economic growth.

The Rapid Development of China's Economy and All-Around Development of the Sino–U.S. Relationship at the Beginning of the Twenty-First Century

The golden opportunity that Macao meets is the historical trend of the overall rising of developing countries at the beginning of the twenty-first century. Economic strength, a representative of the overall rising national strength of developing countries like China and India, will form the changes of the underlying trend at the twenty-first century.

And China's performance is more prominent. After entering into the twenty-first century, on the solid basis of reform and opening up policy for more than twenty years, the Chinese economy has witnessed a rapid growth. And the economic growth is unprecedented in the Chinese history.

10 percent growth in 2003
10.1 percent growth in 2004
10.4 percent growth in 2005
10.7 percent growth in 2006
11.5 percent growth in 2007
9 percent growth in 2008

As seen in figure 7.1, the economic growth is unprecedented in the Chinese history: it has taken just four years for China to surpass the world's second-largest trading nation. The trade surplus in 2006 was $117.4 billion. (The first eight months in 2007 was $161.7 billion.) By the end of September 2009, foreign exchange reserves were $2.1 trillion.

It was predicted that, by the year 2010, China would become the world's largest exporting country. The contribution rate of the Chinese economy to

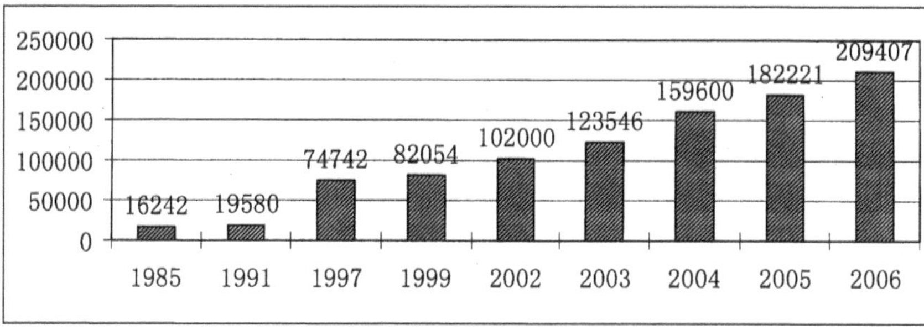

Figure 7.1. China's Gross Nation Product (hundred million RMB)

the world continued to grow more than 20 percent and by the end of 2009, the rate was up to 40 percent.

For the next fifteen years, China will enter a period of "consumer explosion," and, possibly, may become the world's largest market. The determination of the Chinese government to develop its economy is firm, and the goal is solid; this may help the government to achieve the target.

The strategic goal raised at the seventeenth National Congress of the Communist Party of China (CPC) is, by the year 2020, to achieve the goal of building a moderately prosperous society in all respects: quadruple the per capita GDP of the year 2000 by 2020; make China an innovative country; steadily increase the ratio of consumption to GDP; and coordinate consumption, investment, and export to boost economic growth, paying attention to the development of following areas: new countryside building, social equality and justice, cultural construction, the basic livelihood guarantee, the elimination of absolute poverty, health care, environmental protection, and ecological civilization.

But because of historical reasons, China will be in the preliminary stage of socialism for a long time, and the per capita GNP in the year 2005 ranked 111 in the world. Therefore China will still stay in the range of a developing country.

As seen in figure 7.2, with the rapid development of China, foreign economic relations play an important role and one of the most important trade partners is the United States. The economic relationship between the two countries started late, but developed rapidly. The United States is now the only superpower in the world, and it has the strongest national power. It is also the only state that is capable of threatening the world's peace and security; it wields the most prominent influence in international situations.

The United States is the largest economy in the world. At present, it ranks first in its labor productivity, gross domestic products, and the total

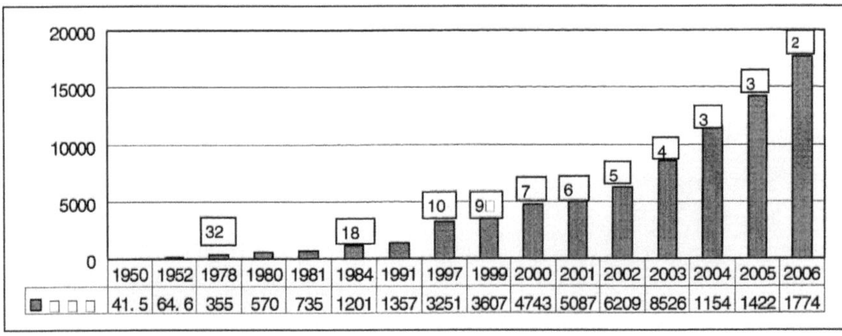

Figure 7.2. Total Volume of Imports and Exports of China and the World Rank (hundred million dollars)

amount of foreign trade. In 2006, the GDP of the United States was about $13 trillion, and the per capita GDP was nearly $40,000. The total amount of importing and exporting goods in 2005 was $2.57532 trillion; compared with 2004, the growth rate was 12.5 percent. The United States is the most influential country in the world, and it is also the country that has the largest impact on China. In China, the Sino–U.S. relationship is the most important bilateral relationship. After entering the twenty-first century, the Sino–U.S. relationship is in its best-ever period in history. At present, the relationship between the two countries is moving forward in a comprehensive and continuing way, and it became one of the most important global bilateral relations to have a great impact on the changes of world and international situations. The main trend of the relationship is cooperation, cooperation in a mutually beneficial way. The common interests of these two countries are expending constantly. The multi-level political connections of the two countries are on the way of being systematic, regular, and timely.

The Sino–U.S. economic and trade relationship is developing rapidly. The total amount of trade between the two countries reached more than $200 billion in 2004. This was the first time the United States surpassed Japan and became China's largest trade partner, and China became the United States' third-largest trade partner. The financial links of these two countries are also very close: China is now the largest holder of American financial bonds, totaling more than $800 billion. The United States has the largest investment in China, including direct investment. The total trade amount between China and the United States was up to $3.3274 trillion in 2008, an increase 10.5 percent compared with the previous year.

The Sino–U.S. relationship, the economic and trade relationship included, is developing in an all-around way. Against this background, Macao, as a place that is in a unique location and policy advantage, develops in a rapid way.

Behavior and Cooperation of China and the United States with the Developing Economy of Macao in the Beginning of the Twenty-First Century

After the return of Macao, the fundamental state policy of "one country, two systems" was implemented strictly, and the fruitful management and ability of Macao SAR government has been extensively praised. The position which Macao has and policy advantages are explained and developed.

The specialties of Macao: Except diplomatic affairs and national defense affairs that belong to People's Central Government, the current social and economic systems and lifestyle and basic law of Macao enjoy high-level autonomy, including administration, legislature, independent judicial right and the right of final judgment, financial independence, and the SAR government, which is made up of locals. Macao will continue to act as the free port and independent tariff districts, keeping and developing economy, culture relations, and so forth with various countries, areas, and relevant international organizations. The clauses in "Basic Law" are all implemented, and Macao will be steady for the long term.

This political prospect is very beneficial to investment. And the SAR government of Macao, in these nine years, supported by central government, has improved the investment climate in a more cost-effective manner, set up and completed the regulation system, and held multiple large-scale international activities: the sports meeting of east Asia, Portuguese-language countries' sports meeting, applying for the cultural heritage of the world, which has improved its international popularity greatly. Especially, in the year 2001, Macao SAR announced the policy concerning the open of gambling and lottery industry. In 2002, the introduction of the policy of the open lottery industry has attracted U.S. large capital investment, which accelerated the economic change of Macao. According to statistics, the total foreign trade amount was 38.8 billion Macao dollars in 1999 and was up to 59 billion in the year 2008. It's surprising that the total amount almost doubled in ten years' time.

American investors noticed and utilized investment value of Macao very early. On September 25, 2000, not too long after the return of Macao, the consul general of America in Macao, Gao Lesheng, said that the United States hoped to further strengthen cooperation with Macao and, as the consul general of America in Macao, encouraged American officers to visit Macao to understand the unique history and culture of Macao and see the achievements of the Macao Special Administrative Region. On September 25, a Hong Kong American Chamber of Commerce delegation composed of eight people visited Macao for the first time, meeting with business leaders and high-ranking officials of the special region government of Macao.

Before this, the U.S. government had already reached a cooperation memorandum which attacked illegal transshipment of fabrics with the Macao Special Administrative Region.[4] In November 2005, in order to meet the increasing need of U.S. investment, the Macao branch of the American Chamber of Commerce in Hong Kong came into existence, aiming to promote U.S. trade and Pearl River Delta of China, with the hinge point centralized in Macao.

Macao has become the connecting stage of American businessmen in South China, News in May 29, 2007 (reporter Liang Wei Hao). President of South China American Chamber of Commerce Harry brought a large delegation with more than 150 businessmen who participated in Zhuhai and Macao investment communication fair. These enterprises come from all fields, including logistics, travel, hi-tech, and real estate. This was the largest trade delegation to come to Zhuhai for exploration in recent years. Harry says, Macao and Zhuhai are totally different economies, their economic complementary is very strong, if two places can further strengthen cooperation, the business opportunity will be limitless. The American Chamber of Commerce of South China has more than 1,100 members, most enterprises have sound rewards from their investment. Among them there are 100 members in Zhuhai, which all make profit. Harry says: We often encourage American enterprises to come to China to make investment. The investment repayment in Macao or Zhuhai of our trader's group is very ideal. All receive the best repayment within shortest time. According to the investigation of the association of trade, in the following three years, the member intends to continue investing 140–170 hundred million dollars in South China. By the end of 2007, Macao has attracted huge foreign investment and the amount was up to 63.02 billion Macao dollars in which most of the investment comes from the United States.

The Exhibition Economy of Macao Has Sound Development

The government of Macao has hosted trade-consulting meetings for many years. Macao has grown more and more strong in this respect in recent years. The twelfth Macao International Trade Investment Fair (MIF) held in "golden road (Venetian of Macao) Convention and Exhibition Center," October 18–21, 2007, was a main economic and trade activity. It was also a grand occasion of international economy and trade of Macao. The number of exhibitions of this MIF was 889, an increase of 273 percent over the eleventh MIF, which had 326 exhibitors. The exhibitors came from thirty-one countries and areas such as the Chinese mainland, Portugal, Brazil, Angola, Mozambique, Bissau, Cape Verde, East Timor, United States, Canada, Australia, Austria, Czech, Germany, Hungary, Holland, Poland, Spain, Britain, Chile, South Africa, Dubai, Egypt, India, Pakistan, Japan, Thailand, Hong Kong, Macao, and Taiwan; the number of exhibiting countries increased 48 percent compared with last session.[5] With the promotion of Macao government, the convention economy has grown rapidly. In recent years, many international conventions were held in Macao like G2E Asia, International Telecomp, and the Indian Movie Festival. In the first three seasons of 2009, there were 1,040 conventions held in Macao and more than 420,000 participants were involved. For instance, the Venetian Macao–Resort–Hotel invested by Las Vegas Sands Co., which opened in 2007, is not only the largest casino in Macao but also the largest convention center, which also includes large shopping malls and theaters.

The Lottery Industry of Macao Is the First Place in the World

In recent years, with the guidance of Macao government concerning the lottery industry, in order to build the new gambling house–comprehensive facility hotels, six lottery companies around the globe invested about $20 billion altogether.[6] It is mainly American capital among them. The economic benefit brought by the development is the speed of the lottery industry of Macao, which leads the world. By the end of 2006, the lottery industry gross income in Macao had already exceeded Las Vegas, reached $7 billion, and leaped to the largest market for lottery in the world.[7] The Macao government planned to merge three major parts of hotel, convention and exhibition, and gambling together, devoted to turning Macao into international travel, meeting, and exhibition center. President of Jinsha group William White says, there have been not so many outstanding brands to get together at the same time and same place in the world so far, creating an international tourist attraction together. It took Las Vegas seventy-five years to develop into an international amusement city. And the company will finish the goal and realize this ideal in three years in Macao.[8]

With the opening of the lottery industry, tourism grew rapidly. The financial reserves in Macao are seven times as those of the year 1999 in, for example, the tourist hotel industry, catering industry, retail industry, transportation industry, and entertainment industry. The GNP of Macao has reached a high position in Asia.[9] The GNP rose from 110,000 Macao dollars in 1999 to 313,000 Macao dollars. The average monthly income rose from 5,100 Macao dollars in 1999 to 8,000 Macao dollars in 2008. The fiscal surplus rose from 2 billion Macao dollars in 1999 to 100 billion Macao dollars in 2009. The annual population of tourists rose from 6.9 million to 23 million.[10]

Why, when U.S. investment was nearly zero before the return of Macao, and only about three hundred Americans were there,[11] does the United States invest tens of billions dollars in Macao after coming back? Besides the reason described above, the achievements also come from the economic liftoff of China's mainland and strong support from central government. After the return of Macao, its economic link with the Chinese mainland became closer and it has become an important component of the economic region of South China. Macao is a pivot of international network of communication lines and domestic network of communication lines of China now. The Sea–Air–Land stereoscopic traffic extends in all directions. Chinese mainland urban airborne vehicles can reach Macao in three hours; the land route in Pearl River Delta can reach Macao in three hours. And Macao is receiving support and incentive measures from the central government in the area of domestic industry, domestic region integration, regional health care, and food hygiene, among others.

There are two concrete measures very favorable to Macao which really make the international lottery industry excited. One is "come freely." At present the inhabitants of forty-four cities are permitted to travel to Macao, and the RMB allowed to carry abroad has been raised, and so also the exchange volume. The mainland visitors continually come to Macao, increasing Macao's prosperity; in 2006, the number of mainland tourists reached 22 million. The other is that China has stopped "one-day gambling runs in border port" in 2003, which settled the situation of "gambling houses abroad besiege China" completely. These are the most direct and the most effective support to the lottery and entertainment industry of Macao.[12]

The development of Macao in 2009 was more prosperous. The Chinese central government authorized Macao to have the right to use 1.0926 square KMs on Hengqing Island of Guangdong Province. The land will be used to construct the new campus of the University of Macao. The Chinese central government granted "Reform of the Pearl River Delta Region Development Plan (2008–2020)" so as to build one of the most competitive business circle of metropolis cities within Guangdong, Hong Kong, and Macao by the year 2020.

Macao Plays a Special Role in Sino–America Trading Ties

Macao Becomes the Largest Direct Investment Place in China for American Capital

Investments from America have obvious characteristics in Macao area. First, in the years since 2002, investors have already realized a repayment of principal. The investment cycle was short and amazing. Second, American capital investment in Macao is all direct investment, which established the legal person of enterprises, undertook the business risk, and made repayment from the market, not indirect investment, which has different market risks. Third, the investment number is enormous. The international capital cost, relying mainly on American capital, reached $20 billion. This is rare in Sino–America history of thirty years of trading ties. Calculated according to the investment place, I'm afraid that no one has obtained so much direct investment in China's mainland cities.

Fourth, investment trade is single, and trade "entertainment industry of lottery," which wants special management by countries all over the world.

Macao is Another New Connection Passway in South China for Sino–America Economic and Trade Relationships

American capital entering Macao area makes China–U.S. strategy attitudes on trading in South China change on a large scale. Sino–America trading ties have added another new contact passway. Though there were two contact passways in South China in the past, Hong Kong and Macao, Sino–America trading ties mainly used the connection of Hong Kong for a long time, which appears the situation of "valuing harbor more than Macao." But during the several years after the Macao return to China, the trading tie between Macao and United States has changed—namely, potential strategic investment is showing especially and Macao is improving in the importance of Sino–America trading ties greatly. And because of the history contact of Macao and Portuguese-language countries, Portuguese-language countries in the West will more or less make use of economic and trade connections between China and the United States to aggravate the passway, following Macao's stated platform function.

Macao is Another New Connection Platform in Sino–America Trading Ties

In Macao investment from the United States increased and the Sino–America increase in capital and goods, commercial activity in and out of South China through Macao also increased, which made Macao a new contact platform in Sino–America trading ties. Because of historical reasons, the platform mainly functioned in politics in the past, mainly with Hong Kong as the core in China's foreign trading tie. So there was phenomenon of "valued harbor more than Macao" in the twentieth century. After entering the twenty-first century, because of the development at full speed of Macao's economy, its growth rate of average annual national product increased quicker than that of Hong Kong. The per capita national income of Macao is close to 30,000 Macao dollars, which ranks first place in the four economic zones of both sides of Taiwan Strait. This increased Macao's status in economy connection, and this kind of importance is strengthened because of the characteristic of the economy of Macao: lottery amusement, commercial convention and exhibition, tourism, and leisure.

Macao is the Showcase of China's Peaceful Development

The development of the economy of Macao is due to the development of the economy of the mainland, which cannot leave the fundamental state policy of "reform and opening-up." The fundamental state policy of "reform and opening-up" can only be proposed and carried out in peace developing period. In other words, the development of China's mainland is peaceful development,[13] which has not only caused great change of the continent but also caused great change in the surrounding area. The development of the economy of Macao is a result of the mainland's great change. According to the experts, the middle class of China will grow from less than 300 million people at present to more than 600 million people in 2020. China's peaceful development will produce a bigger middle class, and this middle class will generate an important impact on social stability and development conversely. Namely, they can make development and peace of China continue, which will promote Macao's prosperity. As a result, Macao will become the showcase of China's peaceful development naturally. In addition, this is also the successful example of "one country two systems." On November 13, 2009, the Research Center for One Country Two Systems of Macao Polytechnic Institute conducted a survey indicating 59.77 percent of 1,052 interviewees above eighteen years old found the practice of Macao "Very Successful" or "Successful."[14]

Macao is the Crossing Area of the World Where China and the United States Enhance Trust and Reduce Misgivings

Macao is still playing the special function of enhancing trust and reducing misgivings in Sino–America trading ties.

This is because it is the one area that develops steady and very sensitive capital to peace to invest a huge sum of money in the lottery entertainment industry, which has very high expectations for capital security. Without considerable trust, investment won't be successful. Going with the connections of Sino–America trading ties becoming closer and closer, the difference and contradiction between both sides will increase, even may produce the conflict, which needs a suitable regional place to increase trust and clear up the scattered suspicion. Macao has been the crossing area of the cultures between East and West for several hundred years, so Macao can become the crossing area of the world to enhance trust and reduce misgivings.

Look into the future about Macao: it will develop constantly, will form the pearl associations of Hong Kong and Macao. The development of Macao brings prevention of lopsided development, prevention of the society being out-of-balance, prevention of insufficient management, and prevention of inappropriate adjustment.

Notes

1. *Asian-Africa Forum*, vol. 6, 2007, p. 57.
2. The China-Portuguese Joint Declaration was one of the key documents concerning Sino–U.S. relations.
3. Zhang Lili, *China's Foreign Relation of the Twentieth Century* (Lanzhou: Gansu People's Press), 474–75.
4. See *People's Daily*, September 27, 2000.
5. Macao Information Bureau.
6. Ocean network.
7. China: Macao. February 15, 2007, xinhuameitong.
8. New Bulletin, March 23, 2003.
9. Rong Yongqi, paper in *Macao Daily*, December 11, 2009.
10. Lang Ran, paper in Xinhua Macao Newspaper, December 14, 2009.
11. Zaobao, Singapore, September 23, 2007.
12. China review, page 57, 2007, 3.
13. China review, Hong Kong, 2007, 3.
14. "Can Kao Xiao Xi," edition 9, December 15, 2009.

CHAPTER EIGHT

An Evaluation of Macao's Gambling Industry: With Special Reference to American Investment

T. J. Cheng and Sixin Sheng

Introduction

The past decade was the golden age of Macao's economic growth, and gambling industry was the largest contributor. To a great extent, the boom of gambling business benefited much from Macao's liberalized industrial policy, especially U.S. investment. In 2002, Macao's Special Administrative Region (SAR) government decided to open its gambling market for international competition; prior to that, Macao's gambling industry was monopolized by Stanley Ho (何鸿燊) for four decades. By and large, this opening policy has been successful: just four years thereafter, with US$7.2 billion gross gaming revenues in 2006, Macao replaced Las Vegas as the largest casino city in the world.[1] Indeed, the gross revenue in the gambling market has increased dramatically since the liberalization of gambling industry in 2002 (see table 8.1).

The introduction of international competitors has not only improved the service quality of the local gaming industry, but also exerted positive influence over Macao's tourism industry. Theme park–style hotels, free shuttle buses, non-smoking rooms, paid-vacation for casino employees, and many other new things have been introduced to Macao by investors from Las Vegas. The number of visitors jumped sharply to 27 million in 2007 from 11.5 million in 2002. Although Macao saw a slight fall in visitors' average length of stay from 1.3 nights in 2000 to 1.1 nights in 2007, the number of overnight

Table 8.1 Gross Revenue from Different Gaming Activities 2003-2009 (MOP Million*)

Items	2003	2004	2005	2006	2007	2008	2009 First Qtr.
Games of Fortune	28,672	41,378	46,047	56,623	83,022	108,772	26,019
Greyhound Racing	74	84	67	67	98	186	45
Horse Racing	1,004	1,566	636	437	403	501	90
Chinese Lottery	3	5	7	7	6	6	2
Instant Lottery	0.07	0.03	0.03	0.03	0.02	0.003	0
Sports Lottery - Football	510	442	333	327	273	304	72
Sports Lottery - Basketball	52	36	44	60	44	57	25
Total	30,315	43,511	47,134	57,521	83,847	109,826	26,252

* 1 US$ = 8 MOP
Source: Macao SAR Gaming Inspection and Coordination Bureau, www.dicj.gov.mo

guests showed an upward trend in recent years, and accordingly local hostels improved their occupancy rate. In addition, the visitors' per-capita non-gambling spending also went up from 2005 to 2008 (see table 8.2).

Partly because China wants Macao to be a showcase of "one country, two systems" for Taiwan, Macao's economic development has also gained strong support from the Chinese government since its return to China in 1999. In 2003, China and Macao finalized the Agreement on Macao/Mainland Closer Economic Partnership Arrangement (CEPA, 内地与澳门关于建立更紧密经贸关系的安排).[2] According to this agreement, Chinese government provides Macao a package of preferential treatments in trade, finance, tariff, investment, and tourism. Meanwhile, Macao has benefited greatly from these preferential treatments as a result of China's high-speed economic growth. More and more Chinese people flock to Macao for gambling and tours, the two pillars of Macao's economy. Mainland China has become number 1 inbound tourist source of Macao since 2003, followed by Hong Kong and Taiwan (see figure 8.2). Table 8.3 also shows that visitors from mainland China have the strongest purchasing capacity among Macao's visitors.

As of March 2009, Macao had thirty-one casinos owned by six operators[3]: Galaxy Casino (银河娱乐), S.J.M. (澳门博彩股份有限公司), Melco Crown (皇冠), MGM Grand Paradise (美高梅金殿), Venetian Macao (威尼斯人), and Wynn Resorts (永利) (see table 8.4 as well as

Table 8.2 Gaming Industry's Spill-over Effect on Macao's Tourism

Year	Number of visitors	Average length of stay in Macao (days)	Per-capita spending, MOP (excluding gambling)	Number of overnight guests in hotels	Hostel occupancy rate (%)
2000	9,162,212	1.3	1,367	2,689,843	57.6
2001	10,278,973	1.3	1,389	2,766,853	60.7
2002	11,530,841	1.2	1,454	3,154,801	67.1
2003	11,887,876	1.2	1,518	3,043,505	64.3
2004	16,672,556	1.1	1,633	3,956,154	75.6
2005	16,979,124	1.1	1,523	4,121,088	70.9
2006	21,998,100	1.1	1,610	4,680,854	72.2
2007	27,003,370	1.1	1,637	5,739,734	77.2
2008	22,907,724	1.1	1,729	6,537,661	74.5

Source: The Statistics and Census Service of Macao

Table 8.3 Per Capita Non-Gambling Spending of Visitors by Place of Residence (in MOP)

Location	2005	2006	2007	2008
Mainland China	3,078	3,215	3,080	3,571
Southeast Asia	1,458	1,418	1,452	1,864
Taiwan	1,336	1,494	1,447	1,361
United States	1,317	1,318	1,304	1,075
Oceania	1,042	1,172	1,267	1,093
Hong Kong	898	955	1,085	1,109
Japan	952	871	995	967
Europe	824	894	905	1,008

Source: The Statistics and Census Service of Macao

appendices 8.1 and 8.2). Galaxy Casino is controlled by Lui Che-Woo's family (吕志和家族). Stanley Ho owns S.J.M. and is affiliated with another two casino companies: (1) Stanley Ho' son, Lawrence Ho (何猷龙), joined hands with Australian Publishing & Broadcasting Limited to form Melco Crown; (2) Stanley Ho's daughter, Pansy Ho (何超琼), worked in partnership with MGM Mirage Inc. (a Las Vegas–based casino giant) to establish MGM Grand Paradise.[4]

As the Macao government's initial goal was to turn Macao into a Las Vegas–style gambling destination, American capitals were introduced into Macao's gaming market. Besides MGM Grand Paradise, which has American investment, Venetian Macao and Wynn Resorts are solely founded by Las Vegas–based casino operators (Las Vegas Sands and Wynn Group). The previous monopolist, S.J.M. today still owns the largest number of casinos (see table 8.4), but its market share shrank to 26 percent in 2008 from 100 percent in 2002 due to fierce competition from American operators, who now account for half of the market through modernized operations and management.

Table 8.4 Number of Casinos in Macao: 2003-2009

CONCESSIONAIRES	2003	2004	2005	2006	2007	2008	2009 First Qtr.
S.J.M.	11	13	15	17	18	19	19
Galaxy Casino, S.A.	-	1	1	5	5	5	5
Venetian Macao, S.A.	-	1	1	1	2	3	3
Wynn Resorts (Macao) S.A.	-	-	-	1	1	1	1
Melco Crown Gaming (Macao) Ltd. *	-	-	-	-	1	2	2
MGM Grand Paradise, S.A.	-	-	-	-	1	1	1
TOTAL	11	15	17	24	28	31	31

*Formerly known as "Melco PBL Gaming (Macao) Ltd." The new name was effective as of June 2008.
Source: Macao SAR Gaming Inspection and Coordination Bureau, www.dicj.gov.mo

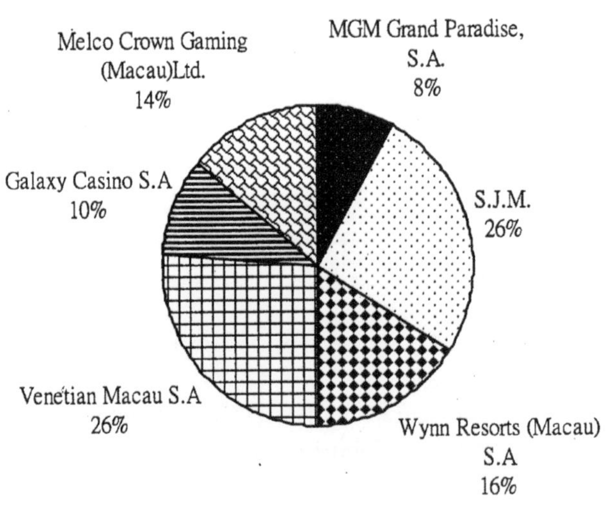

Figure 8.1. Gambling Market Share in Macao: 2008, Calculations from six casino companies' financial reports in 2008

As a response to the challenge from American competitors, Melco Crown just opened a new casino resort on June 1, 2009, the US$2.4 billion City of Dreams (新濠天地). This resort, sitting on the Cotai Strip[5] (appendix 8.2) directly opposite the Venetian, features a 420,000-sq ft complex with 516 gambling tables and a 175,000-sq ft shopping mall.

The Impact of the Global Financial Crisis

Table 8.1 reveals that Macao's gross gambling revenue for the year of 2008 increased 31 percent to MOP$110 billion (around US$13.7 billion), compared to MOP$84 billion (around US$10.6 billion) in 2007. However, Macao's gambling industry has still witnessed glaring downturn trends in the global financial crisis.

First, the number of visitors sharply declined from 27 million in 2007 to 23 million in 2008, the first in visitor reduction since the liberalization of the gambling industry in 2002 (see figure 8.2). This downward slide in tourist arrivals would probably continue in 2009 in view of the financial crisis and H1N1 flu (swine flu). As Macao's gambling business is heavily dependent on China, any hiccup in China's economy is likely to have a direct adverse impact on Macao's economy.

Second, with dwindling tourist arrivals, casinos have to reduce gaming tables and slot machines to cut their operation costs. Compared to the peak in 2007, gaming tables and slot machines in Macao's casinos were reduced by 377 and 1,296 respectively in the first quarter of 2009.

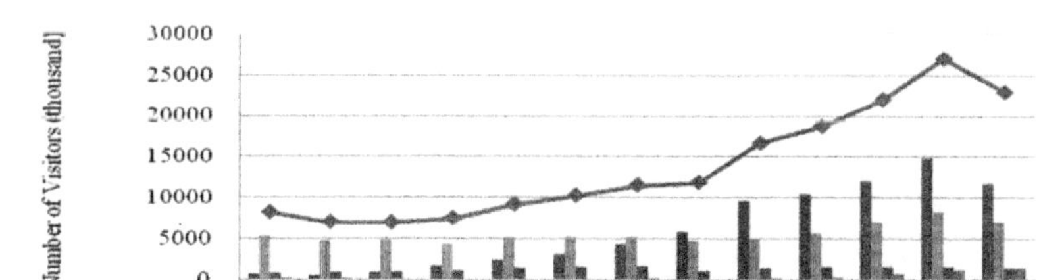

	96'	97'	98'	99'	00'	01'	02'	03'	04'	05'	06'	07'	08'
Mainland China	604	530	817	1645	2275	3006	4240	5742	9530	10463	11986	14866	11595
Hong Kong	5206	4703	4722	4230	4955	5196	5101	4623	5051	5615	6941	8174	7009
Taiwan, China	759	909	817	985	1311	1452	1533	1023	1287	1483	1438	1444	1315
Southeast Asia	234	176	109	116	142	150	170	147	261	396	693	1179	1470
Total	8151	7000	6949	7444	9162	10279	11531	11888	16673	18711	21998	26993	22908

Figure 8.2. Vistor Arrivals by Place of Residence: 1996–2008
***Source:* The Statistics and Census Service of Macao**

Third, the global financial crisis has hard hit Las Vegas casino operators and seriously affected their investments in Macao. From the peak in 2007, Wynn Group's market value shrank by 62 percent and MGM Mirage's stock price was reduced by 83 percent at the end of 2008. The market value of Las Vegas Sands even shrank to 6 percent. Sands is reportedly on the verge of bankruptcy and had to stop its ongoing construction projects in Macao and lay off 11,000 employees. [6] To improve fluidity, Sand even tried to sell some of its non-gambling assets in Macao.

The market value of local casino operators, such as Hong Kong–listed S.J.M., Galaxy Casino, and Melco Crown, has been reduced by more than 50 percent. Due to the global financial crisis, they also had to suspend development plans and cut costs. In the first quarter of 2009, there were no new casinos opened in Macao, maintaining thirty-one casinos in 2008 (see table 8.4).

In the financial crisis, almost all countries and regions have been actively looking for new economic growth, and opening gambling industry is regarded as an option for some Asian economies. Singapore already legalized gambling business in 2005. Its casino resort project invested by Sands is going ahead even in the financial crisis, leading to the suspension of Sands' development plan in Macao. Singapore has also the potential of attracting Chinese gamblers who used to patronize Macao's casinos.

Taiwan is another important region that may constitute a real threat to Macao's gambling industry in the near future. The proposal had gone through a long-term debate before being passed in Taiwan's parliament in January 2009 in the wake of the financial crisis. This legalizes gambling on Taiwan's offshore islands of Kinmen (金门), Matsu (马祖), and Penghu (澎湖).[7]

Given improving China–Taiwan relations, Taiwan is poised to have easier access to mainland visitors. In addition, Taiwan owns an excellent geographic location to compete with Macao for Hong Kong and mainland Chinese gamblers and tourists. This will considerably weaken (see figure 8.2) Macao's competitiveness in the gambling industry in the future.

Table 8.5 Number of Gaming Tables and Slot Machines: 2003-2009

Items	2003	2004	2005	2006	2007	2008	2009 First Qtr.
Gaming Tables	424	1,092	1,388	2,762	4,375	4,017	3,998
Slot Machines	814	2,254	3,421	6,546	13,267	11,856	11,971

Source: Macao SAR Gaming Inspection and Coordination Bureau, www.dicj.gov.mo

Controversial American Investment in Macao

American investment in Macao's gambling industry is a controversial issue. It was widely believed that American investment promoted Macao's gambling industry in terms of scale and service, while some people argued that the U.S. investment in Macao leaded to over-competition in gambling industry and imbalanced development of Macao's economy. There is no denial that competition between casino operators has become fiercer as the market is no longer monopolistic and that situation does challenge Macao's traditional supervision system on the gambling industry. However, that is not to say American investment should be responsible for unfair competition. On the contrary, it would rather say that American investment impelled Macao's gambling market to perfect itself, because supervision organizations have to adjust institutions and response to deviant business behavior. In addition, American casino operators contributed much to Macao's gambling market with new business operations and ideas, which improved the development level of Macao's gambling industry.

A more sensitive debate is whether American investment in Macao's gambling industry was economic or politicaly motivated. In 2007, the *Macao Monthly* published a cover story titled "What Has Venetian Brought About to Macao?" It says:

> The two American casinos are mainly targeted at mainland Chinese. It is very clear in their minds and they have prepared well for dealing with these customers. For those gamblers coming from China, especially the VIP group with sufficient capital, the American casinos could provide with satisfactory services. . . . For such an important social group, if they have been controlled in the hands of Americans, where is China's political and economic security?[8]

In late 2006 and early 2007, several Hong Kong and Macao media reported the potential American threat to Macao's and China's economic security and political independence. According to some reports, it even attracted enough attention in Beijing to dispatch specialists to Macao for further investigation.[9] We have so far not seen any official conclusion on this issue yet, except for a very brief, and somehow self-contradictory, statement in President Hu Jintao's report to the concluded seventeenth Party Congress in Beijing. It says, "(We) actively support Hong Kong and Macao to develop their foreign relations, (but) definitely oppose foreign powers to get involved into Hong Kong and Macao's affairs (積極支持香港、澳門開展對外交往，堅決反對外部勢力干預香港、澳門事務。)."[10]

However, there are other business owners in Macao who are pretty optimistic on the American investment in Macao gambling business. One of them is Mr. Chen Zhijie, CEO of Nanguang Group, one of the most influential Chinese state companies in Macao. He says:

> Macao has to rely on those several foreign investments, especially their management and worldwide networks, and this makes Macao ride on the express train of economic development. We have to be used to the new current of development, cannot still cherish the memory of the previous little peaceful town any more.[11]

It is well known that monopoly can easily result in corruption and stagnation, and only competition can bring about price going down, service going up, and quality improvement. Marxist–Leninist description or the market law from ancient to modern times, from China to abroad, have all proved it to be the unchangeable truth, but there are still some who do not listen.

Reform and opening-up policy is the current tide of the world, and also the motivator of the development both in Mainland China, Hong Kong, and Macao. The problems emerged during the development are actually the by-products produced by the incompletion of the reform and open policy, rather than consequences from the reform and open policy themselves.

There are many reasons underlined in the incompletion of reform and opening policy in Macao. Here we may list two of them: one is due to knowledge deficiency; the other is that vested interests make various obstacles to hinder further reform. Knowledge problems arise from errors in theory or thoughts, and that could be resolved by theoretical breakup. It should be comparatively easier because we are in a time having no theoretical taboo, and in a place where people enjoy the superiority of "one state, two systems." But in the reality, theoretical creation is not easy at all, sometimes there are obstructions and risks.

Compared with the knowledge deficiency, the problems of vested interest and interest re-distribution is more difficult to deal with. Social development always brings about interest restructuring and reorganization. If we say that theoretical breakthrough needs scholarly debates and experiments through practice, then, struggles over interests need long terms of gaming on "survival of the fittest" to see the final direction.

Looking ahead, the role of U.S. investment played in Macao's economy would become smaller than before. As we have mentioned above, American casino operators seem to be retreating from Macao's gambling market and shifting their strategic location in the Asia–Pacific region from Macao to other places such as Singapore. Besides the global financial crisis, reasons for the retreat of American investment have also something to do with the limitation of Macao as a casino destination. Compared with Singapore as a city-state that owns sole discretion to make decisions, Macao's public policy is subject to China's central government to a large extent. In that sense, casino operators in Macao actually have to deal with Macao SAR government and central government of China at the same time. Nevertheless, Chinese central government's policy adjustments to Macao's economy are often not predicable so that political–economy risk in Macao is larger than that of Singapore. Moreover, there are also explicit signals that the central government asks Macao to diversify its economic structure and get rid of its over-dependence on the gambling industry. Thus, one can expect that it will be more and more difficult for American casino investment to influence Macao's economy as a whole.

More Challenges to Sustainable Development

Apart from the financial crisis, Macao's gambling industry is facing other challenges to its sustainable development. One of the biggest challenges arises from policy restrictions from Mainland China. The soaring gambling industry dominates Macao's economy and public finance, taking away large portions of financial resources and human capitals, and thus restraining other industries' development in Macao (see table 8.6).

The Chinese government is afraid that an over-expansion of the gambling industry would adversely affect Macao's economic and social stabilities in the long run. Meanwhile, many mainland Chinese businessmen and government officials are often found to be involved in money laundering, problem gambling, corruption, and other scandals in Macao's casinos. To cool down the gambling economy, China has tightened relevant financial regulations and the policy of Individual Visit Scheme (自由行政策),[12] greatly reducing

Table 8.6 Government Revenue and Working Population in Gaming Industry (MOP Million)

Year	Government Revenue	Revenue from gaming industry	Gaming revenue/ government revenue	Gaming industry staff/ working population
2002	10,206	7,765	76.0%	----
2003	13,260	10,579	79.7%	----
2004	18,159	15,236	83.9%	9.7%
2005	20,438	17,318	84.7%	13.0%
2006	25,135	20,600	78.7%	16.1%
2007	40,694	30,948	75.5%	19.5%
2008	51,076	41,986	82.2%	23.7%

Source: Macao SAR Statistics Monthly & Yearbook, 2002–2008

mainland Chinese visitorship and gambling activities in Macao. The impact on market confidence is also real, as Macao's success in the gambling industry largely relies on mainland China's policy support and gamblers.

Furthermore, the Chinese government seems bent on tempering Macao's gambling industry. The chief executive of Macao has been asked to tighten regulations on the gambling industry and improve Macao's economic structure. China has also made great efforts in helping Macao diversify its economy. Besides the Zhuhai–Macao Cross-border Industrial Zone (珠澳跨境工业区) inaugurated in 2006, China is also working with Macao on two other proposed projects, namely, the Hong Kong–Zhuhai–Macao Bridge project (港珠澳大桥工程) and joint development of Hengqing Island with Zhuhai (珠澳联合开发横琴岛). The former will stimulate Macao's logistics and trade industry and promote Macao's economic integration with Guangdong and Hong Kong, while the latter will give Macao more land resources to develop a diversified economy (see appendix 8.2). There will be no casinos on Hengqing Island, and the new campus of University of Macao has started to build. However, it still waits to see how Hengqing Island could change Macao's economy structure. The management of the island and the co-operation with Zhuhai and Guangdong governments are also tough problems that would pose various challenges to Macao.

The gambling industry of Macao has also been criticized for its over-dependence on Chinese VIP gamblers who are often the victims of problem gambling. Moreover, the game of baccarat, which constitutes more than 80 percent of gambling revenue, is said to be a major source of problem gambling "characterized by many difficulties in limiting money and/or time spent on gambling which leads to adverse consequences for the gambler, others, or for the community." (See figure 8.3.)

It is alarming that more and more local people become problem gamblers as well. According to a survey in 2003, about 2 percent of Macao's residents were problem gamblers. People who are male and have "monthly income lower than MOP 8,000, and a casino gambler" have the maximal tendency of becoming gambling addicts.[13] Another recent survey shows that there was an alarmingly high rate (around 60 percent) of gambling among youths (thirteen-to-twenty-nine age group) in Macao, mostly school drop-outs or youngsters who do not have jobs; 6.1 percent of them were probably problem gamblers at the time of interview.[14]

Indeed, casino operators in Macao are now under tremendous pressure to change their ways of running their gambling business. Local communities, legislators, and scholars are calling for *responsible gambling* that emphasizes "policies and practices designed to prevent and reduce potential harms as-

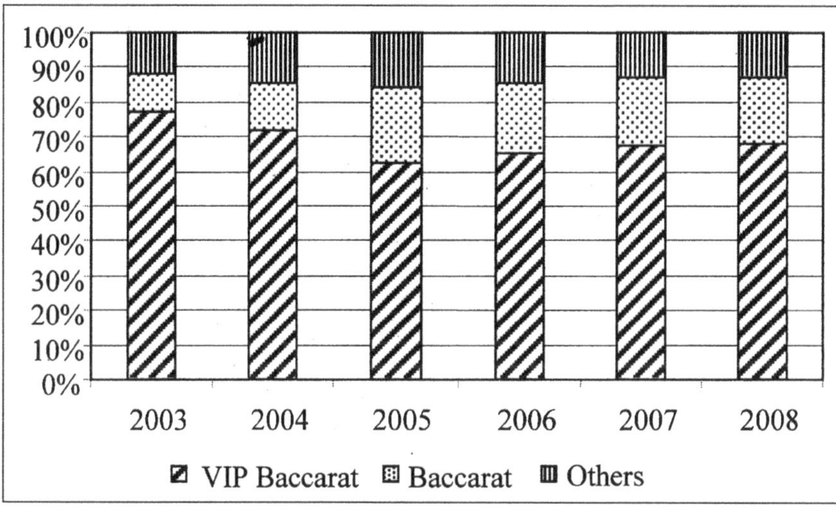

Figure 8.3. Gambling Revenue by Types of Game
***Source:* Macao SAR Gaming Inspection and Coordination Bureau**

sociated with gambling."[15] In this framework, gambling enterprises are required to invest a large amount of money in promoting consumer protection, community and consumer awareness and education, and provide efficacious treatment for problem gamblers; they will have to look for alternative markets and revenues for the sake of sustainable development.

However, implementing a responsible gambling model may not come easy as a result of the already high operational cost. Compared to the wagering tax rates in Singapore (15 percent), South Korea (30 percent),[16] and other Asian casino destinations, Macao's tax rate for the gambling industry is quite high (around 40 percent); this has hurt Macao's competitiveness in attracting casino investments and gamblers. Although Macao's casino operators have been asking for some tax concessions in the financial crisis, Macao's SAR government stands firm on its wagering tax rate.

To summarize, the gambling industry's sustainable development in Macao is quite doubtful. With the above-mentioned challenges and problems, Macao's gambling business would probably go through a recession in the future. Thus policy attention and cautious measures should be given to the present crisis.

Policy Conclusion

Urgently, Macao SAR government needs to take action to reinforce its supervision and regulations on the gambling industry, and avoid casino companies' operations in the crisis that would violate Macao's law and economic stability. Especially, Macao should prevent American capitals from retreat on a large scale, as that would significantly hurt Macao's gambling industry and market confidence. Meanwhile, casinos in Macao should diversify their tourist sources to offset visitor reduction from mainland China, and the casinos also can be developed as multifunction complexes, which provide not only gambling entertainment but also more comprehensive services for visitors and businessmen, such as conventions and exhibitions, show business and other art performance, theme parks, and cartoon and animation, among others. Macao government may consider giving special tax concession in order to encourage these gambling companies to diversify their business.

For the issue of problem gambling, Macao should legislate for responsible gambling as soon as possible, and the law needs to regulate the behaviors and responsibilities not only for the casino business, but also for the government agencies and the public, especially for the school and continuing education system. In particular, the law should request the establishment of "responsible gambling service centers" that can help and prevent problem gamblers. Such service centers should not be subject to casino companies or government agencies because of conflict of interest, and they would better run by independent NGOs operated by local residents and/or communities. However, the government and casino companies should provide funds and cooperate with these centers. Macao may benefit from relevant experience and practices in Australia and Las Vegas.

As discussed before, Macao's public finance is dominated by gambling tax revenue. Macao has also not completed a fiscal reserve system at this moment. As a result, Macao's financial security is exposed to the risk of the gambling industry's recession. Hence, on the one hand, Macao SAR government should establish fiscal reserve system in case of future needs; on the other hand, it also needs to improve its economic structure in order to diversify tax sources. Particularly, the Macao government should try to attract more foreign non-gambling investments, and support local medium and small enterprises in trade, clothing, and other existing industries. Furthermore, Macao also needs to explore some new economic sectors, such as the cultural industry and Internet industry, which have the potential to become the new economic growth points in Macao. A more aggressive proposal is setting up a government investment corporation based on Macao's foreign exchange reserve (US$16.2 billion in January 2009[17]). This corporation could focus on business opportunities in mainland China, and invest gambling and tourism industries in some new casino destinations.

Finally, when diversifying its economy, Macao should make full use of the Chinese government's policy supports and actively engage in China's regional economic integration (especially in the region of the Pearl River Delta). In order to develop a diversified economy, the Macao government needs to attach much more importance to education than before, as presently local residents' educational level[18] and skills cannot satisfy the requirements for introducing new economic sectors. At the same time, Macao should try to attract more foreign talents to develop Macao's economy. In that sense, Singapore's foreign talent policy is a very good model for Macao's reference.

References

Agreement on Macao/Mainland Closer Economic Partnership Arrangement (内地与澳门关于建立更紧密经贸关系的安排). Available from: www.china.com.cn/chinese/zhuanti/hkmainland/426259.htm; tga.mofcom.gov.cn/subject/cepanew/index.shtml (accessed August 14, 2009).

Blaszczynski, Alex, Robert Ladouceur, and Howard J. Shaffer. 2004. "A Science-Based Framework for Responsible Gambling: The Reno Model." *Journal of Gambling Studies*, 20(3): 301–17.

Cheng, T.J. 2009. *Introduction to Sociology of Gambling*. Beijing: Social Sciences Academic Press. *The Cooling Gambling Industry Calls for Countermeasures Urgently* (博彩业"寒潮"来袭宜急谋对策). Available from: news.xinhuanet.com/gangao/2008-11/24/content_10403112.htm (accessed August 14, 2009).

Feng, Jiachao and Meibao Wu. 2003. *The Survey Report on Macao Residents' Gambling Behaviour* (澳门居民参与博彩活动调查报告). Institute for the Study of Commercial Gaming, University of Macao.

Feng, Jiachao, Meibao Wu, and Zhicheng Gao. 2005. *The Survey Report on Macao Youth's Gambling Behaviour* (澳门青年参与博彩活动调查报告). Institute for the Study of Commercial Gaming, University of Macao.

Gambling Research Australia. 2005. *Problem Gambling and Harm: Towards a National Definition*. Available from: www.gamblingresearch.org.au/CA256902000FE154/Lookup/TenderBriefs/$file/PartB%20ID%20PG%20at%20Venue.pdf (accessed August 14, 2009).

Liu, Weiguo. 2009. *The Foreign Reserve of Macao Hit US$16.17 Billion* (澳门外汇储备达161.7亿美元). Available from: news.xinhuanet.com/gangao/2009-02/28/content_10915089.htm (accessed August 14, 2009).

Macao Overtaking Las Vegas as the Biggest Casino City in the World (超拉斯维加斯 澳门首次正式成为全球最大赌城). Available from: news.xinhuanet.com/tai_gang_ao/2007-04/05/content_5938120.htm (accessed August 14, 2009).

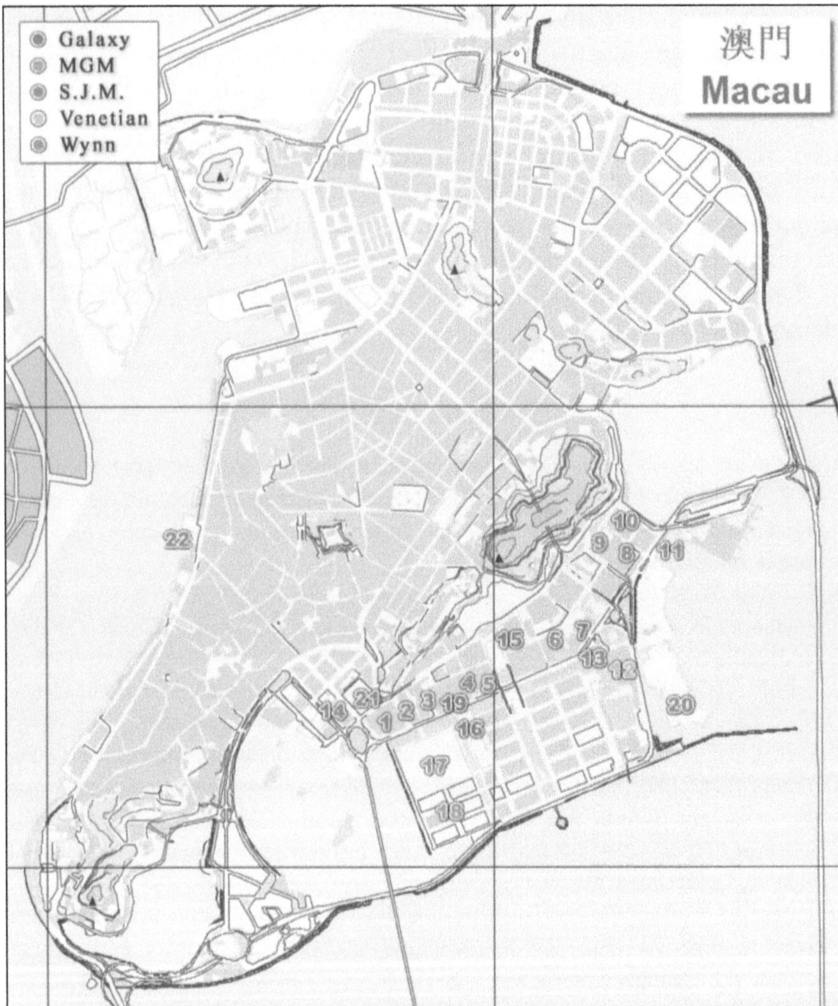

Appendix 8.1 Location of Macao Casinos (Macao Island)

1.Lisboa (葡京娱乐场); **2.Kam Pek Casino**(金碧娱乐场); **3.Casino Fortuna** (财神娱乐场); **4.Diamond Casino** (钻石娱乐场); **5.The Legend Club** (励骏会娱乐场); **6.Kingsway Casino** (金域娱乐场); **7.Waldo Casino** (华都娱乐场); **8.Golden Dragon Casino** (金龙娱乐场); **9.Casa Real Casino** (皇家金堡娱乐场); **10.Jai Alai Casino** (回力娱乐场); **11.Macao Palace** (皇宫娱乐场); **12.Sands Casino** (金沙娱乐场); **13.Oriental Casino** (东方娱乐场); **14.Casino Emperor Palace** (英皇宫殿娱乐场); **15.Casino Rio** (利澳娱乐场); **16.Galaxy StarWorld** (星际娱乐场); **17.Wynn Macao Casino** (永利娱乐场); **18.MGM Grand Macao Casino** (美高梅金殿超濠); **19.Casino de Presidente** (总统娱乐场); **20.Babylon Casino** (巴比伦娱乐场); **21.Grand Lisboa** (新葡京娱乐场); **22. Ponte 16** (十六浦娱乐场).

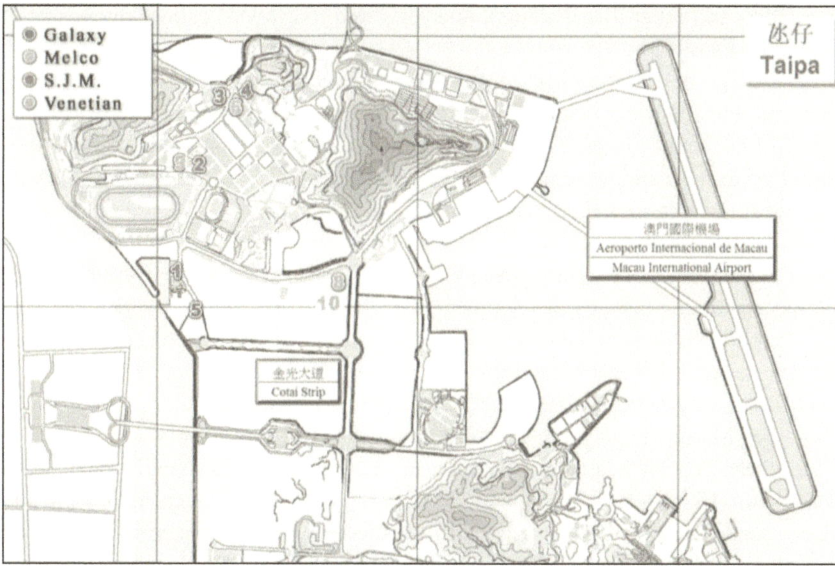

Appendix 8.2: Location of Macao Casinos (Taipa and Road Central)
1. Casino Marina Infante; 2. Grandview Casino; 3. Casino Taipa; 4. Greek Mythology; 5. Grand Waldo Casino; 6. Crown Macao; 8. Venetian Casino; 9. Hotel Taipa Square Casino; 10. Four Seasons Hotel Plaza.

Notes

This paper has been originated from an article titled "Overall Assessment of the American Investment in Macao Gambling Industry," presented by T. J. Cheng at the "International Conference on Macao and Sino–U.S. Relations," which was held December 11–12, 2007, STDM Auditorium, International Library of the University of Macao. In later years, we redrafted it substantially with the new title for contribution to this book project.

1. news.xinhuanet.com/tai_gang_ao/2007-04/05/content_5938120.htm.

2. Please refer to china.com.cn/chinese/zhuanti/hkmainland/426259.htm for the full text. In addition, besides this agreement, Chinese government and Macao SAR signed another five supplementary agreements after 2003: tga.mofcom.gov.cn/subject/cepanew/index.shtml.

3. In 2006, Macao government announced that it would not issue new gambling concessionary besides the six existing operators.

4. In May 2009, New Jersey Cason Control Commission deemed that Pansy Ho was "an unsuitable partner" (implicitly saying that Pansy Ho was involved in money

laundering and other illegal affairs), and suggested that MGM Mirage disassociated itself from Pansy Ho.

5. The proposed Cotai strip on the Taipa Island was motivated by Macao's government, with the intention to transform Macao into a multipurpose resort (hotels, conventions, retails shops, golf, etc.). However, Cotai Strip plan has not been successful up to now, and more than 75 percent of Macao's gaming revenue still comes from downtown casinos (i.e., Macao Island).

6. news.xinhuanet.com/gangao/2008-11/24/content_10403112.htm.

7. According to Prof. Liu Daiyang (刘代洋), one of the major consultants for Taiwan's gambling industry development, Penghu probably will be the first place to run gambling business in Taiwan in two or three years. However, a recent suffrage in Penghu in late 2009 has refused the gambling legalization proposal, see: www.bbc.co.uk/zhongwen/trad/china/2009/09/090926_penghu _casino.shtml.

8. See *Macao Monthly*, no. 128, September 2007, 9–10.

9. Please see Ji Shuoming: "American Power Mushrooms in Macao," *Asia Weekly*, vol. 19, no. 46, November 13, 2005, and other related reports in Hong Kong, Macao, and Taiwan media. It was said that these reports have successively roused attention in the Center; therefore we see the tightening up of free traveling for mainland Chinese, and also the speech made by Hu Jintao on the Party Congress. It seems to me, however, these above mentioned analyses are too subjective, do not match to the impression I've received.

10. See: cpc.people.com.cn/GB/64093/67507/6429854.html.

11. See the cover story of *Phoenix Information News*, November 30, 2007.

12. For example, in the past, Chinese visitors with Hong Kong SAR entry permit could enter Macao as well, but this policy has been invalidated since September 1, 2008; Guangdong provincial government also significantly reduced travel visas to Macao in 2008. This control on travel visas to Macao was recently applied to other Chinese provinces and regions, making the "golden weekend" in Macao a thing of the past. Individual Visit Scheme (自由行政策) refers to the policy that allows mainland tourists in eligible cities to visit Macao on an individual basis instead of in tour groups; however individuals still need to apply for visa for entry into Macao under this policy. This policy been in effect since 2003.

13. Feng Jiachao and Wu Meibao, *Investigation Report on Macao Residents' Participation in Gaming Activities*, published by Institute for the Study of Commercial Gaming (ISCG, 2003). 冯家超、伍美宝，《澳门居民参与博彩活动调查报告》，澳门大学博彩研究所，2003年10月.

14. Feng Jiachao, Wu Meibao, and Gao Zhicheng, *Investigation Report of 2004 on Macao Youth's Participation in Gaming Activities*, published by Institute for the Study of Commercial Gaming (ISCG, 2005). 冯家超、伍美宝、高志成，《澳门青年参与博彩活动调查2004报告》，澳门大学博彩研究所，2005年4月.

15. Gambling Research Australia (2005), *Problem Gambling and Harm: Towards a National Definition*. gamblingresearch.org.au/CA256902000FE154/Lookup/TenderBriefs/$file/PartB%20ID%20PG%20at%20Venue.pdf.

16. Alex Blaszczynski, Robert Ladouceur, and Howard J. Shaffer, "A Science-Based Framework for Responsible Gambling: The Reno Model," *Journal of Gambling Studies*, 20, no 3. (2004): 308.

17. news.xinhuanet.com/gangao/2009-02/28/content_10915089.htm.

18. Up to 2008, only 21 percent of the labor force in Macao received a college education, although the labor force already included a number of foreign workers who had a good education. Please refer to the data on www.dsal.gov.mo/pdf/work/chinese/2_EmpEdu_a.pdf.

CHAPTER NINE

Learn from the Nevada Model to Reform Macao's Casino Regulatory System

Wang Wuyi

Introduction

There are always worries about natural conditions which might form "bottlenecks," blocking or limiting developments. As a matter of fact, on the way of its development, Macao's casino industry is really encountering several "natural bottlenecks," such as land, labor, transportation, water, and other infrastructures. However, besides those, there is another bottleneck, an "institutional bottleneck" that is also negatively impacting its development, which is Macao's casino regulatory system.

Casino industry is a policy-driven industry. It is up to the government to decide whether, where, what kind of, and how many casinos a jurisdiction can have.[1] Casino owners and operators have to design their operation structure to match the legal and regulation structure that governs them.[2]

Since 2004, there have been three important changes within Macao's casino market: market size has expanded drastically; market structure has changed from a monopoly to a competing kind; and the way of operating casinos is internationalized from its traditional and local pattern. It was the Macao government as well as its new gaming policy, so-called gaming liberalization, that actually made the changes. In other words, gaming liberalization is not driven by economic forces but policy changes. (Wang, 2005)

On the other hand, the change of industrial base and market structure demands further change of governance structure. Macao's gaming regulatory system is too old, or too traditional, to satisfy the new industrial base and new market structure. (Eadington and Siu, 2007)

Comparing the Nevada model, this work is to examine Macao's current casino regulatory system as an "institutional bottleneck."

Why Use the Nevada Model?

First, any gaming regulatory system of any gaming jurisdiction in the world, including Macao, more or less has learned or absorbed some ideas from the Nevada model when constructing its own gaming regulatory system.[3] Being aware of Nevada's gaming regulatory system is a shortcut to learn, know, and understand the main stream of world gaming regulatory systems, and hence to find Macao a effective model in diagnosing and reforming its own gaming regulatory system.

Second, gaming liberalization has opened the door of Macao's gaming market to Nevadan investors, who take approximately a half market share of the whole now. If Macao government eventually decides to reform or redesign its gaming regulatory system, as suggested by this study, the operational and managerial features of these newcomers must be put into consideration. Nevertheless, their operational and managerial structure are largely related to and influenced by the gaming regulatory system under which they are regulated in their home country. Under regulation by Nevada Gaming Control Board for a long time, these Nevadan casino tycoons have been trained to be the kind of entrepreneurs who inherently have the tradition to comply with law. From their behavior and actions, we can clearly see the imprints and heritage left by their home regulator, Nevada Gaming Commission and Nevada Gaming Control Board. So, a simple way to learn about Macao's new regulated entities is to gain knowledge of the regulatory system under which they have been operating.

Along with the change of industrial base, should the superstructure, the gaming regulatory system, also change? Hopefully it is not too late to bring up this question. It seems that no one has realized the fact that Macao's current gaming regulatory system has some contradictions or shortcomings that form a kind of "institutional bottleneck" and negatively affects the operation and development of Macao's gaming industry.

The institutional contradictions or shortcomings with Macao's gaming regulatory system are explored below. If we have not found the right solutions to overcome the contradictions or shortcomings so far, at least we should acknowledge their existence. To address these problems to the public and to begin more discussion for solving the problems are the purposes of this chapter.

Counting Tax or Reporting Tax?

Efficiently collecting tax is the major function and purpose for any casino regulatory system.

First, collecting tax is the ultimate motivation for almost every jurisdiction in the world to decide to legalize casinos. Without fiscal revenue, most of the gaming jurisdictions would choose not to open or would shut down their casinos.

Second, as with the first important function, every gaming regulatory system in the world is constructed to make certain that gaming tax is fully and efficiently collected. Without the task of colleting tax, establishing a gaming regulatory body would basically become unnecessary and the rest of the regulatory functions could be simply undertaken by a regular policing body.

Third, the design of a gaming regulatory system is determined by the design of its gaming taxation system. Before 1982 when Macao's casino company was taxed by annual flat rate, Macao did not even need a gaming regulatory agency.

Macao's major gaming tax item is similar to that of Nevada and most jurisdictions in the world, all on gross casino revenue (casino win).[4] The real difference between the taxation systems of Macao and Nevada is the ways the gaming taxes are collected. Since 1983 when Macao changed its taxation system from flat rate to gross casino revenue, Macao's gaming regulatory agency DICJ[5] began sending "counting team(s)" to casino company(s)'s counting rooms to count the taxable take on a daily basis. Whereas, since 1945 when Nevada state legislature imposed a 1 percent tax on each casino that generated gross casino wins over $3,000 per quarter, Nevada's gaming regulatory body, the county sheriff in the beginning and Gaming Control Board (GCB) later on, has adopted a kind of tax report system. The regulator just distributes the tax report forms and stays in office and waits for casinos to report their win and account taxable. Casinos report and turn in their tax monthly. Macao's counting tax and Nevada's reporting tax, each has its pros and cons, and each has been based on its historic and objective conditions. The following describes the two taxation systems respectively.

In Nevada, casinos are required to file tax report forms before the twenty-fourth of the month to report the gross casino revenue as well as the total amount taxable of the previous month. Regulator officials do not need to go to casinos on the scene to actually count the money. What they need to do is just stay in office and wait for casinos to honestly report and pay whatever they should pay to the government.[6]

This way has its obvious advantages: low taxation cost and it's easy for the government to collect. However, to efficiently exercise it, there are three conditions.

First, casino licensees, since 1968, are statutorily required to establish a set of accounting and managerial procedures called "internal control" based on the standard made by the regulator. Each casino licensee must submit a written system of internal control that describes administrative and accounting procedures; duties and responsibilities of personnel, organization, and structure; and physical safeguards and controls and detailed operating procedures as they relate to the gaming areas. The function of the internal control is to help the regulator easily trace back through the casino's internal financial flow to inspect, audit, and verify if the tax is correctly calculated and reported. (Kilby, Fox, and Lucas, 2005, pp. 39–41) Nevada Gaming Control Board stipulates that if it is found that a casino does not calculate its tax by the method that is stated in its reported internal control system, the regulator retains the right to use its own method to calculate tax for the casino. When an intentional tax evasion is found, criminal law would take care of it.

Second, casinos are licensed by location, not by corporation. Logically, a gaming licensee should also be a taxed unit. In Nevada, the government licenses the casino and hence taxes the casino. In Macao, however, the government licenses the casino company and hence taxes the company. Licensing by location is the key precondition to exercise a gaming tax report system because this system relies on exercising an internal control system. Yet the system is technically not exercisable on a multi-casino basis. It has to be on the basis of "one location, one set of internal control." For instance, SJM has twenty casinos now. Obviously it is infeasible to tie the whole bunch of casinos by one internal control system.[7]

Third, the society has a sophisticated legal system and culture. Only when legal punishment is so serious and the risk of evading tax is so high that it is worth to report and pay gaming tax honestly, the "wait-for-casinos-to-report" taxation system would work. Macao's count-tax system, on the contrary, does not have this kind of legal culture.

Counting gaming tax on the scene has been the taxation system since 1983 when Macao changed from levying gaming tax by flat rate to by casino win.[8] It works like this: the gaming regulatory body DICJ sends patrol staffs to every casino to watch every step of the internal financial flow and managerial frame, to count the casino win every day.[9] Every casino company must designate a counting room and all subordinate casinos send their win to the room to count with members of counting team present. The casino company remitts its gaming tax monthly according to the amount that is counted and calculated daily.

We do not clearly know that if Macao is the only jurisdiction in the world that adopts such a silly way to collect gaming tax, but we do know that even a rough collection like this also has its advantages: First, it is easier to prevent casinos from evading tax, so the counted outcome is sort of reliable. Second, it does not need an internal control system that a tax report system must have, so it is good for the casino to lower its operational cost. Third, it helps avoid fatal conflicts between the regulator and the regulated. This is especially important when there was only one casino firm in Macao's gaming market. In order not to give the casino firm chances to commit tax cheating and hence create a confrontation and a governance crisis, it might a good way for the government to grab the money and clear the bill right after the money comes out.

Macao's special way of collecting gaming tax was based on Macao's special historic conditions: all casinos belong to one gaming company; the government licenses and taxes the gaming company rather than every individual casino.

Now, however, Macao's gaming market has drastically changed. Macao currently has thirty-four casinos owned by six gaming companies and there will be more casinos participating the fast-expanding market in the near future. This implies that the historic conditions which resulted in the counting tax system do not exist any longer. If the number of casinos increases to fifty and game tables increase to 7,000, then the tax-counting work will be horribly costly. In addition, the ownership joining, license-leasing arrangement and gaming concession or sub-concession collaboration, and so on, have become so complicated, under which there will be many more institutional conflicts coming up. For example, a casino running under a concessionaire or sub-concessionaire could not really have a share of ownership but just rent the concession from it. Does the concession renter need to open a separate counting room for the regulator to count tax or just mix up with all other casinos that really belong to the concessionaire as one counting unit? The more the casinos, the more money counters that DICJ needs to hire to meet the demand. The larger the counting crew, the higher will be the watching, patrolling, counting, and administrating cost. Moreover, the regulator has to hire staff to watch the watchers. It will become more and more difficult to prevent the casino patrollers and money counters from corruption.

It seems that it is the time for Macao to give up its traditional way of collecting gaming tax and start to learn and adopt Nevada's gaming tax report system. Recently, in fact, DICJ did make a set of "Internal Control Standard" and distributed it to every casino company. Every casino company has started to design and make its own internal control system according to DICJ's standard. Of course this is not a difficult task for those Nevadan investors because the Macao standard is simpler than what they used to practice in their home state. Yet it is little harder for those Macao- or Hong Kong–based casino firms. It seems that Macao government is pushing things toward the direction of a reporting tax system. Or otherwise if the Macao government still wants to keep the old counting tax system, it does not make sense to force the casino firms to spend some operational cost to maintain a "deaf ear."

However, can Macao really exercise a tax report system? Would a system smoothly exercised in other jurisdictions automatically work in Macao? Does an internal control standard make a sufficient condition for tax report system to be feasible in Macao?

The answer is "no."

There is a critical difference, cultural difference, between the two societies. Macao does not have the legal culture that Nevada has. In other words, the legal system in Macao is not as serious as that in Nevada. Chinese culture is a kind of "personal culture" whereas American culture is a kind of "institutional culture." Understanding this point is very important in designing or reforming Macao's gaming regulatory system. In China, any institutional elements, laws, governmental policies, or stipulations are compromisable or negotiable. If a governmental or judicial official enforces the law or policy "too" seriously, the punished one would take that as a personal (not institutional) offense and hate him personally. So no one wants to be hated for just doing his job. With such a mentality, if a government official knows that the data on a tax report from a casino is not true or some of it is made up, very likely he would choose to close his eyes and pretend to be unaware. Would he be fired by his superior for being intentionally ignorant? Most likely, no. The superior also does not want to be hated for firing a subordinate. In Chinese culture, as an official, loyally working for the government is not always worth the conflict. An inter-institution conflict can easily become an inter-person conflict. As a government official disciplines or punishes someone according to law, he does not expect to be "forgiven" by his "victim" when he just say "I am just doing my job." If Macao really adopts a gaming tax report system, then most likely casino companies would keep testing the seriousness of the new system by going further and further in making up the taxable account, and the regulator would keep compromising and compromising with the typical Chinese wording "not as an example for next time" (下不为例) until it reaches the point that however much is reported is what accepted. The same institution on different cultural grounds will work differently.[10]

Based on this cultural ground, the Macao gaming regulator body has to grab its share at the first step before the money flows into casino's financial maze, before the casino faces stronger temptation to make up the tax report, before the regulator has to confront and punish tax cheaters. In Nevada, the way of gaming tax collection is designed to prevent cheating by punishing. In Macao, however, the way of gaming tax collection is designed to prevent punishing by preventing cheating. Macao people do not like confronting and punishing.

Cultural differences between the two societies are too inherent and stubborn to overcome. A tax report system is good but not necessarily feasible in Macao. Counting tax is feasible in Macao but not good. How should this contradiction be solved?

Licensing Casinos or Licensing Casino Companies?

With more and more casinos and a larger and larger industrial base, Macao's gaming regulatory system is facing another dilemma: how to license the industry—by location or by corporation? The former is the Nevada way and the latter is the way Macao has been doing it. This issue is also related to the taxation issue discussed in the last section. As we mentioned, only when licensing casinos by location can the internal control standard and hence the tax report system be adopted.

By the end of June 2009, Nevada Gaming Commission had issued 2,882 licenses of five categories.

Among them, 428 are non-restricted licenses. Holders of this kind of license can do any kind of gaming business including table games, slot machines, sports booking, race track, and so on, excluding lotteries.

There were 2,097 restricted gaming licenses and 59 slot route operator licenses. When a non-gaming company, such as a supermarket or a grocery store, wants to put some slot machines (no more than fifteen) on its premise, it needs a restricted license. The licensee does not run those slot machines but collaborates with a licensee of "slot route operator" on a profit share basis. The slot route operator is the real runner of the slot machines.

There were 292 licenses for gaming equipment manufacturers and gaming product distributors.

In terms of number of licenses, it seems Nevada has many more gaming facilities than Macao. However, as we know, in Macao, one gaming licensee can legally open and run many casinos. In Nevada (and almost everywhere else in the world), one licensee can run only one casino. MGM in Nevada has about twenty casinos, of which seven are located at the Strip, every one of which has a license. The system of one casino, one license has its obvious advantages from the view of regulation.

First, the government can easily tax the licensee. You tax whom you license—this is a general principle of gaming regulation. You license the casino, you tax the casino; by the same token, you license the casino company, you tax the casino company. The former is the way Nevada does and the latter is that Macao does. The key is that, in order to establish a tax report system, an internal control system needs to be established, yet an internal control system can only be built on the basis of location. It is technically impossible for a casino company to weave all its, say, twenty casinos into one internal control system. Therefore, the right way of taxing and licensing casinos is by location instead of by corporation.

Second, the regulator can easily distinguish and discipline the responsible entity in terms of obligation. In regard with disciplining casinos, the "capital punishment" is revoking license. Under the by-location licensing system, whoever has done something wrong so its license should be revoked, the regulator would just punish the individual casino, not the whole company. Dealing with an individual casino is much easier than dealing with a casino company especially when the company forms a big franchise and is subject to the "too big to fail" principle.

Third, it is easier for the regulator to deal with casino property transactions. In Nevada's gaming history, there have been many casino property buyouts. A casino hotel belongs to A gaming company yesterday and is bought out by B gaming company today—this kind of property transaction happens almost every year in Nevada. Some Nevadan gaming giants, such as Wynn, even specialize in doing such kind of business: buying an old casino hotel and imploding it and building up a new mega resort on the site and selling it to somebody else to run it. When this kind of transaction happens, the taxed entity remains the same. What the Nevada Gaming Control Board needs to do is just license the new owner of the location. Just imagine that if Nevada casino industry was not licensed and taxed by location but by corporation as Macao does now, those frequent property transactions would trouble the regulator: whenever there is a property buyout, the regulator must follow the transaction to uninstall the transacted property from its old owner's taxation integration and install it into the new owner's.

While talking about the advantages of Nevada's by-location licensing system, we are also talking the disadvantages of Macao's by-corporation licensing system, and we are also expressing the necessity for Macao to adopt the by-location licensing system.

Under Macao's one-company, one-license system, what should the Macao government do if MGM–PansyHo or PBL–MELCO joint ventures break up again as SANDS–GALAXY did seven years ago? What if a gaming company goes bankrupt or insolvent and closes? Should the government automatically cancel its license or allow it to sell or rent out its license?

Theoretically speaking, it can be concluded that Macao should change its gaming licensing system from by-corporation to by-location in order to establish internal control systems, to establish an efficient gaming taxation system, to establish a flexible casino property market, to modernize Macao's gaming regulatory system.

However, practically speaking, to reform Macao's gaming licensing system is not that easy. There are six concession or sub-concession contracts in the way. The concession contracts of SJM and its sub-concessionaire MGM will end in 2020. The concession contracts of the other four of the big six will end in 2022.

Who Should be Licensed?

In Nevada, the Gaming Control Board not only licenses casino institutions but also casino owners and some management personnel. In other words, the Board actually issues two kinds of gaming licenses, one of which is for legal persons and the other is for natural persons (Casiello and Jones, 1999).

When an applicant applies for opening and running a casino, the applicant(s), the owner(s), is subject to a big investigation on his personal background tracing back twenty-five years. That is why, under such an individual licensing system, foreigners are rarely awarded licenses.[11]

More over, besides the owner(s), some "key employees" also can be called to apply for licenses. The concept "key employee" is defined by the terms down below:

Any individual who makes more than $75,000 annually;
Any individual who can approve the use of rim credit;
Any individual who can extend a player's credit limit by the greater of 10 percent or $1,000;
Any individual who can recommend or approve the settlement or write-off of a credit instrument;
Any individual who has the authority to hire or terminate supervisory casino personnel;
Any individual who is a gaming or security shift manager;
Any individual who has the authority to authorize complementaries for other than food or beverage, examples include complimentaries extended for rooms or airfare;
All individuals with the authority to manage the following departments: accounting, food and beverage, cage, credit and collections, personnel, internal audit, security, surveillance, entertainment, sales, and marketing;

Any individual who can enter into a contractual arrangement that is binding on the licensee and is reportable under Regulation 8.130 (Transaction Reports);
Any individual who has been represented to the Board or Commission by the licensee as being important to the operation of the gaming establishment;
Any person who individually or in conjunction with a group formulates management policy. (Kilby, Fox, and Lucas, 2005)

Every licensed casino must make its key employee list according to the terms above and submit it to the Investigation Division of the Gaming Control Board. The division will select some individuals, usually not many, from the list and call for interviews. And then, based on the impressions from the interviews, the board will select some individuals from the interviewed and require them to deposit some investigation fees and start the license application procedures. During the investigations, if someone's background is too complicated and hence the investigation takes longer, those bad-lucks could be required to add more money. Some key employees can even receive the same strict investigation as the boss.

With the worldwide gaming development, most gaming regulatory bodies in the world have adopted the licensing individual system. At least, every state of the United States is exercising it. The regulator licenses and controls the top-rank ones and lets go ordinary personnel, which implies the bigger a boss is, the more seriously he would be investigated, the more restricted his license would be, and the more money he would need to pay for the investigation. Casino owners, board directors, presidents, and CEOs, among others, must apply for a license. The key employees would be licensed selectively.

Macao, however, the gaming regulator traditionally does not investigate and license individuals. After gaming liberalization, in order to make Macao's gaming market work better or at least look better, Macao government decides to license those VIP junket operators. In addition, in order to make sure all dealer positions are occupied by Macao legal residents only and to protect employment opportunities from illegal foreign laborers, in 2007, Macao government decided to license the table game dealers. But the casino big bosses and managerial employees are not required to apply for licenses. This kind of upside-down licensing system creates a unique world.

How Many Regulatory Bodies, Four or One?

Nevada's gaming industry is regulated by only one regulatory body, Nevada Gaming Control Board. Whoever owns a casino, finances a casino, collaborates with a casino, is employed by a casino, or gambles in a casino, all are regulated by the same board. In Macao, however, there are four governmental bodies in charge of different aspects of casino regulations. Gaming Inspection and Coordination Bureau (DICJ) regulates the casinos and VIP room contractors; the Judiciary Police (PJ) polices gamblers; the Labor Affair Bureau (DSAL) is in charge of licensing table game dealers; and even the Commission Against Corruption (CCAC) also has a policing function when a chip-stealing is committed by a casino employee.

One or four regulatory bodies, which is better?

One regulatory body system has obvious advantages.

First, putting all the regulatory functions together under one ceiling would be good for all regulatory divisions and staffs to communicate and share information and responsibilities. For example, on the Website of Nevada Gaming Control Board, there are three sets of black lists, "Excluded," "Wanted," and "Denied." Once someone is labeled by one casino as an "unwelcome" person, he could be put on the "excluded" black list by the government and can never walk into any casino property in the United States. However, in Macao, every casino company has its own "excluded" black list and, without regulator's coordination, don't share the information. A bad guy might be excluded by one casino firm but he still can go in other properties. The reason that Macao does not have an official and universal black list is because no one knows which gaming regulatory body, DICJ or Judiciary Police or Commission Against Corruption, is responsible for establishing the black list.

Second, one regulatory body system is good for specializing and professionalizing the leadership of the regulatory body. Casino business is not something like the IT industry that demands very skillful regulators; however, to regulate casinos, special and professional knowledge is still needed, especially for its leadership. Most casino fraud or other crime cases are complicated and hard for regular police to deal with. The Enforcement Division, Nevada GCB, has some very professional experts who have knowledge in dealing with gambler fraud. But in Macao, while each of the three regulatory bodies should have such experts, none of them really has one.

Third, one regulatory body system is good for unifying prosecution and other judicial matters. Sometimes, one crime case is committed by several parties together. A money laundering case could be a conspiracy between a gambler and a casino boss (Mills, 2002); a dealer and a gambler can collude to cheat casino. In Macao, this kind of case would be sued by two regulatory bodies separately as two cases. It is costly and inefficient. The Enforcement Division, Nevada GCB, however, not only has experts to catch the criminals, but also has professional prosecutors and attorneys to exercise the enforcement. They can sue whatever kinds of crimes committed by whatever kinds of criminals: gamblers, casino employees, casino bosses, and so forth.

Fourth, one regulatory body system is good for simplifying administration facilities and saving administration cost.

Who is Responsible for Regulating Junket Rollers?

Macao's casino industry has an unique sector, VIP room contractual system, by which over half of the casino revenue is generated. Almost all VIP gamblers are recruited and ushered by so-called junket rollers. Now there are more than 10,000 of them wandering around six casino firms, thirty-four casinos, and hundreds of VIP rooms to sell their customers to whoever gives them higher commission rate. Before gaming liberalization, these self-employed people were actually regulated by the casino firm STDM. Once more than one casino firm emerged in Macao's gaming market, the former monopolist automatically ceased his regulatory function and handed it over to the governmental regulator. However, the government has not taken it over yet. Now, none of the guys can be officially identified, and hence, no one knows who should be responsible to regulate them and how to regulate them.

The one-company, one-license system has been Macao's tradition for seventy years. As a matter of fact, this system used to play a very positive role in trimming Macao's gaming market at the time when Macao had a population of 40,000 and 200 gambling booths. When the original license was issued to the first casino monopolist seventy years ago, the Portuguese government actually was sharing its regulatory power and function with the licensee. So it is not completely correct and fair to just regard the only casino firm then simply as a monopolist enterprise. In some sense, it also can be regarded as a "second government" in terms of regulating the whole industry, especially the junket rollers.

Gaming liberalization, however, has broken the "monopoly" but kept the one-company, one-license system. This means the SAR government is facing a dilemma: none of the six licensees can still keep performing as a "second government" to help the "first government" to rule the junket rollers and the government itself also does not know how to regulate them.

Conclusion

The freer a gaming market is, the stricter it should be governed.

Gaming liberalization does not only mean more casinos, more gamblers, more employees, and more money, but also means a more standardized and modernized regulation system. When the industrial size expands and the market structure changes, we must change the way of regulating it. We can not just simply copy the old regulation system.

The larger the industrial base, the tighter and harder the "institutional bottleneck" will work.

There is no way to avoid the inevitability of reforming Macao's gaming regulatory system.

One-company, one-license system must be changed into one-casino, one-license.

The tax counting system must be changed into a tax reporting system.

Casino bosses must be licensed.

Regulatory bodies must be integrated into one entity.

Junket rollers must be leashed.

References

Casiello, Nicholas, and Marie Jones (1999). *International Casino Law, New Jersey* 3rd Edition. Las Vegas: Institute for the Study of Gambling and Commercial Gaming.

Eadington, William R., and Ricardo Siu (2007). "Between Law and Custom—Examining the Interaction between Legislative Change and the Evolution of Macao's Casino Industry," in *International Gambling Studies*, 7 (1), 1–28.

Kilby, Jim, James Fox, and Anthony Lucas (2005). *Casino Operations Management* 2nd Edition. New York: John Wiley & Sons, Inc.

Liu, Pin Liang (2002). *Aomen Bocaiye Zongheng (Vertical–Horizontal Perspectives of Macao's Gaming Industry)*. Hong Kong: Joint Publishing.

Mills, John, and Jannet Vreeland (2002). "Suspicious Transaction Reporting: An Update." Working paper: University of Nevada, Reno.

Wang, Wuyi (2005). *Duquang Kaifang de Zhidu Fansi (Rethinking Macao's Gaming Liberalization from a View of Institutional Economics)*. Macao: Macao Polytechnic Institute Publishing.

Wang, W., and W. R. Eadington (2008). "The VIP-Room Contractual System and Macao's Traditional Casino Industry." *China: An International Journal*, 6–2, P1–24.

Notes

1. There is no other industry in the United States or in any other more or less free market economy where the profitability of companies is so overwhelmingly dependent on what the law permits, requires, and prohibits. The profitability of a gambling company depends to an enormous extent on what the law says rather than simply on what the public wants.—*Introduction to the Study of Gambling and Public Policy* (Peter Collins, UK, 2002)

2. Of course, the government cannot design its gaming regulatory system completely based on its "free will." Any gaming regulatory system in any jurisdiction more or less reflects its geographic, cultural, and other objective conditions.

3. "Nevada: the Birthplace of Modern Gaming." (Kilby, Fox, and Lucas, 2005, p. 1)

4. As we all know, the tax rates of the two jurisdictions differ much, from Macao's 35 percent to Nevada's 6.75 percent. In addition, Macao government also levies about 4.5 percent of casino win for supporting several local civil projects. This is a tradition inherited from STDM era.

5. DICJ stands for Gaming Inspection and Coordination Bureau. Most names of official agencies in Macao are abbreviated from Portuguese not from English. So it is unlikely to figure out what an abbreviation really stands for in English.

6. As a matter of fact, in the United States, not only gaming tax, but almost all kinds of taxes are collected in this way.

7. Among the seven divisions of Nevada Gaming Control Board, there is one called "Tax and License Division." That tax and license are put together in one division shows the close connection between the two functions.

8. Before then, Macao's gaming tax was a flat rate, which was not literally a kind of tax but a kind of license fee.

9. Sometimes even more often.

10. Since the end of 1970s when so-called reforming and opening started to overthrow China's socialist system, Chinese intellectuals, especially economists, have been worshipping the academic concept "institution." They believe that all differences between China and America are just institutional differences. If China established America's institutions, China would become another America in the world. For many years, Chinese young students, populous workers, government officials, and even communist leaders have been brainwashed by this methodology.

11. In 1987, a Japanese tycoon Jinji Yasuda bought the grand casino Aladdin on the Strip and obtained a two-year conditional license, which made him a commercial hero. Unfortunately, two years later in August 1989, Nevada Gaming Commission revoked his license because he refused to tell the commission where he borrowed the money. Along with some commercial mistakes, Aladdin filed bankruptcy four days after the revocation. Three month later, Jinji Yasuda died of cancer. On the list "revoked and denied" on the Website of Nevada Gaming Control Board, the man's name is still there. The date revoked is August 24, 1989. www.lvstriphistory.com/ie/alad66.htm; gaming.nv.gov/documents/pdf/denials_revocations_list.pdf.

12. Most abbreviated names of Macao institutions are from their Portuguese origins and cannot simply be figured out by their English contexts.

PART IV

MACAO AND THE UNITED STATES: BEYOND THE BILATERAL

CHAPTER TEN

A Chinese Perspective of Macao and Sino–U.S. Relations: A Case Study of the Banco Delta Asia Affair

Hou Ying

The Sino–U.S. relations are undoubtedly one of the most important bilateral relations in the world today, which to a great extent consists in the interwoven interests between the two states in almost every corner of the world. After the handover of Macao to China in 1999, the entry of a large scale of American capital into this area has contributed to rapid growth of local economy, which has greatly enhanced Macao's international status. However, the role of Macao in the Sino–U.S. relations has not seemed significant until the Banco Delta Asia (BDA) issue surfaced in 2005, which for the first time involved Macao into the swirl of the Sino–American wrestle. The questions are: Why did the affair take place in Macao? Was it accidental? If not, what is the role of Macao in Sino–U.S. relations after its handover in 1999?

Taking the BDA issue as a case study, this chapter tries to argue that Macao can play a special role such as intermediate and buffer in China–U.S. relations. In the first part, this chapter will review the BDA affair. The second part will analyze the subtle Sino–U.S. relationship reflected by the issue and China's strategies. The third part will study the significance of the "one country, two systems" operation on China's foreign relations. The fourth part will analyze the special role of Macao in Sino–U.S. relations under the "one country, two systems" arrangement.

The BDA Affair

Banco Delta Asia is a Chinese family-owned bank in Macao with total assets of 420 million HK dollars. Early in 1994, $250,000 counterfeit notes were detected in BDA when several North Koreans tried to deposit them in the bank. Although the bank reported it to the local police as well as U.S. government, the incident finally ended up with nothing conclusive. Later, the forged U.S. dollars resurfaced in Macao after the handover in 1999. But it was not until September 15, 2005—after the undercover investigations with the codenames of Royal Charm and Smoking Dragon—that the U.S. Treasury Department designated BDA a "primary money laundering concern" and described it a "willing pawn" of North Korea engaging in illicit activities.[1]

Although Stanley Au, the owner of BDA, publicly refuted the designation at once,[2] the U.S. action against BDA led to a run on the bank and about $133 million—equal to 34 percent—of deposits were drained out of the bank from September 15 to 21.[3] In order to stabilize the local financial system, the Macao monetary authority took over the bank by appointing three delegates to help manage the bank and adopted stricter anti-money laundering measures, including freezing $25 million related to North Korean accounts[4] and suspending all commercial ties with North Korean companies. Meanwhile, the Macao government commissioned Ernest & Young, one of the Big Four auditors in the world, to audit BDA and found no evidence that BDA knowingly help North Korea launder money.[5]

The U.S. sanction against BDA aroused the ripple effect. Afraid of being excluded from American financial systems, many other banks around the world, especially those in China, Japan, Thailand, Vietnam, and Singapore, later took similar tougher measures against North Korea, "creating an informal financial embargo of the country."[6] Moreover, DPRK found its legitimate business had also been influenced. "DPRK banks and traders reportedly are having difficulty finding other lenders to conduct their overseas business."[7] The Zokwang Trading Company, which had acted as the de facto consulate of DPRK in Macao, "closed its headquarters on the fifth floor of an office building near Banco Delta Asia," and relocated in Zhuhai, a city abutting Macao within China's border.[8] In sum, it seems that the U.S. action against BDA "hit North Korea where it hurts."[9] Just as some observers point out, "Because the North Korean leadership placed so many of their foreign exchange eggs in the BDA basket, the sanctions on BDA that prompted the closure of these accounts have had an unusually effective impact. . . . It is not just the amount of funds tied up that matters, it is the disruption of their system for transferring foreign exchange for meeting critical needs of the regime."[10] Kim Kye-gwan, vice minister of the Ministry of Foreign Affairs in DPRK and chief negotiator for North Korea in the Six-Party Talks, later told Christopher Hill, the U.S. assistant secretary of state for East Asian and Pacific Affairs at that time, that the BDA issue was of importance[11] and the U.S. financial sanctions against North Korea made the North Korean leaders feel their blood had congealed.[12]

Though the United States insisted that the BDA designation had nothing to do with the Six Party Talks, North Korea reacted sharply by refusing to return to talks until the Americans lifted these financial "sanctions." As a result, a series of bilateral negotiations between the United States and the Democratic People's Republic of Korea (DPRK) were launched in 2006 and 2007, which contributed to the signature of the February 13 agreement. But the DPRK refused to implement the agreement until it received the $25 million frozen in the BDA.

In order to urge North Korea to dismantle its nuclear facilities, the United States took steps to return the funds to the former. March 14, 2007, despite the petition submitted by BDA for demanding the withdrawal of the Treasury Department's rule,[13] the U.S. Treasury Department finalized the rule under Section 311 of the Patriot Act against BDA by prohibiting "all U.S. financial institutions from maintaining correspondent accounts for BDA" and barring "BDA from accessing the U.S. financial system, either directly or indirectly."[14] As far as the $25 million was concerned, the United States let the Macao government decide whether to unfreeze the funds or not.[15] Then Daniel Glaser, the U.S. Treasury Department's deputy assistant secretary for Terrorist Financing and Financial Crimes, went to Macao to discuss with related officials on the BDA issue. March 19, 2007, in a statement on its Web site, the Macao monetary authority announced to release the funds after studying the information provided by the U.S. Treasury Department.[16] On the same day, Daniel Glaser announced that the United States and DPRK had reached "an understanding on the disposition of DPRK-related funds frozen at Banco Delta Asia."[17] The United States, according to the proposition of DPRK, agreed to transfer the frozen funds in BDA into an account of North Korea's Foreign Trade Bank at the Bank of China (BOC) in Beijing.[18] However, in order to protect its own prestige and being afraid of the American retaliatory acts, the Bank of China refused to accept the funds.[19] On the other hand, DPRK insisted on transferring the funds through another foreign bank as a means of re-entering the international financial system.[20] Finally, with the guarantees of the U.S. Treasury Department, the assets were transferred to the New York branch of the Federal Reserve Bank and then to the Russian Central Bank. The latter in turn forwarded the funds to Russia's Far East Commercial Bank, or Dalkombank, in which Pyongyang had an account.[21] June 25, 2007, the DPRK announced it received the funds, and three months later, Macao monetary authority returned BDA to Stanley Au. But the American Treasury sanction against BDA has not been lifted yet, so that the latter "remains unable to conduct operations using either American or Hong Kong dollars."[22]

The Subtle China–U.S. Relationship and China's Strategies

For Pyongyang, the BDA affair came to a conclusion, as the fund dispute resolved; but for Beijing and Macao, the BDA affair is of significance, considering the U.S. Treasury sanction is still in operation.

First and foremost, the BDA affair reflects the common ground and divergence between China and the United States on the North Korean nuclear issue. On one hand, both China and the United States share common interests in the denuclearization of the Korean peninsula. On the other hand, China and the United States diverge on the strategy toward the North Korean regime. The United States inclines to adopt coercive measures to press DPRK to abandon its nuclear program and even to change the Kim Jong Il regime, while China, out of the geopolitical concern, prefers to maintain the North Korean regime in order to keep a stable and peaceful Korean peninsula. Thus, China may try to help the DPRK "realize soft land in economy and politics"[23] by trading with the latter and providing the convenience for it to interact with the international system. In this case, it is not surprising that North Korean companies had been active in Macao, China's semi-liberated area under Portugal's administrative control before 1999 and the Special Administrative Region (SAR) since 1999, until the Macao authority adopted stricter measures toward North Korean companies.[24] This also partly explains why BDA has had more than two decades of open business relations with "a range of North Korean government companies and entities"[25] such as the Zokwang Trading Company—the once de facto consulate of DPRK in Macao—until it was suddenly charged by the U.S. Treasury Department of engaging in illicit activities in 2005.[26]

Second, the BDA issue reflects the complex interweaving interests and contradictions between China and the United States, which DPRK has made the best of to gain what it wants. As mentioned above, China and the United States have convergence and divergence on the North Korean nuclear issue. The different policies between China and the United States toward DPRK make it possible for the Kim Jong Il regime to seek survival in the interstice between the major powers in international politics. Especially, as the old ideological ally of China, the isolated regime had freely gone into business, engaged in foreign activities and "generate[d] sufficient funds to keep the regime afloat"[27] in Chinese enclaves such as Macao, which is inconspicuous and had the financial system in line with international practice, until the U.S. Treasury Department's designation against BDA.[28] But the U.S. sanctions against BDA, which aimed to tighten the screws on North Korea's finances, once again had Washington confronting Beijing, since the United States targeting BDA inevitably will influence the financial stability of Macao—which the Chinese government is concerned about most—and BDA as a Macanese private bank "has the implicit backing of the Chinese government."[29] Particularly when the U.S. government forced Stanley Au to sell his bank, China stealthily supported Stanley Au in resisting American pressure.[30] And finally, North Korea got the funds it claimed, while BDA bore the punishment from the United States. Many observers thus believed BDA was an unfortunate victim of international political struggles,[31] but others further questioned the real motives of the United States to target BDA, considering the timing of the American punishment on the bank was precisely during the swift growth of American capital in Macao.[32] On all accounts the BDA affair made Beijing at least consider it as an alert for the infiltration and interference of American forces into Macao along with the entrance of American capital to this region.[33]

Third, the BDA affair also reflects China's pragmatic and dual strategies toward the United States. If the most heated question discussed in the United States today is how to respond to a rising China, the latter also faces the question of how to deal with the United States in the course of its rise. For the Chinese government, economic development and social stability are its primary concerns, which has respect to the ruling status and regime survival of the Chinese Communist Party (CCP). In this purpose, China focuses on economic aspect and integration into the global order when developing its foreign relations, so as to gain a favorable international environment and to bandwagon the globalization for Chinese modernization. Considering the U.S. dominant role in international affairs today, China has attached importance to the Sino–American relations and sought to cooperate and sometimes accommodate the Americans to avoid face-to-face confrontations on one hand. On the other hand, China also actively develops relations with other countries—including those "rogue" or "evil" ones in terms of the United States—in order to balance and cope with some deep contradictions or so-called structural contradictions resulting from geopolitics and different interests demands between China and the United States. Just as some scholars point out,

> There seem to be two dominant policy perspectives at the base of Beijing's strategy in this unipolar world; both hope for accommodation with the United States, but they differ over the possibility of maintaining cooperation over the long term. Given that level of uncertainty, China seems to have chosen the prudent course of avoiding unduly antagonizing the United States while establishing a web of relationships with other states and state-based bodies that could serve to provide China with a degree of leverage were this to prove necessary—for example, in the case of conflict with the United States over Taiwan, or United States attempts at coercion or containment of China.[34]

Likewise, out of its own national interests considerations, China has cooperated with the United States on the denuclearization of the Korean Peninsula while adopting an engaging policy with DPRK by offering a relatively tolerant environment in the Chinese territory for the North Koreans to be in touch with the international system. A good illustration is the frequent appearance of North Koreans in Macao before the occurrence of the BDA affair. Actually, according to some open reports, Macao has been an important platform for North Korea to conduct foreign liaison in East Asia since the 1950s.[35] But after the BDA affair took place, the Zokwang Trading Company "closed its headquarters on the fifth floor of an office building near Banco Delta Asia," and relocated in Zhuhai, a city abutting on Macao within China's border.[36] And recently most of North Korea's commercial beachheads have shifted to Malaysia.[37] Moreover, after the U.S. Treasury Department accused BDA of money laundering in 2005, China took a cooperative position with the United States by tightening up financial policy against money laundering on one hand, but quietly defended Stanley Au against American pressure of selling the bank on the other hand. And finally, when the U.S. Treasury maintained the ruling against BDA, the Chinese government only expressed "deep regret" on the U.S. sanction,[38] avoiding any direct confrontation with the United States. But later, the refusal of BOC to help to transfer the unfrozen funds to Pyongyang not only is out of the commercial reputation consideration, but also reflects China's misdoubt to the United States, since the experiences of BDA let BOC have reason to be worried about the U.S. retaliatory measures in the future and China absolutely will not let one of its Big Four state-owned banks risk "losing access to the world's most important economy"[39] when China is trying to further engage in the international financial system.

In addition, the BDA affair reveals the high dependency of North Korean businesses on China's financial system and Washington's targeting BDA seems to hit the right nail on the head on bearing upon Pyongyang. Then, aiming at North Korea's nuclear and missile tests in 2009, the Obama administration did not hesitate to raise again financial leverage and push other countries, especially China, to participate in these sanctions against the Kim Jong Il regime.[40] As a result, the five individuals and five institutions of North Korea punished by the United Nations Security Council (UNSC) seem to be a repeat of BDA: the United States considers China the key to twist the arms of the North Koreans; and China only agreed to punish DPRK after revising the UNSC Resolution 1874, which demonstrates again Beijing's pragmatic and dual strategies toward Washington.

In sum, the BDA affair tells a lot about Sino–American relations and China's foreign strategies, which are both flexible and pragmatic. Meanwhile, taking place in one of the SARs, the BDA issue is of consequence to the operation of "one country, two systems."

The Unexpected Role of "One Country, Two Systems" Operation

"One country, two systems" has become a major feature of China's political regime, which demonstrates the "practical and realistic" style of Chinese leaders in solving the problems left over by history. Actually, during the early days of People's Republic of China, the Chinese leaders were not eager to get the two regions back. Under the policy of "planning for the long-term, utilizing sufficiently" framed by the first generation of Chinese leaders, the two regions have acted as "the two nostrils" of the mainland by providing materials urgently needed for the national reconstruction as well as communicating with the mainland and Western countries. In the era of reform and opening up, Deng Xiaoping's "one country, two systems" enables the two areas to continue to play an intermediary role between the mainland and the world after their return to China. Under this context, the BDA affair shows that the "one country, two systems" policy has not only contributed to the stability and prosperity of both the whole country and the two SARs, but also made the Chinese government more flexible in managing internal and external affairs.

Particularly, the arrangement of "one country, two systems" makes it possible for the Chinese government to enjoy more flexibility when dealing with the often two-faced United States. Compared with China's unitary regime, the U.S. institutional arrangement enables it to realize its diverse, even conflicting interests.[41] Both the American government and Congress can affect foreign affairs, as they often need to speak for different interest groups or have different concerns out of their different stance. This is also the case between different departments within the U.S. government. For example, on the BDA issue, the State Department and the Treasury Department had different concerns. The former, concentrating on denuclearizing North Korea, hoped to unfreeze the funds as soon as possible in order to urge the DPRK to implement the February 13 Agreement, while the latter stuck to punishing BDA in order to frightened other foreign banks and thus led to a delay of the transfer of the funds to Pyongyang. Likewise, China also had different interests on the North Korean nuclear issue. On one hand, China is in favor of the denuclearization of the Korean peninsula. On the other hand, China opposes the severe sanctions against the King Jong Il regime, which would otherwise lead to the unrest of the Korean peninsula and thus threatens China's own border stability. "The Chinese are most concerned about the collapse of North Korea leading to chaos on the border."[42] Moreover, if DPRK provoked a war with the United States, China undoubtedly "would bear the brunt of any military confrontation on the Korean peninsula."[43] In this case, when DPRK depended on China to be in touch with the international system, the two SARs—which enjoy a high degree of autonomy in administrative, legislative, and judicial areas under the "one country, two systems" regulation and are internationalized in business and legislation—will be more appropriate than the Chinese mainland for the North Korean activities. In this sense, the "two systems" to a certain degree helps the Chinese government to better handle some dilemmas which potentially will bring both benefits and costs to China on one hand, and help to enhance China's strategic status in East Asia on the other hand. And once some problems emerged, such as the sanctions imposed by the U.S. Treasury Department on BDA, it would not do great harm to China's entire economic development and social solidity which are crucial to the legitimacy and regime survival of CCP. In an interview, David Asher, a former senior U.S. State Department official dealing with the Kim Jong Il regime, stated a similar point that BDA "was an easy target in the sense that it was not so large that its failure would bring down the financial system."[44] In addition, Beijing kept a low profile and let the Macao authority handle the BDA affair under the relevant provisions of "one country, two systems," thus enabling the Chinese government to be more flexible in dealing with Sino–U.S. relations on this issue.

However, even under "one country, two systems," the two SARs—Hong Kong and Macao—have had different experiences after their handovers. Many studies have focused on Hong Kong's political, economic, and social development and its role in China–U.S. relations. By comparison, Macao has attracted less attention and its role in Sino–American relations seems unclear. But the BDA affair reveals that Macao, owing to its inconspicuousness, has been a place where multiple forces congregate, and its special role in Sino–U.S. relations thus deserves to be explored.

The Special Role of Macao in Sino–U.S. Relations

Compared with Hong Kong, Macao has its own advantages, which enable it to play a special role in Sino–U.S. relations. At first, having a more pro-Beijing political culture, Macao enjoyed a smoother relationship with the central government. Early after the December 3, 1966, event, pro-Beijing forces were firmly rooted in Macao. Since then, the co-existence and cooperation of the Portuguese Macao government and pro-Beijing interest groups have made Macao a "semi-liberated region." After the smooth handover in 1999, Macao kept a relatively harmonious relationship with Beijing, which let Beijing not need to overtly intervene into its internal affairs. Therefore, although the exposure of North Korea's illicit activities in Macao more or less put China into an awkward situation, the Chinese central government was still able to be free of direct intervening into the BDA affair.

Second, owing to the cultural, historical, and geographical advantages, Macao has maintained a closer relationship with Taiwan than Hong Kong has, which makes it possible for Macao to play a special role in communicating with the Chinese Mainland and Taiwan. In fact, although the pro-Taipei forces were expelled after the December 3, 1966, event, the sharing Matsu culture and tens of thousands Fujian descents offered an access for Macao and Taiwan to rapidly restore their ties since the end of the 1980s. In February 1990, the Taiwan authority founded the Taipei Trade and Tourism Office in Macao, indicating the resumption of its official and semi-official activities in this region. In 1995, the opening of the Macao–Taipei line gave impetus to trade and personnel exchange between Macao and Taiwan, and contributed to the rapid increase of Taiwan tourists visiting the Mainland via Macao. Nowadays Taiwan is the third-largest source of tourists visiting Macao, only after the Chinese Mainland and Hong Kong.[45] And many of the Macanese social elites received their education in Taiwan. Increasingly close economic and financial ties as well as frequent personnel exchange between Macao and Taiwan thus have made Macao an important intermediary between the two sides of the cross straits. Moreover, the navigation between Macao and Taiwan—through which the planes of Air Macao only need to change their flight number at Macao International Airport in the course of the flight from Taipei to the cities of the mainland and vice versa—has indirectly realized direct flight between the Mainland and Taiwan before the daily direct charter flights began at the end of 2008.

In this context, both the Chinese government and Taiwan authority attach importance to the special role of Macao in communicating between the two sides of the cross straits. For the Chinese government, then Vice Premier

Qian Qichen publicly proclaimed Macao's special role in the cross-strait exchanges in 1998.[46] The seven basic policies he announced at the Fifth Plenary Session of the Preparatory Committee for the Macao Special Administrative Region (MSAR) for handling the relations between Macao and Taiwan after Macao's return to China laid the basis for the development of Macao–Taiwan relationship thereafter. In 2002, the Association for Relations Across the Taiwan Strait (ARATS) set up its first transfrontier office in Macao, so as to make use of Macao's special role to develop exchanges with Taiwan in the context of which the Taiwan authority disavowed the "common understanding in 1992" as well as ARATS, and Straits Exchange Foundation (SEF) could not resume dialogue and negotiations at that time. Almost at the same time, the Taipei Economic and Cultural Center in Macao was allowed to directly accept applications of mainland residents and foreigners for the Entry Permit to Taiwan. For the Taiwan authority, its Legislative Yuan passed the Act Governing the Relations with Hong Kong and Macao in 1997, in order to specify Taiwan's relations with Hong Kong and Macao after their handovers. According to this act, the Taiwan authority considers Macao as the third area after December 20, 1999, and emphasized its intermediary role in communicating the two sides across the Taiwan Strait. Later, following Macao's return to China, the Taiwan authority also declared three principles—reciprocity, continuity, and the rule of law—to guide Taiwan's interaction with Macao.[47] The Taipei Trade and Tourism Office, Macao, attached to Taiwan's Foreign Ministry was also changed to Taipei Economic and Cultural Center attached to Mainland Affairs Council (MAC), thus suspending the sensitive dispute over the name of Taiwan institutions and encouraging the Taiwan–Macao relationship to be more pragmatic.[48] On this basis, the Macao–Taiwan relationship continued to steadily develop, and Macao became a special channel communicating both sides cross the Taiwan Straits. Many important negotiations, such as the negotiations on the Spring Festival charter flights of Taiwanese businessmen in 2005 as well as negotiations on cross-strait tourism in 2006 and 2007 were held in Macao and thus set up the Macao Consultation Model which is characterized by government authority but promotion and consultations are on a non-governmental basis. Besides, Macao is so small and inconspicuous that it is easy for the two sides cross straits to avoid the media's attention and keep a low profile in handling cross-strait relations. In 2009, MAC urged the Macao government to set up a liaison office in Taiwan in order to strengthen bilateral relations and exchanges.[49] In this sense, just as some studies point out, "Taiwan has become more concerned about the development of Macao–Taiwan relationship, which makes Macao partly replace the functions of Hong Kong."[50]

Third, compared with Hong Kong, as small as it is Macao is an area at which all kinds of forces converge. As mentioned above, North Koreans have long been active in Macao until the U.S. Treasury ruling against BDA. The Zokwang Trading Company acted as the consular of the DPRK in Macao before its withdrawal and Kim Jong-nam, Kim Jong Il's eldest son, hung his hat in this "low exposure" place.[51] Moreover, according to many public reports, BDA has about thirty years of commercial relations with North Korea, including helping the North Koreans resell gold to Hong Kong and Germany.[52] Although the reselling through Macao takes more time and brings fewer benefits for the Pyongyang regime than the direct selling on the Hong Kong market, North Korea still chose this way of selling its gold, because it "felt more at home in Macao than in Hong Kong."[53]

In addition, after the Macao government liberated its casino industry in 2002, the entrance of large-scale American capital not only enhanced U.S. interests in this region but also raised American voices and concerns. Among the six casinos operating concessions granted by the Macao government, American capital occupies 41 percent, ranking first in the distributing structure of the concessions.[54] In fact, the United States has always been Macao's largest export market. But Macao–U.S. relations seemed insignificant until American companies including the Las Vegas Sands, Wynn Resorts, and MGM Mirage invested in Macao. In 2004, Sands Macao, the casino constructed by the Las Vegas Sands at a cost of US$240 million, opened and had a turnover of more than 10 million pataca within only ten hours. In the following forty-four days, its average daily profit was up to 4.16 million pataca, and the principal capital was recovered within less than nine months.[55] Later, the Venetian Macao Resort Hotel, opening in 2007, was another investment of Las Vegas Sands in Macao at a total cost of US$ 2.4 billion, and contains 3,000 suites, 111,000 m^2 of convention space, 149,000 m^2 of retail as well as an arena with 15,000 seats for entertainment events. The luxurious casinos and various entertainment services attracted visitors in the vicinity of Macao, and boosted the market share of the American casinos in this region. It is reported that there are about 600 billion RMB flowing out from the Chinese mainland to the American casinos in Macao every year.[56] At the same time, the market share of these American casinos has steadily increased year by year. In the first half of 2008, the market share of all the casinos invested by American companies, including Las Vegas Sands, Wynn Resorts, and MGM Mirage, has attained 61 percent, and the number of employees working in these casinos accounts for 60 percent of Macao's total employees in gaming industry.[57] In this context, the growing American capital has increased the concerns of the American government in this region. Washington is reported to have made a request to Beijing for the establishment of the consulate general in Macao, but the Chinese government has not declared its stands and really worries about the intervention of the United States into Macao's affairs on the pretext of protecting American interests.[58] In this sense, the BDA affair has more or less sounded the alarm to the Chinese government, since many analysts, including some governmental advisors, believe the timing and the motive of the American government to target BDA were suspicious.[59] Actually, according to David Asher, the former American senior official, although American investigations "point to almost every bank in Macao" and "the evidence of money laundering by the Macao branch of the Bank of China was 'voluminous,'"[60] the U.S. Treasury Department finally blacklisted only BDA instead of the larger banks in Macao in order to "avoid the excessive damage to the financial system of Macao and a resultant clash with China."[61]

In sum, it is reasonable to believe that Macao can play the role of diplomatic "experimental field" in China–U.S. relations. In other words, when the two countries face some uncertainty and complexity, they need to adjust to and accommodate each other. In this case, one small place like Macao can act as a go-between to solve complex or extraordinary issues, with the price acceptable for both sides.

Conclusion

The BDA affair reflects the subtle and complicated Sino–American relations, and demonstrated the advantage of the "one country, two systems" regulation on helping China handle relations with the United States. With pragmatic strategy, China may seek to cooperate with the United States in order to be further integrated into the U.S.-dominant world order and to benefit China's modernization on one hand. On the other hand, out of considerations for its own interests, China also developed relationships with some countries defined as evil by the United States. However, it is quite possible for China that this two-way strategy will bring both benefit and loss. Compared to U.S. institutional arrangements which can help Americans to realize their conflicting interests, the unitary nature of the Chinese political regime seems to be ineffective in achieving contradictory goals. In this regard, the "one country, two systems" operation, even though it originally was not planned for this kind of function, objectively makes up for the deficiency of the Chinese political regime, which enables China to enjoy more flexibility in the diplomacy. Moreover, under the "one country, two systems" regulation, Macao, compared with Hong Kong, has maintained a relatively smoother relationship with the central government and has played a special role in cross-strait relations, which makes it possible for Macao to act as a buffer between China and the United States in the sense that any dispute involving these two countries in Macao often can be resolved locally, thus avoiding a face-to-face confrontation between the two countries.

Meanwhile, it is also worth noting that other issues similar to the BDA affair may occur in the future, because of the expansion of American capital and the increase of American interests in this region. Therefore, it is necessary for both Macao and Beijing to draw lessons from the BDA affair. However, how Macao can play a more effective role on the Sino–U.S. relationship still deserves further study.

Notes

1. See Dick K. Nanto, "North Korean Counterfeiting of U.S. Currency," Congressional Research Service, June 12, 2009, www.fas.org/sgp/crs/row/RL33324.pdf (accessed October 10, 2009).

2. Wang Yan, "Hui Ye Ying Hang Yu Chao He De Nie Yuan" (The Evil Fate between Banco Delta Asia and North Korean Nuclear Issue), *China News Week*, no. 14, 2007: 50–51.

3. Reuters, "Action on Macao Bank May Hit Sino–U.S. Ties," February 17, 2006, article.wn.com/link/WNA17A5633A5FE69014AAAC106A3EEC50C97?source–templategenerator&template=macaopost/rs2.txt (accessed November 15, 2007).

4. These accounts encompass twenty North Korean banks, eleven North Korean trading companies, nine North Korean citizens, eight Macao-based companies doing business with North Korea and two Macao residents (Donald Greenlees and David Lague, "The Money Trail That Linked North Korea to Macao," *The New York Times*, April 11, 2007, www.nytimes.com/2007/04/11/world/asia/11cnd-macao.html?_r=1&oref=slogin (accessed November 20, 2007). Some of these accounts were speculated to belong to some top brass of DPRK and had even been kept secret from Kim Jong-Il, the imperator of North Korea. (Dick K. Nanto, "North Korean Counterfeiting of U.S. Currency," 10)

5. Ernest and Young, "Banco Delta Asia S.A.R.L Report to the Administrative Committee," December 16, 2005. media.mcclatchydc.com/smedia/2008/01/08/15/E_Y_Report_Redacted_1_.source.prod_affiliate.91.pdf (accessed October 10, 2009). See also Dick K. Nanto, "North Korean Counterfeiting of U.S. Currency," 12.

6. Ibid.

7. Dick K. Nanto, "North Korean Counterfeiting of U.S. Currency," 10.

8. John J. Tkacik, Jr., "Is China Complicit in North Korean Currency Counterfeiting?" The Heritage Foundation, April 20, 2006, www.heritage.org/Research/AsiaandthePacific/wm1046.cfm (accessed November 20, 2007)

9. David Lague and Donald Greenlees, "Squeeze on Banco Delta Asia Hit North Korea Where It Hurt," January 18, 2007, www.nytimes.com/2007/01/18/world/asia/18iht-north.4255039.html?_r=3&pagewanted=2 (accessed October 10, 2009).

10. Quoted from David Lague and Donald Greenlees, "Squeeze on Banco Delta Asia Hit North Korea Where It Hurt."

11. Wang Yan, "Hui Ye Ying Hang Yu Chao He De Nie Yuan" (The Evil Fate between Banco Delta Asia and North Korean Nuclear Issue), 51.

12. Sun Guanzhu, "'Wu He Kai Fang' Xiang Yao Cheng Gong, Xian Yao Jie Jue Zhong Guo De 'Chao Xian Bei Lun'" (To Make the Denuclearization and Opening Up Succeed, China's North Korean Paradox Should Be Resolved Firstly), *The Daily NK*, July 6, 2009, www.dailynk.com/chinese/read.php?cataId=nk00200&num=4300 (accessed October 20, 2009).

13. John McGlynn, "Banco Delta Asia, North Korea's Frozen Funds and U.S. Undermining of the Six Party Talks: Obstacles to a Solution," *Japan Focus*, June 9, 2007, www.japanfocus.org/-John-McGlynn/2446 (accessed October 10, 2009); Lee Jeong Hon, "Analysis: N. Korea's Macao funds," *United Press International*, April 24, 2007; and David Lague, "Macao Bank Challenges U.S. Ban as Politically Based," *The New York Times*, April 17, 2007, query.nytimes.com/gst/fullpage.html?res=9D0DE4D9113FF934A25757C0A9619C8B63 (accessed October 10, 2009).

14. "Prepared Remarks of Stuart Levey under Secretary for Terrorism and Financial Intelligence," U.S. Department of Treasury, HP-314, Mar. 14, 2007, www.treasury.gov/press/releases/hp86.htm (accessed November 20, 2007).

15. "Ruling on Macao Bank Unlikely to Derail North Korea Talks," State Department's Bureau of International Information Programs (IIP), March 15, 2007, www.america.gov/st/washfileenglish/2007/March/20070315182643zjsredna0.3443109.html (accessed October 10, 2009).

16. David Lague, "Bank Freeze Stalls North Korea Talks," *The New York Times*, March 22, 2007, www.nytimes.com/2007/03/22/world/asia/22cnd-korea.html?pagewanted=1 (accessed October 10, 2009).

17. "Treasury Statement on the Disposition of North Korea-Related Funds Frozen at Banco Delta Asia," Institute for Corean–American Studies (ICAS), March 21, 2007, www.icasinc.org/2007/2007l/2007ldlg.html (accessed October 10, 2009).

18. Ibid. See also "U.S. announces to release frozen fund of DPRK for humanitarian use," *Xinhua Net*, March 19, 2007, news.xinhuanet.com/english/2007-03/19/content_5866110.htm (accessed October 10, 2009).

19. "Bank of China Refused to Incept the Frozen Funds of North Korea," *Zaobao*, March 22, 2007, www.zaobao.com/special/newspapers/2007/03/hongkong070322h.html (November 20, 2007).

20. Anna Fifield, "North Korea may get back cash—at a price," *Financial Times*, May 16, 2007, www.ft.com/cms/s/1cd01926-03cf-11dc-a931-000b5df10621.html (accessed November 20, 2007).

21. "North Korea Confirms Fund Dispute Resolved," *The Financial Times*, June 25, 2007, us.ft.com/ftgateway/superpage.ft?news_id=fto062520070526481576&page=1 (accessed November 20, 2007).

22. Donald Greenlees, "Blacklisted Bank to Return to Original Owner," *The New York Times*, September 29, 2007, www.nytimes.com/2007/09/29/world/asia/29bank_web.html?ex=1348718400&en=e614e1ee340e9c06&ei=5124&partner=permalink&exprod=permalinkNo (accessed October 10, 2009).

23. He Xingqiang, "North Korean Nuclear Issue in Sino–American Relations: A Chinese Perspective," www.kida.re.kr/data/2007/10/18/3(%ED%97%88%EC%8B%B1%EC%B0%BD).pdf (accessed November 20, 2007).

24. Liu Songjie, "Bei Han Ren Zai Ao Men" (North Koreans in Macao), *Phoenix Weekly*, no. 12, May 30, 2007, big5.ifeng.com/gate/big5/www.ifeng.com/phoenixtv/73020791993663488/20070530/908192.shtml (accessed October 10, 2009); John Ruwitch, "Mr. Kim of Macao? North Korea's Family Mystery Deepens," Reuters, February 8, 2007, www.reuters.com/article/topNews/idUSHKG33402620070208?pageNumber=1&virtualBrandChannel=0 (accessed October 10, 2009); Barbara Demick, "No more gambling on North Korea," *Los Angles Times*, April 6, 2006, www.latimes.com/news/printedition/la-fg-macao6apr06,1,5374376,print.story?ctrack=2&cset=true (accessed November 20, 2007).

25. David Lague and Donald Greenlees, "Squeeze on Banco Delta Asia Hit North Korea Where It Hurt."

26. Wang Yan, "Hui Ye Ying Hang Yu Chao He De Nie Yuan" (The Evil Fate between Banco Delta Asia and North Korean Nuclear Issue), 51.

27. Bertil Lintner, "Tunnels, Guns and Kimchi: North Korea's Quest for Dollars—Part II," *Yale Global*, June 11, 2009, yaleglobal.yale.edu/content/NK-quest-for-dollars-part2 (accessed October 10, 2009).

28. Liu Songjie, "Bei Han Ren Zai Ao Men" (North Koreans in Macao).

29. Tim Johnson, "Macao Tycoon Wants His Bank Back," *McClatchy Newspaper*, July 6, 2007, www.mcclatchydc.com/227/story/17620.html (accessed October 10, 2009).

30. Ibid.

31. Ibid. See also Liu Songjie, "Shen Mi De Hui Ye Yin Hang" (Mysterious Banco Delta Asia), *Phoenix Weekly*, no. 12, May 30, 2007, big5.ifeng.com/gate/big5/www.ifeng.com/phoenixtv/73020791993663488/20070530/908191.shtml (accessed October 10, 2009).

32. Ji Shuoming, "Mei Guo Shi Li Ao Men Jue Qi Bei Jing Pai Yuan Diao Cha Ying Bian" (The American Forces Emerge in Macao, Beijing Sends Out for Investigation), *Asia Weekly*, vol. 19, no. 46, November 13, 2005, www.yzzk.com/cfm/Content_Archive.cfm?Channel=ae&Path=2203390622/46ae1a.cfm (accessed October 10, 2009).

33. Ibid. See also Tim Johnson, "Macao Tycoon Wants His Bank Back."

34. Rosemary Foot, "Chinese Strategies in a U.S.–hegemonic Global Order: Accommodating and Hedging," *International Affairs*, vol. 82, no. 1 (2006): 93. Shi Yinhong, a Chinese scholar, also put forward similar opinions on China's diplomatic

strategies named as "Dual Contact-Balance" (shuang chong lian xi zhi yue). See Shi Yinhong, "The Fifteen Years of China's American Foreign Policy and Strategies: Evolution, Experiences, and Problems" (zhong guo dui mei wai jiao he zhan lue shi wu nian: yan hua guo cheng, ji ben jing yan he shang cun wen ti), in Shi Yinhong, *International Politics and Statecraft (guo ji zheng zhi yu guo jia fang lue)* (Beijing: Peking University Press, 2006), 214.

35. Liu Songjie, "Bei Han Ren Zai Ao Men" (North Koreans in Macao).

36. John J. Tkacik, Jr., "Is China Complicit in North Korean Currency Counterfeiting?"

37. Li Heyuan, "Bei Han Mao Yi Ju Dian Cong Ao Men Yi Zhi Ma Lai Xi Ya" (North Kean's Mercantile Beachhead Shifted to Malaysia), *The Chosun Ilbo*, July 15, 2009, chn.chosun.com/big5/site/data/html_dir/2009/07/15/20090715000013.html (accessed October 10, 2009).

38. "China Expressed Deep Regret on the U.S. ruling against Banco Delta Asia," *Xinhua Net*, March 15, 2007, big5.xinhuanet.com/gate/big5/news.xinhuanet.com/world/2007-03/15/content_5852456.htm (accessed November 20, 2007).

39. Donald Greenlees and David Lague, "The Money Trail That Linked North Korea to Macao."

40. Daniel Dombey, and Demetri Sevastopulo, "U.S. Talks Tough on North Korea," *Financial Times*, June 8, 2009, www.ftchinese.com/story/001026868/en (accessed October 10, 2009).

41. See Yufan Hao, *Dilemma and Decision: An Organizational Perspective on American China Policy Making* (Berkeley: Institute of East Asian Studies, University of California, 1997).

42. Quoted from Jayshree Bajoria, "The China–North Korea Relationship," Council on Foreign Relations, July 21, 2009, www.cfr.org/publication/11097/#p5 (accessed October 10, 2009).

43. Jayshree Bajoria, "The China–North Korea Relationship."

44. Donald Greenlees and David Lague, "The Money Trail That Linked North Korea to Macao."

45. Guo Jianqing, "Xin Shi Ji De Ao Tai Guan Xi Jiang Jin Yi Bu Cu Jin Liang An Guan Xi De Fa Zhan" (The Macao–Taiwan Relationship in New Century Will Help Bolster The Cross-Strait Relations), China Internet Information Center, August 10, 2001, ganzhi.china.com.cn/chinese/TCC/haixia/50161.htm (accessed October 10, 2009).

46. Yong Yi, "Chong Fen Fa Hui Ao Men Zai Liang An Guan Xi Zhong De Te Shu Zuo Yong" (Fully Play Macao's Special Role in Cross-Strait Relations), *Journal San Wa Ou*, July 17, 18, 19, 2003, www.waou.com.mo/wa/2003/07/20030717a.htm, www.waou.com.mo/wa/2003/07/20030718a.htm, www.waou.com.mo/wa/2003/07/20030719a.htm (accessed October 10, 2009).

47. "Macao Return Brings Opportunity," *Taiwan Aujourd'hui*, December 24, 1999, taiwanauj.nat.gov.tw/ct.asp?xItem=17708&CtNode=122 (accessed October 10, 2009).

48. "Taiwan Changed the Name of Its Office in Macao," *BBC Chinese Net*, December 27, 1999, news.bbc.co.uk/chinese/simp/hi/newsid_570000/newsid_579900/579932.stm (accessed October 10, 2009).

49. Deborah Kuo, "Macao Urged to Set Up Liaison Office in Taiwan," *The China Post*, July 27, 2009, www.chinapost.com.tw/china/local-news/macao/2009/07/27/218002/Macao-urged.htm (accessed October 10, 2009).

50. "The Development of Macao–Taiwan Relations and the Changes of Hong Kong–Taiwan Relations," China Internet Information Center, July 6, 2007, big5.china.com.cn/overseas/zhuanti/xgtwgx/2007-07/06/content_8488367.htm (accessed November 23, 2007).

51. Liu Songjie, "Bei Han Ren Zai Ao Men" (North Koreans in Macao).

52. Liu Songjie, "Shen Mi De Hui Ye Yin Hang" (Mysterious Banco Delta Asia). See also Ricardo Pinto, "Special Report: Korea Meltdown," *Macao Business*, August 1, 2006, www.macaobusiness.com/index.php?id=539 (accessed November 20, 2007).

53. Ibid.

54. Wang Wuyi, "Ao Men Bo Cai Ye Fa Zhan" (Macao's Gaming Industry), in Hao Yufan and Wu Zhiliang, eds., *Blue Book of Macao: Annual Report on Economy and Society of Macao 2008–2009* (Beijing: China Social Sciences Academic Press, 2009), 45.

55. Chen Xuefeng, "Huo Xi? Fu Xi? Mei Zi Zheng Zai Kong Zhi Ao Men Du Ye" (Bad Fortune? Good Fortune? American Capital Is Controlling Macao's Gaming Industry), *Kan Shi Jie (World View)*, no. 23, December 2007, www.gotoread.com/s/e/?vo=6576&p=20 (accessed Oct. 10, 2009).

56. Ibid.

57. Yu Xiaoli, "Mei Zi Mou Qiu Kong Zhi Ao Men" (The American Capital Seeks to Control Macao), *World News Journal*, January 23, 2009, gb.cri.cn/12764/2009/01/23/145s2406043.htm (accessed October 10, 2009).

58. Ibid.

59. Ibid.

60. Donald Greenlees and David Lague, "How a U.S. Inquiry Held up the North Korea Peace Talks," *The New York Times*, April 11, 2007, www.nytimes.com/2007/04/11/world/asia/11iht-bank.4.5238231.html (accessed October 10, 2009).

61. Donald Greenlees and David Lague, "The Money Trail That Linked North Korea to Macao."

CHAPTER ELEVEN

Macao's Unique Role in Cross-Straits Relations

Jianwei Wang

As a small enclave, Macao's role in "big" domestic and international events and development is often neglected or downplayed. Compared to Hong Kong, international media's coverage of Macao is almost non-existent. However, in recent years, an obscure Macao bank's role in the inflammatory North Korean nuclear crisis suddenly brought Macao to the forefront of the world's attention. By the same token, although Macao probably is not a major player in the political game between Beijing and Taipei, it nevertheless occupies a quiet but unique position in cross-strait relations, which has always been the most critical issue in U.S.–China relations.

This chapter intends to take a preliminary look at some trends in the post-1999 Macao–Taiwan relations and the unique and even indispensable role Macao has played in cross-strait relations. The main proposition is that different from Hong Kong which often encountered difficulties in its relations with Taiwan after the handover, Macao's usefulness in cross-strait relations actually has been enhanced rather then weakened after 1999. In a sense, the practice of "one country, two systems" in Macao serves both as a window to showcase this bold initiative as well as a facilitator in promoting cross-strait relations in an interesting way.

Macao Connection

Historically Macao's relations with Taiwan were much closer compared to Hong Kong. The contact between Macao and Taiwan initiated and engaged by both Chinese and Westerners could be traced back to the sixteenth and seventeenth centuries. The Hokkien Chinese from the southern part of China's Fujian province migrated to both Taiwan and Macao around that period of time. They shared the same local dialect and many cultural customs and maintained close ties with each other even since.

After the establishment of People's Republic of China, for long time Portugal maintained official relations with the KMT government in Taiwan and therefore the Macao government allowed Taiwan's official diplomatic presence in Macao and protected pro-Taiwan forces and activities. Particularly after Great Britain recognized PRC in 1950, the KMT government moved its diplomatic mission to Macao and intensified its effort to build Macao into an anti-communist base to collect information about China and to penetrate and subvert the communist control in the mainland. Taiwan's intelligence agency had extensive presence in Macao and pro-Taiwan organizations and associations were also supported and cultivated.[1] In 1965, the Chinese government protested against Taiwan's intelligence activities in Macao, the Portuguese authorities had to close Taiwan's diplomatic missions in Macao.[2]

The Macao–Taiwan relations were also influenced by the politics within the mainland China. In the late 1960s, influenced by the political upheavals of the Cultural Revolution in China, the pro-Beijing forces in Macao launched the "December 3rd" uprising in 1966 and forced the Portuguese authorities to drive out all the Taiwanese institutions, associations, and officials. In 1975, Portugal switched diplomatic recognition from Taiwan to Beijing and began to improve its relations with China. The Portuguese authorities in Macao banned all activities by the Taiwanese intelligence and pro-Taiwan organizations against China in the enclave. As a result of all these developments, Macao–Taiwan relations had been completely cut for more than twenty years.

By the late 1980s, Beijing softened its hard-line policy toward Taiwan and declared the policy of "peaceful unification." In the meantime, Taiwan's leader Chiang Ching-guo made a decision to allow Taiwanese to go back to the mainland to visit their separate families and relatives. Under such new circumstances, without objections from China, the Macao government allowed Taiwanese to stay in Macao for twenty days without visa.[3] Taiwanese businessmen gradually returned to Macao and pro-Taiwan groups resumed their activities there. In 1990 Taiwanese authorities set up the Taipei Trade and Tourism Office in Macao formally re-establishing its official representation.[4] Since then, private economic and cultural exchanges between citizens of the two localities have been quickly expanded. Taiwan's universities, foundations, and civil societies established wide-ranging contact with their counterparts in Macao. Starting from 1995, the annul conference on Macao–Taiwan relations began to be held in Macao and Taipei alternately. Religiously Macao and Taiwan also maintained very close ties. People in both places share the same belief in the Goddess Matsu of the Sea. In recent years, the Macao government holds annual cultural and tourist festival of Matsu and thousands from Taiwan go to Macao to participate in the festival.[5]

Thanks to the flexible policy of the Macao government, Taiwanese could enter Macao without visas and Macao also serves as a transit point for further trips to mainland China. Taiwan is also lenient to Macao residents visiting Taiwan. Many Macao youngsters go to Taiwan to receive higher education. The Taiwan government takes this very seriously. The concerned agencies have established various scholarships to attract the Macao students and hold school fairs in Macao every year attracting thousands of high school students, parents, and people of all walks of life. The students who applied for universities in Taiwan increased from six hundred in 1990 to five thousand in 2000.[6] Many of the graduates come back to Macao to work in various occupations including the government thus providing a bank of talents who understand Taiwan better and therefore are better suited to managing Macao's relations with Taiwan.

A sizable Macanese laborers find jobs in Taiwan. Some 20,000 people from Macao were working in Taiwan before the handover.[7] Although there are few direct Taiwan investors in Macao, Taiwanese businessman often use Macao as a springboard to invest in Zhuhai, Zhongshan, and other cities in western Guangdong. Particularly after the Macao–Taiwan air link became operational, about 800,000–900,000 Taiwanese went to Macao to do either tours or business every year.[8] The human traffic was not just limited to ordinary people. Many high-level Taiwanese officials, including the vice president, director of the Mainland Affairs Council, visited Macao before the transfer of political power in Macao in 1999.[9]

According to the statistics by Taiwan's Mainland Affairs Council, before the handover of Macao to China, the socioeconomic and cultural relations between the two places had become quite close and dense. Some 6,000 students went to Taiwan to study in the ten years before the handover, while more than 30,000 Macao residents worked in Taiwan, making up 7 percent of the total 430,000 population. Since the start of the air links in 1995, Macao became the second mid-way stop for travelers between the two sides of the Taiwan Strait, next only to Hong Kong. In 1997, more than 900,000 travelers flew to Macao. In 1998, 54.77 percent of all travelers arriving in Macao came from Taiwan. Macao also acted as a magnet for Taiwanese investment in mainland areas surrounding Macao with 315 Taiwanese factories and companies located in Zhuhai and another 400 in Zhongshan and nearby counties in China's Guandong province. The bilateral trade had also risen from merely $97 million to $360 million in 1998. Taiwan was the fourth-largest trading partner of Macao in Asia.[10]

Macao Formula

For all these and other reasons, before the handover in 1999, authorities on both sides of the Taiwan Straits were aware of Macao's uniqueness in cross-strait relations and made efforts to work out a post-1999 formula that could maintain the special status of this mini island in cross-strait relations. From the very beginning, both Taipei and Beijing seemed to be more flexible and less political in their policy toward Macao.

In 1995 Chinese President Jiang Zemin issued a landmark eight-point proposal on Taiwan policy in which he systematically laid out the basic ideas of the Chinese leadership in resolving the Taiwan issue and proposed to hold negotiations with Taiwan to end the state of hostility between the two sides under the principle of "one China" and to realize China's peaceful unification.[11] As a response to Jiang Zemin's proposal, then Taiwan President Lee Tung-hui came up with a six-point proposal[12] in which he particularly mentioned that both sides across the Taiwan Straits should jointly safeguard prosperity and promote democracy in Hong Kong and Macao. In that proposal he acknowledged that Hong Kong and Macao are integral parts of the Chinese nation and Taiwan would maintain normal relations with, participate in affairs related to both of them, and provide better services to compatriots there after the handover. Lee's proposal also emphasized the important role that Hong Kong and Macao could play in cross-strait relations as the "transit points" between the mainland and Taiwan. More specifically, Taiwan promulgated regulations to manage its relations with Hong Kong and Macao in 1997.[13] Taipei decided to treat Macao as a "special area" or "third place" different from the mainland and not to limit the Taiwanese people's freedom to visit Macao after the handover. The government mission would also remain in Macao after it was returned to the mainland.

On the mainland side, Beijing also adopted a more flexible and pragmatic formula in handling the post-19999 Macao–Taiwan relations. In 1999, on the eve of Macao's handover, Chinese Vice Premier Qian Qishen announced "seven articles" regarding post-1999 Macao's relations with Taiwan.[14] In the articles, he stipulated that the Macao SAR's various official relations with Taiwan could continue after 1999 upon the approval of the central government. All Taiwanese institutions could stay in Macao under "proper" names.

The economic, cultural, and other functional private exchanges between Macao and Taiwan would experience no change. Taiwanese visitors could enter Macao according to the local laws and regulations, basically meaning that the visa-free policy for the Taiwanese visitors would remain intact. The air and sea links between Taiwan and Macao could also continue to operate as "regional special lines."

In sum, both sides were willing to assign Macao a special position in the post-1999 cross-strait relations. Chinese Taiwan affairs officials reiterated this intention many times after the 1999 transition and took concrete measures to illustrate that point. In early 2002, mainland China's semi-official Association for Relations across the Taiwan Strait (ARATS) set an office in Macao. This is the first office ARATS ever created outside of mainland China. ARATS officials explained that the reason for setting up such an office in Macao was to provide better services to the visitors from Taiwan who enjoy visa-free entries to Macao and come in large number producing more practical issues that need expeditious care. It is also a channel to maintain communications with various political parties in Taiwan. More important they point out that Macao's relationship with Taiwan is a special part of cross-straits relations after its turnover to China in 1999. Macao can play special roles and influence in cross-strait relations.[15] After the ARATS set up its office in Taiwan, Taiwan's Mainland Affairs Council discussed several times to set an office of SEF (Strait Exchanges Foundation)—ARATS's counterpart—in Macao as well. The purpose of that is to facilitate informal contacts and meetings between political leaders from both sides under the name of "inspecting the office work." So far it has not happened yet. If it does, that will be another breakthrough in cross-strait relations.[16]

Due to the practical and goodwill policy of both sides, Macao–Taiwan relations in various areas have grown rather than shrank after the turnover. For instance, the number of Taiwanese tourists to visit Macao increased 33.4 percent in 2000 compared to 1999, the year Macao was changed hands.[17] The scale and number of exchange activities and events between the two sides had increased annually from about 30 immediately after the turnover to about 200 in 2008. Most of these events took place in Macao. Civilian visits have also become more active. From 2002 to 2007, on average about 20,000 tourists from Macao visited Taiwan and the number reached more than 30,000 in 2008. The number of high school graduates going to Taiwan to attend college and universities has increased from 197 in 2000 to more than 1,000 in 2009. Currently there are more than 3,000 Macao students studying in Taiwan. Trade and other economic relations maintained a momentum too. In terms of bilateral trade, the Macao–Taiwan trade increased 2.7 times in

2000 compared to 1999, reaching 2.6 billion PTC (Macao dollars). The Taiwanese side enjoyed a huge surplus of 1.7 billion.[18] While Macao's trade only occupies a very small fraction in Taiwan's foreign trade, Taiwan is a big factor in Macao's tourist business. Since the handover, the bilateral trade had maintained at a level of about $300 million and reached $435 million in 2008.[19] Between 2002 and 2004, Macao Airline's cargo transportation reached 114 flights every week. Macao also became the window and platform for Taiwan to introduce and promote its featured local products to the mainland.[20] As mentioned earlier, before the handover, Taiwan business established 315 Taiwanese factories and companies located in Zhuhai and another 400 in Zhongshan and nearby counties in China's Guandong province. By the end of 2000, however, Taiwan businessmen set about 1,500 factories in the western Guangdong province with $1 billion investment.[21] Thanks to the smooth development of Macao–Taiwan relations, the Taiwanese authorities in their annual reviews of the situation in Hong Kong and Macao tend to have more positive evaluation of Macao and Macao–Taiwan relations compared to Hong Kong.[22] In terms of Taiwan's relations with Hong Kong and Macao, it can be said that in certain functions, Macao replaced Hong Kong after the handover.

Macao Model

The more cooperative and flexible spirits between Beijing and Macao before Macao's return to China was exemplified in negotiating the air link between Macao and Taiwan in 1995. The negotiation was conducted with the endorsement from the Portugal government in Macao at that time. Initially the Taiwanese side wondered if the negotiation was worthwhile as Taipei was not sure if the agreement on the air link could survive the 1999 handover due to possible political difficulties. But Beijing demonstrated enough goodwill and flexibility on the issue and expressed its willingness to strike a deal with Taiwan. Because there was no formal official channels between the two sides, Beijing suggested that the negotiation should be carried out by private airlines and the government should not be directly involved. But in practice, government officials from both sides participated in the negotiations. The key issue was whether the Air Macao plane could fly all the way from Taiwan to Macao and then to Beijing or Shanghai without changing flight or aircraft. Initially Taipei was concerned as it could be interpreted as a sort of direct flight across straits, which was a violation of the Taipei's official policy of three "nos" at that time. But eventually Taipei accepted the scheme suggested by Beijing that the problem could be resolved by changing the flight number without changing flight.[23] So this practice of no flight-changing practice for onward travel to Mainland China from the same flight originating from Taiwan was considered no trivial breakthrough in cross-straits exchanges as it actually is a kind of "indirect direct flight" between Taiwan and China.[24] The air link agreement has made Macao the second air hub after Hong Kong for travelers to Mainland China from Taiwan. This successful experiment of "one aircraft all through" was late dubbed the "Air Macao model."

The establishment of the direct air route between Macao and Taiwan greatly facilitated the civilian exchanges between the two places. According to Taiwan's statistics, before the opening of the Macao–Taiwan air link in 1995, Taiwanese travelers to Macao were numbered less than 16,000. After the air link was put into operation, the number of travelers to or through Macao rapidly increased. The total number of passengers in 1996 alone was 4.4 times more than the accumulated figure between 1986 and 1995 added together.[25] Another study shows that before the opening of the air link, the highest figure for the Taiwanese to visit Macao was 15,000 in 1995. This figure jumped to 300,000 in 1996, more than 1 million in 2000, and reached 1.271 million in 2002.[26] The "one aircraft all through" and inexpensive airfare were the main attractions to Taiwanese tourists and business people. Many Taiwanese in the past went to the mainland via Hong Kong and now they preferred Macao instead. Therefore, before the realization of "three direct links" between Taiwan and the mainland in 2009, Macao, together with Hong Kong, remained the two major transit hubs for the Taiwanese traveling to Mainland China.[27]

The significance of this model went beyond Macao–Taiwan relations. It sets an example for the Hong Kong–Taiwan negotiation on the post-1997 air link in 1995 and 1996, resulting in similar "indirect direct flight."[28] Moreover, it also laid down a foundation for broader cross-strait consultations and negotiations on broader functional issues under the condition of no official contact between the two sides. After President Chen took office in 2000, no official contact was assumed between the two sides because of the political stalemate on the issue of "one China." Even semi-official bodies such as SEF and ARATS suspended their contact. In the meantime, however, the demand and pressure for "three links (direct postal, airline, and trade links)" and other functional exchanges were fast growing in both the Mainland and Taiwan, particularly when a large number of Taiwanese began to work and live in the Mainland. Beijing did not want to have any official contact with the Chen government. On the other hand, to win the heart and soul of the Taiwanese population it did hope to see some progress made to facilitate the flow of people back and forth between the two sides. Under such circumstances, the "Air Macao model" was rediscovered and Macao was once again picked up as an ideal place for the experiment of low-profile and semi-official negotiations on functional issues between the two sides.

In January 2005, after a brief discussion of merely two hours between the civil aviation organizations from both sides in a small conference room in a Macao hotel, a historical agreement was reached to temporarily lift a ban on direct flights across the Taiwan Straits to allow charter flights during the Chinese Lunar Year in 2005, which facilitated the reunion of families of those Taiwanese who live in the mainland. This deal broke the fifty-six year history of no direct air flight between the two sides across the Taiwan Straits.[29]

The negotiation on chart flights in Macao was conducted between private Mainland China and Taiwan organizations with middle-level governmental officials from relevant departments involved in their non-government capacity. No formal document was signed and there was only a memorandum of consensus which was brought home by the negotiators. Upon the approval from the respective authority, the memorandum was implemented by the concerned parties on both sides. No government officials from the State Council's Taiwan Affairs Office, ARATS on the mainland side and from Mainland Affairs Council and SEF were present. Chinese officials even did not want to call it "negotiation" but rather used the word of "communication."[30] Such a practice was later called a "Macao model." The "Macao model" opened the door for the both sides to engage in direct negotiations on cross-strait functional issues without formal official contact. After the successful experiment of this model, Chinese officials asked for the application of the same model in the consultation on cross-strait passengers and cargo charter flights and the issue of allowing mainland tourists to visit Taiwan. At the CPC–KMT economic forum held in April 2006, both sides agreed that the talks on all functional issues involving finance, agriculture, and tourism should be conducted according to the "Macao model."[31] The recently signed cross-strait financial MOU was also negotiated and signed according to the "Macao model."

Macao Approach

As discussed earlier, because of the flexibility of the "Macao formula" in handling the transition of Macao from a Portuguese colony to a PRC Special Administrative Region (SAR), the economic, cultural, and other functional relations between Macao and Taiwan were not adversely affected by the handover. Instead these socioeconomic and cultural ties obtained new momentum. In terms of broader cross-strait relations, Macao operates as a special bridge between the Chinese mainland and Taiwan for economic and trade relations. The direct air route linking Macao with Taiwan is very economic for Taiwanese investors. They can reach Zhuhai or Zhongshan from Kaohsiung or Taipei within a matter of just a few hours. Macao can also assist in attracting capital, new technologies, new management skills- and business-related information from Taiwan to the Pearl River Delta in many other ways as it, as the SAR, enjoys many special policies for economic and trade ties between Macao–Taiwan from the central government. Many Taiwanese business people have expanded their operations into the mainland via Macao because of the Special Administrative Region's unique location and highly beneficial position as a connection between different economic areas.[32]

But more remarkably for Macao is that its official relations with Taiwan have not just survived, but also strengthened after the 1999 transition. I would argue this is not just good for Macao, but also beneficial to cross-strait relations in general. Under the guidance of Qian's "seven articles," the Macao SAR handled its political and official relations with Taiwan quite pragmatically and skillfully. As a result, the more relaxed and cordial relationship between the Macao SAR government and the Taiwan authorities is in contrast to the often rocky political relations between Hong Kong and Taiwan. After the handover, although the name of Taiwan's official mission was changed into "Taipei Economic and Cultural Center" without official color, its function has not reduced but expanded. For example, the Taipei Economic and Cultural Center began to accept applications of Taiwan visas from Macao residents and foreigners and to issue entry visas to them in early 2002. It could also handle issuing and changing tourist visas of the mainland residents visiting Taiwan. [33]

The various sections of the Economic and Cultural Center could also directly contact the corresponding functional agencies and departments in the SAR government, therefore various issues involving Taiwanese visitors in Macao could be resolved in real time. This is also more convenient than the situation before the handover. For the same purpose, the functional departments of the Macao SAR also maintain direct contact and relations with their counterparts in the Taiwanese government in Taipei. These functions do not exist for Taiwan's similar agencies in Hong Kong. That is why one veteran observer of Macao–Taiwan relations describes Taiwan's representation in Macao before the handover as "having a name without substance" and that after the handover as "having substance without name."[34]

The personal contact between Taiwanese officials and Macao officials is also more institutionalized. Even the mainland officials from the liaison office of the central government in Macao could informally meet Taiwanese officials from Taipei Economic and Cultural Center on social occasions. In the meantime, in recent years the officials from the Macao SAR also went to visit Taiwan to meet their counterparts to consult on various issues.[35] In recent years, the officials of the Liaison Office of the Central People's Government in the Macao SAR began to visit Taiwan and the number of visits and the level of ranking of these officials have increased.[36]

Macao's entry permission policy for officials and politicians from Taiwan is also more relaxed and nuanced. High-ranking Taiwanese current officials from time to time were allowed to visit Macao in private capacities. For example, the vice chairman of Taiwan's Mainland Affairs Council, Chen Mingtong, was permitted to visit Macao in December 2000 to attend a conference as a "university professor." Other former senior Taiwanese officials could also visit Macao without much difficulty.[37] It is also interesting to note that because of its more relaxed entry policy, many Taiwanese political figures who had difficulty entering China via Hong Kong often ended up visiting the mainland via Macao. Unlike in Hong Kong–Taiwan relations, one seldom hears the story that someone from Taiwan was denied an entry to Macao.[38] This is probably another special role Macao has played in promoting cross-straits personnel changes.

The "regime change" in Taiwan in 2000 immediately after the turnover did not disrupt Macao–Taiwan relations as a lot of people originally feared. Chief Executive Edmund Ho Hau-wah wisely remained silent on Chen Shui-biang's election as the president of Taiwan, and the SAR government tried not to get involved in the bitter quarrel between Beijing and Taipei. Instead it continued to cultivate the functional cooperation between Macao and Taiwan. For example, Macao's SAR government worked together well with Taiwan in the cooperative prevention of the SARS virus and mutual assistance in judicial cases.[39]

These sensible and pragmatic practices by the Macao government in dealing with the Taiwanese authorities walk a very fine line here to draw a delicate balance between the imperatives of "one country" and "two systems" on this very sensitive issue. In a sense, what Macao has achieved so far is also beneficial to cross-strait relations in the long run as it helps more convincingly demonstrate the effectiveness and attractiveness of the "one country, two systems" formula by showing that Macao's way of doing things could be different from Beijing even on an issue like Taiwan.

Macao's Historical Opportunity and Challenges Ahead

The above brief analysis of Macao's relations with Taiwan after its return to China has demonstrated that this small island does have a larger role to play in cross-strait relations. Both Beijing and Taipei seemed to be willing to give Macao a little bit more space to maneuver. The Macao SAR government on the other hand has also utilized its special position well to maximize its interest and influence. In a sense, the stalled political relations between Beijing and Taipei after Chen Shui-biang came to power also provided an opportunity for Macao to play a role as a "third place" where semi-official consultation and negotiations could be quietly carried out. Macao's traditional non-political profile also gave it some advantages that Hong Kong does not have so far as its relations with Taiwan are concerned. As some analysts pointed out, Macao's political ecology is much less complicated than Hong Kong's. Macao does not have strong pro-democracy opposition political forces as Hong Kong does. Although Macao's international ties have been strengthened after the handover, the foreign influence in this enclave is still far weaker compared to Hong Kong. For these reasons, Beijing is far more worried that things may get out of control in Hong Kong than in Macao. As a result it is willing to give Macao more autonomy in handling Taiwan affairs while more reluctant to give Hong Kong the same freedom for fear of the unpredictable political fallout.[40] In short, the Macao model, no matter how limited it is, cracked a door on the otherwise seamless political stonewall between the two sides before 2008, although whether and when this door will be used still pretty much depends upon the political will of the leaders in Beijing and Taipei. When the political climate in cross-strait relations changes for the worse, the "Macao model" is unlikely to reverse the overall negative trend. The sluggish negotiations on passenger and cargo charter flights and tourist issues after Chen Shui-bian trumpeted the referendum on UN bid under name of Taiwan in 2007 demonstrated quite clearly that the application of "Macao model" is still contingent upon the macropolitical atmosphere across the Taiwan Straits.

Overall, however, Beijing's leadership is very positive about Macao's role in cross-strait relations. Wang Yi, director of Taiwan Affair Office of the State Council, at a symposium to commemorate the ten years of Macao–Taiwan relations after Macao's turnover in October 2009, summarized Macao's unique role and function in cross-strait relations.[41] First, Macao plays a role of pioneering exploration. For example, the negotiation on the Macao–Taiwan air link created a Macao model to handle functional affairs by private entities under the principle of "one China." Second, Macao plays the role of bridge to connect two shores of the Taiwan Straits. For many years, Taiwan has maintained its status as the third-largest destination for Taiwan travelers with millions of Taiwanese taking Macao as a transit to travel between the mainland and Taiwan. Third, Macao plays a role to promote unification against Taiwan independence. The rank and file in Macao support China's peaceful reunification and oppose Taiwan's independence, strengthening the mainstream public opinion for peaceful development across the Taiwan Straits. Finally Macao also serves as an example for China's formula of "one country, two systems." Macao's economic prosperity and political stability after the turnover to China can influence the Taiwanese opinion on this formula and facilitate mutual understanding of people across the Taiwan Straits.

Macao's new chief executive Chui Sai On echoed Wang Yi's opinion. He argued that Macao has the prerequisite to promote Macao–Taiwan relations and should contribute to the peaceful unification of the motherland. He made four suggestions to help promote Macao–Taiwan relations: first, to enhance exchange and co-operation between Macao and Taiwan; second, to promote-cooperation between Macao and Taiwan in the areas of business, tourism, convention and exhibition, culture, education, and creative industry; third, to serve as a services and business platform for Taiwan enterprises and its people; and finally, to study methods and mechanism to enhance Macao–Taiwan relations, based on the principle of "one country, two systems."[42]

These remarks indicate that Beijing wants Macao to continue to serve useful and special functions in cross-strait relations while the Macao SAR government is equally willing to do so. Both the Mainland and Macao leaders emphasize that Macao–Taiwan relations are facing new opportunities. Needless to say, after the political power transition in Taiwan in 2008, the circumstances under which Macao plays its role in cross-strait relations has significantly changed. It provides opportunities as well as challenges to Macao. On the one hand, the rapid improvement in cross-strait relations does provide a more favorable macropolitical atmosphere for Macao–Taiwan relations. The increase of non-governmental exchanges between the two places since the thaw of cross-strait relation in 2008 mentioned earlier seems to suggest this trend. Beijing may allow more political freedom and flexibility for Macao to further explore its ties with Taiwan to a higher level. By the same token, the Taiwan authorities are also more willing to use Macao to test the water for new initiatives and to start implementing already-reached deals between the two sides because of Macao's favorable geopolitical conditions. For example, Macao and Taiwan have had judicial cooperation through private channels for a long time. After the third round of talks between semi-official mainland-based ARATS and SEF reached a formal agreement on cross-strait mutual assistance in cracking down on crimes in April 2009, Taiwanese justice and criminal authorities suggested, first, that a criminal liaison office be set up in Macao to implement the agreement by exchanging intelligence on crime and jointly cracking down on crimes. Scholars suggested that the Macao government could actively respond to such initiatives and help institutionalize judicial and criminal exchanges across the Taiwan Straits.[43]

Moreover, some observers even suggest that Macao can provide a platform for the future political negotiations and dialogues across-Taiwan Straits. It has some advantages in this respect. Among other things, it is very easy to enter Macao without being noticed. Unlike Hong Kong, Macao is normally not under the spotlights of international media, inductive to quiet and unofficial exchange of views and dialogues on sensitive political issues. Macao could start with mutual visits of political figures on both sides and explore the feasibility of setting up official representation in the other side.[44] They point out that with the solidifying and growing Macao–Taiwan relations, it is time to normalize official relations between Macao and Taiwan. Macao could consider establishing an official representative office in Taiwan, which has been long been called for by the Taiwanese side. While it is not easy to do so, it is still worth trying given the overall development of cross-strait relations.[45] These and other similar ideas are somehow endorsed by Chinese officials. One senior Chinese Taiwan affairs official stationed in Macao commented that there is a mutual trust between Macao and Taiwan. Macao could cultivate that trust to help promote cross-strait mutual trust. Macao can also use its special environment to provide a platform for both sides to tackle some complex and sensitive issues. He encouraged the Macao government to explore how to regularize and institutionalize Macao–Taiwan communication channels, including setting up an office in Taiwan under proper names.[46]

As both Wang Yi and Chui Sai On mentioned in their remarks, Beijing also intends to use Macao as a display window to sell the formula of "one country, two systems" to Taiwan and as a venue to promote China's unification in the long run. In December 2006, the little tiny Macao hosted a large scale global rally of overseas Chinese calling for China's peaceful unification with more than 1,200 representatives from fifty countries all over the world attending. It is unusual for such a small enclave to hold such a big convention. The intention behind the event, according to the local media, was to use Macao as a living case to demonstrate that the practice of "one country, two systems" has been successful in Macao and people in Macao enjoy a high degree of political autonomy and economic prosperity.[47]

On the other hand, with direct exchanges and links between the two sides of the Taiwan Straits ever increasing and intensifying, Macao's role as an "intermediary agent" in both economic and political senses is likely to decrease in general. This is particularly true in trade and other economic areas. As discussed earlier, economic and trade relations had developed smoothly after the handover. However the upward trend has suffered double hits in the last two years. The world financial crisis adversely affected Macao's tourist and airline industries. Then the mainland and Taiwan reached agreements on direct "three links" in November 2008 and began to implement them in 2009, which brought another challenge to Macao's economy and its economic and trade relations with Taiwan. Although it is still too early to give a complete assessment of the impact of these developments, early signs of negative fallout have emerged. Among other things, the Macao–Taiwan trade growth was negative in 2008 and 2009 with the minus 54 percent in the first ten months of 2009. With the realization of direct postal, transportation, and trade links between the mainland and Taiwan, Macao's role as an intermediary between Taiwan and the mainland has visibly reduced. For instance, the direct cross-strait postal service significantly shrank Macao's profit margin compared to the time all mails and parcels between the two sides had to go through Macao. The gradual normalization of cross-strait trade and investment relations has also weakened Macao's role as a window, platform, and intermediary for capital transaction, logistics, and goods promotion between Beijing and Taipei. Finally the direct air link between the mainland and Taiwan also hit Macao's air and tourist industry hard. The quantity of Taiwan passengers and cargo in the Macao international airport has sharply fallen. Related to that, the tourist market in Macao was adversely affected and consequently Macao's revenue for the gambling business has decreased as well.[48]

Looking into future, while Macao does face some tough economic realities, challenges are always accompanied by opportunities. As a whole the improvement of cross-strait relations will create more favorable conditions and environment for Macao–Taiwan relations. While some old functions of Macao in cross-strait relations may decrease, some new functions for Macao may emerge and grow. For example, when the mainland tourists begin to visit Taiwan in large numbers, it could provide new opportunities for Macao. Many mainland tourists may be interested in visiting Macao on the way back after finishing their tour of Taiwan, thus compensating for the lost Taiwanese tourists to Macao. Air Macao has already begun to explore cooperation with the mainland travel agencies to make arrangements for Taiwan-bound tourist groups to go through Macao at least one way.[49] As mentioned earlier, politically speaking, Macao as a model of "one country, two systems" still has some advantages that the mainland cities or even Hong Kong can hardly beat in making unique contributions to cross-strait relations. Macao–Taiwan relations still have room to raise the level and substance of contacts and exchanges. Most recently some Taiwanese scholars suggested that it is time for Macao's new chief executive Chui Sai On to make the initiative to visit

Taiwan to plan the next ten years of the relationship.[50] If that materializes, that may realize a new stage of Macao–Taiwan relations. Finally one can also argue that the development of cross-strait relations is unlikely to be linear without difficulties and even crises. One also cannot rule out the possibility that pro-independence political force may return to power in Taiwan. Under such a scenario, the "Macao model" may once again play a more visible role as a reservoir, facilitator, buffer zone, and catalyst in cross-strait relations. As one Chinese official put it, "Even when cross-strait relations are tense, Macao–Taiwan relations could still maintain relative stability."[51]

Notes

1. Meng Qingshun, *Hong Kong and Macao and Cross-Strait Relations* (Wuhan, Wuhan Press, 1999), 29–37.
2. Wang Ling, "Macao and Taiwan," *Observing and Thinking*, no. 12, 1999.
3. Ibid.
4. Guo Shuqing, "The Macao–Taiwan relations in the new century will further promote the development of cross-strait relations," big5.china.com.cn/chinese/TCC/haixia/50161.htm.
5. Lin Yuanding, "Make a good use of Macao as a special platform in cross-strait exchanges," *Unification Forum*, no. 2, 2005, p. 50.
6. Guo Jianqing, "The development of Macao–Taiwan relations in the new millenium," *Journal of Fujian Provincial Party School*, no. 1, 2002, pp. 56–58.
7. Wang Ling, "Macao and Taiwan."
8. Lin Chang, *Free Discussion on Macao–Taiwan Relations*, vol. 2 (Macao: Dong Wang Yang Press, 2008), 29–30.
9. Wang Ling, "Macao and Taiwan."
10. "Stability and reciprocity—Republic of China's stance toward Macao 1999," Mainland Affairs Council, www.mac.gov.tw/ct.asp?xItem=54924&ctNode=5940&mp=3.
11. "Jiang Zemin's Eight-point Proposal," January 30, 1995. Taiwan Affairs Office of the State Council.
12. "President Lee Tung-hui's speech at the 10th Plenary of State Unification Council, April 8, 1995," search.president.gov.tw/search-cgi/getfilelist.exe?no=-6&filelist=../tmp/query7831365533074&page=0.
13. "Regulations Governing Relations with Hong Kong and Macao," April 2, 1997, Mainland Affairs Council, www.mac.gov.tw/ct.asp?xItem=51261&ctNode=5915&mp=3.
14. "The basic principles and policies of the central people's government regarding Macao's post-99 relations with Taiwan," Taiwan Affairs Office of the State Council, April 1, 2002, www.gwytb.gov.cn/flfg/flfg0.asp?flgf_m_id=123.
15. "An analysis of Macao's position and roles in cross-strait relations," www.chinataiwan.org/tsh/mtxy/hx/200708/t20070801_395631.htm.

16. Lin Chang, *Free Discussion on Macao–Taiwan Relations*, vol. 2, 145–46.

17. Guo Shuqing, "The Macao–Taiwan relations in the new century will further promote the development of cross-strait relations."

18. Guo Jianqing, "The development of Macao–Taiwan relations in the new millenium."

19. Cheng Jinzhong, "Macao–Taiwan relations are facing rare opportunities," December 17, 2009, news.ifeng.com/taiwan/4/200912/1217_354_1477954.shtml.

20. Chen En and Wang Fang Fang, "The impact of cross-strait three links on Macao–Taiwan trade and economic relations and the way to respond," paper presented at the 1st Macao Forum on Cross-Strait Relations, The Society for Relations across the Taiwan Strait and Between Macao and Taiwan, Macao. Polytechnic Institute, January 11–13, 2010.

21. Lin Chang, *Free Discussion on Macao–Taiwan Relations*, vol. 2, 29.

22. See www.mac.gov.tw/lp.asp?ctNode=5939&CtUnit=4157&BaseDSD=7&mp=3; www.mac.gov.tw/lp.asp?ctNode=5940&CtUnit=4158&BaseDSD=7&mp=3.

23. Jiang Xinli, "Macao' s return and relations between two shores and three locations," www.adanstar.com/FF/108-2196.html.

24. Wang Jingqun, "The position and role of Macao in the development of cross-strait relations," www.cass.net.cn/zhuanti/taiwan_1/zhjia/zhj063.htm.

25. According to Chinese accounting, in the three years from 1995 to 1998, Air Macao alone transported 1,591,354 passengers and 18,562 tons of cargo with 13,361 flights. Wang Jingqun, "The position and role of Macao in the development of cross-strait relations."

26. Wang Jianmin and Chen Jianfeng, "Taiwan-Hong Kong, Taiwan-Macao and cross-strait interactions," *Journal of Asia and African Studies*, no. 6, 2007, p. 56.

27. Lin Chang, *Free Discussion on Macao–Taiwan Relations*, vol. 2, 151–57.

28. Ibid.

29. Phoenix TV comment: "Macao model: it took two hours to break a fifty-six year deadlock," January 16, 2005, www.xmatc.com/atcdata/html/40358.html.

30. He Weiping, "An analysis of Macao model," www.zhongguotongcuhui.org.cn/06tybbs/next070405.htm.

31. "The CPC–KMT forum will follow the Macao model," blog.yam.com/cutting/article/5917963.

32. "Macao—an Ideal Platform for Trade and Economic Co-operation between Guangdong and Taiwan," www.ipim.gov.mo/pt/publication/macaoimage/cover/no36_04.htm.

33. *Xinhuanewsnet*, "Macao 'Taipei Economic and Cultural Center' has been approved to take applications for Taiwan entry permits," January 6, 2002, news.xinhuanet.com/china/2002-01/06/content_226291.htm.

34. Lin Chang, *Free Discussion on Macao–Taiwan Relations*, vol. 2, 19–21.

35. Lin Chang, "The smooth development of Macao–Taiwan relations under the regulation of 'Qian's Seven Articles,'" www.macaodata.com/macaoweb/book262/html/0125001.htm.

36. "Nine Years after Macao's handover: an analysis," March 2009, Mainland Affairs Council, www.mac.gov.tw/lp.asp?ctNode=5940&CtUnit=4158&BaseDSD=7&mp=3.

37. Guo Jianqing, "Macao–Taiwan relations after Macao's handover and their trends of development," www.macaodata.com/macaoweb/book262/html/0133001.htm.

38. Ibid.

39. "Four years after Macao's handover: an analysis," Mainland Affairs Council, EY (November 17, 2004:04:07.0), english.www.gov.tw/e-Gov/pda_index.jsp?categid=78&recordid=78844.

40. Lin Chang, *Free Discussion on Macao–Taiwan Relations*, vol. 2, 44–45.

41. "Director Wang Yi's speech at the closing ceremony of the symposium on "ten years of Macao–Taiwan relations," October 21, 2009, Taiwan Affairs Office of the State Council.

42. "Macao should contribute to peaceful unification of the motherland," December 31, 2009, Government Information, www.dwnews.com/gb/MainNews/2010-01/2010-01-29-15-33-39-614.html.

43. Dong Yuhong, "Some thoughts on Macao's role in the peaceful development of cross-strait relations," www.waou.com.mo/detail.asp?id=40078.

44. Ibid.

45. "Discussing the grand strategy of peaceful development at the moment of the 10th anniversary of Macao–Taiwan relations after return," October 21, 2009, www.ChinaReviewNews.com.

46. Cheng Jinzhong, "Macao–Taiwan relations are facing rare opportunities."

47. *Macao Daily*, "Macao hosts the rally for peaceful unification with great significance," December 14, 2006, www.chinareviewnews.com.

48. Chen En and Wang Fang Fang, "The impact of cross-strait three links on Macao–Taiwan trade and economic relations and the way to respond," paper presented at the 1st Macao Forum on Cross-Strait Relations, The Society for Relations across the Taiwan Strait and Between Macao and Taiwan, Macao. Polytechnic Institute, January 11–13, 2010.

49. Ibid.

50. "Time comes for Chui Sai On to visit Taiwan," October 23, 2009, www.ChinaReviewNews.com.

51. Cheng Jinzhong, "Macao–Taiwan relations are facing rare opportunities."

CHAPTER TWELVE

In Search of a Sustainable Gaming Industry in East Asia: A Futuristic Analysis of a Las Vegas–Macao–Sentosa Paradigm in the 10 + 1/10 + 3 FTA

Keelian Huang

To Define Gambling and Gaming Industry

Like wine and gourmet food, gambling has been an important part in social activities since the dawn of human history; it is particularly so in the Chinese civilization. In addition to making love and enjoying good foods, Confucius should perhaps include gambling into what he deems as human nature, too.[1]

With the advent of modern economy, technology, and society, gambling has gradually been "institutionalized" into what we now known as the gaming industry, characterized by its own unique logic, structure, organizations, rules, personnel, activities, and functions. Similar to other industries, gaming industry also has its own specific malpractices and problems, too. Nevertheless, the industry has always been caught in a dilemma, wavering between the extreme of being a powerful industrial sector and that of a controversial one.[2]

The crux of the problem is how to manage gambling and gaming activities within the social system and make its development serve the general interests of the public; without swinging, like a pendulum, between the extreme of moral condemnations and that of shameless utilitarianism.[3]

What is the definition of a "normal" if not a "moral" or a "healthy" industry? Maybe a so-called normal industrial sector within the context of modern day industrialization and urbanization should include the following traits:

1. It originates from what I refer to as a "human pentagon system," which is composed of physiological, psychological, societal, physical, and cosmological systems and is there to serve the individual's needs.
2. It fulfills social needs.
3. It operates in accordance with market mechanism.
4. It operates within the legal systems and abides to law.
5. It follows internal rules and regulations, systems and management, professionals and bureaucracy, checks and balances.
6. It coordinates with and promotes development of other industrial sectors.
7. It makes use of science and technology.
8. It fulfills social responsibility.
9. It offers growth and is not a dying sector.
10. It harmonizes with Mother Nature—that is, an environment-friendly industry.[4]

With this definition, people should have no difficulty to point out that education, healthcare, tourism, recreation, IT, and logistics industries are of healthy and good characters but are mostly caught in controversy about how to characterize the gaming industry. Nevertheless, no industry or trade goes along perfectly with the ten-plus points of prescriptions, while no industry or trade suffers a 100 percent rejection rate either.[5]

For research and practical purposes, we are here to point out that the gaming industry as it is today does not go against the above-mentioned traits, and it should therefore be treated as an industrial sector of modern economy, which will then enable us to go ahead to study its role and its relationship with other industries, and its impact on society.

Without this reasoning, there is no way to understand the current situation and future of the Macao SAR because it is has adopted gaming as its core economy and leading industry.

Macao's Continuous Efforts to Streamline Its Commercial Gambling

Like other trades and industries, gambling is given a different definition and status in different societies during different periods of its social development, which inescapably shaped its structure, functions, and problems. Its operational model is a matter of history and society.

Gambling has been rooted deeply in Macao's history since the Portuguese ruler legalized it in 1847 in order to rescue Macao's loss of strategic position between the East and the West to the British who had successfully established

Hong Kong as an international platform. Coupling with coolie trade, drugs, and prostitution, gambling became an important pillar of Portuguese Macao's vice industries for more than a century, from the 1850s to the 1950s.

The Portuguese administration had tried hard to make good profits out of the gambling operation and establish it as a mainstream industry, or in present-day terms, a leading industry which propels improvement of other branches of the economy. However, legalization and government support did not give new impetus to the gambling trade because it was in existence during a long period of confusion—while China was in domestic chaos under foreign encroachments and Southeast Asia was torn by imperialistic competitions between the Western powers, such as Great Britain, the Netherlands, France, the United States, and Japan.

There was no influx of gamblers or tourists from China Mainland and Southeast Asia to Macao; indicating that an international factor is always a critical part of Macao development.[6]

In the later half of the twentieth century, the Portuguese vice industry model was more or less transformed to combine gambling with tourism when the Sociedale de Tourismo e Diversoes de Macao (STDM), under leadership of Stanley Ho and Henry Fok, was granted full monopoly to give gaming a new face and a new momentum. The STDM model also reflected development in Mainland China and Southeast Asia in the heyday of the Cold War. Chinese from Hong Kong, Taiwan, and Southeast Asia as well as tourists from Japan and the United States constituted the main groups of visitors consuming Macao's gaming services. Although gambling was a very lucrative trade in East Asia, it did not become a modern business institution because the operations were managed more as family businesses, thus limiting their scale, scenarios, and quality of growth.

A new paradigm is needed if Macao's gambling is to be transformed into a new business configuration. By the 1990s, many local economic researchers began to talk about "industry clusters," introducing a core industry with a fringe of industries such a tourism, trade shows, and exhibitions as well as recreation.[7]

Interestingly and paradoxically, gambling takes a greater turn in its development and becomes the current form of institutionalized gaming industry only after Macao's sovereignty was reverted to China, a socialist country which has been a strong opponent to gambling because of its ideology, policy, and moral standard. Article 118 of the MSAR Basic Law has given necessary political endorsement, legal support, and professional status to the gaming industry. It has been, in turn, creating a necessary economic foundation for "one country, two systems."

In order to bring this third paradigm into the scene, a breakup of Macao casino monopoly was needed; and it took place when the Macao SAR government enacted a new law of gaming, termed "Administrative Regulation 26/2001" on August 30, 2001. A researcher of anti-monopoly, Mr. Lau Peng Leung, who promoted diversification, liberalization, and restructuring of the gambling industry in the 1990s was killed tragically in "a car accident" in the neighboring town of Zhuhai. The incident reflected that, like any other reform program, the paradigm shifting was invariably a matter of death and life.[8]

Consequently, Edmund Ho, the then chief executive of the MSAR, gave big coverage of building up a gaming industry in the SAR's new economy in the shortest possible time in his Policy Address to the Legislative Council annually. It is expected that the patronage and privilege given to the gaming industry will enhance its rapid development, which in turn will give necessary supports to other related business, such as entertainment, tourism, conference, exhibition, logistics, and even Chinese herbal medicine, thus ushering in a new economy in Macao in the coming years.[9]

It is undoubtedly with the Beijing blessing and support that foreigners are invited to take part in the efforts of reinventing the gaming industry, thus opening the door to American participation in Macao's gaming industry. Three new concessions were awarded to Wynn, Galaxy, and the Venetian, signaling Macao's important and crucial role in the global economy.[10]

The Macao SAR is Overwhelmed by the Early Success of Its Gaming Industry

The past five years have witnessed the tremendous impact and success of MSAR's development strategy and it is credited as a success of "one country, two systems." For example:

—All the U.S. gaming giants have entered Macao, building their gambling hotel and retail complexes and as exemplified in the case of Las Vegas Sands, enjoyed early success. The three concessions were split into six, without negative reaction and objection from the SAR government.

—The original gaming giant, the Ho family and their associates, was confronted uncomfortably with the invasions and needed to find ways of transforming its business philosophy and management style so as not to be marginalized or even eliminated by U.S. corporations and corporate cultures.

—Macao has virtually become a super construction site, with casino buildings emerging everywhere, particularly in the Cotai Strip.

—Local citizens, particularly the youth population, are overwhelmed by lucrative jobs available in the casinos. There are more new motorbikes and new cars cruising on the narrow streets, leading to unprecedented traffic problems, air and noise pollutions.

—The SAR government was awash by taxation money from the gaming industry which enabled it to announce more tax cuts almost annually. The government has been able to spend easily in such public events as East Asia Sport and other international events. It also gave money to senior citizens. In addition, the MSAR is a pioneer in granting fifteen years free education to its youths in East Asia. The government also decided to build more public low-cost housing for citizens in need, which include young married couples. Macao's gaming revenue is expected to keep increasing in the coming years.

—The government also gave more money to its public servants, teachers, and professionals, including teaching and administrative staff in the higher learning institutes. Nevertheless salary and fringe benefits of the University of Macao staff, for instance, was already comparable to that of their counterparts in the HKSAR, which is reputed to be the best-paid university employees in the world.

—Macao has became an attraction to professionals, skilled and unskilled laborers in the surrounding areas, particularly Southern China and Hong Kong. Chinese from different parts of the world flooded the Macao job market. It was predicted that there will be a labor shortage if Macao's gaming industry is diversified. This manpower movement could again be attributed to the success of "one country, two systems"—that a professional like myself can be taken as someone who has enjoyed transformation of the Special Administrative Zone.[11]

Since a policy of legalization, liberalization, and internationalization of commercial gambling is built tightly into the Basic Law and with blessing from the central government, the MSAR is therefore given a unprecedented opportunity to advance its modernization process rapidly and comprehensively by capitalizing on the gaming industry without a sense of guilt or shame. What it has to do is to make necessary efforts so as to prevent a "gambling only" scenario from happening, and to carve for itself scrupulously a unique position in China as well as East Asia in sustainable development.[12]

Between the "Dutch Disease" and "Diabetics": The MSAR Elites' Helplessness in the Configuration of the Frenzy Process

Nevertheless, the MSAR's success story recently turned sour or became controversial, when a senior government minister was arrested in December 2006. He was put on trial for his alleged corruption over the last few years. There was also a mass demonstration on May Day in 2007 which ended in police opening fire at the "troublemakers."

Undoubtedly, these scandals seriously damaged the MSAR government; it was losing face, public confidence, and support which it enjoyed only two to three years ago.

This dramatic downturn for the MSAR government also signaled a new page of social development that paradigm shift and its implementation could turn into a political dispute overnight between the government and the general public.

A case in point is Dr. Ieong Wan Chong, who is a senior member of the Chinese National People Congress and member of the MSAR Basic Law Committee appointed directly by the Standing Committee of the NPC, and director of the Macao Study Center at the University of Macao as well as founding chairman of the Union of Macao Scholars.

In his recent writing delivered to a seminar on the current state of the gaming industry, like many of his colleagues and peers, he was perplexed and disturbed by the booms and proliferations of the gaming complexes. Understandably, he was uneasy about U.S. participation and a possible domination of the gaming industry which could cause a negative impact on the Macao–China–U.S. relationship.

Dr. Ieong's criticism is actually tantamount to ways and means of putting the so-called paradigm shift into practice for the MSAR new economy in the coming decades:

1. In accordance with Article 118 of the MSAR Basic Law, Macao is allowed to develop its unique tourism and entertainment industries for overall interests of the general population. It requires the government to pursue a diversified approach, namely, to promote tourism, gaming, and other related industries simultaneously; the "gambling only" policy is technically against the Basic Law. For the time being, the gaming industry has not lived up to expectations that it fosters other branches of economy.

   On the contrary, it is consuming others, particularly small and medium industries in the sense that it received the best pieces of lands and most of the manpower. There is saying that the "dragon head" is eating up its own "tail" and "body"; ending up possibly nothing but a "head," that is, the MSAR could one day become a one-trade economy or simply a gambling economy.

2. The MSAR government should therefore introduce comprehensive legislations and conduct necessary regulatory controls with regard to the gaming industry, preventing it from strangling the growth of other industrial sectors.

   If a policy of diversification and internationalization is to be promoted, more open and equal opportunity should be offered to the latecomers, including China's investors, to participate in building up a new economy for the MSAR.
3. While enjoying a near monopoly of manpower, the gaming industry should be required by laws and regulations to offer its employees necessary training programs as well as new job orientation and training should they leave their positions. This can prevent the gaming industry from discharging its employees and forcing them into long-term unemployment.
4. The government should see to it that a few U.S. companies should not be allowed to monopolize the Macao gaming market as reflected in the Sands and the Venetian's early success.

What underlines Dr. Ieong's concern is a looming takeover of the Macao gaming industry by U.S. interests as represented by Wynn, MGM, and Las Vegas Sands because of their aggressive global strategy, capital investment, and management style.

He refers to a recent point made in President Hu Jintao's Opening Address to the XVII Party Congress of the CCP that necessary precautions and measures be taken as soon as possible against possible foreign interventions with the domestic affairs of the HKSAR and MSAR.

Specifically in the MSAR case:

—Will U.S. participation lead to its domination of the MSAR gaming industry?

—Will this possible domination encourage the United States and some of their local associates to go into MSAR domestic affairs, including participating in legislative elections?

—Will this political presence motivate further the "U.S. Group" to diversify and extend its activities into Mainland China by trying to promote U.S.–style human rights, democracy, and religious movements?

—Drawing parallel to the U.S. military bases in East Asia during the Cold War, will Macao become a center for the United States to build up a ring of commercial gambling hubs surrounding China, positioning from Japan, Korea Peninsula, the ASEAN, and Australia, which aims at making easy money from the numerous Chinese gamblers?

—In other words, will the MSAR gaming industry become a new battle field between U.S. hegemony and China's rise to a world power, between Pax Americana and Pax Sinica, between the West and the East?[13]

"Las Vegas Model" to be Explored as a Business Strategy

As a matter of fact, the above-mentioned "conspiracy theory" reminded us that a study of the U.S. gaming industry in East Asia, particularly its involvement in the MSAR, constitutes a new dimension of the U.S.–China relation.

During my term as founding director of the Institute for Sustainable Development at the Macao University of Science & Technology (MUST–ISUS), I had tried hard to promote such a *Project on the Macao–U.S. Relations* within the framework of China–U.S. relations. Due to lack of funding, the project did not become a reality but it is fortunately taken over by Prof. Hao Yifang, Dean of Faculty of Social Science & Humanities at the University of Macao, who spent considerable efforts to organize the "International Conference on 'Macao and Sino–U.S. relations'" on December 11–12, 2007.[14]

Being on staff of the SSRC–UMAC, I have many opportunities to conduct many academic discussions with Dr. Ieong about the MSAR development strategy. We inevitably talk about the U.S. role in the gaming industry, having many agreements and many differences.

For instance, while taking Dr. Ieong's argument seriously, I prefer to move away from the "conspiracy theory"; namely, not to politicize it and turn it into an ideological issue but treating the U.S. involvement as a matter of economic affairs. It is argued that, with the so-called Las Vegas business model, we can configure development phenomena in Macao, formulating a new paradigm for Macao to build up a multi-industry economy in the coming years.

What is the "Las Vegas Model?" The following quotations are indicative:

> If Las Vegas had once been retrospective in inventing itself, its capacity for reinvention is entirely prospective.

> The factology and chronology of the Strip's bricks and mortar are but a part of the story. The transformation is profoundly conceptual as well. After the failed attempt to attract families, the lord of the lemmings configuring the city's zeitgeist perceived that much of the world's tourism is driven by the quest for

> good cuisine, shopping, and Culture (with a capital C). Not to worry. If, prior to the 1990s, Las Vegas was known more for its cheap buffets than pricey gourmet dinning, today there is scarcely a noted name within the world's culinary Who's Who absent on the Strip. With lightning speed Las Vegas has emerged as a major gastronomic destination. Presently, four of the seventeen five-star restaurants in the entire United States are on the Strip, and it is awash with future contenders. Similarly, virtually all of the world's purveyors of luxury retail items, particularly clothing and jewelry, have outlets on the Strip. Caesar's Forum, with its price of $1,300 per square foot for leased space, is the world's greatest concentration of luxury retail outlets. In recent tourists' surveys, shopping ranks first as the reason for visiting Las Vegas (gambling was third, behind entertainment.

In fact, Las Vegas's diversified and bourgeois approach should be an envy of its MSAR counterparts. Only days before writing this chapter, a troop of riot police were called to confront a group of angry tourists from Northern China, creating yet another scandalous event which may indefinitely taint the image of Macao.

Cheap tours from Mainland China have recently plagued Hong Kong, Macao, and Southeast Asia tourism industries. Hundreds of the so-called tourists were deliberately deserted by their local guides on the streets, who claimed innocently that the tourists refused to buy anything in the designated stores that were selling mostly junk, pirated, and fake goods. Since the Mainland tourists enjoyed a free trip or a trip with minimal charge of travel and accommodation costs, their underpaid guides and bus drivers expect them to spend lavishly, for which the shop owners will then reward them accordingly, and these commissions constitute decent incomes of the tourism personnel.

Recent incidents of this nature indicate that cheap and low-level tourism will eventually derail leisure, retail, and entertainment industries in Hong Kong, Macao and Southeast Asia; not to mention the fact that an influx of bogus tourists would inevitably consume limited public services available to the local citizens and cause law and order problems for the host communities.

It could become a lose-lose scenario for the locals and the visitors: a scenario that is alarming to China as well as its neighboring areas, including the HKSAR and MSAR, a scenario that deserves forward-looking planning and management.

To avert the possible incidents and accidents so as to usher in an "Era of Chinese Tourists," perhaps there are more to learn from Las Vegas practices:

> The tourist in Las Vegas is now recruited (indeed practically conscripted) into the endless army of flaneurs traversing, consuming, and photographing the

> Strip's sensory overload of which they are an integral component. Arguably, there is no better place on the planet for people watching; no greater display of polyglot, multicultural variation. In the process their common experience serves as a king of gigantic blender producing a smoothie that oozes in two-directional fashion. The effect is altogether antithetical to the circularity and intimacy of the passeggiata or paseo around some Mediterranean or Latin American town square. Rather, the Strip stroller moves lineally from one sight to the next in an unfolding journey of new discovery. The return to point of origin (one's hotel) is more likely to be effected by taxicab than on foot . . .
>
> It has become commonplace to discuss Las Vegas in terms of "disneyfication," reference being to the use of exotic historical, futuristic and geographic theme. . . . Finally, Las Vegas has now achieved the capacity to be both self-sustaining and proliferating phenomena.

If the so-called Las Vegas model is valuable and relevant, it is for Macao's emerging trade to learn more about reinvention, authenticity, sustainability, and social responsibility so as to transform a place for gambling into a place of business, industry, and conventions eventually.

The definition or configuration of a new gaming industry for Macao can best be illustrated with the following quotation:

> The point that critical obsession with authenticity (or the seemingly obvious lack thereof) when contemplating Las Vegas is not only a statement of the obvious; it is entirely beside the point. Las Vegas is no more nor less a human invention than Rome, Paris, or San Francisco. Nor are the latter devoid of simulacra; indeed they are replete with them. When a city imports and displays an attraction (say an Egyptian obelisk), erects a neoclassical public building, or constructs a tract of Tudor homes, it is scarcely celebrating local tradition or "authentic" cultural distinctiveness.
>
> What does distinguish Las Vegas from Rome, Paris, or San Francisco, then, is not an invented tradition (as if there could be any other kind), but rather its tradition of invention. That is, within less than a century, Las Vegas, despite its inhospitable location and improbable prospects, emerged as the major tourism destination any where with the power to influence, if not configure, a significant portion of future world tourism. Las Vegas, through its capacity to reinvent itself, if not spontaneously then nearly so, is the antithesis of tradition. In its present incarnation, it is not simply composed of simulacra (pace Hughes), it has critically amassed them into an unprecedented configuration. In the process, Las Vegas has become the sole, and hence authentic, representation of its unique self: a success that is both envied and now emulated in varying degrees by other aspiring (and established) destinations. In its signatured critical massing of simulacra, Las Vegas is now, ironically, more paradigmatic than parasitical.[15]

Another "Tale of Two Cities": Macao and Singapore Join Hands in Promoting a 10 + 1 Paradigm for East Asian Gaming Industry

On my part, there is no urge to deify Las Vegas and other U.S. experiences. Nonetheless, if suspicions and anxiety about the U.S. gaming industry's grand design and global strategy in East Asia, as seen in Dr. Ieong and his associates' arguments, are to be handled properly, it might not be a bad idea to configure the so-called Las Vegas Model in the following terms:

1. It is operated within the legal boundary set by federal and state laws; a pure business practice without involving itself in local politics and foreign affairs.
2. It is clear of underworld manipulation and not becoming a façade of crimes and money laundering.
3. It is managed with market mechanism, with "corporate America" going into the gaming business, and "the incursion of respectable financial institution into casino financing."
4. It is a true gaming destination "with all its architectural complexity and heterogeneity."
5. It is also a major gastronomic destination and a great concentration of luxury retail outlets.
6. It is "a place for gambling gradually being transformed into place of industry conventions."
7. It is the largest and most attractive exhibition and conference center in the country.
8. It is a place capable of inventing and reinventing itself; of achieving "the capacity to be both self-sustaining and proliferating phenomena."[16]

This # VI (1, 2, 3, 4, 5, 6 . . .) configuration is basically identical to that of the above-mentioned # I (1, 2, 3, 4, 5, 6, 7, 8, 9, 10 . . .) which could be turned into a "Las Vegan–Macao–Sentosa Paradigm" if we try to streamline prospectively a booming industry in East Asia in the coming decades.[17]

Singapore's entry and participation in December 2009 is believed to be a epoch-making event for the gaming industry in East Asia.

First, Singapore expects China will "become the largest tourists generating country in Asia"; "the development of China's outbound tourism market is changing the tourism pattern of Asia-pacific and that of the globe."

Second, "to satisfy the spending habits of mainland Chinese," in addition to reinventing a vibrant and exciting shopping venue, Singapore will enter the two main gaming segments for the Mainland Chinese market; namely, the VIP gaming segment and the mass market segment:

> This includes leveraging on their own network and having strong marketing and branding efforts. Las Vegas Sands, Corp which won the bid for Marina Bay IR and runs the Sands Macao Casino must not see Singapore as a competitor but as a strategic partners . . . offer complimentary travel packages to mainland Chinese high rollers in Sands Macao who wish to visit Marina Bay Sands and vice versa.
>
> We can appeal directly to the high rollers by virtue of the outstanding experience that Singapore can provide. High rollers are used to the excellent service and VIP treatment in practically every casino that they visit and they will be looking out for new experiences when making their choice of destination. One of the factors under consideration for the high rollers would be availability of an experience that is beyond just gaming. In other words, they will also consider the attractiveness of the sights, sounds and activities that the destination can offer. To this end, Singapore on its IRs, tourism attractions, good infrastructure, and excellent service demands.

Nevertheless, Singapore is also taking the middle segment into serious considerations:

> China's rapid economic growth has led to a growing middle class that can afford to gamble. The availability of cheaper and easily accessible transport tools have also increased the number of potential players. . . . According to a recent report by Morgan Stanley, visitors to Macao have consistently spent around 70 percent of the money on gaming, 25 percent on F&B, shopping and 2 percent on accommodation.

While making low price accommodation and cheap food available to Chinese tourists so that they could maximize their gaming expenses, Singapore will also interest them with themed shopping outlets and cultural events "to provide an experience that is beyond gaming. The casino, retail, F&B, entertainment zones should be interconnected seamlessly to provide an integrated and memorable experience."

Singapore is following the case of MSAR and is aware of the positioning and defining dilemma that troubles Macao:

—Is Macao destined to be a "gambling only" destination?
—Is Macao destined to be a "lower level" gaming destination?
—What does it mean to an economy and society if all these scenarios become a reality?

—Is Singapore equipped to turn herself into a more interesting, diversified, and better gaming destination?

To a pragmatic country like Singapore, the answer to the abovementioned question is to increase its competitiveness in her tourism by studying behavior and psychology of the prospective clients and restructuring Singapore's management style and even its sociocultural systems accordingly:

> The VIP market is a highly lucrative one that the Singapore IRs cannot afford to ignore. There is a high level of competition for this small segment and the IR operators must rely on several strategies such as the use of junket operators, leveraging on their own network and cross-marketing with their other casinos in the case of Las Vegas Sands. The mass market segment is set to increase rapidly with the rise of the middle class in mainland China and it will be the strongest area of growth for the Singapore IRs. To this end, the Sentosa IR should leverage on its natural geography as a tropical island and focus on the development of water-related activities that appeal greatly to the mainland Chinese tourists. These include the development of beaches, resorts, water sports and recreation activities as will as leisure boating activities. The growing in-between segment, of Chinese with "gaming spending power" that is below the VIP level and above those of the mass-market, is potentially the most lucrative customer base to target as exclusive private facilities, personalized service and not extremely noisy or quiet gaming environment but with moderately "people atmosphere" (人氣) will appeal greatly to this group of Chinese customers.[18]

A "Mariana Bay front–Sentosa Model" is taking shape:

—The gaming industry is to be structured fully into Singapore economy and its development strategy.
—A comprehensive scheme is introduce specially for the development of gaming industry.
—In addition to the development of two Integrated Resorts (IRs), Mariana Bay and Sentosa, three southern isles are to be designated to be gaming sites. The sites are more or less isolated spots from the local residential centers so as to minimize social costs and to maximize "economic growth stimulating tax revenues."[19]
—U.S. institutions are invited to help draw blueprints, to train personnel, and to devise ways of meeting specific needs of consumers, particularly for those from Mainland China.[20]
—For its long-term development, while the "Las Vegas Model" is emulated, the MSAR will be taken as a business partner.

—Chinese visitors are targeted and they are split into two different segments. There is a common theme: while introducing a comprehensive range of facilities and putting up a "gambling plus" presentation, it caters to different needs of the VIP market and mass market.

—The United States is invited to enter the science with different groups going to one of two places; and they are supposed to operate within the Singaporean legal framework and reinforce the Singaporean establishment.

A Las Vegas–MSAR–Sentosa Paradigm to Be Formulated for the 10 + 1 FTA

Singapore learned selectively from Las Vegas's mature experience on the one hand and also from Macao's chaotic practices on the other hand; but it is wise enough to ally itself strategically with both.

> Singapore IR operators must take a proactive approach in attracting high rollers. This includes leveraging on their own network and having strong marketing and branding efforts. Las Vegas Sands, Corp which won the bid for Marina Bay IR and runs the Sands Macao Casino must not see Singapore as a competitor but as a strategic partner. Sands is spending a lot of time and money into the Marina Bay Sands projects and they should spend equal amount of attention to cross-market the Marina Bay Sands with Sands Macao. It is also in the interest of the gaming operator to host his VIPs in different and new cities to keep the gaming experience refreshing and to build customer loyalty and sustained interest. For example, Sands can offer complimentary travel to mainland Chinese high rollers in Sands Macao who wish to visit Marina Bay Sands and vice versa.

Since the gaming industry is a very special and unique business with a competitive market, there will be jealously and conspiracy between Las Vegas, Macao and Singapore.

If cutthroat competitions are to be avoided, China is believed to have a critical and crucial role to play in formulating a trilateral relationship, or a triple cooperation regime:

—Chinese outbound tourism is the main supply of consumers of East Asia's major tourist, gastronomic, shopping, and gaming destinations.

—Macao's gaming industry prospers because of China's "one country, two systems" and many other privileged policies. If the MSAR becomes the world's largest gaming revenue generator then China will logically be the

"Super Power of Gaming Industry." Ways and means of exerting its influence could become a matter in China's regional as well global strategy.

—Diversification and internationalization of the MSAR gaming industry require bringing Las Vegas and Sentosa into the operational scheme. By doing so, the MSAR might not become a gaming-only destination, or a "lower level" gaming industry, which will work against China's national interests.

—A trilateral relationship in the East Asian gaming industry, with the MSAR as a key player, will place China in a strategic position when a ring of gaming hubs emerge in the coming decades in East Asia; all targeting gamblers from Mainland China.[21]

—Las Vegas's and Singapore's approach to replace "gambling only" policy with "gambling plus" is more desirable and practical. It should be capable of meeting various needs of China's outbound tourists who are destined to be more sophisticated and diversified. The theory of development indicates that as Chinese tourists become more well off and better educated, more of them will move away from the "gambling only" syndrome which has plagued Macao since the 1840s.[22]

It is therefore a logical conclusion that eventual introduction of the trilateral gaming institutions first into the ASEAN plus China Free Trade Arrangement/10+1 FTA and then into the ASEAN plus China, Korea, Japan/10+3 FTA is a matter of reality and necessity for China.

To do so, it is also because of the following considerations regarding regional cooperation within the globalization framework[23]:

1. There is a platform for the 10 + 1/10 + 3 members to deal with policy and urgent matter regarding the gaming industry, if a situation requires it.
2. There is to be a common understanding that no person, no group, no corporation, or no country should monopolize the gaming industry in East Asia.
3. Business is business: no group or nation should use its influence in the gaming industry to conduct money laundering, ideological campaigns, and political infiltration in East Asia.[24]
4. No criminal group should be allowed to manipulate the gaming industry.
5. Development of gaming industry should not be disturbed excessively by politics, law, and morality; it should not distort local economy and society.
6. Prevention of pathological gambling should be dealt with at the 10+1/10+3 level.[25]

7. In addition to the MSAR, Singapore could also become an East Asian service center of research, teaching, consultation, and arbitration for matters regarding the gaming industry.

The Gaming Industry is to Serve Individuals as well as Social Development

If a "Las Vegas–Macao–Sentosa" trilateral approach is to be a foundation on which an East Asian Paradigm for gaming industry can be gradually formulated, the underlying messages are very clear:

—Since gambling is considered a congruent part of human nature, it is to be tackled by means of industrial and public services by an open, regulated, and functional approach.
—Since human nature is a complex of diversity, it is realistic and idealistic that the "gambling only" approach should be discarded; instead, a "gambling plus" approach should be in its place.
—A "gambling only" policy is also undesirable to economic and social developments; a "gambling plus" policy leading to gaming industry is perceived to be more constructive to sustainable development.
—China and the United States can work together in promoting a "gambling plus"/"gaming industry" policy both in Macao and East Asia, making another important dimension of the Sino–U.S. relation.
—Through the 10 + 1/10 + 3 framework, China is offered good opportunity to promote "gambling plus"/"gaming industry" policy, making the gaming industry helpful to regional cooperation and sustainable development.
—Due to its almost unlimited supply of consumers, proper handling of gambling and gaming activities of the Chinese people is believed to be crucial to China's efforts to introduce a "Harmony China," a "Harmony Asia," and a "Harmony World"[26] (October 12, 2007, SSRC–UMAC, MSAR; Revised on January 1, 2010, HKSAR).

Notes

1. T. J. Cheng talks about human nature and gambling in his article, "Introduction to Sociology of Gambling," in *2006 Conference Proceedings of an International Conference on Gaming Public Welfare* (Hereafter "GIPW Conference Proceedings"), pp. 219–27. Prof. Cheng has this to say about gambling and the Chinese community:

> Abovementioned stereotype comes from the deeply-rooted traditional culture, especially the long term impact of rural society and Confucianism. But in modern society, no matter

> China or overseas, even in those areas which gambling is either illegal or semi-illegal, gambling activities or covert gambling activities are becoming popular by days. Completely and absolutely banning gambling is not only impossible, but also unnecessary, even bringing some negative consequences. . . . The social function of gambling has been fundamentally changed, and it is still changing now in many other places. In Macao, because of its historical effects and special position, gambling has not only been protected by the government, but also been designated as Macao's key industry. Therefore, in Macao, to research and develop sociology of gambling, has certainly access to the advantage of climate, geography and personal support, thus we are just on a correct time to do this job (p. 223).

The conference is organized jointly by the China Center for Lottery Studies at Peking University, Macao Polytechnic Institute, Macao Insitutte for Tourism Studies, and Macao Tourism and Casino Career Center annually.

2. William R. Eadington, "Lessons from the West: What the Experience of Legalization of Gaming in America and Europe can Teach Asian Countries," in *2004 GIPW Conference Proceedings*, pp. 14–27.

Prof. Eadington has this argument,

> Under the best circumstances, gaming industries are likely to remain moderately to significantly controversial in any jurisdictions among some members of the general public, and some policy-makers, because of ongoing moral concerns about gambling in general, and because of perceived or real negative social consequences of expanded gambling. The best way to overcome this stigma is to support a regulatory structure that has greatest potential to protect areas of the serious public concern (p. 26).

3. Peter Collins, "Harnessing Commercial Gambling to Economic Development," in. Ibid., pp. 29–38.

Prof. Collins says that, in order to "secure the objective of harnessing the creativity of the (gaming) developers and thereby of maximizing benefits to the public it is necessary to have competitive process"; and, it is essential to have an adjudication process which is (a) transparent, (b) fair, (c) rational, and (d) demonstrably in the public interest" (pp. 36, 37).

4. How to make commercial gambling and gaming industry "socially responsible," or, to give the industry a face of "social responsibility," is apparently a challenge to elites of that business world. It is so important because it is "an imperative to the long-term viability and role of commercial operators of gaming." See Rohan J. Martin, "Strong Social Responsibility: An Imperative to the Long-term Viability and Role of Commercial Operators of Gaming," in *2004 GIPW Conference Proceedings*, pp. 542–61; Jennifer Shattley, Dean Hestermann, Robert Landouceur, James Whelan, and Car Braunlich, "Harah's National Responsible Gaming Programs: Policy, Technology, Training, and Evaluation," in *2006 GIPW Conference Proceedings*, pp. 124–29.

5. Interestingly, in the GMPW 2004, 2005, and 2006 Conference Proceedings, there is only one article that defends commercial gambling and gaming industry strongly and righteously: Katherine Spilde, "The Social Benefits of Casino Gambling," in *2004 GIPW Conference Proceedings*, pp. 350–76.

Her conclusion should please leaders in Australia, Las Vegas, Macao, Singapore, and possibly in Mainland China, too:

> While the positive social impacts of casino gambling are sometimes difficult to measure quantitatively, it is clear that many jurisdictions are translating gaming employment and revenue into significant positive social change by investing in social and physical infrastructures and governmental reform. These investments ease the burden on state and federal assistance plans since community members are able to find meaningful employment, often for the first time. Communities that host casinos or are located in the region also benefit significantly from the gambling industry's ability to attract new spending and provide additional employment opportunities (p. 374).

6. There are a great numbers of well-written articles studying transformation of commercial gambling into gaming industry in Macao as seen in the *2004*, *2005*, and *2006 GIPW Conference Proceedings* and *Journal of Macao Gaming Research Association*. Apparently, more and more scholars in Mainland China join the rank of research on Macao gambling and gaming institutions.

7. Lau Pun Lap, chairman of the Macao Economic Association and a member of the MSAR Legislative Council, has an article arguing that commercial gambling be turned into a new "Industrial Cluster" if the MSAR is to maintain its competitiveness in the gaming area.

8. Lau Peng Leung's book was published a year after his sudden death. It is in Chinese; full of insightful stories and documents, it is considered to be the first book on the development of commercial gambling in Macao and it certainly deserves to be translated in to English and other languages for this matter.

9. For instance, in his *2007 Policy Address* the CE spent a considerable amount of time to talk about the rapid development of the gaming industry and its impact on socio-economic change in Macao; trying hard to convince both the local population and the central government that the MSAR is moving away from "gambling only" to a "gambling plus" policy.

Tainted by corruption and bad management, readjustment and reorientation of this lead industry have become a very serious challenge to the then MSAR ruling elites if they are going to have sustainable leadership and good governance of the city for the rest of their terms, which was to end December 2009.

10. It is a point well taken that China takes efforts to support and protect the MSAR prominent status as a center of commercial casino; and HKSAR has not given any blessing to intrude into this lucrative business (see "HK 'won't build casinos' to compete with Macao," in *The Macao Post Daily*, September 17, 2007, p. 1).

11. Businessmen and scholars in Macao are perplexed about Macao's rapid development as well as social problems caused by the gaming industry (see for instance the two articles in the *2006 Journal of Macao Gaming Research Association*).

12. Glenn James McCartney, "Casino as a Tourism Redevelopment Strategy: The Case of Macao," in *Journal of Macao Gaming Research Association* 2, April 2005, pp. 40–52.

Prof. McCartney's conclusion is:

> The liberalization process has presented Macao with a strategic milestone in its tourism development cycle, with several destination planning and management challenges emerging as a result. How Macao now repositions itself will have implications on how tourism will develop in the coming years and the destination image that will be portrayed internationally, requiring equal and equitable collaboration and corporation with all of Macao's gaming and tourism stakeholders in reaching the initial objectives behind the liberalization process (p. 49).

13. Dr. Ieong's article is written in Chinese. 楊允中, <產業的特殊性与法監管的重性>; 發表于 "博彩業快速增長對澳門經濟及社會的影响" 學術研討會. 文章有曰:

"中國有句古老成語: '成也蕭何, 敗也蕭何'. 事實上, 討論博彩業似乎也可借用這一模式: '成也博彩, 敗也博彩'. 澳門博彩業近年急速發展是否伴有病態基因實耐人尋味: 投資*2.65*億美金的金沙賭場*2004*年*5*月開幕時掀起一陣熱浪, 開幕當日集團在紐約股市上揚*61 percent*, 不到*8*個月投資已全部返本. 這在國際上極為罕見. 三年之后, *2007*年*8*月, 威尼斯人度假村開幕就更加匪夷所思, 單是世界各地探訪記者竟超過*2000*名, 其設備之豪華, 其規模之龐大, 其設計之新穎等方面可能都是前所未有的紀錄. 如果按老闆如意算盤, 這間投資*24*億美元打造的'巨無霸' 可在三, 五年內返本. 在對比澳門与拉斯維加斯時, 安德森說: '金光大道將被唯一一間賭場運營商壟斷, 那就是金沙集團.' 澳門博彩市場被其中一間所壟斷的可能性絕不應排除, 但恐怕另一一種可能性依然存在, 那就是巨大包袱也可能令超大規模的賭場不堪重負. 如出現前兩種可能之中的任何一種, 澳門所受打擊將不容低估 . . .

14. When I formulated and tried to launch the MUST–ISUS's Project on the Macao–U.S. Relations, Dr. Ming K. Chan, senior researcher at the Hoover Institutions, Stanford University, was asked to give advice and he has been very helpful to my approach.

I introduced Dr. Chan at the "International Conference on 'Macao and Sino–U.S. Relations'" in which he presented a well-written paper on "Sino–U.S. Links with a Twist: Historical and Contemporary Perspective on American Relations with China's Hong Kong and Macao."

15. The quotations come from William A. Douglass and Paulina Raento, "The Tradition of Invention: Conceiving Las Vegas," in *Annals of Tourism Research* 31, no. 1 (2004), 7–23.

16. Macao scholars are also studying the implications of the "Las Vegas Model" for the MSAR gaming industry. Among them, there are Prof. Zeng Zhonglu and Prof. Wang Wuyi at the Macao Polytechnic College. Their articles were written in Chinese *[*曾忠祿, <澳門与拉斯維加斯差異分析>; 刊 <<澳門博彩>>, 第三期, 頁*16–27*; *(2)* 曾忠祿, <美國內華達州博彩區位法律及其對澳門的借鑒意義>; 發表于澳門大學澳門研究中心主辦 "公共行政建設与法制完善" 學術研討會 *(2007.11.)*; *(3)* 王五一, <賭場 "豪華競賽": 產業兩樓性制造的市場失敗>; 發表于澳門學者同盟主辦, "博彩業快速增長對澳門經濟及社會的影响" 學術研討會*]*.

17. Many Macao scholars are also studying Singapore's forthcoming operation of gaming industry and worry about cutthroat competition between the cities.

18. All the quotations on Singapore's IRs came from Yong Kwek Ping and Fu Wenhao Kelvin, "With the Two Integrated Resorts (IRs) in Singapore due for Completion in the Next Few Years, How Should the IRs Align Their Strategies to Attract the Increasingly Affluent and Outbound Tourists or Businessmen from China?" in *2006 GIPW Conference* Proceedings, pp. 71–82.

19. Jamie Leonard, "Building Casinos in the Best Possible Place: Geographic Information Systems and Minimizing Social Cost," in *2006 GIPW Conference Proceedings*, pp. 17–22.

Prof. Leonard has this to say in his conclusion:

> One of the most important features of a casino is its location, a feature that is largely manipulated by zoning, legislation, circumstance, and jurisdiction. Contemporary technology affords the researcher the ability to combine known elements in order to answer questions that are asked for the benefit of society, it is entirely possible to discover the ideal casino location based upon a GIS model to minimize social cost and maximize revenues base upon already available information published through econometric studies and marketing reports. Through the collaboration of econometric regression and Geographic Information Systems, the casino of the future can be strategically placed based upon precision modeling to minimize social costs while simultaneously maximizing economic growth stimulating tax revenues (p. 21).

20. Singapore IRs are formulating their own model by learning from the Las Vegas paradigm with the psychology and behavior of Chinese customers taking into consideration as indicated in the following quotation:

> Tourism institutes also have a very important role in improving the service standards in Singapore. The largest hotel course in the United States, the University of Nevada, Las Vegas (CCI), has set up its first international campus in Singapore offering hospitality management courses. Courses should focus on understanding consumer behavior and developing effective communication skills. The importance of communicating effectively traverses the whole tourism industry. To this end, developing service staff who can converse confidently and smoothly in Mandarin will enable them to communicate effectively with mainland Chinese. Moreover, understanding the consumer behavior of mainland Chinese will give service staff a better understanding of the customer. This also helps to prepare and boost the confidence of service staff should tricky situations arise.

21. China became the prime target of the East Asian gaming industries: while worrying about losing billions and billions of dollars to foreign investors, she is also unwittingly placed in a strategic position to influence the course of this emerging business ring (see M. Mark Michalko, "Challenges and Opportunities Facing the Gaming Industry in the Asia–Pacific Region," in *2006 GIPW Conference Proceedings*, pp. 41–54; and Henry Chan, "The Trend of the Gaming Industry in Asia Pacific," in *2005 GIPW Conference Proceedings*, pp. 35–46).

22. In his *2007 Policy Address*, Dr. Edmund Ho, the MSAR CE, tried again and again to argue that his administration is learning hard from various models to move Macao away from "gambling only" to "gaming plus," and building up the gaming industry systematically.

23. In the *Charter of the Association of Southeast Asian Nations* (published in November 2007, in Singapore), the ASEAN, with its "One Vision, One Identity and One Caring and Sharing Community" (preamble), talks about the need for developing "friendly relations and mutually beneficial dialogue, cooperation and partnerships with countries and sub-regional, regional and international organizations and institutions" (Article 41).

24. If U.S. participation in Macao's gaming industry worries such prominent figures as Dr. Ieong about its political implication so much, it should be in the interests of U.S. corporations, the MSAR and, above all, interests of Macao–U.S. relations and China–U.S. relations that gaming industries both in Macao and East Asia should be treated primarily as business operations; no politics, ideology, and ethnocentricity involved.

Otherwise, they have to read the following nationalistic and xenophobia quotations from the Dr. Ieong's article carefully:

> 在中共七大政治報告里指出: '積極支持香港, 澳門開展對外交往, 堅決反對外部勢力干預香港, 澳門事務'. 确保香港, 澳門長期繁榮稳定, 是執政黨在新形勢下治國理政的重大課題, 上述要求正是落實相關國策的五個內容之一. 外部勢力或外國勢力要干預港澳事務, 必然在內部尋找代理人, 港澳極個別人要賣國求榮, 也必然投靠外國勢力. 從澳門來講, 隨著博彩業開放, 澳門經濟多元化, 國際化程度也空前提高, 社會結構和基本理念也日趨多元化, 這無疑是經濟發展与社會進步的重要標誌, 但与此同時也伴生諸多消極現象, 為發展与進步付出前所未有的巨大社會成本.

> 對于蓄意干預澳門內部事務的企圖和行為, 可能存在不同情況, 不同表現形式. 有些志在壓跨其他企業並進而以澳門為大本營建構全球博彩王國的國際大亨, 會否在經濟上得手后進一步擴大其政治, 文化影响力, 澳門官民恐怕都要打醒精神, 拭目以待: 如果置基本法原則性規定于不顧, 置本地整体利益于不顧, 甚至制造事端意慾借機干預澳門特區內部事務, 那絕對是不明智的, 恐怕也是絕對做不到的. 因為不僅澳門社會這一關過不了, 中央政府也不會袖手旁觀的. 澳門是個功能不減的傳統中外交中心, 澳門居民對寬容, 友善, 和諧的理解是充分而深刻的. 對尊重澳門特區政府, 尊重澳門居民基本權的外來投資者, 他們的合理合法經營所得是會受保護的. 澳門唯小, 但容量龐大, 微型經濟大有作為; 居民數量不多, 但心地善良, 氣量頗大. 當然, 澳門人也是有頭腦, 有智慧的一群, 凡是同現代文明背道而馳, 有霸權味道, 對澳門特區及其廣大居民基本權益構成侵犯時, 絕不會等閒視之. 因為擴大博彩業開放的主旨是引入公平競爭, 加速發展, 提升社會福祉, 因為基本法所設定的, '本地整体利益' 是條不可超逾的底線, 所有澳門博彩市場競爭的參与者都應有一個服務澳門的大前提, 即不可單向地期望變澳門為自己的搖錢樹, 或把澳門變作為意慾控制東方世界的墊腳石. 總之, 博彩業快速發展引發一些暫時性亂象, 如果有人估錯形勢, 伺機蠢蠢欲動, 妄圖改變回歸業已年的現實, 那也不能得逞 . . .

25. As seen in numerous articles published by the *2004*, *2005*, and *2006 GIPW Conference Proceedings* and various issues of the *Journal of Macao Gaming Research*

Association, almost all scholars in Macao have shown serious concerns for pathological gambling caused by casino industry.

26. President Jingtao Hu, in his *Opening Address to the XVII Congress of the Chinese Communist Party*, has promised that China's socioeconomic development will be always beneficial to other economies, particularly economies of the developing world. 10 + 1 FTA is undoubtedly the most important part of China's global strategy *[*<<胡錦濤十七大報告全文>>,<<澳門日報>>, *2007*年*10*月*22*日, *C10-14*版; 有曰: "我們堅持把中國人民的利益同各國人民的共同利益結合起來,秉持公道, 伸張正義"*]*.

CHAPTER THIRTEEN

Macao and Chinese Foreign Relations: A Possible Platform for China and Portuguese-Speaking Countries

Iong Hoi Sun

The Chinese Initiatives

Economic Interdependence

China's initiatives to pursue linkage with PSCs are due to the fact that China and PSCs are becoming more interdependent, especially in economic aspects. Joseph S. Nye and Robert O. Keohane defined "dependence" as "a state of being determined or significantly affected by external forces," and "interdependence" simply means "mutual dependence," which refers to situations characterized by reciprocal effects among countries or among actors in different countries.[1] The PSCs having a population of 230 million are the potential buyers and consumers of Chinese products; on the other hand, China's entry into the markets of PSCs has assisted in boosting investment and in adding value to their assets. Interdependence between China and the Portuguese world is viewed from China's dependence on the PSCs for an abundant supply of resources; in return, the PSCs are mutually dependent on China for their assistance to exploit their untapped resources or gain leverage to negotiate better deals. In recent years, China's dependence on PSCs for the supply of energy resources has increased immensely. In the past, China was the largest oil exporter in East Asia; however, due to rapid economic development and urbanization, it is now the world's second-largest energy consumer after the United States. Based on the figures released by the National Bureau of Statistics, China's energy consumption increased 4 percent to the equivalent of

2.85 billion metric tons of standard coal in 2008. Due to the global economic crisis, this was the least growth in three years compared with 7.8 percent in 2007 and 9.3 percent in 2006. In addition, China's oil consumption keeps on rising; the total oil consumption in 2008 was 360 million tons. However, China's domestic oil production was only 190 million tons, with an increase of only 2.2 percent compared to 2007. Given China's limited domestic reserves of most fuels except coal,[2] in order to sustain economic growth and maintain social stability, China must maintain the expansion of oil imports. China's net import of crude oil was 178 million tons in 2008, up 9.6 percent and net imports of oil products rose by 15 percent to 38.9 million tons.[3] Therefore, it is not surprising for China to expand its foreign access to resource-rich countries to secure a long-term energy supply, and it is no doubt for China to put in the priority of her foreign policy to seek cooperation with them. In addition, countries in the Persian Gulf traditionally have been the largest oil supplier to China; however, due to ongoing political instability and the U.S military preponderance in and around the region, China has started to diversify its foreign supplies, and to shift her dependence on the Middle East and Central Asia to the resource-rich countries in Africa, Southeast Asia, and Latin America.[4] PSCs such as Angola, Mozambique, Brazil, and Timor-Leste are the potential source of energy supporters to China; for instance, Angola is the second-largest oil producer in Africa and has taken over Saudi Arabia to become the largest oil supplier to China in recent years.[5] Therefore, the establishment of linkage with Portuguese countries provides China with the opportunities to expand its energy sources. In addition, it is believed that the mineral deposits in countries like Angola, Brazil, Mozambique, and East Timor have not yet been developed and determined fully. In such way, China can help to exploit the resources by providing them with the technology. As the world's manufacturing kingdom, China has a huge demand for other mineral resources. It is known that China's combined share of the world's consumption of aluminum, copper, nickel, and iron are going to reach near 40 percent by 2010,[6] the Portuguese-speaking countries are known to have rich reserves of mineral resources, like iron, nickel, aluminum, phosphate, and bauxite, among others, which can meet the needs of China.[7]

While China is dependent on the resource rich Portuguese world, some of the Portuguese-speaking countries are also relying on China for the export of finished products and consumer goods such as textiles and electronic products. For example, in 2008, bilateral trade between Brazil and China reached $36.44 billion, increasing 55.9 percent over 2007. In April 2009, China for the first time overtook the United States to become the leading export market for Brazil and the trade between both countries reached $3.2

billion.[8] In fact, bilateral economic relations with the Portuguese world has been strengthened and improved in recent years. In 2003, China and the seven PSCs held their first ministerial-level official meeting in Macao, the crucial achievement was the signing of the "Action Plan for Economic and Trade Cooperation," which established the mode of cooperation between the participating countries in the future, covering areas such as inter-governmental cooperation, investment and enterprises cooperation, trades, agriculture and fishing, construction and infrastructure, natural resources, and human resources. The trade volume between China and the Portuguese world in 2002 was only $6.1 billion; after the signing of the bilateral agreement on trade and commerce, trade volume has risen to $34 billion in 2006, with Brazil and Angola being the largest trading partners among the Portuguese world (see table 13.1). Recognizing the great potential in bilateral trade between China and Portuguese-speaking countries, especially the latter's export to China, in 2006, at the second ministerial-level official meeting, China and seven Portuguese-speaking countries adopted a new "Action Plan for Economic and Trade Cooperation" in Macao, stressing that economic and trade relations are the core and basis of the exchanges among member countries of the Forum, and striving for increasing the bilateral trade volume to $45–50 billion by 2009.[9] Bilateral trade between China and PSCs already reached the target of the New Action Plan to $46 billion in 2007 (see table 13.1). In the first ten months of 2008, the bilateral trade between China and PSCs was nearly $66 billion,[10] exceeding the designed target by $16 billion.

A Multilateral Foreign Policy Approach

In addition to economic interdependence, China's initiative to establish linkage with PSCs is a representation of China's approach of a multilateral foreign policy. In the post–Cold War era, international relations has been featured by a structure of uni-polarity, with the United States as the major superpower, many of the international standards and game of rules were shaped by the large nations, small states and developing countries often have less right to say. Recognizing the fact that developing countries can only survive through "active participation," Chinese foreign policy has adjusted the longstanding approach of "independent foreign policy" toward a multilateral and multipolar world development process.

In an era of globalization, China understands that only by integration and multilateral cooperation can it exert an "influence towards the rule of international organizations and regimes so as to ensure their qualification in relation to the priorities of China's own national economic development."[11] The

Table 13.1 Import and Export Value of China and Portuguese-Speaking Countries (US.$10,000)

Year	2002		2003		2004		2005		2006		2007	
Country (Region)	Total Import and Export Value	±%	Total Import and Export Value	±%	Total Import and Export Value	±%	Total Import and Export Value	±%	Total Import and Export Value	±%	Total Import and Export Value	±%
Total Value	62,076,808	21.80	88,120,729	37.1	115,479,162	35.7	142,211,761	23.2	176,068,645	23.8	217,383,301	23.5
Portuguese-Speaking Countries	605,641	25.05	1,102,923	82.11	1,827,063	65.7	2,318,561	26.9	3,408,187	46.9	4,635,338	36.0
Portugal	38,363	15.5	60,098	56.7	86,930	44.7	123,586	42.2	171,353	38.7	221,081	29.0
Brazil	446,944	20.9	798,856	78.7	1,235,898	54.8	1,481,729	20	2,029,997	37	2,970,504	46.4
Angola	114,835	49.6	235,173	104.8	491,087	108.8	695,462	41.6	1,182,748	70.1	1,411,998	19.4
Mozambique	4,849	45.9	7,171	47.8	11,944	66.8	16,504	38.1	20,774	25.9	28,411	36.8
Guinea-Bissau	450	-45.7	1,235	174.2	602	-51.2	579	-3.8	508	-2	745	31.2
Cape Verde	184	-16.9	260	41.1	275	5.8	519	88.9	1,009	94.6	1,470	45.7
Sao Tome and Principle	16	-87.7	22.9	47.5	156	582	55	-64.7	122	121.4	178	46.1
Timor-Leste	--	--	107	--	171	60.1	127	-25.5	1,676	1,215.90	951	-43.3

Source: Ministry of Commerce of the People's Republic of China, zhs.mofcom.gov.cn/tongji2008.shtml

step-by-step learning process of China's engagement in international organizations has further reflected China's multilateral foreign policy approach. In the initial period after the establishment of the People's Republic of China, China was excluded from mainstream international politics; the recognition of China by the United Nations in 1971 marked the transition point for China's involvement in international affairs. In the past decades, China has been gradually fitting into the global environment by adjusting the domestic laws and regulations and improving their compliance to international standards. Apart from growing participation in the United Nations, there has been increasing activism of China to involve itself in Asian regional institutions, especially the Association of Southeast Asian Nations (ASEAN). ASEAN and China are partners in various regional and international forums, such as the ASEAN Regional Forum, ASEAN + 3 (China, Japan, and South Korea), Asia–Europe Meeting, and the Forum for East Asia–Latin America Cooperation. China was ASEAN's first major partner to sign the Treaty of Amity and Cooperation in Southeast Asia in 2003; it was also the first country to sign a framework agreement with ASEAN for the establishment of a free trade area in 2002.[12] Besides, ASEAN and China were each other's major trading partner. In 2008, China's total import value from ASEAN reached $117 billion, an increase of 7.9 percent compared to 2007, while export reached $114.1 billion, an increase of 20.7 percent.[13] In order to further cooperation and dialogue between ASEAN, a memorandum of understanding was signed in April 2005 covering areas of cooperation in translation crimes and other areas of economic, tourism, and energy cooperation,[14] another Memorandum of Understanding in regard to information sharing and media cooperation was also signed in 2008.[15] In other aspects, China also advocated the Shanghai Cooperation Organization (SCO) that included the countries in Eurasia, aiming to a progressive "regrouping and cooperation mechanism"[16] to promote a multipolar development in international relations. Over the past few years, the organization has served as a forum for military and security issues, intelligence sharing, energy cooperation, as well as counterterrorism and drug trafficking among member states. In military aspects, the SCO has pursued a number of military exercises, such as a peace mission anti-terror drill in 2007 near Russia's Ural Mountains, the joint exercise was intended to show the will and determination of SCO members in action to crack down on terrorism.[17] In term of energy cooperation, recognizing Central Asia as one of the world's energy reserves, SCO member states sought greater energy cooperation through preferential energy agreements. All these actions confirm the claims about China's current strategy, which involves a growing participation in regional and international organizations that might have been viewed as suspicious in the past, but have come to have been seen recently as more beneficial for Chinese economic, security, and other objectives.[18]

In the new millennium, the regional spectrum of China's multilateral foreign policy approach is extending across Asia to Africa and Latin America. It is also clear in the Chinese policy and diplomacy's advice to Third World countries that they must find ways to maximize the opportunities of economic globalization while retaining their sovereign options through participation in international rule making and remaining politically wary of the agenda-setting activity of the developed states.[19] In recent years, China and some of the developing countries have continuously sought cooperation opportunities. For example, the Ministerial Forum between China and African countries (FOCAC) was held respectively in 2000, 2003, and 2006. The objective of the Summit aims to build a new type of China–Africa strategic partnership featuring political equality and mutual trust, economic win-win cooperation, and cultural exchange. The forum served as a key platform and effective mechanism for collective dialogue and pragmatic cooperation, a series of cooperative plans have been achieved in the forum. Apart from Africa, China's connection to the Portuguese world was first initiated in 2003 with the First and Second Ministerial Conference of the Forum on Economic and Trade Cooperation between China and Portuguese-speaking Countries held in Macao in 2003 and 2006. These forums have allowed China to establish links and connections with multiple countries working in concert on a given issue and in areas of common interests. In the era of globalization, China's linkage with the world has extended from Asia across the continent to Latin America and Africa, the cooperation program and action plan set forth in the forum have allowed multiple countries, having diversified backgrounds, to cooperate toward the goal of achieving mutual benefits, which draws up a new blueprint for future cooperation between China and multiple regions in all fields in the new century.

Enhancement of Cooperation for the Developing World

Ever since the 1970s, there has been much debate on the issues of North–South divide; due to the fact that many of the Third World countries were previously colonized by the West, their development remained in a poor and underdeveloped situation. When the northern industrialized counterparts had already been exporting manufactured products and engaged in advanced economic activities, denied with advanced technologies for production, many of the LDCs can only rely on the export of raw materials and resources in order to survive, thus remaining in the primary stage of production. Such situations can be viewed by the capitalist world system that industrialized countries are the core, leaving the less-developed and underdeveloped states in the semi-periphery and periphery, thus staying in a subordinate position in the world capitalist system. The North–South divide has resulted in the situation that the LDCs had to accept the poor deals Western countries forced on them and relied on the West for the transfer of technology and export of manufactured commodities. This uneven development has led the South to a widespread agreement on the New International Economic Order (NIEO) to seek multilateral cooperation between the North and the South. Despite the fact that the NIEO did not result in a great success, in recent years, there has been increasing cooperation among the developing states themselves.

As stipulated by the *Human Development Report 2008* of the United Nations Development Program (UNDP), in measuring Human Development Index, 179 countries of the world are divided into three groups: high human development, medium human development, and low human development. Among the countries being evaluated, 75 of them are categorized as high development, while the rest of 104 are categorized as medium and low development. Of the PSCs, except for Portugal (ranked 33) and Brazil (ranked 70), which are categorized as high development, China and the rest of the other PSCs are categorized as medium and low development.[20] In this era, although China and most of the PSCs are still considered to be developing countries, their intimate cooperation has a broad implication and strategic importance for South–South cooperation. As China becomes a rising power in the world, it can take a leading role in assisting the developing countries and in promoting a balance growth in world development. In recent years, China and other developing countries as strategic partners have developed trust and supported each other. There were frequent diplomatic visits between the leaders of China and PSCs to exchange views on bilateral relations and issues of common interests, agreements for further bilateral cooperation have been signed. Since 2001, the Chinese president and premier have met with the presidents and other higher-level officials of Angola, Cape Verde, Mozambique, and Brazil, among others. Such bilateral exchanges and visits can further strengthen the close connection between both sides, and to a further extent create a new atmosphere for South–South cooperation. For example, in an official visit to Brazil in 2006, the chairman of the Standing Committee of the National People's Congress (NPC) Wu Bangguo expressed his view on the importance of bilateral cooperation between China and Brazil. "As the largest developing countries in the eastern and western hemispheres respectively, China and Brazil have common interests in international affairs, and hold the same or similar views on major international or regional issues. Further agreements on Sino–Brazilian economic and trade cooperation will be signed to push forward the strategic cooperation and inject new vitality into the development of bilateral strategic partnership."[21] On August 25, 2007, the Brazilian vice president also met with Chinese Vice Foreign Minister Lin Jinzhang, and both sides agreed to continue in strengthening multilevel dialogue and communication, deepening all areas of exchanges and cooperation, and making unremitting efforts for in-depth development of bilateral ties.[22]

Apart from frequent diplomatic visits, China is also providing assistance to many of the developing countries of the Portuguese world. The Chinese government has granted subsidy and provided aid to encourage the domestic state-owned enterprises to invest in and establish business relations with the African countries of Mozambique and Angola. For instance, Chinese government has attempted to encourage and assist Chinese companies to invest in Africa and provide reciprocal arrangements for African companies in China. This strategy has prompted China's business sector to invest abroad and at the same time solidified China's relations with many developing countries.[23] China is also known to be involved in basic welfare such as road construction, bridging, hospitals, and health facilities in Portuguese-speaking countries, and assisted them in agriculture development and infrastructure construction. For example, in 2004, China agreed to extend $2 billion in credits to Angola for the reconstruction of the nation's east–west railroad that was destroyed by civil war.[24] In February 2007, China agreed to increase government-funded scholarship quotas for Mozambican students and assist Mozambique to build schools in rural areas and malaria prevention and treatment centers.[25] Besides, the Chinese government has expanded the range of imports from Cape Verde that enjoy favorable tariff treatment and assist Cape Verde to build two country schools.[26]

It is pointed out that China's approach to win Third World endorsement for policies is its design to achieve the PRC's fundamental strategic and economic goals.[27] However, in a time when the Western world has reduced development aid year after year, China has promised to double aid by 2009 without insisting on onerous conditions to the Third World nations. Chinese assistance to the Third World countries is important for them to build up national strength; it is of strategic importance for building mutual trust and promoting South–South cooperation by creating conditions for a balanced growth in world development. By the joint effort to promote mutual interests among the developing world, it is hoped to push the international political and economic order to develop in a more fair and reasonable way.

In the year 2008, even in times when the global economy was suffering from downturn and financial crisis, trade and economic cooperation between China and the PSCs were still growing at a rapid pace, more and more infrastructure and business missions were initiated between Beijing and PSCs. In fact, this positive trade relationship was made possible by the Chinese recognition of the opportunity for growth in Africa. As it is known, China has helped to add much value to the assets of the Third World, for example, the modernization of the International Airport in Mozambique was carried out on funding provided by the Chinese government, which aimed to increase the airport's current passenger capacity. Besides, large Chinese companies are involved in the Angolan national reconstruction program, which is estimated to be $5 billion. In addition, the two biggest airlines in Angola and China began to organize scheduled flights in 2009.[28] Besides, the president of Angola visited China two times in 2008 with a view to boost bilateral cooperation in areas of infrastructure, transport, health, and education.[29] Apart from Angola, it is forecasted that the Chinese government is looking for trade opportunities in Cape Verde, seeing the potential of the country in its level of development and availability of infrastructures and so forth.[30] In December 2008, businesspeople from logistics, ports, fishing, and information technology in Shenzhen visited Cape Verde to study the possibility of investment. The increasing investment and assistance of China in the continent has allowed the Third World countries to build up their infrastructures, so as to attract more business opportunities. Such phenomenon is described by Edward Friedman as the flying geese paradigm,[31] in which China could be the driving force for African countries' development in the short term and China's involvement in Africa could cause the continent's economy to grow. It is further claimed that, despite increasing South–South cooperation, China does not pose as a leader of the Third World; it tries to achieve a balance between promoting its own fundamental interests and representing those of the developing world. In fact, it represents China's attempt to redistribute the global power by its continuing effort to shift the current locus of global power from the United States to a more differentiated, multipolar environment.[32]

Macao Platform: Potential and Strength

The favorable conditions offered by Macao's political and economic system together with the cultural and language linkages composed to be the unique features for Macao to be the service platform.

Political and Economic Advantages

The preferential political and economic environment has equipped Macao to play the role of facilitating and enhancing the connection between China and the PSCs. As long as in the period under Portuguese administration, due to the Portuguese connection with Europe and Latin America, Macao as a non-sovereign entity has already maintained extensive close relations with various countries and regions in the world. After the handover, in accordance with the Basic Law and under the principle of "one country, two systems," Macao can still maintain and develop relations, conclude and implement agreements with foreign states and regions and relevant international organizations in the appropriate fields, while regulating negotiations at the diplomatic level regarding the region to be conducted by the central government (Article 135). In this sense, the authority of Macao to participate in international organizations and establish external relations is guaranteed by the Basic Law even after its return to Chinese sovereignty. At present, four of the PSCs, Brazil, Portugal, East Timor, and Cape Verde, granted visa free entry to holders of Macao passports, thus allowing free movement of human resource and personnel exchange between Macao and PSCs. At the same time, Portugal and Angola have set up consulates general in Macao, while Cape Verde, Mozambique, and Guinea Bissau have appointed honorary consuls in Macao. As the only region within Chinese territory to possess the unique linkage with the PSCs, the highest authority in Beijing decided to utilize Macao as to serve as a platform for China's growing economic and strategic interests in the Portuguese world.

Apart from the special privilege of the political system, Macao's economic environment has provided it with the potential to be the service platform. Since the mid-nineteenth century, situated at the estuary of the Pearl River Delta Region, Macao was a famous entreport of sea trade. Although Macao's position was gradually taken over by its Hong Kong counterpart, it still maintains its popularity as a free trade center. After the handover, Macao continuously modified its investment environment to attract foreign investment. Compared to neighbors, like Hong Kong, Taiwan, or Korea, Macao has a low property and labor cost, and in addition, Macao is a well-known offshore financial center—the minimum registered capital in Macao is MOP$25,000 (approximate to $3,125), the operation of offshore service business in Macao is provided with tax incentives, and they are exempted from income tax, industrial tax, and stamp duties.[33] In addition, giving its well-developed telecommunication and financial system, and a legal framework that is similar to that of the European market,[34] these advantages can help Macao to serve the needs of economic and trade cooperation between China and the PSCs.

Furthermore, under the doctrine of "one country, two systems," Macao enjoys preferential policies offered by the central government to the Special Administrative Regions. In January 2009, the National Development and Reform Commission released the Development Plan for the Pearl River Delta for 2009–2020, with the development of Hengqing Island in Zhuhai,[35] and the construction of the Hong Kong–Zhuhai–Macao Bridge listed as the priorities for the endorsement of the plan, in such way there will be a wide spectrum of opportunities for potential investors and businesses in the Pearl River Delta region. The preferential policies by the central government have further allowed Macao to integrate into the regional market and consolidate its platform function.

A Long-Standing Connection

Historically and culturally, Macao has established a long-standing connection with the Portuguese world. First of all, Portuguese is one of the official language, and many of the civil servants and businessmen in Macao are fluent in both Chinese and Portuguese languages. Second, a number of Portuguese companies such as banks and lawyers are providing services in Macao. There are also a number of Portuguese investments in the major areas of public utilities such as telecommunications and electricity.[36] Third, a large number of local Macao people have migrated to Brazil and Mozambique, which gives them knowledge of the cultures and customs there.[37] Fourth, the Portuguese culture and way of living has been embedded in the social environment of the Macao society, for instance, Portuguese cuisine has become Macao's famous gastronomy. In addition, many of the Portuguese-style buildings and architectures were being renewed and preserved by the Macao government in a way to demonstrate the unique features of Sino–Western cultural integration in Macao. Furthermore, there is other evidence showing the close connection between Macao and PSCs. For example, in 2002, during the East Timor occupation by Indonesia, Macao has provided shelter for Timorese in Macao.[38] Besides, in 2002, Macao also attracted a Portugal association (Forum of Portuguese-speaking Entrepreneurs–FELP), a non-profit and non-governmental organization which has branches in seven PSCs, to set up headquarters in Macao. In addition, some large scale activities of the PSCs have chosen Macao to be the host city, which included the twenty-third Conference for Portuguese Language Capital Cities Association—UCCLA[39]—held in October 2007, and the thirty-fourth National Congress of the Portuguese Association of Travel Agencies—APAVT[40]—held in 2008. The former congress has been hosted for its third time in Macao while the latter has been hosted four times in Macao, thus demonstrating the close connection between Macao and the PSCs.

The Increasing Popularity

Since the opening of the gaming industry in 2002, Macao has been growing into an international and metropolitan city; the entry of the U.S. investment into Macao has further strengthened its potential to serve as the platform, especially for convention and meeting purposes. As the construction of newly invested casinos and other entertainment facilities have gradually completed, many of them are equipped with large scale convention and meeting venues. For example, the largest new convention facility development in the Venetian complex on the Cotai Strip is featured with a 15,000 fixed-seat plenary hall, 25,000 square meters of meeting complex, and 74,682 square meters of new exhibition space, which is one of the largest convention and exhibition centers in Asia.[41] The existing facilities together with others under construction are expected to add strength to Macao's potential for conventions and exhibition purposes and also assist in boosting Macao to attract more high-yield events. Furthermore, Macao's ability to act as the coordinator and organizer for international events is being consolidated in recent years; several large scale and international sport events such as the 2005 East Asian Games, the 2006 Lusophony Games, and the 2007 Asian Indoor Games have been hosted in Macao, which further consolidates Macao's ability in holding international events and also in gaining international recognition, thus creating a positive image and giving confidence around the world to utilize Macao as a service platform.

The Potential Platform

Since the initiation of the first ministerial-level official meeting between China and Portuguese-speaking countries in 2003, Macao has served as the platform between China and Portuguese-speaking countries. At present, Macao has been the platform for economic and trade cooperation, and also served as the liaison platform. As cooperation between China and Portuguese-speaking countries gets more intensive, it is believed that Macao's platform function will be more prominent and diversified.

Platform for Bilateral Trade and Economic Cooperation

The most obvious function performed by Macao to serve the interests of China and the Portuguese world is the platform for trade and economic cooperation. Having the potential of historical linkage and a flexible economic system, together with the strength of language ability, Macao can serve as an intermediary to facilitate bilateral trade and provide enterprises for Portuguese-speaking countries that hope to enter or expand the Chinese market with the necessary consultation and financial support services. One of the obvious achievements for enhancing economic cooperation between China and PSCs is the initiation of the Forum on Economic and Trade Cooperation in 2003, which was a milestone for China and PSCs in the new era. The Action Plan signed seeks to establish common development in seven areas related to inter-governmental cooperation, investment, and enterprises co-operation; trades, agriculture, and fishing; construction and infrastructure; and natural resources and human resources.

In recent years, as bilateral trade between China and the Portuguese world increases year by year, China and the PSCs have demonstrated an increasing level of economic interdependence. However, for Macao, the level of inter-dependence with the PSCs is relatively low, Macao is not the major trading partner with most Portuguese-speaking countries, Macao's trade with Portuguese-speaking countries is limited to Portugal and Brazil. The total trade volume with Portugal was $22 million in 2008, while the total trade value of Macao and Brazil was $20 million in 2008, which was limited to imports of foodstuffs and beverages to Macao from Brazil (table 13.2).[42] As Macao focuses on the development on tertiary industry, services, and gaming, there is no urgent need for large consumption of energy and natural resources to facilitate industrial development; on the other hand, many of the poor and underdeveloped regions of the Portuguese world cannot afford to consume Macao's exports and tourism-related services. Despite the fact that Macao and the Portuguese world do not have immediate concern for cooperation, possessing the advantages of being a regional monetary, financial, consultation, and convention center, Macao can achieve a higher level of sustainable growth and development by utilizing itself to serve as a platform for transit trading and re-export. In 2008 the total re-export value of Macao reached $805 million, of which 27.1 percent was re-export to Mainland China. In addition, Macao is well known for having a low tax rate, besides, the stable investment and economic environment has attracted large amounts of foreign direct investment. The flows of foreign direct investment in 2007 reached $1.65 billion, a 2.7 percent increase compared to 2006.[43] In fact, Macao has a number of very important Portuguese companies such as banks and law firms, which can provide service for the PSCs. Apart from a favorable economic environment, Macao also enjoys favorable and special privileges and policy arrangements in trade and investment offered by Mainland China, with CEPA as one of the examples, it is a Free Trade Area (FTA)-like arrangement concluded between Mainland China and Macao, two separate customs territories within a single sovereign state. In conformity with the WTO principles and rules, CEPA provides Macao service suppliers an earlier access to the mainland market, earlier than the timetable China committed to the WTO.[44] Therefore, potential manufacturers from PSCs can utilize Macao to set up production firms and export the products to the mainland to enjoy special custom reduction.

Since the signing of the "Action Plan for Economic and Trade Cooperation" in 2003, there has been increasing recognition and utilization of Macao as a service platform by the PSCs. For instance, in October 2008, the Portuguese-owned company Sociedade Industrial de Macao (SIM) set up a roasting coffee factory in Macao, in a project focused on exports to China and providing services in Asia.[45] In addition, at the meeting with some 200 Macao and Pearl River Delta businesspeople in June 2008, the Brazilian secretary for foreign trade, Welber Barral proclaimed that "the role of the Forum for Economic and Trade Cooperation between China and the Portuguese-speaking countries based in Macao was important in the strategy of greater economic proximity between Brazil and China via Macao." This is especially important when Brazil is planning to boost trade relations with China based on infrastructure work and logistics projects (airports and ports). As far as it is known, both sides have already reached agreement and the "China Agenda—Positive Action for Sino–Brazilian Economic and Trade Relations" was launched.[46] Furthermore, more and more PSCs are planning to set up local offices in Macao to utilize its platform function. For example, as early as 2005, Brazil planned to set up a permanent institution in Macao to be a "base for entry for Brazilian companies in the Macao market,"[47] given the country's interest in promoting the sale of farm products in Macao and southern China. It is also known that another Brazilian association, the São Paulo Commercial Association (ACSP), also plans to open a representative office in Macao to support small and medium-sized Brazilian companies that want to work in Mainland China.[48] Owing to Brazil's economic structure and the growing cooperation with China, a stronger economic and trade cooperation between Brazil and Macao will surely raise Macao's profile in the Portuguese-speaking world and attract other Portuguese-speaking countries to expand their business in the Mainland China market by making use of Macao as a platform.

Apart from the Portuguese-speaking countries' interests to utilize the Macao platform, in recent years, Macao investors have shown their presence in the Portuguese world, especially in the finance sector. In June 2008, a Mozambique bank Moza Banco was launched, which involved an initial capital of $15 million from Macao.[49] The bank will be involved in investment, corporate, and private banking, but the main purpose of the Macao-based

Table 13.2 Macao's Import and Export Value to Portuguese-Speaking Countries
***MOP$8 is approximately equal to US$1 (MOP$10,000)**

Year	2004		2005		2006		2007		2008	
Country (Region)	Import	Export	Import	Export	Import	Export	Import	Export	Import	Export
Total Value	2,790,401.50	2,256,108.30	3,134 ,029.30	1,982,334.20	3,652,730.29	2,046,126.53	4,311,385.90	2,043,057.87	4,303,421.9	1,602,540.30
Portugal	11,556.54	2,165.92	10,502.64	1,621.48	13,224.28	721.55	15,128.69	274.48	17,134.81	556.91
Brazil	9,263.06	52.36	5,503.14	258.32	6,151.39	2,263.98	10,278.66	691.28	14,996.52	1,066.43
Angola	-	465.51	-	-	-	-	-	0.54	17.59	-
Mozambique	-	-	-	-	0.70	0.36	248.90	-	-	-
Guinea-Bissau	-	-	-	-	-	-	-	-	-	-
Cape Verde	-	-	-	-	-	-	0.058	-	1.49	-
Sao Tome and Principle	-	-	-	-	-	-	-	-	-	-
Timor-Leste	-	2.0	3.07	-	63.43	-	249.33	-	145.38	-

Source: Statistics and Census Service (DSEC), Macao SAR, //www.dsec.gov.mo

company is to establish itself as one of the main biofuel producers worldwide based in Angola, Mozambique, and Guinea Bissau. Considering the great potential of the Portuguese world for agricultural and geo-mining, Macao's investment in the Portuguese world can provide them to gain access to long-term financial support and technological assistance to develop their manufacturing activities.[50] In the first half of 2008, Macao was seventh among the biggest investors in Mozambique while China ranked ninth. In addition, cooperation with PSCs are beneficial for Macao to diversify its industrial structure; for instance, Macao can import relevant raw materials, such as timber or diamonds from Angola, Brazil, or East Timor, in cooperation with the enterprises in the Pearl River Delta responsible for the manufacturing process, and Macao's back office acts as a supporting function for marketing, packaging, and design.

Platform for Liaison and Organization of International Events

As the only region in China that has historical and cultural links with PSCs, Macao was designated to host the first ministerial-level official meeting between China and Portuguese-speaking countries. This forum was the first kind to be organized by the Chinese Ministry of Commerce, and Macao SAR was the event coordinator. The Forum concluded to set up a permanent secretarial office in Macao to take up the role for further contact and liaison, as well as to follow up with the actions of the Forum and continue with the consultations with the Portuguese-speaking countries on the organization of different kinds of economic and trade activities. The secretarial office to be stationed in Macao is of vital significance to further strengthen Macao's platform function for maintaining close connection between China and PSCs. Due to the October 2003 Forum, Macao SAR successively signed various cooperation agreements with counterpart organizations and business associations in Portugal, Brazil, and other Portuguese-speaking countries. Besides, a joint cooperation agreement has been reached among Macao, China Council for Promotion of International Trade (CCPIT), and the trade promotion institutions and business associations of Portuguese-speaking countries, which established a mode of co-operation for all the signatories, covering market research, trade links, investment promotion, trade information exchanges, the setting up and updating of a "database of trade and investment projects," and the annual "Businesspeople Meeting for the Commercial and Economic Co-operation" to be hosted on a rotation basis by the signatory countries and regions.[51] The Meeting of Businesspeople for Economic and Trade Cooperation between China and the Portuguese-speaking countries has been held four times, previously in Luanda, Lisbon, Maputo, and Praia, and brings together businesspeople and representatives to explore business opportunities.[52]

Possessing the language ability and a long-standing cultural linkage with Portugal and other Portuguese-speaking world, Macao can act as an intermediary for the arrangement and organization of bilateral exchanges and visits in order to maintain intimate contact and harmonic cooperation environment for both sides. Since 2002, the Macao Trade and Investment Promotion Institute of the Macao government, together with local commercial organizations have arranged business delegations to the Portuguese-speaking countries including East Timor, Brazil, and Cape Verde to visit the major association of traders, government ministers and various important commercial organizations and chambers of commerce to seek further cooperation in potential areas. In an official visit to Mozambique in 2002, some useful business matching sessions arranged for the Macao delegates to have private meetings with the entrepreneurs in respective areas; both sides signed a pact in regard to pharmaceutical product development. Besides, as a liaison platform, Macao has assisted investors from Mainland China to be familiarized with the PSCs; for instance, Macao has arranged delegations and entrepreneurs from PSCs to visit the Pan Pearl River Delta Region and in October 2005, Fujian and Macao joined hands for a business mission to FACIM (Maputo International Trade and Investment Fair) in Mozambique. The delegation visits not only provide a good chance to have a comprehensive understanding of the market conditions and investment environment of the Portuguese world, it can also enhance bilateral cooperation and further strengthen Macao's platform function.

In addition, Macao can also serve as an interface to create investment opportunities through the organization and coordination of international events. For instance, the Macao Trade and Investment Fair (MIF) is held each year by the Macao Trade and Investment Promotion Institutes. Exhibitors from China, especially Guangdong provinces and Pearl River Delta Region, Hong Kong, and Macao are invited to set up exhibition counters and to participate in major economic activities like trade negotiation, product displays, and business matching in order to exchange business information. In recent years, by fully utilizing Macao as a platform for China and PSCs, a special theme area was created for the Portuguese-speaking countries, including exhibition counters, buyer's corner, negotiation area, seminars, business matching sessions, and so forth. This is a good opportunity for the participants to interact and co-operate with each other in order to attract economic and trade organizations, government institutions, corporations, traders, and investors from around the world.

Challenges and Constraints

Owing to historical proximity and language ability, together with the advantage of Macao's knowledge of the cultures and customs of both Chinese and Portuguese environments, such potential has made Macao to be designated as the service platform. As an intermediary, Macao can provide the necessary legal consultancy and assist in the translations and business procedures. Besides, the rapid economic development in recent years has enhanced Macao's international reputation and the U.S. investment in gaming industry has assisted Macao with the infrastructure to facilitate its liaison function. However, Macao is just at the beginning of its role as the service platform, and there are still many constraints and weaknesses Macao needs to overcome and take into considerations.

The Lack of Human Resources

The U.S. investment in the gaming and entertainment sector has led to a rise of reputation of Macao in Asia, and more and more international events and activities are hosted in Macao. Although the gaming industry has facilitated Macao with the necessary convention and meeting venues for the organization of these activities, however, limited by its small population, Macao is faced with the problem of the lack of human resources. Presently Macao is importing labor from the Mainland and other countries to fill the need of the local development. In 2008, the total population of Macao was 540,000, and the total number of working labor was 320,000, of which 92,161 were imported labor, which accounted for 28.8 percent of the total labor force, showing a high reliance of imported labor force.[53]

In order to utilize Macao as the liaison platform between China and PSCs, Macao needs a large number of personnel who are proficient in both Chinese and Portuguese languages. Although Macao was under Portuguese administration for 400 years, the number of Macao people who are proficient in the Portuguese language is very limited. Those who are proficient in Portuguese are the older generation of Portuguese and their Macanese generation. According to the survey by the Macao Development Strategy Research Center in 2005, even though Portuguese is one of the official languages, only 3 percent of Macao people know how to speak, read, and write it, 10 percent knows very little of it, and nearly 85 percent do not know any.[54] At present, since Portuguese is one of the official languages in Macao, the documents of the local government are normally represented in both Chinese and Portuguese languages, and sometimes English. Therefore, the use of Portuguese language is quite limited to government and other large-scale enterprises, while other small and medium enterprises and local communities normally do not use it. As economic and trade cooperation between the mainland and Portuguese-speaking countries are increasing year by year, the role of Macao as a service platform is becoming more prominent. It is expected that the use of Portuguese will be extended to other private sectors in the near future,[55] and there will be a higher demand for professionals in both Chinese and Portuguese languages. In order to maintain a sustainable development as a service platform, the Macao government can actually encourage and subsidize students to receive training in the Portuguese language; local institutions can also help to enhance language proficiency by providing language courses in Portuguese. In addition to this, the government can consider importing professional personnel who are proficient in the Portuguese language from Portugal or China to fill the demand.

Transportation and Logistics Network

As an economic and trade cooperation platform, Macao plays an important role in the promotion of bilateral trade. Through the organization of business matching sessions and delegation visits, Macao has assisted both Chinese entrepreneurs and enterprises from PSCs to find potential partners for trade and economic cooperation. It is believed that with the release of "the Development Plan for the Pearl River Delta for 2009–2020," regional cooperation within Southern China will further be enhanced. In order to serve as an economic and trade platform and meet the increasing demand of regional cooperation, Macao is required to develop a sophisticated logistics and transportation network. According to statistics information, Macao's volume of containerized cargo has increased rapidly in recent years. In 2008, logistics services both in and out the border gate and Cotai checkpoint recorded a rise of 67 percent compared to 2007 (see table 13.3). Despite the fact that Macao has the basic transportation network including an international airport and container harbor and land transportation network linked with Mainland China through the border gate, the existing transportation network is of small scale and cannot meet the demand of future development. For example, the existing International Airport of Macao has direct flights covering only eleven destination points of Mainland China, Taiwan, Singapore, Thailand, Vietnam, Malaysia, Japan, Australia, Indonesia, Philippines, and Korea, with the total number of flights at 46,036 in 2008.[56] The flight destinations and airlines covered by the existing Macao International Airport are very limited and do not yet cover major destinations of the Portuguese-speaking countries; despite that Macao International Airport successfully handled ten charter freighter services from Macao to Angola in August 2008.[57] There are not yet any long-term flights established between Macao and PSCs. In addition, most of Macao's container traffic is related to the South China region, and even though Macao has two harbors (the inner harbor and the Ka Ho Harbor), its throughput capacity is far smaller than the nearby region of Hong Kong.[58] For example, seaborne freight movement in Hong Kong was 24,494,000 TEUs in 2008; while Macao's seaborne transit movement was only 126,335 TEUs, demonstrating the relatively weak seaborne transit capacity of Macao.

In order to strengthen Macao's logistics capacity under the demand of huge scope development, in 2001, construction began on the Macao Logistics Center, located near the international airport; a total area of 23 hectares completed in two phases is hoping to solve the increasing demand of cargo transit.[59] For continuous development, Macao should continue strengthening its logistic and transportation network. In 2008, consensus was finally reached among the three sides on the construction of Hong Kong–Zhuhai–Macao Bridge since it was first proposed in 1982. Once completed, the bridge will enhance connections of Hong Kong and Macao with other cities and port facilities in the Pearl River Delta in southern China. The tentative schedule will commence in the year 2011 and is hoping to be completed by 2015 or 2016.[60]

Barriers of a Small Territory

The third challenge facing Macao being a service platform is its small territory, which limited Macao's development in many aspects. As a small territory, there is a lack of human resources in supplying the demands of the fast-growing economy. As a small territory, Macao lacks extra land area to

Table 13.3 Gross Weight of Containerized Cargo (Tonne)
***Since 2007, the containerized cargo has included the figures from Trans Border Industrial Park.**

	Containerized Cargo at Border Gate and CoTai Checkpoint (Land)		Containerized Cargo at Inner Habour and Ka Ho Habour (Sea)		Air Cargo at Macao International Airport (Air)	
	In	Out	In	Out	In	Out
2003	9,809	1,590	159,172	74,450	20,220	68,449
2004	14,947	3,548	134,855	61,034	29,586	105,786
2005	15,375	5,479	163,085	45,517	27,957	96,366
2006	21,902	5,682	200,555	56,853	24,225	89,003
2007*	37,662	10,439	230,071	54,880	22,758	69,625
2008	70,403	10,286	253,341	53,937	16,705	41,548

Source: The Statistics and Census Service (DSEC), Transport, Storage and Communications Statistics, Macao SAR, www.dsec.gov.mo

facilitate the construction of large firms to support the manufacturing industry. As a small territory, Macao can only concentrate on the development of some major industries, so by adhering to the gaming and service industry as the leading industry, many of the local firms and enterprises as well as the local resources have switched to support the gaming sector. In 2008, 78,900 people were employed by the gaming and service sector alone, comprising the largest percentage (24.4 percent) of the total working labor force.[61] This has resulted in a highly autonomous industrial structure that is not favorable for Macao's sustainable development. Macao's economy will easily fluctuate if there is any defect with the gambling sector. To serve as a platform for China and PSCs, Macao needs to maintain a stable and sustainable environment, therefore, Macao should maintain a steady growth of its gaming sector while trying to diversify its existing industrial structure.

At present, Macao acts as two major platforms between China and PSCs, namely the platform for economic and trade, as well as the platform for liaison. The original objective for China to utilize Macao as the service platform was to increase bilateral trade and economic cooperation between China and PSCs. It is obvious that there were successful achievements between China and PSCs, of which bilateral trade increased from $11 billion in 2003 to $46 billion in 2007. However, for sustainable and long-term development, Macao has to strengthen existing platform functions while seeking to diversify other potential platforms. As it is known, Macao and PSCs, especially with Portugal, has a long-standing connection, the fusion of the long-standing historical legacies and cultural elements between Macao and Portugal are worth preserving and promoting. In such a way, Macao should broaden its focus of service platform not only on economics and trade, but further extend cooperation into other aspects such as cultural, science, and education.

Conclusion

Owning to the long-standing cultural and historical linkages with Portugal, it is Beijing's determination to utilize Macao as the service platform for the enhancement of economic and trade cooperation between China and PSCs. The ministerial-level official meetings and the "Forum on Economic and Trade Cooperation between China and Portuguese-Speaking Countries" were carried out smoothly with remarkable results through the joint efforts of the member countries. As the event coordinator for the Forum, Macao is said to have fulfilled its platform function to serve Chinese interests by keeping up an intimate contact and liaison among the member countries, so that the mechanism of the forum can be continued and cooperation can be deepened. Through the organization and arrangement of all kinds of delegation visits and economic activities, bilateral trade between China and PSCs has risen to a higher level since the signing of the "Action Plan for the Economic and Trade Cooperation." In return, by being utilized as a service platform, Macao has gained much experience in organizing international events and activities, which can further enhance its reputation and popularity among Asian countries. The increase in popularity can further strengthen Macao's platform function, giving confidence to both Chinese and foreign enterprises to invest in Macao. In addition, by operating as the service platform, Macao has to diversify its structure and strengthen its potential sector such as logistics and financial services to support the need of an ever-growing market for China and PSCs, thus maintaining a continuous and constant development for Macao society.

Notes

1. Robert O. Keohane and Joseph S. Nye, *Power and Interdependence* (Peking: Pearson Education Asia Limited and Peking University Press, 2004).

2. In 2008, the national reserve of crude oil was 1.34 billion tons, natural gas 647.2 billion cubic meters, and coal 23.1 billion tons, www.stats.gov.cn/tjgb/ndtjgb/qgndtjgb/t20090226_402540710.htm (accessed February 26, 2009).

3. Data on the consumption of other resources in 2008 were: Crude oil consumption gained 5.1 percent to 360 million tons, coal gained 3 percent to 2.74 billion tons, natural gas rose 10 percent to 80.7 billion cubic meters, www.stats.gov.cn/tjgb/ndtjgb/qgndtjgb/t20090226_402540710.htm (February 26, 2009).

4. Loro Horta and Ian Storey, "China's Portuguese Connection," in *YaleGlobal*, yaleglobal.yale.edu/display.article?id=7634 (accessed June 22, 2006).

5. "Angola Overtakes Saudi Arabia as Biggest Oil Supplier to China," www.bloomberg.com/apps/news?pid=newsarchive&sid=aqJ3Wjxs.OWs (accessed April 21, 2008).

6. David Zweig, *China and the World Economy: The Rise of a New Trading Nation*, paper presented at the World International Studies Association, Ljubljana, Slovenia, July 24, 2008.

7. David Zweig and Bi Jianhai, "China's Global Hunt for Energy," *Foreign Affairs*, (September/October 2005) www.cctr.ust.hk/articles/200509-10_workPaper5.htm.

8. "China surpasses U.S. to become Brazil's biggest trading partner," news.xinhuanet.com/english/2009-05/05/content_11316255.htm (accessed May 5, 2009).

9. "China, Portuguese-speaking countries adopt new 3-year cooperation Action Plan," english.peopledaily.com.cn/200609/25/eng20060925_306047.html (accessed September 25, 2006).

10. Ministry of Commerce of the People's Republic of China, zhs.mofcom.gov.cn/tongji2008.shtml.

11. Ronald C. Keith, *China as a Rising World Power and its Response to "Globalization"* (London and New York: Routledge, 2005), 2.

12. "Fostering a Millennium-Old Relationship," *Beijing Review* 43, www.bjreview.com.cn/expert/txt/2006-12/19/content_50995.htm (accessed October 26, 2006).

13. National Bureau of Statistics of China, www.stats.gov.cn/tjgb/ndtjgb/qgndtjgb/t20090226_402540710.htm (accessed February 26, 2009).

14. www.aseansec.org/ASEAN-SCO-MOU.pdf.

15. "China, ASEAN sign MOU on information, media cooperation," china.org.cn/international/2008-10/17/content_16629268.htm (October 17, 2008).

16. Ronald C. Keith, *China as a Rising World Power*, 4.

17. "SCO military forces start 2nd phase of anti-terror joint drill," english.people.com.cn/90001/90777/6237437.html (accessed August 12, 2007).

18. Robert G. Sutter, *Chinese Foreign Relations, Power and Policy since the Cold War* (Lanham, Md.: Rowman & Littlefield Publishers, Inc., 2008), 5.

19. Ronald C. Keith, *China as a Rising World Power*, 2 and 6.

20. *Human Development Report 2007/8*, United Nations Development Programme UNDP.

For the statistical update of 2008 HDI figures, China ranked 94, Cape Verde ranked 118, Sao Tome and Principle, Angola ranked 157, Timor-Leste ranked 158, Guinea-Bissau ranked 171 and Mozambique ranked 175.

21. "Wu Bangguo Meets with Brazilian President Lula," Ministry of Foreign Affairs, www.fmprc.gov.cn/eng/wjb/zzjg/ldmzs/gjlb/3473/3475/t270476.htm (August 31, 2006).

22. "Brazilian Vice President Meets with Chinese Vice Foreign Minister Li Jinzhang," Ministry of Foreign Affairs, http://www.fmprc.gov.cn/eng/wjb/zzjg/ldmzs/gjlb/3473/3475/t355992.htm (August 25, 2007).

23. David Zweig and Bi Jianhai, "China's Global Hunt for Energy."

24. James Brooke, "China link to Portuguese," *The New York Times*, October 22, 2004.

25. "Hu Jintao Holds Talks with His Mozambican, Counterpart," Ministry of Foreign Affairs, http://www.fmprc.gov.cn/eng/wjb/zzjg/fzs/gjlb/3044/3046/t297442.htm (accessed February 9, 2007).

26. "Wen Jiabao Meets with Cape Verde President," Ministry of Foreign Affairs, www.fmprc.gov.cn/eng/wjb/zzjg/fzs/gjlb/2934/2936/t319629.htm (accessed May 15, 2007).

27. Samuel S. Kim (ed.), *China and the World, Chinese Foreign Policy Faces the New Millennium* (Boulder, Colo: Westview Press, 1998), 152.

28. "Scheduled flights between Angola and China starting in 2009," www.ipim.gov.mo/ipim_content001/en/ccpsc/06-08_3.htm#351 (accessed December 18, 2008).

29. "China: Angolan President in Beijing to boost cooperation," www.ipim.gov.mo/ipim_content001/en/ccpsc/06-08_3.htm#351 (accessed December 16, 2008).

30. "China: After Angola, the Chinese government looks on Cape Verde as new economic partner," www.ipim.gov.mo/ipim_content001/en/ccpsc/06-08.htm#5 (accessed May 13, 2008).

31. The flying geese model maintains that the process of industrialization occurs in a pyramid formation, with one country as the leading power, followed by other, less advanced economies, and then by still less industrialized economies, each benefiting in their turn from the comparative advantages, and receiving investment from economies on the level above. "Role of China in Africa similar to that of Japan in Asia, according to American Expert" www.ipim.gov.mo/ipim_content001/en/ccpsc/06-08_3.htm (accessed December 15, 2008).

32. Ann Kent, "China's International Socialization: the Role of International Organizations," in *Global Governance*, vol. 8, no. 3 (July–September 2002), 349.

33. Tax Incentives for Operating Offshore Service Business, www.ipim.gov.mo/ipim_service_detail.php?tid=188&.

34. The legal system in Macao is broadly based on Portuguese law, and part of the civil law tradition of continental European legal systems.

35. On June 27, 2009, the ninth session of the Standing Committee of the eleventh National People's Congress (NPC) passed a bill to authorize the Macao Special Administrative Region (SAR) to have jurisdiction over the new campus of the University of Macao (UM) on Hengqing Island, Guangdong Province, Mainland China. It will cover approximately one square kilometre (100 hectares). UM Newsletter, Vol. 53 (July 9, 2009), um2.umac.mo/apps/pr/eNewsletter.nsf/showtopics/2009-51-001?open.

36. "Portugal's Trade Commissioner for Hong Kong and Macao, Manuel Geraldes, Says the Special Administrative Region functions as an Important Service Center and a Bridge for Trade, Investments and Tourism," www.ipim.gov.mo/en/ccpsc/01-02_04.htm.

37. "Exclusive Interview with the Assistant Minister of Commerce of the People's Republic of China, Mr. Chen Jiang," www.ipim.gov.mo/en/ccpsc/01-02_04.htm.

38. "Eduardo Ambrosio, Head of the Forum of Portuguese-speaking Entrepreneurs in Macao, is Adamant that Untapped Markets in Portuguese-speaking Countries Have Great Potential for Development," www.ipim.gov.mo/pt/relation/otherinfo.htm#4.

39. The UCCLA is an international association to promote understanding and cooperation between its members through economic, cultural, scientific, and technological sharing to improve the living standard of the member countries. It includes twenty-six member countries and forty-three enterprises.

40. The National Congress of APAVT is a main highlight in the annual agenda of the Portuguese tourism industry. APAVT is the most representative association of Portuguese tourism, and since its foundation in 1950 has played a fundamental role in the development of tourism in Portugal; industry.macaotourism.gov.mo/en/pressroom/index.php?page_id=172&year=2008&sp=0&id=2172.

41. Macao Government Tourism Office, www.macaotourism.gov.mo.

42. Statistics and Census Service (DSEC), External Merchandise Trade Statistic 2008, www.dsec.gov.mo.

43. Statistics and Census Service (DSEC), Direct Investment Statistics 2007, www.dsec.gov.mo.

44. The first phase of CEPA was signed on October 17, 2003, and came into effect on January 1, 2004. To enrich CEPA's contents as well as broaden its commitments, the Mainland and Macao signed the Supplement to CEPA, the Supplement II to CEPA, the Supplement III to CEPA, the Supplement IV to CEPA, the Supplement V, and the Supplement VI to CEPA on October 29, 2004, October 21, 2005, June 26, 2006, July 2, 2007, July 30, 2008, and May 11, 2009, respectively. The coverage of CEPA mainly consists of three parts, they are: (1) trade in goods, with Mainland agrees to apply zero tariff to all goods of Macao origin, starting from January 1, 2006, except for goods that are prohibited from imports into the Mainland; (2) trade in services, in which Mainland has progressively provided preferential treatment on market access to forty service sectors; and (3) trade and investment facilitation, which involves cooperation in areas of trade and investment promotion, customs clearance facilitation, etc. Macao Economic Services, www.economia.gov.mo/web/DSE/public?_nfpb=true&_pageLabel=Pg_EETR_CEPA_S&local=en_US.

45. "Macao: Portuguese-owned company opens coffee roasting factory in Macao," www.ipim.gov.mo/ipim_content001/en/ccpsc/06-08_3.htm (accessed October 23, 2008).

46. "Macao: Brazil wants a base in Macao to increase exports to China," www.ipim.gov.mo/ipim_content001/en/ccpsc/06-08_2.htm (accessed July 8, 2008).

47. "Macao: Brazil wants a base in Macao to increase exports to China."

48. "Brazil: Sao Paulo Commercial Association to open Office in Macao to act in Mainland China," www.ipim.gov.mo/ipim_content001/en/ccpsc/06-08.htm (accessed June 2, 2008).

49. The main shareholders of the Mozambique bank are Moçambique Captiais (with 51 percent share), a local company of Moçambique and Geocapital, a Macao-based company whose shareholders are Macao business tacoon Stanley Ho and Portuguese businessman Jorge Ferro Riberiro. "Stanley Ho and Ferro Riberior's Geocapital Focuses on Biofuels," www.ipim.gov.mo/ipim_content001/en/ccpsc/06-08.htm (accessed June 9, 2008).

50. "Stanley Ho and Ferro Riberior's Geocapital Focuses on Biofuels."

51. "Visit to Brazil by a Macao Entrepreneurs' delegation, to strengthen economic cooperation links," www.ipim.gov.mo/en/publication/newsletter/220/220_1.htm (accessed August 1, 2005).

52. "Cape Verde: Cape Verde wants to be link between China and Portuguese-speaking countries," www.ipim.gov.mo/ipim_content001/en/ccpsc/06-08.htm (accessed May 29, 2008).

53. Statistics and Census Service (DSEC), www.dsec.gov.mo, Demographic Statistics.

54. Macao Development Strategy Research Centre, *Report on the Quality of Macao's Citizens 2005* (Macao: Macao Development Strategy Research Centre, 2006) 20–21.

55. "Professional in Chinese and Portuguese languages entering into private sectors," *Macao Daily News*, April 16, 2009.

56. Statistics and Census Service (DSEC), Transport, Storage and Communications Statistics 2008, www.dsec.gov.mo.

57. "Macao: Cargo airline flies between Macao and Angola," www.ipim.gov.mo/ipim_content001/en/ccpsc/06-08_2.htm (accessed August 29, 2008).

This was the first time the Macao airport realized operation of full freighter services to a Portuguese-speaking country in Africa. Singapore-based Jett8 Airlines Cargo carried out the charter freighter operation, shipping approximately 900 tons of cargo to Angola with its Boeing 747-200F freighter flights.

58. Hong Kong Port Development Council, www.pdc.gov.hk/chi/statistics/hongkong.htm and Macao Statistics and Census Services, www.dsec.gov.mo/getAttachment/be98f86c-7391-4d19-895f-1547bb3b90d6/E_ETC_FR_2009_M04.aspx.

59. "Logistics," www.ipim.gov.mo/en/subpage.asp?include=runbusiness/potential.htm.

60. "Agreement reached on bridge link funding," www.hktrader.net/200803/lead/lead-HKMacaoBridge200803.htm (accessed March 3, 2008).

61. Statistics and Census Service (DSEC), http://www.dsec.gov.mo (Employment Survey 2008).

PART V

MACAO AND HONG KONG IN SINO–U.S. RELATIONS: A COMPARISON

CHAPTER FOURTEEN

Sino–U.S. Links with a Twist: Historical and Contemporary Perspectives on American Relations with China's Hong Kong and Macao

Ming K. Chan

Hong Kong hit global headlines on July 1, 1997, when the British colony reverted to the sovereignty of the People's Republic of China (PRC). Its retrocession on that date had some interesting historical U.S. links. Macao's December 20, 1999, transfer from Portuguese to Chinese rule also attracted world attention. In fact, the 1843 opening act in Sino–U.S. official relations began in Macao. U.S. interfaces with both cities are vital yet often ignored dimensions of Sino–U.S. dynamics that deserve to be explored.

After 1949, British Hong Kong was a pawn in the Cold War, vulnerable to pressures from the West and the PRC that exploited its geopolitical importance and economic utility. After China and Britain, the United States constituted a very crucial yet often disturbing third external influence in Hong Kong's precarious existence. Shaped by U.S. containment of Communist China policy and its support of the Republic of China (ROC), U.S.–colonial Hong Kong ties encompassed sensitive issues like refugees, trade controls, naval visits, and anti-PRC propaganda and covert operations. Despite UK attempts to stay neutral in the Chinese civil war, Hong Kong as a Chinese society was tied to the mainland and Taiwan was entrapped in the Beijing–Taipei crossfire complicated by U.S. involvement.

Unlike Hong Kong that eclipsed it as an international port for China trade, Macao under Portuguese rule remained in the backwater drawing little U.S. interest. Macao survived World War II as a neutral haven. Until

1974, Lisbon did not recognize the PRC but kept official ties with Taipei. While Portugal complied with the U.S.–UN embargo against the PRC, Macao thrived in Mainland China trafficking. Sharing similar fates, Macao's 1966 upheaval preceded Hong Kong's 1967 leftist riots. Then Macao's 1999 transfer to Chinese rule followed Hong Kong's 1997 reversion. Replicating the 1992 U.S.–Hong Kong Policy Act to ensure the city's autonomy in U.S. functional ties under PRC sovereignty, the United States passed the 2000 U.S.–Macao Policy Act. U.S. interfaces with China's Hong Kong and Macao are key facets of Sino–U.S. relations as their post-colonial performance reflecting China's globalization and marketization advance. Much more than in the Hong Kong SAR, U.S. inputs are drastically transforming the Macao SAR.

In view of the substantial discussion on various aspects of U.S.–Macao relations in the preceding thirteen chapters of this volume, this chapter, as one of the chapters with a Hong Kong comparative focus, will by design begin with a historical delineation focused more on U.S. links with Hong Kong than those with Macao, then follow with analytical coverage of U.S.–HKSAR and U.S.–MSAR dynamics since the late 1990s. This essay's five sections will first sketch U.S.–Hong Kong ties since the 1840s with emphasis on the post-1949 era. The second and third sections focus on U.S. interfaces with China's Hong Kong and Macao. The fourth section magnifies the HK/MSAR factors in PRC–U.S. realpolitik. The final section prospects the future of U.S. links with Hong Kong and Macao.

Historical Sketch of Hong Kong in Sino–U.S. Ties

Hong Kong becoming a British colony was part of the imperialist assaults that impaired modern China's national interests in the 1842–1942 "century of humiliation." After Britain defeated China in the 1839–1842 Opium War, the 1842 Treaty of Nanking ceded Hong Kong Island to the British to become a China trade hub.[1] The treaty opened five ports on China's southeast coast to British trade that started the "treaty ports" system with special privileges (low tariffs and extraterritoriality) for foreigners.[2] The first Sino–U.S. accord, the Treaty of Wanghsia, was signed on July 3, 1843. Wanghsia (Wangxia) is an area in Macao, then a Portuguese enclave on the Pearl River's western estuary. In the Kun Lam Temple forecourt U.S. envoy Caleb Cushing signed the treaty with Chinese officials to gain similar rights to trade and reside in the ports open by British gunboat diplomacy. It also granted the U.S. extraterritoriality and "most favored nation" (MFN) treatment.[3]

The British took Kowloon (a peninsular across the harbor from Hong Kong Island) in the 1860 Peking Convention that settled the 1856–1860 Second Opium War in which Anglo–French forces occupied Guangzhou and ransacked China's capital Beijing. Then in 1898 the British expanded into the New Territories (NT, an area north of Kowloon to Shenzhen River's south bank) that constituted the bulk of the colony's domain but was on a lease, unlike the two earlier ceded parcels. This NT lease came amid the imperialist "scramble for concessions" after China's defeat in the 1894–1895 Sino–Japanese War. As rewards for aiding China in the "Triple Intervention" that refuted Japan's demand on Liaodong in the 1895 Treaty of Shimonoseki, Russia, France, and Germany each carved a "sphere of influence" of economic rights in China. Keen to maintain geopolitical dominance, the British expanded into the NT. As the Western powers' new turfs were only leased areas but not permanently ceded Chinese land, the NT was on a ninety-nine-year lease set to expire on June 30, 1997. This also reflected the U.S. entry as a new Pacific power.

Victorious in the 1898 Spanish–American War, the United States took the Philippines and moved into Asia. Alarmed by the powers' division of China into exclusive spheres of influence, the United States advocated an "Open Door Policy" against further permanent alienation of China's territory to prevent its dismemberment. The NT lease paralleled the U.S. "Open Door" spirit. But for the powers' rivalry and the "Open Door," the NT might have come under British control differently and Hong Kong's reversion to China could have occurred sooner or later, but not necessary in 1997. A U.S. scholar suggests another factor behind the NT expansion as the U.S. Navy used Mirs Bay north of Kowloon as a staging site for its attack on the Spanish fleet at Manila Bay in 1898. "The presence of the U.S. Asiatic Fleet gave impetus to British fears regarding Hong Kong's security and their subsequent demands . . . for additional territory to shield the colony."[4]

The influx of Mainland Chinese with skills, capital, and business networks transformed Hong Kong under British rule into a thriving hub for China and Asia trade and trans-Pacific shipping that attracted foreign business, including a sizable American presence. Until the 1930s, Hong Kong functioned as a prime disembarkation port for Chinese overseas migration and major supply center for Chinatowns abroad, including those in the United States.[5] In 1865 Americans were among the founders of the colony's largest bank, the Hong Kong and Shanghai Banking Corporation (HSBC), which was among the first foreign banks to open offices in the United States, with a branch in San Francisco in 1875 and in New York in 1880. U.S. banks arrived in Hong Kong in 1902, and later on Citibank, Bank of America, and American Express operated profitable local branches.[6]

American speculation in 1905 about creating a new anchorage at Guangzhou with rail link to Wuhan in central China prompted the British to accede to long-ignored Chinese desires to build the Kowloon–Canton railway that opened in 1910, lest Hong Kong be displaced as China's premier southern port.[7] From 1937 to 1941, Hong Kong was the Asian terminus of Pan Am's China Clipper trans-Pacific passenger service. The small American community in Hong Kong contributed much to the colony's development. A U.S. missionary (Jehu Lewis Shuck) from Macao founded the island's earliest Christian church in 1842. The U.S. opened the first foreign consulate in the colony the next year. The Russell & Co. was one of the largest trading firms in nineteenth-century Hong Kong.[8] Yet it was Mainland China with its vast potentials rather than Hong Kong or Macao that attracted most U.S. efforts. In the 1860s U.S. missionaries founded schools in Guangzhou with branch campuses added later in Hong Kong and Macao that still exit.

U.S.–Hong Kong Links from World War to Cold War

Hong Kong's growth lasted a century until Japan invaded the colony on the same day as it attacked Pearl Harbor. Hong Kong fell on Christmas Day 1941 to endure three years and eight months of brutal Japanese occupation. Between 1942 and 1945, Hong Kong's future was a sensitive issue among the ROC, the UK, and the United States. Hong Kong's colonial status was viewed in an ambiguous light as President Franklin Roosevelt pushed for post-war decolonization. U.S. demand on Hong Kong's return to China after the war (to be pledged by the British in the January 1943 UK–ROC friendship treaty) provoked Prime Minister Winston Churchill's famous line, "I am not His Majesty's prime minister to preside over the liquidation of the British Empire."[9] In refuting U.S. envoy to China Patrick Hurley's call for Hong Kong's return to China, Churchill retorted that it could only be done "over my dead body," as the UK insisted on its recovery even by force.[10]

When the Pacific War ended in August 1945, Hong Kong's status remained precarious. Roosevelt died in April 1945 and his successor Harry Truman was not keen to press for Hong Kong's return to China. Churchill was out of power after the July 1945 UK general election but Clement Attlee's Labour cabinet intended to restore British rule in Hong Kong. Preoccupied with asserting Kuomintang (KMT) control over former Japanese occupied areas against Chinese Communist Party (CCP) domination, the ROC under Chiang Kai-shek was not prepared to militarily contest the British "recovery" of Hong Kong. With U.S. consent and ROC acquiesce, British Rear Admiral Cecil Harcourt sailed with a Royal Navy flotilla into Hong Kong harbor on August 30, 1945 to take the formal Japanese surrender in

Hong Kong on September 16, representing both the UK and Chiang as the Supreme Allied Commander, China–India–Burma Theater.[11]

In contrast to Hong Kong's wartime trauma, Macao escaped Japanese attack as Portugal stayed neutral in World War II and Tokyo was forewarned that aggression against Macao would provoke retaliation against Japanese immigrants and their descendants in Brazil. In fact, Macao became a haven for war refugees from Hong Kong and Mainland China who inflated the enclave's population to more than half a million.

Post-war Hong Kong under restored British rule was soon flooded with mainlanders escaping the Chinese civil war. The colony became entrapped in new Sino–U.S. politics upon the October 1, 1949, founding of the PRC after the CCP defeated the KMT and forced the ROC regime into exile on Taiwan. The 1949 regime change in Mainland China drastically altered U.S. perception of colonial Hong Kong in the Cold War. The United States utilized Hong Kong as a valued strategic asset in its Containment of Communist China. The CCP's opposition to Western imperialism and capitalism challenged the colonial rule and global-linked market economy of this British enclave on Chinese soil populated with Chinese people. Beijing's ideological imperative could be fused with militant Chinese nationalism to undermine Hong Kong's status quo. The external threats from the mainland and the internal threats from leftist partisans worried the UK and allies.

The mainland threats were partially countered by a reinforcement of the local garrison with additional UK forces. The Communist threat to Hong Kong changed with developments elsewhere. In the 1950–1953 Korean War British forces under the United Nations (UN) banner fought the PRC "volunteers" while the U.S. 7th Fleet's patrol of the Taiwan Straits prevented CCP attack on Taiwan but prolonged the Chinese civil war. The Korea conflict lessened mainland pressure on Hong Kong to such an extent that the newly reinforced 30,000-strong UK garrison redeployed some of its troops to Korea.

In a pragmatic survival strategy for Hong Kong with its ethnic-cultural and geoeconomic realities as a natural part of Guangdong, London did its best to prevent the mainland refugee-inundated colony from becoming a Chinese civil war battlefield. Hong Kong's necessary dealings with the Communist mainland (mainly Guangdong) were treated by the colonial regime as basic neighborhood interfaces over the usual cross-border issues. Despite UK diplomatic recognition of the PRC, the colonial authorities tied to maintain strict neutrality and complete impartiality toward the CCP and KMT partisans, often with legal means to ensure local order and neighborhood peace.[12]

With the CCP–KMT hostility settled into a cross-strait stalemate after 1953, the colonial regime moved to prevent Hong Kong from becoming a Cold War beachhead. Delinking Hong Kong from both the Chinese civil war and the Cold War would yield it more room to maneuver. The United States' entry as an active player in Hong Kong's defense could complicate its deliberate detachment from both conflicts; hence the British courting of the U.S. in Hong Kong's defense might be counter-productive. To deter Communist attack and to boost local morale and overseas confidence in Hong Kong, London sought strategic cooperation with the United States, whose Containment policy seemed a ready platform to mobilize its powerful military to buttress the British hold on Hong Kong under Beijing's shadow, a case supposedly akin to the U.S. defense of Taiwan. The Five Powers' (UK, the United States, France, Australia, and New Zealand) joint strategic planning did link Hong Kong to Communist threats to British Malaya, Singapore, Borneo, and French Indochina. In 1954, the Five Powers plus Pakistan, Thailand, and the Philippines formed the Southeast Asia Treaty Organization (SEATO) but Hong Kong was excluded from its coverage. Hong Kong's security remained a UK responsibility without firm U.S. defense commitment.

U.S.–UK Divergence on Hong Kong Defense

Hailed in Cold War rhetoric as "Asia's Berlin" on Communist China's "Bamboo Curtain," Hong Kong seemed vital to the U.S. anti-PRC calculus. Despite lip-servicing, the United States was never committed to militarily protect the colony. The sharpest 1950s–1960s U.S.–UK discords in Asia–Pacific had been over the two islands of Hong Kong and Taiwan.[13]A major U.S.–UK rift arose over UK diplomatic recognition of the PRC on January 6, 1950 (and ended ROC diplomatic ties but retained a consulate in Tamsui near Taipei), while the United States continued its recognition of Chiang Kai-shek's ROC in Taipei as the legitimate government of China.[14] The United States criticized the UK decision that broke the ranks of the anti-Communist NATO alliance. London justified it on the need to deal with Beijing on Hong Kong matters, to protect its vast investments in Mainland China, and to improve the security of its Southeast Asia domains (all with large Chinese population).[15]

London, however, did not press its Commonwealth "industrial democracy" siblings, Australia, New Zealand, and Canada (a NATO state and U.S. neighbor sharing a joint air defense) to follow its example as they had no Hong Kong responsibility. Despite Hong Kong's geopolitical reality, the United States criticized British near-sightedness for discounting the prospect that PRC regime might be short-lived. Meanwhile, enjoying a "free ride" in British Hong Kong, the United States made optimal use of the colony for anti-PRC activities that could provoke Communist retaliation. The Hong Kong–Beijing–Taipei triangle remained a major cause for serious U.S.–UK discords in Cold-War Asia for two decades.[16]

The U.S. consulate-general in Hong Kong (USCG) was the largest U.S. consulate overseas and the largest in the colony. USCG personnel at one point numbered more than 860 according to the colonial regime that tried to limit its size. Closure of the U.S. embassy and consulates in Mainland China after 1949 led to the transfer of many U.S. "China Hands" and their operations to the colony.[17] The USCG hosted staff from various U.S. agencies that had little to do with Hong Kong but were using it as a prime listening post and peeping hole into the mainland. Besides being an intelligence gathering hub, Hong Kong was a production center for U.S. anti-Chinese Communist propaganda materials and a base for U.S.-linked covert anti-PRC operations, like commando raids and sabotage by KMT agents with CIA ties.[18] Such U.S. undertakings created headaches for the colonial regime as sandwiched between an unfriendly neighbor and a trouble-making ally.

Despite its provocative anti-PRC efforts staged in or through the colony, the United States refused to militarily defend Hong Kong even in case U.S. activities triggered PRC retaliations, either taking Hong Kong by force or fermenting disturbances through its supporters inside the colony.[19] Hong Kong as a non-democratic colonial entity undermined British claim on U.S. military aid to defend its hold on the enclave. Hong Kong's real strategic value in U.S. eyes was mainly that of a convenient port and intelligence-gathering hub on Communist China's fringe. In the absence of a bilateral treaty or collective security pact with explicit obligations, the United States refused to commit its military to defend an ally's colony. In contrast, the 1954 U.S.–ROC Mutual Defense Treaty stipulating U.S. military defense of Taiwan against Chinese Communist threats was a major breakthrough in U.S. support that prolonged the ROC's survival until today.

Seven key factors shaped the U.S. assessment of Hong Kong's security risks: First, its most likely threat would come from within, hence direct U.S. military aid would be of limited effect. Second, British defense of Hong Kong was part of the overall UK strategy for its Southeast Asian domains facing CCP threat, against which London was confident of its capability (as in Malaya). Third, Beijing's reliance on Hong Kong's economic contributions should minimize the possibility of unprovoked PRC attack. Fourth, Beijing's reunification agenda prioritized Taiwan, Hong Kong, and Macao. The U.S. defense guarantee for Taiwan should benefit Hong Kong. Fifth, the uncertainty of allies' (the United States, NATO, and Commonwealth) military and economic responses following an attack on Hong Kong constituted a powerful deterrent to Beijing.

Sixth, Hong Kong's colonial status diminished U.S. enthusiasm to defend remnants of European empires. Seventh, Hong Kong interests should be subsumed under the larger overall U.S. anti-PRC objectives.[20]

U.S. defense underwriting of the colony in the 1950s and 1960s might not be a blessing as this would subject Hong Kong to PRC reprisals. Paradoxically, without U.S. defense guarantee, Hong Kong would be less a threat to Beijing amid British attempts to separate the Chinese civil war from the Cold War in the colony's functioning and to detach the enclave from entanglements in both conflicts. Still British handling of sensitive Taipei-related matters, from disputed Chinese aircraft ownership to KMT agents' anti-PRC sabotage, inevitably involved the United States.[21] Hong Kong's security underlined British approach to Western anti-PRC operations and tied the colony to external crisis engaging the United States, PRC, and ROC. In the early 1950s London opposed U.S. military actions against the PRC-like air raids or naval blockade as "a sea blockade would provoke the Chinese Communists to attack Hong Kong. To hold Hong Kong would require sizeable air, land and naval forces, which would not be available if the blockade was undertaken."[22]

After the PRC entered the Korean War in November 1950, the possibility of KMT forces attacking Mainland China alarmed London, which tried to prevent the Korean conflict from spreading to Taiwan and escalating into a general war. As the UK defense chiefs conceded the inadequacy of British forces to hold off a full-scale Chinese Communist attack on Hong Kong, the Colonial Office concluded that wider UK Far East strategic interest would compel them to wholeheartedly (even at the risk of losing Hong Kong) support the United States if the latter were forced to defend Taiwan against a PRC attack.[23] The prospect of U.S. military aid to the colony amid U.S. anti-PRC operations becoming a provocative liability was real as Hong Kong had been deemed indefensible by the United States.

In October 1949, President Truman approved a National Security Council (NSC) recommendation that the United States should not "provide military support to the British for the defense of Hong Kong in the event of a Communist military attack."[24] This stance remained through the 1950s as under President Eisenhower the United States never committed to militarily defend the British hold on Hong Kong. There were limits to the effects of U.S. military deterrence (that would mainly be symbolic and psychological) to buttress British rule in Hong Kong against potential Chinese Communist threat.[25] On Hong Kong's security concerns, the best London could expect was U.S. emergency evacuation aid.

Yet even the proffered U.S. evacuation assistance was problematic. As a May 1952 NSC note revealed, the United States would offer "assistance to the

British to cover an evacuation from Hong Kong, if required," and the United States "should consider taking unilateral action" against Communist China even without UK support.[26] A NSC 1959 scenario planning yielded this finding: In case of an emergency when and if Hong Kong were to come under Communist attack, the United States would be willing to consider, but definitely not as a firm commitment, the possibility of landing aircraft and ships to help evacuate important persons from Hong Kong. Top priority evacuees would be U.S. citizens, then British officials and other British Commonwealth personnel if they were "white."[27] No spin of Cold War logic could justify such racism in the U.S. "helping hand" priority as the local Chinese being "non-white" were not entitled to be evacuated by the United States.

Amid the Anglo–U.S. entente after the 1956 Suez debacle that confirmed Britain's decline as a world power, there was an October 1957 secret agreement between Eisenhower and British Prime Minister Harold Macmillan that the United States would regard Hong Kong as a U.S.–UK "joint defense problem." In exchange for this U.S. gesture, London would not support, without U.S. consent, Beijing replacing Taipei in China's UN representation. This deal's details remain secret but it is unlikely that it entailed any firm U.S. military commitment.[28] The Hong Kong–Taipei link in U.S. strategy was obvious as three U.S. consuls general in Hong Kong later became U.S. ambassadors to Taipei.[29]

Saying the colony was "in friendly hands" was of great strategic value to the United States; a June 1960 NSC "Statement of U.S. Policy on Hong Kong" stated that U.S. defense umbrella should not cover Hong Kong.[30] A June 1960 NSC minutes noted Eisenhower "said that if the UK became so weak that it was not able to suppress civil disturbances in Hong Kong after we had . . . provided assistance and supplies, he was unable to see why we should intervene with U.S. forces" as he "believed that if the British were about to lose Hong Kong as a result of civil disturbances, Hong Kong would be such a completely hostile place that there would be little use in attempting to retain it" and he "felt that if the disturbances were purely civil disturbances, the UK would be able to deal with them . . . even if instigated by the communists" as "the British would be near the end of their power if they were compelled to ask for U.S. troops to suppress civil disturbances in Hong Kong." Thus he proposed that "a decision as to whether or not to provide U.S. forces to prevent loss of British control of Hong Kong in the event of major civil disturbances should be made in the light of conditions prevailing at the time" as "he was not ready to order the intervention of U.S. armed forces in the event of civil disturbances in Hong Kong unless there was a showing that Chinese Communist forces were involved."[31]

Eisenhower's stance was borne out in mid-1967 when Hong Kong was engulfed in violent anti-colonial riots unleashed by Beijing supporters. Exploiting grassroots grievances, these leftist outbursts were partly fueled by the PRC's Cultural Revolution radicalism and by Portuguese capitulation to Chinese demands in Macao after a late 1966 leftist riot. Through stern police measures with UK army assistance and supported by the local Chinese community, the British managed to restore order by fall 1967.[32] Confident of its counter-insurgency capability, London did not request U.S. military aid. Still some locals believed that "the ultimate savior of Hong Kong is the United States" and cited as proof U.S. 7th Fleet warships anchored off Hong Kong harbor.[33] Yet this might represent routine R&R (relax and recreation) visits by U.S. forces. Hong Kong's role as a U.S. forces' favorite R&R port in the 1966–1975 Vietnam War repeatedly drew Beijing's wrath. Hence, it would be risky for the British to deliberately "stage" such U.S. naval visits as a symbolic deterrent to impress Beijing that might further provoke the local leftists amid the 1967 riots.[34]

In contrast to Hong Kong forty miles away, the much smaller Macao under Portuguese rule survived in the backwater off international limelight, seemingly almost ignored by Lisbon and the rest of the world. Without stationary U.S. consular presence, the USCG–HK has covered Macao matters since 1843. Of far less strategic prominence, Macao lived through World War II as an unmolested neutral enclave. Under the anti-Communist Salazar regime, Portugal did not recognize the PRC and Lisbon kept official ties with Taipei until 1974. As NATO states, the United States and Portugal were Cold War allies with their ties reinforced by the London–Lisbon alliance under the 1368 Treaty of Windsor. While Portugal complied with the anti-PRC embargo, Macao thrived as a major 1950s–1960s smuggling loophole in contrabands traffic running vital supplies to the Communist mainland. Despite the sharp disparities in the UK and Portugal's global clout and in their South China enclaves' relative strategic and economic significance, the fates of Hong Kong and Macao intertwined. The early 1967 Portuguese regime's capitulation to Chinese demands in Macao after the late 1966 leftist riot was a prelude to Hong Kong's mid-1967 leftist disturbances and forewarned the British not to yield, much to U.S. relief.

U.S.–Hong Kong Socioeconomic Ties

Colonial Hong Kong enjoyed extensive ties with the United States in tourism, migration, education, trade, investment, technology, shipping, and air links. It hosted a sizable pool of U.S. businessmen, missionaries, journalists, and professionals, some with their families. American popular culture invasions came via Hollywood movies, songs, and TV programs (since local broadcasting began in 1957). Movies shaping U.S. popular images of postwar Hong Kong underpinned the growth of tourism. U.S. films like *Love Is a Many-Splendored Thing* (1955) and *The World of Suzie Wong* (1960) both feature William Holden as the U.S. white knight romancing local Chinese women. The Suzie Wong myth remains an icon in local tourist lore.[35] By the 1960s Hong Kong was a favorite destination for jet-age U.S. tourists, who ranked first in terms of arrivals and spending in the colony where Hilton opened the largest hotel with 900 rooms in 1963.[36]

On Hong Kong's humanitarian front, U.S. missionaries' and NGOs' volunteers run schools, clinics, and welfare programs for the local poor and mainland refugees. Some supported Hong Kong as a surrogate recipient for many such pre-1949 U.S. private efforts in the China mainland. The 1949 CCP victory ended many Sino–U.S. people-community interfaces. The closest that these U.S. NGOs could get to China were projects in Hong Kong while some U.S. charities switched to helping Taiwan. A growing stream of Hong Kong students went to the United States for higher education after the war. To reassert British dominance "in the face of growing American influence" was a key reason to reopen the colonial University of Hong Kong in 1946.[37] U.S. church groups and academic bodies aided two of the three colleges (founded by exiled mainland scholars) that in 1963 formed the Chinese University of Hong Kong (CUHK) for local Chinese high school graduates who otherwise would attend Taiwan or mainland universities). A Chinese economist from Berkeley was its first president and many of its teachers hold U.S. degrees. The United States has been the most common graduate study destination among CUHK alumni.

U.S. policy toward Hong Kong's 1950s refugee crisis validated criticisms of U.S. exploitation of this humanitarian crisis for propaganda gains instead of rendering practical assistance to million-plus Mainland Chinese refugees who fled to the colony to escape Communism. The United States was unhelpful toward the UN High Commission for Refugees' (UNHCR) attempt to deal with Hong Kong's situation, like the Hambro Mission.[38] The Committee to Aid Refugee Chinese Intellectuals (ARCI, a New York-based body with CIA funding) offered exiled anti-Communist Chinese intellectuals resettlement in Southeast Asia where they could influence the local Chinese communities. In 1954 the U.S. State Department Far East Refugee Program kept a field staff in Hong Kong to oversee funding for the United States and other voluntary agencies in refugee aid. To embarrass and discredit Beijing while gaining "political and psychological advantages" in a battle of hearts and minds was the main reason behind

U.S. support of APCI activities in Hong Kong. British officials were highly skeptical of the ARCI's motives and actions.[39]

The Vietnam War's end triggered an exodus of Indochina refugees into Hong Kong when the first batch of 3,743 "boat people" arrived in May 1975. As pressure on ethnic Chinese in newly unified Vietnam intensified, the numbers of those fleeing to Hong Kong grew, reaching 66,000 in the first half of 1979. An already overcrowded Hong Kong's inability to cope spatially and financially with this influx under the UK "open port" policy forced London to seek an international burden-sharing solution to resettle these boat people in the UK, Australia, Canada, Europe, and the United States.[40] This crisis continued into the early 1990s, then involving mostly "illegal economic immigrants" who were sent home under UN-sponsored aided repatriation to prevent their remaining in Hong Kong beyond mid-1997 against Beijing's warning. The United States was not too helpful in this crisis.[41] U.S. Vice President Dan Quayle on a 1991 stopover even condemned Hong Kong for "mistreating" these "refugees," forcing an embarrassed USCG to issue a quick correction to emphasize that his words did not accurately reflect official U.S. policy.

In its global anti-Communist crusade, the United States used Hong Kong as a production and coordination center of anti-PRC literature, mostly in Chinese language produced by the U.S. Information Service (USIS) for distribution to Southeast Asia Chinese communities.[42] Under the colonial regime's tight rein (to avoid provoking Beijing) against local dissimilation of these items, the bulk of such anti-PRC literature produced in Hong Kong was "consumed" overseas. Such Cold War U.S. "soft power" projection via Hong Kong complemented its "hard power" tactics like covert anti-PRC sabotage launched through Hong Kong.[43] In between "soft" and "hard" tactics was the 1951–1953 Truman-era U.S. patronage of the "Third Force" movement among anti-Communist but also anti-Chiang Kai-shek elements exiled in Hong Kong. Besides funding their anti-PRC media and research-publication programs, the CIA also sponsored guerrilla raids on the mainland.[44]

Hong Kong's economic reorientation under U.S. sanction is another mixed legacy of the colony's uneasy but vital U.S. links. Six months after the Korean War broke out in June 1950, the United States imposed a trade embargo against Mainland China, thus cutting off Hong Kong's mainland trade, particularly in strategic materials, medicine, and other provisions that could aid PLA military operation in Korea. It became an UN embargo in mid-1951 with UK compliance. Soon Hong Kong's blood line, its historically crucial China trade, evaporated.[45] To survive economically after its role as China's leading entrepôt diminished, Hong Kong was forced to transform itself into a manufacturing hub of light consumer goods for export with the United

States as a major market. After the United States imposed quotas on Hong Kong textile-garment exports in 1958, the UK and Western Europe followed suite. Hong Kong then diversified into electronics, watches, toys, and other products. By the early 1960s, Hong Kong's success in selling its industrial products triggered retaliation with restrictive import quotas imposed by the Kennedy regime.

Despite U.S. anti-Communist rhetoric and proffered support of Hong Kong as a free city, the colony that has no tariff or trade barrier allowed almost any U.S. products to be sold freely while its own products could not be exported above a certain quota into the United States, hardly a free and fair trade example. This moved some Americans who worked in Hong Kong to bitterly criticize U.S. protectionism with double standards and high-handed treatment as its embargo forced Hong Kong to switch to industrial production, but this "Asia's Berlin" received meager U.S. beneficial import allowance to compensate for its forfeited China trade.[46] Particularly harmful were the restrictions on U.S. raw materials exported to the colony least they be transferred into the Communist mainland. Hong Kong endured the U.S. embargo's triple effects—loss of China entrepot traffic, restricted U.S. materials for local manufacturing, and cumbersome "non-PRC origin" certification of local products for export. Trade controls were the USCG–HK's second key task, after "China Watching" intelligence but ahead of its propaganda efforts. Governor Alexander Grantham implored London to appreciate the greatest threats for Hong Kong's stability, security, and prosperity did not come from Beijing but from U.S. trade controls.[47]

The United States outranked the United Kingdom as Hong Kong's top trade partner with $560 million in 1966 two-way exchange. Importing U.S. farm products and electronic components, Hong Kong exported to the U.S. plastic flowers, toys, textiles, and clothing. The United States invested over $100 million in the colony where some 400 U.S. firms operated, including 150 regional headquarters. Hong Kong earned $52 million from supplying uniforms to the U.S. military in Vietnam.[48] The 1974 Multifiber Arrangement forced Hong Kong to further diversify its overseas markets and its products as the United States remained its largest export market. After 1976 Hong Kong benefited from reduced U.S. tariffs under the Generalized System of Preferences. By then, U.S.–Hong Kong economic interfaces expanded into financial service with Citibank the colony's fourth-largest bank and the largest U.S. firm. Hong Kong business also expanded in the United States. In 1978, HSBC acquired New York's 350-branch Marine Midland Bank (the thirteenth-largest U.S. bank) to become the world's fifteenth top bank.[49] Soon, China's reform would alter the U.S.–Hong Kong dynamics.

U.S. Interface with China's HKSAR

U.S. concerns for Hong Kong geared up in late 1984 when, after two years of tough negotiations, London and Beijing signed an accord mandating Hong Kong's retrocession to China upon the NT lease expiration on June 30, 1997. Besides the United Kingdom and the PRC, the United States was the most concerned third power in Hong Kong's "transition to 1997" saga as it was keen to help post-1997 Hong Kong retain its global hub viability.

U.S. Response to Hong Kong's 1997 Retrocession

Despite its lack of formal standing, the United States closely monitored the 1982–1984 Sino–British talks while both powers confidentially briefed the United States on the talks' progress to court its support for their respective stance.[50] Supporting the Sino–British accord, the United States had three basic objectives for its economic, political, and strategic interests toward China's HKSAR: first, preserve advantages for U.S. economic interests; second, promote democracy in Hong Kong and through it Mainland China, with related emphasis on human rights, civil liberties, and the rule of law; third, as Beijing's "one country, two systems" model for the HKSAR and the MSAR also aimed at Taiwan's reunification.[51]

The desire to fill in the British void led to stronger U.S. support for Hong Kong democratization, especially after the June 4, 1989, Tiananmen Incident. The PLA's armed suppression of Beijing's pro-democracy activists triggered a serious crisis of confidence in Hong Kong, where "Today's Beijing, Tomorrow's Hong Kong," became a popular slogan as none could guarantee that PLA tanks would not one day roll over local democrats in Hong Kong streets. June 4's detrimental impact on U.S.–PRC relations intensified U.S. concerns for Hong Kong. No longer the "inactive super power" the United States engaged with new proactive measures.[52] In the pre-1997 exodus of Hong Kong families seeking safe haven abroad, Canada was their top migratory destination and the United States came third after Australia.[53] This was due to tight U.S. migration control. Until the 1970s, the United States allocated to Hong Kong an annual immigrant quota of 600, which was increased to 2,000 in 1983 and then raised to 10,000 in 1991 and 20,000 since 1994, due to the post-1989 shift in U.S. approach to Hong Kong. Besides quota enlargement, the United States added a deferred immigrant visa (valid until 2002) in order to stem the "brain drain" affecting Hong Kong in the transition to 1997.[54]

Co-sponsored in late 1991 by Senators Mitch O'Conner and Albert Gore, passed by Congress and signed into law by President G. H. W. Bush in August 1992, the U.S.–Hong Kong Policy Act (USHKPA) aims at treating post-1997 Hong Kong as an autonomous and distinct entity from the PRC mainland in economy, trade, transportation, travel, sociocultural exchanges, and other functional dealings with the United States. It required the State Department to report to Congress in 1993, 1995, 1997, 1998, 1999, and 2000 on developments in Hong Kong. The USHKPA implies that in case of soured PRC–U.S. relations, Hong Kong as a distinct entity could be legally exempted from U.S. sanctions on the China mainland. In a sense, this was akin to the special post-1978 U.S.–Taiwan ties. When President Carter switched U.S. diplomatic recognition from the ROC to the PRC in early 1979, tremendous conservative pressure to strengthen the unofficial U.S.–Taiwan ties resulted in the 1979 U.S.–Taiwan Relations Act. Minus the Taiwan Act's arms sales and defense provisions, its bilateral functional treatment is similar to the USHKPA. While displeased, Beijing realized Hong Kong's serious crisis of confidence and it should not undermine Hong Kong's global linkages that had been useful to China. Not wishing to depress U.S.–PRC relations in a U.S. election year as it preferred "old friend" Bush's re-election, Beijing did not protest too strongly against the USHKPA, an unusual device to preserve the HKSAR's special status in U.S. law with implied interference in PRC domestic affairs. To some, this act proves U.S. desires to detach Hong Kong and its South China hinterland from Beijing's control, like U.S. designs for PRC frontier regions—Tibet and Taiwan.[55]

After Tiananmen, Beijing was alarmed by international support for British sunset democratization in Hong Kong that might become a Western Trojan Horse penetrating the China mainland. Beijing's concerns intensified after the Berlin Wall's collapse and Eastern Europe's liberation in late 1989 and the USSR's 1991 demise. As the PRC became the sole major Communist state, U.S. pro-Hong Kong democracy gestures were viewed by Beijing as hostile attempts to "internationalize" Hong Kong. Beijing condemned the last (1992–1997) British governor Chris Patten as "sinner of a millennium" for his democracy push. On his U.S. visits, Patten was warmly received by President Clinton, the secretary of state, and congressional leaders, who all praised his reform.[56] Hong Kong democratic advocates were also stigmatized as "Western agents" who intended to subvert CCP rule in China through foreign-supported local democratization.

By 1996, U.S. economic links with Hong Kong become considerable as the largest base (with 31,000 U.S. citizens residing) of American economic operations in Asia. Hong Kong was the tenth largest export market ($14 billion in 1996) for U.S. goods, especially farm products, amid a $24 billion two-way trade (for a $4.1 billion U.S. surplus) with Hong Kong ranking thirteenth among U.S. trade partners. U.S. investment totaled $14 billion in Hong Kong where 1,000 plus U.S. firms operated (450 as regional HQs). Annually, seventy U.S. Navy vessels with 45,000 sailors came for R&R, and more than 700,000 U.S. tourists visited Hong Kong. Some 14,000 Hong Kong students were enrolled on U.S. campuses in 1996 when the USCG–HK issued 170,000 business and tourist visas.[57]

Mixed scenarios of Hong Kong under Chinese rule were aired by U.S. observers in a "Hong Kong Watching" game amid a proliferation of literature on its 1997 blues. A particularly notorious media piece foretelling the city's post-1997 fate is "The Death of Hong Kong" by Louis Kraar (*Fortune*, June 26, 2005).[58] Most of such doomsday forecasts turned out to be far off the mark; Kraar's view shaped U.S. media coverage of Hong Kong's reversion.[59] Most agreed that U.S. "ability to affect the course of events in Hong Kong seemed marginal unless the United States decided to confront Beijing more directly."[60]

U.S.–HKSAR Economic Ties

As a PRC's SAR since mid-1997, Hong Kong remains a free port, global financial center, regional service hub, and China market gateway. Appreciative of Hong Kong as an exemplary free-trader, the United States ranks second in the HKSAR economy after Mainland China. The United States is the second-largest export market for HKSAR products and its fifth-largest import source. Total HK's U.S. trade reached $65.38 billion in 2008—domestic exports $2.41 billion, re-exports $43.64 billion, and imports from United States $19.32 billion (of which $11.9 billion re-exported) while the United States was the second key destination ($43.64 billion) in the $350 billion HKSAR re-export trade (mostly from the PRC mainland).[61]

As a free market yielding hefty U.S. trade surplus, Hong Kong is the United States' fourteenth-largest export market for goods and services. In 2008, Hong Kong imported $1.2 billion worth of U.S. food products, making it the United States' seventh-largest and third-fastest-growing food products market.[62] An attractive locale for U.S. business, some 1,380 U.S. firms operated in Hong Kong in mid-2009, mainly in trading, banking/finance, and transport, employing a quarter of million locals. In mid-2008, Hong Kong hosted 311 regional headquarters and 612 regional offices of U.S. companies, including major U.S. banks, insurance firms, transporters, and multinationals like AIA, American Express, Citibank, Exxon, Federal Express, HP, IBM, Marriott, Microsoft, and 3M. The top fourteen U.S. banks all have offices in Hong Kong with $88 billion aggregate assets from Hong Kong accounts in 2007.[63] Walt Disney built its third overseas theme park in Hong Kong, a $1.8

billion joint project with the local government that opened in 2005, employing some 15,000 workers.

The United States, with a total stock of $47 billion in late 2008, is the fifth-largest external investor in Hong Kong. Many Hong Kong firms have invested in various U.S. locations and sectors, like properties, hotels, restaurants, trade, manufacturing, banking, and services, amounting to more than $4 billion in 2006.[64] Well-known Hong Kong firms with presence in the United States include the Peninsula Group (hotel), the Bank of East Asia (banking), Lee Kum Kee and Vitasoy (food-beverage producer), and Café de Coral (fast food chain).

At end-2008, some 60,000 U.S. nationals resided in Hong Kong.[65] Eight U.S. states have representative offices in Hong Kong, where six U.S. port authorities have a presence. The HKSAR government runs Economic & Trade Offices in Washington, D.C., New York, and San Francisco, its Trade Development Council has New York and Los Angles offices, and the Hong Kong Tourism Board also has offices in New York, Los Angeles, and San Francisco.

Amid panic reaction to the stalled Sino–British negotiations on Hong Kong's future, the Hong Kong dollar exchange rate plummeted to a historic low of US$1 to HK$9.7 in autumn 1983. This undermined local and international confidence in Hong Kong and negatively impacted its trade-reliant economy. The colonial authorities in October 1993 pegged the local dollar to the U.S. dollar at HK$7.8 to US$1, where it remains. This U.S. dollar peg has been repeatedly affirmed by HKSAR and PRC officials since 1997.[66]

Wall Street players and U.S. media condemned as dangerous anti-free market intervention the HKSAR authorities' unprecedented $15 billion purchase of local blue chips shares in August 1998 to combat speculative attacks on the Hong Kong dollar's U.S. peg. Bitter memories of similar attacks in late 2007 (that triggered stock market plunge, property price collapse and sky-high inter-bank overnight rates) compelled the Tung regime to act decisively in 1998 with its huge reserves and Beijing's support. Its success in repelling external speculators (mostly U.S. hedge funds and market manipulators) and in earning handsome profits ($4.5 billion in six months) on the shares silenced the critics who turned to sing its praise.[67] In 2006 Chief Executive Donald Tsang's announced departure from the colonial era "positive non-intervention" stance provoked criticisms for tarnishing its "laissez-faire capitalism" from U.S. critics like Milton Friedman.[68] The Wall Street–triggered 2008–2009 global financial crisis, besides hurting HKSAR economic growth with curtailed exports, also provoked fierce protests from thousands of local small investors who struggled to recover losses in derivatives issued by collapsed New York investment bank Lehman Brothers. The local economy's rebound as significantly aided by Mainland China's 8 percent plus GDP growth further diminished the U.S. local clout.

U.S. Political Concerns

With strong interest in Hong Kong's reversion and post-1997 development, especially in promoting democracy, preserving freedom and the rule of law, maintaining cooperative law enforcement ties, and U.S. Navy ships' port of call access, the United States has been attentive to HKSAR politics under the "one country, two systems" formula. The United States is well aware of its demonstrative effects on Taiwan. When Deng Xiaoping first unveiled the formula, Beijing would let Hong Kong and Macao become its first and second exemplifiers with Taiwan's reunification as its ultimate target. Yet more than 90 percent of Taiwan residents have viewed its Hong Kong and Macao experience negatively.[69]

Despite rapid economic growth, the PRC remains a one-party Leninist state while Hong Kong enjoys a partially democratic system offering similar freedoms as in many Western democracies with a British-style common law legal system. Similar to the 1980s, the United States has since 1997 kept up its voice to support Hong Kong's autonomy with further democratization under Chinese rule. The National Democracy Institute (NDI, funded by the non-partisan National Endowment for Democracy) runs a Hong Kong office to host policy forums, conduct workshops on electoral tactics, and publish survey and research findings. U.S. officials have closely monitored HKSAR elections and human rights, which are key subjects in the State Department's annual Human Rights Report.[70]

In 2002–2003 the Tung regime tried to enact a national security law to protect PRC state interests (as stipulated by HKSAR Basic Law Article 23). This sparked heated debates on draft provisions that might infringe civil liberties, human rights, and press freedom. Popular discontents galvanized half a million protesters who rallied on July 1, 2003, to oppose the bill. This political earthquake shocked Beijing, forced the shelving of the bill and hastened Tung's exit as chief executive in March 2005, twenty five months before his term expired.[71] In June 2003, U.S. Consul General James Keith aired strong concern for the draft bill. He also encouraged reforms toward universal suffrage, a point that all his predecessors and successors have reiterated. Besides State Department–USCG comments there were congressional hearings on HKSAR development. The U.S. media vividly covered the Article 23 protests and related political stories.[72] Such U.S. gestures provoked resentment from Beijing, whose HKSAR supporters rebuked U.S. "interference."[73]

Almost every two years, HKSAR democrats like Martin Lee will call on U.S. officials, testify in Congress, lecture on campuses, and meet with NGOs and the press to promote awareness of their efforts for democracy and human rights. Pro-Beijing circles repeatedly label them "traitors courting foreign support" and accused them of accepting U.S. funds. Ironically, the pro-Beijing flagship party DAB (Democratic Alliance for Betterment of Hong Kong) dispatched its cadres to learn first-hand U.S. elections and enrolled them in a course ran jointly by CUHK, Tsinghua University, and Syracuse University in 2002.[74]

Legal, Functional, and Sociocultural Interfaces

Hong Kong's judicial independence with a British-style common law legal system has been a top U.S. concern as the HKSAR legal environment directly affects vast U.S. economic interests in an open market with fair competition, free information flows, and basic freedoms and civic liberties for U.S. citizens. Hong Kong's rule of law has been regarded as the bedrock to anchor multiple U.S.–HKSAR institutional links on exports controls and transnational law enforcement cooperation.[75] After the 9/11 terrorist attacks on the United States, no other Asian–Pacific jurisdiction has complied more fully with U.S. demands with effective cooperative measures on counter-terrorism and anti-weapons of mass destruction proliferation, on top of anti-organized crime efforts and the interdiction of drug trafficking, money laundering, pirated goods smuggling, and illegal immigrants from Mainland China into the United States. Hong Kong was hailed as the U.S. Container Security Initiative's best partner. More than thirty U.S. Homeland Security agents from the U.S. Transport Security Administration are stationed in Hong Kong, the world's second-busiest container port and a regional economic lynchpin for the United States and its allies.[76] Due to Hong Kong's cooperative vigor, Asia–Pacific seafaring traffic passing through its harbor has been relatively secure, affecting some 10 percent of all goods imported by the United States (with much of the huge volume of Mainland China products to the United States transiting it).[77] Still, the United States was alarmed by Beijing's dark shadow compromising HKSAR judiciary independence and rule of law as in the 1999 HKSAR residents' mainland children right of abode case.[78]

U.S.–HKSAR cooperative efforts also cover public health and environment concerns with bilateral agreements and joint programs on vital areas.[79] Facilitated by the 2002 Civil Aviation Agreement, some ninety passenger non-stop direct flights each week link Hong Kong with major U.S. cities besides extensive air cargo services by air freighters and couriers. In 2007,

1.23 million U.S. tourists visited Hong Kong.[80] The U.S. is a favorite destination in Hong Kong's outbound tourism that often combines family reunion with vacation in North America. Many among the younger locals embrace a vital area is the U.S.–HKSAR social-cultural ties. Harvard MPA alumnus Donald Tsang visited the United States as chief executive in 2005, as chief secretary in 2003, and as financial secretary in 2001. His two top cabinet secretaries are both U.S. educated. The American Chamber of Commerce–Hong Kong with 2,000 plus members is busily engaged in Greater China with more than 200 programs per year. Founded in 1925, the American Club Hong Kong serves its 2,400 members at two club sites. American popular cultural inputs of all styles, from movies, pop music, and TV programs to fast food and clothing. U.S. "soft core" influences are so pervasive that one could hardy imagine the HKSAR entertainment scene without vivid U.S. images, sounds, and tastes.

As a prime higher education provider, the United States has attracted a sizable influx of Hong Kong students that numbered more than 8,000 in 2008–2009, ranking Hong Kong the fifteenth-largest worldwide source of international students in U.S. universities. A smaller pool of HKSAR students are enrolled in U.S. high schools. More than 60,000 Hong Kong students were educated in the United States before 1997.[81] Hong Kong hosts various U.S. university alumni organizations that include returnee alumni and those who come to work. Some 1,000 U.S. students study annually at various HKSAR universities that in 2008 received U.S. professors while eleven HKSAR students and scholars went to the United States as Fulbright scholars.[82] Numerous U.S.-trained faculty and staff fill HKSAR tertiary campuses. Many are Hong Kongers who obtained their degrees in the United States and returned home to serve, some as president (at CUHK, Hong Kong University of Science and Technology, Lingnan University, University of Hong Kong, and the private Chui Hai College). Only two of the eight pubic-funded local tertiary campuses have a non-U.S.-trained president as the once dominant British influence has been eclipsed by a strong U.S. presence. In 2012 the HKSAR undergraduate course will shift from a UK-style three-year to a four-year program akin to the United States and PRC–Taiwan.

As part of the historic Cantonese diaspora, there are major Hong Kong Chinese communities in the United States, like those in San Francisco, Los Angeles, and New York. In a sense, they are "Hong Kong towns" where Hong Kong-style Cantonese dialect radio and TV programs are popular while California North/South and East Coast editions of *Sing Tao*, a mainstream Hong Kong daily are easily available, featuring local Chinese community news and advertisements besides Hong Kong–PRC–Taiwan news.

U.S. Interests in Macao since 2000

The United States has no stationary consular presence in Macao as the USCG–HK has handled Macao matters since 1843. Until recently, to most Americans, Macao was a sleepy small costal city with old churches, exotic temples, and flashy casinos, all laced with Iberian charms worthy of a day trip from Hong Kong. Patterned after the 1992 USHKPA, the United States enacted the U.S.–Macao Policy Act of 2000 to stipulate that the United States "should contribute to Macao's ability to maintain a high degree of autonomy" as "the continued economic prosperity of Macao furthers U.S. interests in the PRC and Asia," "support for democratization naturally applies to U.S. policy toward Macao," and "the human rights of the people of Macao are of great importance to the United States." Those are not empty words as the U.S. presence in post-colonial Macao has been of increasing significance. Initially, except for improved public order after the suppression of gang violence, little seemed to have changed in Macao after its 1999 transfer to Chinese rule. But breakthroughs since 2004 have drawn global media to chronicle U.S. transformational effects on Macao.[83]

Casinos constitute the key pillar of Macao's tourism industry. The forty-year gambling monopoly held by tycoon Stanley Ho's Sociedade de Turismo e Diversoes de Macao (STDM) expired and was replaced by a multi-franchise system in 2002. Of the three new franchises, Stanley Ho's Sociedade de Jogos de Macao (SJM, 80 percent owned by STDM) got one while one each went to Las Vegas gaming tycoons Sheldon Adelson (initially joined with HKSAR investor Chi-wo Lui) and Steve Wynn. After a subdivision of each franchise into two, there are now six gaming franchises in Macao.

Until spring 2004, there were eleven casinos in Macao, all STDM/SJM-operated to offer a variety of games twenty-four hours a day. With multiple franchises, two new casinos opened in mid-2004, the $265 million, 800-table Sands-Macao (of Adelson's Las Vegas Sands Corporation, LVS) and the Galaxy (operated by the Lui family). Several large casino-hotels, including the $1.2 million deluxe 600-room Wynn-Macao, started business in 2006. In September 2007, LVS inaugurated the $2.4 billion, Venetian-Macao with a massive (1.2 million square feet) convention center attached to the world's largest casino (800 tables and 6,000 slots machines in 550,000 square feet of gambling space, thrice over the largest Las Vegas casino) and the 3,000-suite hotel (Macao' largest). A year later, LVS opened next door the deluxe Four Seasons Hotel-Macao with a modest casino (of 175 tables). To compete with the U.S. entries, SJM initiated several major projects like new flagship Grand Lisboa (240 tables, 480 slot machines, 420 rooms) that opened in late

2006. With 32 percent of the local gaming market in fall 2009, the SJM is the largest operator with twenty casinos, mostly small to mid-size. The Stanley Ho family secured two of the three new gaming sub-franchises, one each for daughter Pansy and son Lawrence (whose Melco runs a string of slot machine Mocha Clubs). Melco Crown (a joint venture with Australian PBL) built a casino-hotel on Taipa in 2007 and the $2.1 billion City of Dreams resort-entertainment complex with two casinos and three hotels (including a 791-room Grand Hyatt) that opened in 2009 in Cotai (a reclaimed area linking Coloane and Taipa islands). Pansy partnered with U.S. giant MGM-Mirage to build the $1.3 billion, 600-room MGM-Grand Macao that began business in late 2007.

In Macao's current array of thirty-three casinos, 4,610 gaming tables, and 14,175 slot machines, M/HKSAR interests claimed a 40 percent market share (SJM 27 percent, Galaxy 13 percent) in October 2009 while the United States (LVS 24 percent, Wynn 17 percent) and foreign-partnered operators (Melco 10 percent, MGM 9 percent) took 60 percent.[84] The three U.S. giants operate five casino-hotels (with 2,545 tables, 9,911 slot machines, and 4,850 rooms). Four other U.S.-chain hotels (Best Western, Hyatt, Holiday Inn, and Westin) offer a total of 1,657 rooms. Few in outlets but large in size and market share, U.S. inputs have generated phenomenal growth with breakthrough transformation of Macao into a Las Vegas–style gaming–resort–convention hub. Sands-Macao was so profitable to recap its initial investment a year after its 2004 opening and help the New York Stock Exchange listing of LVS shares in 2006. Breaking Stanley Ho's monopolistic hold on Hong Kong–Macao ferry links, LVS has since fall 2007 run its own Cotai Jet catamaran fleet from Hong Kong to Taipa terminal near Venetian-Macao. In late 2007, LVS' Macao casinos briefly overtook SJM to top MSAR gambling revenue.

The U.S. slice in Macao's growing gaming pie expanded until the fall 2008 global financial tsunami. If able to proceed on schedule, LVS's $12 billion Cotai Strip master-planned development of ten more hotels with casinos for 21,000 rooms with world hotel brands (including U.S. chains Conrad, Fairmont, Hilton, Holiday Inn, InterContinental, Sheraton, St. Regis, and Traders) would be completed by 2012. Wynn has planned a $4 billion project of four to six hotels in Cotai where MGM has also contemplated another outlet. U.S. giant Harrah's Entertainment also has planned a Caesars Golf Macao resort. With assorted new projects by HKSAR interests, Macao would have the largest number of casinos in the world to exceed the U.S. total gambling setup by 2013. In 2006 Macao's $7.2 billion gross gaming intakes exceeded Las Vegas. As the world's biggest gambling market, Macao's $13.7 billion gross gaming intake in 2008 outsized Las Vegas and Atlantic

City combined, while the MSAR government collected $4.95 billion in direct gaming taxes, 68.65 percent of its total revenue of $6 billion.[85]

The American Chamber of Commerce–Macao was inaugurated in May 2007. The three U.S. gaming giants are well represented in this eighty-member new chamber—a Venetian–Macao executive is a vice president while MGM and Wynn senior figures are among its eight governors. The U.S. government has reportedly requested the opening of a local consulate. Until now the USCG–HK has covered Macao concurrently. China's response would partly depend on getting a new PRC consulate in some U.S. city but more crucially on how Beijing views the U.S. role in Macao's transformation. Prompted by perceived excessive and unhealthy foreign influence, PRC Vice President Xi Jinping on his January 2009 visit warned the local folks to guard against external interference in Macao internal affairs. Potential foreign threats helped to justify the MSAR's early 2009 enactment of a national security law. (In contrast, fierce opposition to the HKSAR version of this law forced the Tung regime to shelve its enactment in mid-2003.)

In spring 2008, Beijing intervened to cool Macao's runaway boom under U.S.-fueled "casino capitalism." As Beijing ordered, Edmund Ho in April placed an indefinite ban on new casino constructions. In May Beijing imposed tighter controls on Guangdong's Individual Visitor Scheme tourists who could visit Macao only once every two months and their permits for Hong Kong would be invalid for Macao. This reduced the pool of mainlanders (including corrupt officials and state enterprise executives) patronizing Macao gambling that would often involve money laundering and constitute an undesirable outflow of Chinese funds into foreign-owned casinos.

The fall 2008 global depression led to sharp decline in Macao's tourist arrival, hotel occupancy, and property price. The trend of huge increases in visitor arrivals (26.99 million in 2007) ended in 2008 (22.9 million). Gross gaming revenue decreased from January 2008's P10.4 billion peak to February 2009's P7.99 billion. Unemployment hit 3.8 percent in March 2009 while private consumption, investment, and exports receded. In November 2008, the financially stricken LVS halted construction on its Cotai Strip's half-finished lots 5 and 6. This might signal a receding tide of U.S. "casino capitalism" in Macao and if that becomes a long-term trend, this would render Beijing's alarmist scenario for any "Havanization" of China's Macao premature and off the mark.

Buoyed by Mainland China's economic rebound and relaxed exit controls, Macao enjoyed an unexpected gaming–tourism revival in August–October 2009. With an unprecedented single month intake of $1.42 billion in August (and $1.35 billion in September), MSAR gross gaming revenue rose 22.3 percent in 2009 third quarter to a record $4 billion (from $3.25 billion a year earlier).[86] This upsurge continued into October with an all-time high $1.575 billion in gross gaming intake (a 42 percent jump over a year ago). Macao's boom and Hong Kong stock market upsurge yield a golden opportunity for the recession-dragged and debt-ridden U.S. gaming giants to raise much-needed cash. Wynn-Macao's early October 2009 Initial Public Offering (IPO) listing in the Hong Kong Stock Exchange (HKSE) raised $1.63 billion. The highly leveraged LVS aimed to raise $3.35 billion in its November 30, 2009 HKSE IPO in order to resume its stalled Cotai Strip sites #5–6 (6,000 hotel rooms) construction.[87] These should bond U.S. investments in Macao closely with Hong Kong to tap the huge Mainland China capital market as STDM, Galaxy, and Melco are already HKSE-listed. Not only has U.S. input remade Macao's economic landscape, but Macao has become the cash cow crucial to the U.S. giants' survival. Their third quarter 2009 Macao net revenue (Wynn $474 million and LVS $840 million) contrasted very sharply with their dwindling U.S. domestic intakes.[88]

In bilateral trade, the United States has been the MSAR's second-largest trading partner, after Mainland China. In 2008, Macao's domestic exports to the United States totaled $84 million (much less than 2007's $108 million, 2006's $115.6 million, and the peak $142.7 million in 2004), making the United States its largest export market. Meanwhile, Macao imported $298 million worth of goods (down from 2007's $303.6 million) from the United States, its sixth-largest supplier, whose exports to Macao have increased substantially in the past half decade (from $109 million in 2003) amid a boom partly fueled by U.S. gaming investment. Macao's continuous double-digit GDP growth during 2002–2008 has yielded higher purchasing power for its populace and opportunities for U.S. products like equipment and materials for casino-hotel projects. As the MSAR's second-largest external direct inward investor (after Hong Kong), the total stock of U.S. holdings in Macao reached $3.16 billion in 2006 ($1.23 billion that year alone). In 2007, U.S. firms operated thirty-one enterprises in Macao that attracted 202,137 U.S. tourists that year and 203,191 in 2008 (0.9 percent of the total 22.9 million arrivals).[89]

Since 2004, a local concern has been would Uncle Sam's fist follow the pocket book into Macao amid its rapid U.S. investment-fueled transformation. In a June 2004 interview with this author, MSAR Chief Executive Edmund Ho said he would rather prefer Macao to be kept out of global headlines as they often invited foreign interference.[90] In September 2005, the U.S. Treasury Department accused Macao's Banco Delta Asia of illicit dealings with North Korean interests. The U.S. Treasury blacklisting of that bank forced the MSAR authorities to take over its operations. Senior U.S. officials visited Macao to demand tightening controls. As its currency, the Pataca, is indirectly pegged (via its Hong Kong dollar link) to the U.S. dollar (at US$1 = P 8), Macao is vulnerable to U.S. pressure. Macao's offshore financial role as a low tax zone and a free port with no foreign exchange control has also triggered external alarms. At the April 2009 G-20 London financial summit, French President Nicholas Sarkozy threatened to place Hong Kong and Macao on the list of "tax havens" for international sanction. PRC President Hu's stern objection and U.S. President Obama's mediation deflated this French attempt as these two SARs' finance services are properly regulated by their monetary authorities.[91] It seems that China's Macao has joined Hong Kong as a target in Sino–foreign discords.

Hong Kong and Macao in U.S.–PRC Relations

Hong Kong and Macao have been shaped by and caught in the crossfire of the much larger and complex Sino–U.S. power politics, whose imprints on both SARs are discernable in their economic, military, and financial security interfaces in recent years.

Lobbying for China's MFN

As a crucial economic issue affecting Sino–U.S. relations and Hong Kong's own interests, Hong Kong officials and democratic activists contributed to the PRC's retaining its vital Most Favor Nation (MFN) or Permanent Normal Trade Relations (PNTR) status with the United States. Besides heightened concerns for Hong Kong's reversion to China and its post-1997 fate, the altered U.S. approach toward the PRC after the Tiananmen Incident entailed official sanctions that included linking the PRC's human rights condition with the renewal of its MFN trade status under U.S. law from 1990. Being the largest market for Chinese exports since the PRC's 1978 reform, the United States has been of critical economic importance to China's growth and development. For instance, 31 percent of the PRC's exports went to the United States in 1995.[92] Also since the 1980s, Hong Kong has been increasingly dependent on the Mainland economy both as the premier entrepot for Sino–foreign trade and as the largest external investor in the export-oriented industries in South China (where much of its own manufacturing had relocated). Hence during 1990–2000, when the PRC trade status came up annually on the U.S. congressional agenda, Hong Kong officials in both the final colonial and the first HKSAR regimes vigorously pleaded for the U.S. renewal of China's MFN status.

The United States had no bone to pick with Hong Kong as the world's freest trader much appreciated by U.S. trade officials. When Hong Kong persuaded the United States not to sanction China's trade for human rights record, its message was hard to ignore. If the United States were to impose sanctions on U.S.–PRC trade, these measures would penalize or even cripple Hong Kong's economy at a very critical juncture in its problematic transition to 1997. An April 1997 Hong Kong official estimate projected serious economic damages from the non-renewal of the PRC's MFN status to the tune of costing it two-fifths to three-fifths in GDP growth rate with a loss of 86,000 jobs and some $31.8 billion in re-export trade values (6–8 percent of Hong Kong's total re-exports).[93] President Bill Clinton, who in May 1994 delinked MFN from China's human rights, cited the critical impact on Hong Kong when he unconditionally renewed China's MFN status in 1995 and 1996.

Even Hong Kong democrats like Martin Lee had consistently supported renewal of the PRC's MFN status until the PRC's accession to the WTO in November 2001 ended this debate. Hong Kong democrats wished Beijing would appreciate their unquestioned patriotism on this score. Since the mid-1980s, in their campaign for faster and fuller local democracy that was seen by China's officialdom as threatening its absolute post-colonial control, they were condemned by Beijing as "unpatriotic" by courting U.S. support to "internationalize" Hong Kong. Their stance on the MFN debate should earn them credit.

Macao Bank's North Korean Tint

The Macao Banco Delta Asia case came as a shocking surprise to many in mid-September 2005 when the Six-Party Talks on North Korea denuclearization hosted by Beijing was progressing toward a breakthrough for peaceful resolution. It seemed odd to see the two different faces of the Bush regime's China–East Asian approach in action. On the one hand, U.S. diplomats were highly appreciative of Beijing's efforts in mediating the North Korea crisis. Yet, on the other hand, the U.S. Treasury Department was trying to pull the legs of China's Macao. As it turned out, Beijing remained focused on the Six-Party talks which did reach a preliminary accord two days later. Meanwhile, the MSAR government exercised great restraint by not issuing an official rebuttal but only sought to clarify the U.S. Treasury Department's public accusations. Within a week, the MSAR chief executive set up an investigation team with the dispatch of Monetary Authority of Macao (MAM) auditors and inspectors to station inside Banco Delta Asia to examine the alleged North Korean funding links. A week later the MAM took over the management of the bank. Few would doubt that the decisive steps of the MSAR authorities were taken with Beijing's approval or under its instructions.

So far, Asian–Pacific diplomatic circle sources have not been able to offer any satisfactory explanation to the seemingly self-contradictory and even potentially counter-productive U.S. double gestures: If U.S. diplomats were supportive of Beijing's positive role in the North Korea nuclear crisis resolution, then why did State Department and the Treasury Department not better coordinate their postures toward Beijing at that critical juncture? On what ground did the United States deliberately air the public charges against the Macao bank's alleged illicit North Korean dealings that inevitably embarrassed Beijing for Macao's tarnished image? Or rather the United States charges against the Macao bank were deliberately intended as an additional squeeze to pressure North Korea.

Had the MSAR government failed to effectively control the situation, there could be a general run on the local banks and that might even spread next door to Hong Kong. If Hong Kong were to experience a bank run, Beijing would have to intervene to maintain stability and financial solvency in its two SARs, with the largest U.S. dollar foreign currency reserve in the world at its disposal. If Beijing and Hong Kong were to pool their U.S. dollar reserves together, it could easily overwhelm almost any speculators. But why was Macao being targeted, perhaps as a pawn or a scapegoat in U.S.–PRC politics? A possible story line might be that as U.S. firms now operate huge casinos in Macao, the U.S. government's financial and law enforcement wings wished to extend their long arm jurisdictions into Macao, should the casinos be used for laundering money or for circulating counterfeit U.S. currency notes that would directly harm vital U.S. interests.

After the Six-Party Accord was signed in spring 2007, North Korea insisted on the full release of its funds (about $25 million) in Macao before it would carry out its stipulated denuclearization efforts. Due to the U.S. Treasury's ban on any foreign commercial bank's dealing with Banco Delta Asia, those funds were not transferred into North Korean hands until autumn 2007 via a U.S. Federal Reserve Bank and a Russian bank. That seemed to put an end to the Macao banking case but the six-month delay in North Korean compliance with nuclear disarmament stipulations did not work to the Bush regime's benefit. Yet, the Banco Delta Asia Chairman Stanley Au is still engaged in U.S. legal proceedings to have its name cleared and the Treasury ban lifted.[94]

There are also two noted U.S.–MSAR casino cases. The first alleges that Adelson got a Macao gaming franchise in 2002 as Beijing's reward for his 2001 lobbying in the United States for China's 2008 Olympics bid with his clout as a Republican Party major donor.[95] The second concerns the Las Vegas-based MGM's partnership with Pansy Ho in Macao projects. Due to Stanley Ho-STDM/SJM's alleged underworld links, Nevada gaming authorities took an unusually long process to approve this partnership in 2006. In May 2009, an official report for New Jersey Division of Gaming Enforcement advised MGM (which runs an Atlantic City casino) to "disengage" from the partnership on the same ground.[96] While Adelson rebutted Stanley Ho's criticisms of LVS' Macao operations as "anti-U.S.," U.S. regulators have cast a watchful eye on Macao's gaming scene.[97]

U.S. Naval Visits to Hong Kong

The 1977 reversion ushered in the HKSAR's new geopolitical reality that placed its defense and foreign affairs in Chinese central government's remit. Under an April 1997 PRC–U.S. agreement, all U.S. Navy requests for HKSAR visits must be submitted in advance for Beijing's clearance. The approved cases are governed by rules on wireless communication, supply provisioning, and ship-to-shore shuttle logistics while in Hong Kong. Depending on the specific junctures in Sino–U.S. ties, permission was given in most cases but refusals and deferrals were not uncommon.[98] The HKSAR in its first decade hosted a total of 322 U.S. naval port calls.[99]

U.S. naval visits to Hong Kong have become a barometer to U.S.–PRC bilateral ties, in particular their military links. The May 1999 U.S. "accidental" bombing of the PRC embassy in Belgrade triggered a nationwide protest in Mainland China and in Hong Kong. As a result U.S. naval visits to Hong Kong did not actualize until September 1999. The April 2001 mid-air collision of a PRC fighter with a U.S. EP-3 surveillance plane near Hainan forced the deferral of U.S. naval visits until July. U.S. military infringements on PRC interests were met with finely calibrated "penalties"—naval visits to Hong Kong denied. The Pentagon suspended military exchanges with the PLA after this incident but developed closer military ties with Taipei, further infuriating Beijing. Improved PRC–U.S. ties facilitated by post-9/11 anti-terrorism cooperation permitted more U.S. naval visits to Hong Kong, which hosted nearly twenty U.S. warships, including two carrier battle groups and the 7th Fleet flagship from July 2001 to March 2002. Yet at times refusal still occurred.

On U.S. aircraft carrier Stennis' ten-ship battle group's late 2001 visit to Hong Kong, Beijing at the last minute refused entry to two nuclear submarines due to terrorist threats. Displeased with an invitation to Taipei's defense minister to a March meeting with Pentagon brass, Beijing on March 18, 2002, vetoed the April 5–9 HKSAR visit by U.S. guided-missile destroyer Curtis Wilbur. On March 27, 2002, State Department spokesman Richard

Boucher (ex-USCG–HK) said that for a routine U.S. naval visit, Hong Kong as a free and open port should be treated differently from other Chinese ports. To Beijing this reflected deplorable U.S. reluctance to accept PRC sovereignty over HKSAR in security matters.

The PRC navy also skipped a planned visit to the United States on its 2002 overseas tour. The March 2002 rumored Beijing refusal of U.S. aircraft carrier *Kitty Hawk*'s HKSAR visit saw a reversal as a deliberate decision in the larger Sino–U.S. calculus. Ahead of Vice President Hu Jintao's April 27–May 3, 2002, visit to the United States, Beijing announced on April 12 approval for the *Wilbur* and *Kitty Hawk*'s HKSAR visit. Despite growing U.S. military support for Taipei, Hu (concurrently PRC Central Military Affairs Commission vice-chair) did not cancel nor defer his icebreaking visit to the Pentagon. Gestures like U.S. naval visits to Hong Kong could be useful strategic signals to defuse PRC–U.S. tensions. A symbolic Sino–U.S. military–diplomatic equilibrium was achieved in spring 2002—while the *Kitty Hawk* and four U.S. warships with a 6,000 crew were sailing into Hong Kong for an April 19–May 5 R&R visit, Hu was greeted upon arrival in Honolulu on April 27 by U.S. Pacific Command Chief Admiral Dennis Blair.

After refusing two U.S. minesweepers' HKSAR visit in late 2007, Beijing's repeated non-approval of *Kitty Hawk*'s Thanksgiving visit to Hong Kong caused concern. When Beijing finally granted its approval on "humanitarian ground" on Thanksgiving Day (November 22) the *Kitty Hawk* had already sailed too far on its home port course to return. As to Beijing's real reasons that compelled the *Kitty Hawk* and its five-ship flotilla's 8,000 crew to miss a planned four-day Thanksgiving reunion in Hong Kong with their families (that especially flew in from its home port in Japan), one explanation was that the PLA was conducting a large exercise off China's southeast coast that caused air flight delays. Displeasure over U.S. arm sales to Taiwan was another reason as Beijing warned the United States to stay away ahead of Taiwan's legislative and presidential elections in early 2008.[100]

All these confirm Hong Kong's crucial if symbolic contribution to China's national interests. As the West's an anti-PRC bridgehead, colonial Hong Kong was a Cold War pawn amid the East–West crossfire. With its great harbor, economic vitality, and cosmopolitan charms, the HKSAR plays a unique role in the PRC's interface with the United States, whose navy has obstructed reunification with Taiwan. U.S. naval presence in Hong Kong has always been a high profile projection of U.S. power. As 7th Fleet commander Vice-Admiral James Metzger said in Hong Kong on December 8, 2000, "U.S. Navy port calls to Hong Kong have also long been an important part of American cooperation in the region, both as a British territory and also as a

SAR of the PRC. In addition to providing welcome rest and recreation for our crew, U.S. Navy ship visits also serve as a visible demonstration of Hong Kong's openness and distinct status as an international city."[101]

Some consider the 1997 reversion rendered Hong Kong a hostage in Sino–U.S. politics detrimental in its U.S. ties. Yet colonial Hong Kong was never a neutral port open to all. It was denied to the "enemy" (PLA) but welcomed "friends" (U.S. Navy) in the Cold War. Although such U.S.–UK "friendship" gestures as the presence of U.S. "warship" in Hong Kong could risk PRC retaliation against the colony, the United States refused to defend it. Its non-neutral past preceded its HKSAR present. Hong Kong's strategic importance as the best South China port makes any foreign military contacts sensitive under its colonial legacy as a product of British gunboat diplomacy. Amid troubled PRC–U.S. relations, the links between warship and friendship are tenuous in Hong Kong harbor and beyond.

Concluding Observations

U.S. public interests, media coverage, and academic attention on Hong Kong and Macao waned after the late 1990s. Only a handful of books on Hong Kong or Macao were published in the United States since then. The Center for Strategic and International Studies started a quarterly *Hong Kong Update* in 1998 but ceased publication in January 2000. Besides posting occasional HKSAR-focused essays online, it released in 2008 the only U.S.-published volume on the HKSAR first decade.[102] The Carnegie Endowment for International Peace funded an online quarterly *Hong Kong Journal*, with an advisory board of four U.S. and one HKSAR members, including a former USCG–HK.

The half million Hong Kong immigrants in Canada have cast a stronger impact on their adopted land than Hong Kongers' imprint in the United States. Canadians of Hong Kong origin have held high offices as governor-general, provincial heads (British Columbia and Manitoba), cabinet minister, and members of parliament. The 300,000 Canadian citizens form the HKSAR's largest foreign community. Unlike the University of Toronto, few U.S. university libraries devoted special efforts to Hong Kong and Macao materials.[103] To draw fruitful reference from its neighbor's enriching HKSAR interface, an economically humbled United States should rearticulate its engagement with an increasingly marketized and globalized China, with finer-tuned sensitivity toward its two SARs, especially Macao.

Lacking consular presence, U.S. ambivalence toward colonial Macao contrasted very sharply with the U.S. "casino capitalism" tidal wave in Macao as a newly rediscovered gem since its 2002 gaming re-franchise. Once the U.S.

gaming firms arrived, their massive investments literally remade Macao in half a decade. Besides new casinos and hotels, the U.S. giants infused new chemistry to transform MSAR from a gaming-tourism den into an attractive convention-exhibition center and business travel destination. Its chain reactions triggered large-scale projects by competing Hong Kong–Macao casino operators that altered Macao's physical landscape amid double digit GDP growth since 2004. Yet the LVS, MGM, and Wynn stories are not entirely positive examples of U.S. input into a rapid, wholesale "Las Vegasation" of Macao. As the Banco Delta Asia case revealed, the MSAR and PRC authorities' alarms at hidden U.S. interests in Macao in a global strategic context seem justified. Macao, much more than "Asia's Las Vegas" and with its special ties to Portuguese-speaking countries, is vital to China's global strategy.

Beijing has tried to reign in the ballooning U.S. influence in Macao to prevent its economic "Las Vegasation" from becoming a dangerous "Havanization" to corrupt local sociocultural fabrics and subvert its docile polity.[104] To reduce U.S. casino capitalism's dominance over Macao's over-heated economy that has been over-dependent on gambling with undesirable social consequences, Beijing has recently regulated MSAR gambling through administrative measures. U.S. casino operators in Macao now face a less rosy outlook with restrictions on casino expansion, tighter gaming controls, uncertain mainland visitor influx and over-capacity (40,000 hotel rooms by 2012). But MSAR–U.S. links are not likely to wane. Seeing the United States as a source for talents needed in socioeconomic upgrading, the MSAR government in late 2007 started awarding grants to Macao students at top U.S. universities. Retiring chief executive Edmund Ho is a Canadian university alumnus, his successor Fernando Chui received his three degrees from the United States.

The U.S. Macao casinos saga and Disney–HK's dismal performance are lessons for U.S. attempts to capture China's leisure market. Disney–HK's perceived "cultural imperialism" of arrogance–ignorance, "unequal treaty" partnership terms, and losses since its 2005 opening led many HKSAR legislators to oppose public funding for its expansion. [105] The building of a $3.6 billion, twice larger Disney–Shanghai to open in 2014 deepens HKSAR marginalization fears in face of the rise of Shanghai, which is designated by Beijing to become China's international finance hub. Viewed by some Hong Kongers as a Disney betrayal, this new Disney–Shanghai will siphon part of Disney–HK's Mainlander traffic. The marketwise and West-friendly HK–MSAR folks should be ideal customers for U.S. products, yet the mixed U.S. records in these two most open, cosmopolitan, and affluent Chinese cities cast shadow on U.S. forays into the PRC market.

The fact that the USCG–HK does not follow the usual norm of coming under the purview of the U.S. Embassy–Beijing but instead reports directly to the State Department denotes the special interest the U.S. government has accorded these two PRC–SARs. This can be a positive sign for more proactive and enlightened U.S. engagements with China's Hong Kong and Macao to advance a mutually beneficial dimension to the larger U.S.–PRC relationship. If Sino–U.S. relations are the most important bilateral ties in global affairs, then Hong Kong and Macao should receive sustained higher priority U.S. attention both in their own right and for their Greater China transformational potentials.

In any future prospect, one must appreciate the historical shadows behind Beijing's alarm on aspects of U.S.–HKSAR and U.S.–MSAR links. Much has changed in Sino–U.S. relations since 1949 but memories still linger to inform current policy analysis. Beijing hardly forgets colonial Hong Kong, a Cold War captive amid the Chinese civil war, was implicated in U.S. anti-PRC activities but without U.S. defense guarantee. U.S. policy toward Hong Kong shifted over time as dictated by crisis reactions. The 1949 CCP victory forced the United States to discard its World War II demand on Hong Kong's return to China. The United States used the colony as an intelligence and subversion base in its Red China Containment. The 1970s U.S.–PRC détente reduced the communist threat to Hong Kong. China'post-1978 reform has lured U.S. business and revived Hong Kong's entrepot traffic. As Hong Kong's 1997 reversion enticed the United States to be more engaged, the Tiananmen Incident led to the 1992 USHKPA and expanded U.S. quota for Hong Kong immigrants. U.S. support for HKSAR democracy and civil liberties entails concern for its rule of law and stalled electoral reform. In such shifts due to changing U.S. interests and priorities, the China factor has remained the overriding U.S. concern to shape its Hong Kong policy and articulate the implications of seemingly "local" events in broader Sino–U.S. dynamics. The U.S. Navy's non-actualized HKSAR visits and Macao's Banco Delta Asia case highlight Hong Kong and Macao's precariousness in global politics. Varying responses to China's impact on U.S. vital interests have prompted the United States to change its Hong Kong stance. U.S. economic and national security interests with specific concern for North Korean money laundering and potential terrorist activities triggered U.S. actions on Macao.

As HKSAR democracy has been regarded by Beijing as a very dangerous subversive weapon in the U.S. agenda to promote democracy in the PRC. Viewed through a "Trojan Horse" prism, Beijing opposed any political internationalization of Hong Kong, especially U.S.-endorsed democratization. Due to intimate HKSAR-mainland interface, the HKSAR democratic Trojan

Horse must be stopped far from the gate to avoid galvanizing mainlanders into similar pursuit. Besides reiterating HKSAR affairs must remain a Chinese domestic matter, Beijing often stresses its preferred vision for the HKSAR as an "economic" but not a "political" city. Ideally, HKSAR external links should be confined to functional-economic exchanges but not potentially subversive ideo-political interface. Beijing's apprehension of HKSAR's political internationalization, particularly its "Americanization," will continue. Beijing might try to find ways to filter out undesirable U.S. ideo-political messages convey through Hong Kong into the mainland in a soft powers battle for the Chinese hearts and minds. Perhaps Hong Kong is already too intoxicated and implicated with a full array of U.S. inputs to be easily redeemed.

Still U.S. links will remain a pillar of the HKSAR-global networks and Hong Kongers' overseas mobility.[106] Hong Kong cannot remain a global city without U.S. interfaces, especially in education, medicine, media, professions, technology, finance, business, transport, and pop culture. Some saw expanding U.S. influence in post-1997 Hong Kong as filling the British colonial void and as a beneficial counter-balance to the "Mainlandization" of the HKSAR. As Hong Kong and Macao approach the 2047–2049 end of their SAR status, their evolution toward preordained merger-convergence with the mainland will predicate upon their internal advancement and external dynamics. Concern for mainland–SAR disparity should be mitigated by the narrowing socioeconomic gaps while the mainland is further globalized and marketized.

Hong Kong's post-1949 dual roles (as China's "window" to the world for functional gains and as the West's bridgehead into Red China) have been drastically altered by the PRC's reform and opening. The PRC's apparent success in direct foreign trade–investment–technology transfer, its external sociocultural exchanges and WTO accession with expanding economic-strategic clouts have combined to redress the Sino–West equilibrium in Hong Kong's global positioning. Against China's economic growth and globalization gains, some may question Hong Kong's traditional role as a China market gateway and service hub cherished by foreign business. Does the world still need Hong Kong as the efficient middleman and vital bridging plank? The recent cross-strait breakthroughs that ushered the mainland–Taiwan "three direct links" not only lessened U.S.–PRC tensions but have also minimized Hong Kong and Macao's middleman role in cross-strait exchange. The HKSAR's continued viability as an economic hub of great value to the PRC partly lies in its being a more global than any other Chinese city. Likewise, Macao enjoys a unique status as the PRC's only international tourist hub with legal gambling. Otherwise, the "two systems" flexibility and potentials under the "one country" sovereignty will not be meaningful. As

Beijing's "one country, two systems" model has also aimed at Taiwan's reunification, concerns for cross-strait dynamics entice the United States to assess its HK/MSAR experience under this model. Reflecting a rising China's domestic objectives and external priorities, the HK/MSAR record is of concern to the United States.

The remote but not impossible scenario of Sino–U.S. conflicts over economic issues or strategic discords adds uncertainty to PRC–U.S. dynamics that inevitably would impact U.S. interface with China's Hong Kong and Macao. The assumption that fallout effects from Sino–U.S. trade frictions might not undermine U.S.–HKSAR interface under the protective USHKPA is questionable as it could not fully mitigate the impact of Beijing's retaliation on the HKSAR economy in a PRC–U.S. trade war. While the USHKPA and USMPA accord special functional status to Hong Kong and Macao as distinct from the China mainland, such differential U.S. treatments of Greater China components cannot mask the their closely intertwined mainland ties. Beijing has viewed Hong Kong and Macao's special status under U.S. law as parallel to the U.S. "unofficial ties" with Taiwan under the 1979 Taiwan Relations Act which Beijing opposed. In the long term, it is crucial for the United States to be seen as a constructive force in Greater China reintegration.

In this context, three key points deserve attention: First how will the HK–MSAR's accelerating mainland integration affect their strategic repositioning globally? Second, to what extent can expanded external links to balance and compliment their intensifying Greater China ties buttress Hong Kong and Macao's functional viability in face of cross-strait détente and competition from other Chinese cities? Third, in case of rupture in U.S.–PRC relations, would there be a return to the Cold War–like confrontation with Hong Kong caught in the middle? Since 1997, the HKSAR by necessity must share a common or parallel stance with Beijing in foreign affairs. Post-colonial Hong Kong is increasingly susceptible to Beijing's dominance while the mainland has been more capable in direct exchange with the capitalist world. As such, does the United States really need Hong Kong any more as the bridge to China? Rather Hong Kong should be appreciated for its own right with valuable geo-strategic and economic assets. Hong Kong and Macao (to be linked via a bridge in 2014) with their 7.5 million residents will remain golbalized hubs at the core of the PRD–South China region of 100 million people, a huge market for U.S. business.

Dark clouds will overshadow U.S.–HK–MSAR ties as long as Beijing suspects the U.S. hidden desire for the continuation of a divided China in a cross-strait split with a Taiwan–mainland peaceful but non-unified coexistence. This colors Beijing's perception of U.S. embracement of Hong Kong and Macao at the heart of a relatively more autonomous and potentially separatist South China region. U.S. intents and motives toward the SARs remain under Beijing's suspicion. While the United States continues to publicly support Hong Kong democratization, the local democrats' perceived "disloyalty" would help justify Beijing's restrains on HKSAR democracy. The U.S.–HK–MSAR links must not be seen by Beijing as a threat to PRC interests. Hence the United States should practice enlightened soft power on Hong Kong and Macao. Even as China welcomes Western functional–economic interface with its SARs, Hong Kong's residual British Commonwealth ties and previous UK–EU contacts constitute dimensions of Western influence beyond U.S. inputs. Likewise, Macao's special ties to Portuguese-speaking countries can enrich China's global outreach.

As China, the fast-rising new Asia–Pacific power, engages the United States, the sole but declining superpower, the global power balance is being redressed with the eventual outcome not necessarily in U.S. favor. As such U.S.–PRC interface will likely become more complex to add extra layers and new tones to Hong Kong and Macao's vital U.S. links amid this recalibration of Sino–U.S. equilibrium. Beijing will permit Hong Kong and Macao's global links as long as they serve China's national interest as Beijing defines it. This is a pragmatic stance just like Beijing tolerated Hong Kong and Macao's colonial status as long as they fulfilled the PRC's utilitarian needs as windows to the outside and links to the non-socialist bloc. To make Hong Kong genuinely global will demand it to transcend colonial heritage, rise above PRD localism and Guangdong–Cantonese parochialism and even move beyond PRC national boundaries and East Asian transnational spheres to become a truly world city. Such transcendence will be affected by how effective Hong Kong and Macao advance their own interest through productive engagement with the United States that will also benefit Chinese national interest.

A major problem in the U.S.–China calculus is their acute lack of mutual trust. Recognizing the urgent need and potential gain in promoting Sino–U.S. understanding through the unique perspectives and upon the superb platform of Hong Kong, ex-HKSAR chief and current Chinese People's Political Consultative Conference vice chair C. H. Tung in 2008 founded a China–United States Exchange Foundation.[107] After his 2007 speech in San Francisco, HKSAR legislator Alan Leong (and 2007 chief executive election candidate) answered a questions on "what should the United States do to help HKSAR democracy" by urging the U.S. public and officials to closely observe HKSAR events but they should not interfere as to avoid deepening Beijing's suspicion of local democrats' alleged "treasonous" foreign links.[108] On the two SARs' contrasting national security law enactment, a PRC legalist condemned "U.S. imperialism" for the HKSAR's Article 23 debacle while another official warned against "external interference" right before President Obama's Beijing visit.[109] These cases pinpoint the HK–MSAR's challenges in nurturing their U.S. ties while advancing Beijing-defined Chinese national interest.

In a sense, recent U.S. policy toward HK and Macao has combined full-scale engagement with China with selective containment of the PRC's communist regime—perhaps a sort of "congagement" fusing containment and engagement core elements.[110] This "congagement" is being actualized in U.S. policy toward China through its HKSAR and MSAR as convenient handle bars and effective transmission belts. In the increasingly crucial soft power realm, neo-containment of China's one party regime still lingers as the United States is both capitalist and democratic. Engagement is vital because the United States tries to use Hong Kong and Macao as the positive extra dimensions to enrich its China interface. Politically, the United States likes to see a fully democratic Hong Kong and a more democratic Macao to sow the "seeds of democracy" in the China mainland, leading it eventually to a more open and liberal polity. However, such ideo-political agenda can be counterproductive by fueling Beijing's deep distrust of U.S. intentions toward its two SARs as offshore Chinese domains with dubious foreign links somewhat akin to Taiwan.

At the epicenter of Sino–global dynamics, Hong Kong and Macao are being remolded by the paired processes of re-integration with the China mainland and a concurrent expansion of China's global reach. Sustained by yields from these processes while contributing to both, Hong Kong and Macao must maximize their potentials in China's domestic transformation while enriching their global links. By the mid-twenty-first century, China's GDP would surpass that of the United States. Ideally, the new Sino–U.S. power realignment should enable Hong Kong and Macao to excel in their reinvented roles with rearticulated functions as Chinese cities with global dimensions and global cities with Chinese characteristics. With an enlightened approach, the United States can be a more positive force in the developmental orbit of Hong Kong and Macao as China's world cities to promote Sino–U.S. cooperation. Indeed, the Hong Kong and Macao folks have already enjoyed nearly all the freedoms that President Obama advocated for the Mainland Chinese in his November 16, 2009, exchange with Shanghai students.[111] On this score alone, the United States should cherish these two very unique Chinese cities as the bright spots in U.S.–PRC relations.

Notes

1. Steve Tsang, ed., *A Documentary History of Hong Kong: Government and Politics* (Hong Kong: Hong Kong University Press, 1995), 16–18, 31–39, on British rule's 1841 start, the 1860 and 1898 extensions; Peter Wesley-Smith, *Unequal Treaty (1898–1947): China, Great Britain and Hong Kong's New Territories*, rev. ed. (Hong Kong: Hong Kong University Press, 1998).

2. On the treaty port system, see John K. Fairbank, *Trade and Diplomacy on the China Coast: The Opening of the Treaty Ports, 1842–1854* (Cambridge, Mass.: Harvard University Press, 1953), and his "The creation of the treaty system," *Cambridge History of China: Volume 11, Late Ch'ing, Part I*, J. K. Fairbank, ed. (New York: Cambridge University Press, 1978), 213–43.

3. On historical U.S.–China relations, see John Fairbank, *The United States and China*, 5th ed. (Cambridge, Mass.: Harvard University Press, 1983).

4. Nancy Bernkopf Tucker, *Taiwan, Hong Kong, and the United States, 1945–1992: Uncertain Friendships* (New York: Twayne, 1994), 198. It also refers to Commodore Matthew Perry wintering in Hong Kong in 1853–1854 while waiting to force open Japan with a treaty for U.S. access.

5. On Chinese migration to the United States via Hong Kong, see Elizabeth Sinn, "The Gold Rush Passenger Trade and the History of Hong Kong, 1849–1867," *British Ships in China Seas: 1700 to the Present*, eds. Richard Harding et al. (Liverpool: National Museums Liverpool, 2004), 129–54.

6. Tucker, *Taiwan, Hong Kong, and the United States*, 198.

7. Tucker, *Taiwan, Hong Kong, and the United States*, 198.

8. Chi-kwan Mark, "American 'China Hands' in the 1950s," *Foreign Communities in Hong Kong, 1840s–1950s*, ed. Cindy Yi-yi Chu (New York: Palgrave/Macmillan, 2005), 170.

9. This is in Churchill's 1942 Mansion House speech; see James Tang, "From World War to Cold War; Hong Kong's Future and Anglo–Chinese Interactions, 1941–1955," *Precarious Balance: Hong Kong Between China and Britain, 1842–1992*, ed. Ming Chan (Armonk: Sharpe, 1994), 100.

10. Steve Tsang, *A Modern History of Hong Kong* (London: I. B. Tauris, 2004), 136; also see K. C. L. Chan, *China, Britain and Hong Kong, 1895–1945* (Hong Kong: Chinese University Press, 1990), 305–23; and Andrew Whitefield, *Hong Kong, Empire and the Anglo–American Alliance at War, 1941–1945* (London: Palgrave, 2001) on the allies' discord on Hong Kong's recovery.

11. Tsang, *A Modern History of Hong Kong*, 137–38.

12. Steve Tsang, "Strategy for Survival: The Cold War and Hong Kong's Policy Towards Kuomintang and Chinese Communist Activities in the 1950s," *Journal of Imperial and Commonwealth History*, 25:2 (May 1997); and Tsang, *A Modern History*, 158. On UK–ROC dealings in Hong Kong, see Steve Tsang, *The Cold War's Odd Couple: The Unintended Partnership between the Republic of China and the UK, 1950–1958* (London: I. B. Tauris, 2006).

13. On 1950s U.S.–UK interface over Hong Kong, see Chi-Kwan Mark, *Hong Kong and the Cold War: Anglo-American Relations, 1949–1957* (Oxford/Clarendon: Oxford University Press, 2004); Johannes Richard Lombardo, "United States' Foreign Policy Toward the British Crown Colony of Hong Kong during the early Cold War Period, 1945–1964" (PhD thesis, political science, University of Hong Kong, 1997); and Tucker, *Taiwan, Hong Kong, and the United States*, 201–14.

14. See Tsang, *The Cold War's Odd Couple*, 31, 34, 76–81, for the British consulate in Tamsui.

15. On London's recognition of Beijing, see Tsang, *The Cold War's Odd Couple*, 18–19, 32–33.

16. On UK–ROC links, see, Tsang, *The Cold War's Odd Couple*. On U.S.–UK discord, see Zhai Qiang, *The Dragon, the Lion, and the Eagle: Chinese-British-American Relations, 1949–1958* (Kent, Ohio: Kent State University Press, 1994); and Edwin W. Martin, *Divided Counsel: The Anglo–American Response to Communist Victory in China* (Lexington: University Press of Kentucky, 1986).

17. Mark, "American 'China Hands,'" 173.

18. On U.S.-linked anti-PRC undertakings by KMT elements involving Hong Kong as a base or launching channel, see Tsang, *The Cold War's Odd Couple*, 112–13.

19. This reflects the views of Governors Alexander Grantham (1947–1957) and Robert Black (1958–1964) in their London dispatches in CO 128 files. Some dispatches are included in this author's manuscript "The PRC Factor and Hong Kong External Links, 1949–1969" (Hong Kong University Press, first draft completed August 2001).

20. See Ming Chan, "Under the Shadow of Containment: Hong Kong in Cold War U.S.–China Security Concerns," *Return of the Dragon: U.S.–China Relations on the 21st Century*, eds. Danny Paau and Herbert Yee (Frankfurt: Peter Lang, 2005), 283.

21. See Zhai Qiang, *The Dragon, the Lion, and the Eagle*, 105–7; and Martin, *Divided Counsel*, 140–43, on the disposal of seventy-one Chinese planes in Hong Kong as the United Kingdom recognized the PRC. U.S. pressure to deny them to Beijing led to UK approval of their sales to a U.S. firm by voiding a Hong Kong court verdict favoring Beijing.

22. Memorandum by the Deputy Director for Strategic Plans, Bradley to the Joint Chiefs of Staff, October 23, 1952, U.S. State Department *Foreign Relations of the United States, 1952–1954*, 12:234. Also see Ming Chan, "Under the Shadow of Containment," 284–85.

23. Tsang, *The Cold War's Odd Couple*, 112–13.

24. As quoted in Mark Roberti, "Deal that Raised U.S. Stake in Hong Kong," *South China Morning Post*, April 12, 1992.

25. Ming Chan, "Under the Shadow of Containment," 288–89.

26. NSC Statement of Policy on U.S. Objectives and Courses of Action with Respect to SE Asia, Report to NSC by the Executive Secretary, June 25, 1952, *FRUS 1952–54*, 12:132.

27. Ming Chan, "Under the Shadow of Containment," 275–96.

28. Roberti, "Deal that Raised U.S. Stake in Hong Kong"; also see Tucker, *Taiwan, Hong Kong, and the United States*, 208–9; and Mark, "American 'China Hands,'" 125–27, 215–17.

29. They were as follows: Karl Rankin—Hong Kong, September 1949–August 1950, and Taipei as chargé d'affaires, August 1950–April 1953, and as ambassador until December 1957; Walter McConaughy—Hong Kong, November 1950–June 1952, and Taipei, June 1966–April 1974; and Everett F. Drumright—Hong Kong, December 1954–March 1958, and Taipei, March 1958–March 1962.

30. National Security Council Report, 6007/1-335, June 11, 1960, in *FRUS 1958–1960*, v. 19, 673.

31. Memorandum of Discussion, 447th National Security Council Meeting, June 8, 1960, *FRUS 1958–1960*, v. 19, 667–71.

32. For a recent study of the 1967 riots, see *May Days in Hong Kong: Emergency and Riots in 1967*, eds. Robert Bickers and Ray Yip (Hong Kong: Hong Kong University Press, 2009).

33. Roberti, "Deal that Raised U.S. Stake in Hong Kong"; Tucker, *Taiwan, Hong Kong, and the United States*, 214, refers to U.S. warships spending 1967 summer in Hong Kong as a show of support to the United Kingdom. Gerald Segal, *The Fate of Hong Kong* (London: Simon & Schuster, 1993), 115, calls the U.S. fleet's visit "an informal military guarantee for the colony."

34. Ming Chan, "New Twist on Gunboat Diplomacy: Sino British American Discord Over U.S. Naval Presence in mid-1960s Hong Kong," *Modern Chinese Naval History: New Perspectives*, eds. Ricardo Mak et al. (Hong Kong: Hong Kong Museum of Coastal Defense, 2004).

35. Gary McDonogh and Cindy Wong, *Global Hong Kong* (London: Routledge, 2005), 71.

36. Tucker, *Taiwan, Hong Kong, and the United States*, 215.

37. Tucker, *Taiwan, Hong Kong, and the United States*, 226.

38. See the mission's report, Edvard Hambro, *The Problem of Chinese Refugees in Hong Kong: Report Submitted to the UNHCR* (Leiden, The Netherlands: A. W. Sijchoff, 1955).

39. Glen Peterson, "To Be or Not Too Be a Refugee: The International Politics of the Hong Kong Refugee Crisis, 1949–1955," *Journal of Imperial and Commonwealth History*, 36:2 (June 2008): 171–96.

40. Tucker, *Taiwan, Hong Kong, and the United States*, 216–17.

41. Tucker, *Taiwan, Hong Kong, and the United States*, 223.

42. Mark, *Hong Kong and the Cold War*, 36–37; and Mark, "American 'China Hands,'" 182–84.

43. See Tsang, *The Cold War's Odd Couple*, 170, on the CIA's involvement with Taipei's anti-Mainland operations involving Hong Kong; also see Tucker, *Taiwan, Hong Kong, and the United States*, 206–7.

44. See Mark, *Hong Kong and the Cold War*, 188–93; and Tucker, *Taiwan, Hong Kong, and the United States*, 206.

45. On UK–U.S. discord over anti-PRC embargo and trade controls, with regard to British position in Hong Kong and Southeast Asia and UK commercial interests, see Martin, *Divided Counsel*, 64–70.

46. A positive view of U.S. trade control's impact on Hong Kong is Matthew Turner, "Hong Kong Design and the Roots of Sino-American Trade Disputes," *The Future of Hong Kong, The Annuals*, vol. 547, ed. Max Skidmore (September 1996), 37–53; also see Mark, *Hong Kong and the Cold War*, chapter 4.

47. Mark, "American 'China Hands,'" 178–82.

48. Tucker, *Taiwan, Hong Kong, and the United States*, 215.

49. Tucker, *Taiwan, Hong Kong, and the United States*, 217.

50. Roberti, "Deal that Raised U.S. Stake in Hong Kong"; James Tang, "Hong Kong in United States–Chinas Relations," *Journal of Contemporary China*, 6:16 (1997).

51. Stephen J. Yates, "Hong Kong's Evolving Role in U.S.–China relations," *Hong Kong Journal*, 10 (April 1, 2008); also Hungdah Chu, "The Hong Kong Agreement and U.S. Foreign Policy," *Hong Kong: A Chinese and International Concern*, eds. Jurgen Domes and Yu-ming Shaw (Boulder, Colo.: Westview, 1988), 189–92.

52. This description is from Segal, *The Fate of Hong Kong*, 112. A post–June 4 U.S. pessimist view on Hong Kong in U.S.–PRC ties is Harlan Jencks, "China's Evolving Interest in the Western Pacific: Korea, Taiwan, Hong Kong and ASEAN," *After Tiananmen Square: Challenges to the Chinese–American Relationship*, eds. Jurgen Domes et al. (Washington, D.C.: Brassey's, 1990), 62–64, 71.

53. See *Reluctant Exiles: Migration from Hong Kong and the New Overseas Chinese*, ed. Ronald Skeldon (Armonk, N.Y.: Sharpe, 1994); and Ronald Skeldon, *Emigration from Hong Kong: Tendencies and Impacts* (Hong Kong: Chinese University Press, 1995) for the pre-1997 exodus.

54. Tucker, *Taiwan, Hong Kong, and the United States*, 222; Danny S. L. Paau, "Hong Kong, China and the United States," *Hong Kong the Super Paradox: Life after Return to China*, ed. James Hsiung (New York: St Martin, 2000), 205; also Segal, *The Fate of Hong Kong* on HK immigration to the United States (121–25) and to Canada (130–38).

55. On comparing Hong Kong with frontier zones Taiwan and Tibet in U.S.–PRC ties, see Michael Oksenberg, "Taiwan, Tibet, and Hong Kong in Sino–American Relations," *Living with China: U.S.–China Relations in the Twenty First Century*, ed. Ezra F. Vogel (New York: Norton, 1997), 53–96; Segal, *The Fate of Hong Kong*, 3, 121, 126. Karl Rankin (USCG–HK and envoy to ROC, 1950–1957) in *China Assignment* (Seattle: University of Washington Press, 1964) refers to a Hong Kong–South China split from Beijing's control in a possible scenario of regional separatism.

56. Christopher Patten, "Our Next Five Years: The Agenda for Hong Kong" (Governor's Address to the Legislative Council, October 7, 1922), para. 125–47, on his electoral reform for 1995. Also see Nancy Tucker, "Hong Kong as a Problem in Chinese–American Relations," *Hong Kong Under Chinese Rule: The Economic and Political Implications of Reversion*, eds. Warren I. Cohen and Li Zhao (New York: Cambridge University Press, 1997), 220.

57. Figures are from Tang, "Hong Kong in United States–Chinas Relations," 421; Kerry Dumbaugh, "Hong Kong's Return to China: Implications for U.S. Interests," *CRS Issue Brief*, (September 18, 1997), 2, and his "Hong Kong's Reversion to China: Problems and Remedies for the United States," *CRS Report for Congress* (March 3, 1997), 8–9, 16 (Washington, D.C.: Congressional Research Service); Wai Ting, "The External Relations and International Status of Hong Kong," *School of Law, University of Maryland, Occasional Papers in Contemporary Asian Studies* 2, 1997 [139], 40–41.

58. Louis Kraar, "The Death of Hong Kong," *Fortune* (June 26, 1995), 118–39.

59. Jenet Salaff and Arent Greve, "A Decade of Responses in North America to the Handover," *The First Decade: The Hong Kong SAR in Retrospective and Introspective Perspectives*, ed. Yue-man Yeung (Hong Kong: Chinese University Press, 2007), 43–64.

60. Dumbaugh, "Hong Kong's Return to China," 1.

61. All these are Hong Kong Census and Statistics Department figures as of September 2009.

62. U.S. Consul General Donovan's November 19, 2009, speech at the Chinese University of Hong Kong.

63. These figures are from the Hong Kong Trade Development Council (TDC) data as of August 2009.

64. The $47 billion figure is from Donovan's November 19, 2008, speech that puts HKSAR firms' U.S. investment at $3.2 billion. The $4 billion figure is from HKSAR official data.

65. This figure is from Donovan's 2009 speech. In HKSAR official data, 28,620 U.S. nationals resided in 2008, but this did not cover those of local origin with full entry-residence rights.

66. Tony Latter, "Reflections on Hong Kong's Monetary Evolution and the Occasional Involvement of the United States," *Hong Kong on the Move: 10 Years as the HKSAR*, eds. Carola McGiffert and James Tang (Washington, D.C.: CSIS, 2008), 96, 102–3.

67. Paau, "Hong Kong, China and the United States," 211–14; Latter, "Reflections on Hong Kong's Monetary Evolution and the Occasional Involvement of the United States," 96–98.

68. See *Wall Street Journal*, October 6, 2006, for Friedman's article criticizing Tsang.

69. See Sonny S. H. Lo, *The Dynamics of Beijing-Hong Kong Relations: A Model for Taiwan?* (Hong Kong: Hong Kong University Press, 2008), especially chapter 9.

70. Bate Gill and Chin-Hao Huang, in "Democracy Agenda May Revive U.S. Interest in Hong Kong," *Hong Kong Journal* (January 1, 2006), pinpoint HKSAR democracy as a Bush regime PRC focus.

71. On Article 23 and Tung's exit, see Ming Chan and S. H. Lo, *Historical Dictionary of the Hong Kong SAR and the Macao SAR* (Lanham, Md.: Scarecrow Press, 2006), 47–56; and Alvin So, "Social Conflict in Hong Kong after 1997," *China's*

Hong Kong Transformed, ed. Ming Chan (Hong Kong: City University of Hong Kong Press, 2008), 240–44.

72. Salaff and Greve says the *New York Times* covers more HKSAR political than economic news.

73. Then HKSAR Security for Security Regina Ip complained to this author in March 2003 that U.S. and Canadian officials were hostile to the proposed bill as if they were British "surrogates."

74. Paau, "Hong Kong, China and the United States," 216, attributes the Democrats' electoral success since 1998 to U.S. campaign aids. On the DAB's U.S. training course, see Sonny Lo, *Competing Chinese Political Visions: Hong Kong vs. Beijing on Democracy* (Westport, Conn.: Praeger, 2010), chapter 8.

75. Wai Ting, "The External Relations and International Status of Hong Kong," 42; Dumbaugh, "Hong Kong's Reversion to China," 13–16; also Joseph Lai, "Free and Secure Trade," and Richard T. Cupitt, "Trade Controls of the Hong Kong Special Administrative Region," as chapter 8 (126–37) and chapter 9 (138–46) in McGiffert and Tang, *Hong Kong on the Move*.

76. See Simon Shen, "U.S.–Hong Kong Relations and the Response to Counterterrorism," Hong Kong Institute of Asia–Pacific Studies Occasional Paper, no. 179 (December 2006) (Hong Kong: Chinese University of Hong Kong).

77. Derek Mitchell, "On the Front Lines: Hong Kong's Role in International Security," in McGiffert and Tang, *Hong Kong on the Move*, 111–13.

78. Danny Paau, "Values vs. Realities? American Attitudes and Policies Toward Hong Kong after 1997," *Tamkang Journal of International Affairs*, 7:1 (Fall 2002), 32–38.

79. Susan Blumenthal, "Hong Kong and the United States: Shared Health Care Challenges and Opportunities," in McGiffert and Tang, *Hong Kong on the Move*, 158–78.

80. U.S. tourist arrival in Hong Kong in 2008 declined 6.9 percent to 1.146 million, due to the recession.

81. Ting, "The External Relations and International Status of Hong Kong," 41.

82. See Donovan's 2008 speech for the figures on Fulbrighters and U.S. students in Hong Kong.

83. On Macao's reversion and post-1999 record, see Ming Chan, "Different Roads to Home: The Retrocession of Hong Kong and Macao to Chinese Sovereignty," *Journal of Contemporary China*, 12:36 (2003); Ming Chan and S. H. Lo, "The Macao SAR's 1st Five Years," *Oriente Occidente*, 14 (September–December 2004); Chan and Lo, *Historical Dictionary*, 283–98; Shiu-hing Lo, *Political Change in Macao* (London: Routledge, 2008).

84. *Macao Daily*, November 5 and 17, 2009, the latter quotes the Goldman Sachs percent share figures.

85. MSAR Financial Services Bureau figures; see www.dsf.gov.mo/Con_Pub/e_ConPub_Fs.htm.

86. See *Macao Daily*, October 2, 2009, for the September 2009 figures; MSAR Government Statistics and Census Service (DSCE) data for the other figures.

87. *New York Times*, October 9, 2009; *Ming Pao*, November 10, 2009; *Standard*, November 16, 2009.

88. *South China Morning Post*, October 14, 2009; and BBC News, October 14, 2009; *Macao Daily*, October 28, 2009; LVS press release, October 29, 2009.

89. From DSCE data, *Macao Year Book 2008* (Macao: Government Information Bureau, 2008).

90. Professor Sonny Lo then at University of Hong Kong also attended this June 6, 2004, interview.

91. *Ming Pao*, *Macao Daily*, and *South China Morning Post*, all April 3, 2009.

92. W. M. Morrison et al., "Most-Favored Nation Status and China," CRS Report for Congress, 96–923E (November 19, 1966), 22.

93. See Wai Ting, "The External Relations and International Status of Hong Kong," 36–38, for Hong Kong's colonial era efforts for the PRC's MFN status.

94. See Sonny Lo, *The Politics of Cross-Border Crime in Greater China: Case Studies of Mainland China, Hong Kong and Macao* (Armonk, N.Y.: Sharpe, 2009), 145–47. This author interviewed Mr. Stanley Au, chair of Banco Delta Asia in Macao, March 2008, on this case.

95. In 2008, Hong Kong businessman Richard Suen, who helped Adelson connect with PRC officials to obtain the Macao license, sued Adelson in Las Vegas for reneging on promised profit from the deal. Suen won a $43.8 million verdict. See *New Yorker*, June 30, 2008.

96. See the story by Steve Green in the *Las Vegas Sun*, May 19, 2009.

97. *Wall Street Journal*, March 9, 2009.

98. This section is based on Ming Chan, "New Twist on Gunboat Diplomacy."

99. These U.S. naval port calls range from 1998's fifty-four to 2003's eleven according to HKSAR official data.

100. *Ming Pao*, October 23, 2007.

101. The full text was released by the USCG–HK's Public Affair Section on the same date.

102. That is, the McGiffert and Tang edited *Hong Kong on the Move* volume published in late 2008.

103. Ming Chan, "Friends Across the Pacific: The Canada–Hong Kong Links in Historical and Contemporary Perspectives," *China Review* (forthcoming 2010).

104. See Ming Chan, "Foreword: Transcending the 'Havanization' Syndrome: Comparative Perspectives on Macao Gaming Development and Societal Transformation," *Dimensions of the Gaming Industry and Social Impact in Macao*, eds. S. H. Lo and Beatrice Leung (Hong Kong: City University of Hong Kong Press, 2010).

105. See the news reports and editorials in Hong Kong Chinese-language dailies *Ming Pao*, *Apple Daily*, and *Oriental Daily*, July 1 and 5, 2009.

106. See Helen F. Siu and Agnes S. Ku, eds., *Hong Kong Mobile: Making a Global Population* (Hong Kong: Hong Kong University Press, 2008); Stephen Chiu and Tailok Lui, *Hong Kong: Becoming a Chinese Global City* (London: Routledge, 2009), chapters 1 and 7.

107. For details on this HKSAR-based private foundation, see its website, www.cusef.org.hk.

108. This author attended Leong's speech. USCG–HK James Cunningham made the same point on Beijing attacking HKSAR Democrats' foreign ties at a HKSAR symposium in Stanford University, November 12, 2007; see his "The Hong Kong SAR at Ten Years and Prospects for the Future," in Ming Chan, *China's Hong Kong Transformed*, 335–41.

109. See *Wen Wei Po*, November 11, 2009, for this criticism of the United States at a November 10 Beijing conference on the MSAR's first decade, right before President Obama's visit. A senior PRC official in charge of HK–MSAR affairs also warned against "foreign interference" in the SARs.

110. This author is indebted to Professor Sonny Lo for this suggestion. Also see Ming Chan, "Core Elements in the Foreign Policy of a Rising China and Key Issues in Sino–American Relations," *China's Rise: Threat or Opportunity*, ed. Herbert Yee (London: Routledge, 2010) for a delineation of PRC–U.S. links that suffer from the lack of mutual trust.

111. *New York Times*, November 16, 2009.

CHAPTER FIFTEEN

Another Tale of Twin Cities: Macao and Hong Kong in Comparative Perspectives

Hu Weixing

Does Macao really matter to Hong Kong, the Pearl River Delta, the Chinese mainland, the Greater China, and major powers like the United States? It never did, but not now. Although the Chinese like to refer (and still do) Macao together with Hong Kong as "Gang Au" (港澳), everybody knew the former Portuguese colony was never as important as Hong Kong to China and other major countries in the world. However, after years of post-colonial transformation as a Chinese Special Administrative Region (SAR), Macao is no longer marginalized, rather, rising up in importance in regional economy, cross-strait relations, and even major power relations. This does not mean, though, that Hong Kong's salience in regional and global economy and in the Greater China sphere of integration has declined, and, instead, changes and development in Macao since its return to the Chinese sovereignty have been remarkable.

Hong Kong Special Administrative Region (HKSAR) was established on July 1, 1997, after the British returned Hong Kong to Chinese sovereignty after more than 150 years of colonial rule. Two years later, Macao Special Administrative Region (MSAR) was founded on December 20, 1999, upon Beijing's resumption of its exercise of sovereignty over Macao. Both HKSAR and MSAR have since then functioned within the "one country, two systems" framework enshrined in the PRC Hong Kong and Macao SAR Basic Laws, respectively. The two SAR Basic Laws are quite similar mini-constitutions, drafted and enacted by the Chinese National People's Congress, to govern the functioning of the two SARs under the "one county, two systems" formula. The SAR Basic Laws guarantee a high degree of autonomy, rule by local people, and the preservation of capitalist economy and free society after the return. However, Hong Kong's post-1997 transformation has encountered enormous problems in the realms of effective governance and sociopolitical stability, while Macao, a much smaller and even "backward" special administrative region, has experienced relatively more stable and prosperous transformation since 1999. The Basic Law and Beijing's "one country, two systems" formula are supposed to provide similar administrative and institutional space for political and economic development in the two SARs. Why did Macao and Hong Kong have distinct transitional experiences after the hand-over? Does it matter for the two SARs? This chapter addresses these issues from a comparative perspective as well as from how Beijing and Washington have handled their policies toward the two SARs.

A Tale of Twin Cities: Macao Was Never Viewed as a Rival by Hong Kong and Now . . .

From Hong Kong's perspective, MSAR was never viewed as rival to its development and competitiveness. To ordinary Hong Kong people Macao is just a place for leisure in weekends and at night. Most people even look down upon Macao, and regard it as a lesser place than Hong Kong. It is backward, poorly governed, with a high rate of crime like those in Third World countries or cross the border to the mainland. Hong Kong has a much larger populace and territory, more advantageous physical and institutional infrastructure, higher standard of rule of law, a more vibrant economy, and mature civil society. Given its enormous advantages over the former Portuguese colony, the Hong Kong government and society have never treated Macao as a serious competitor in the region as well as in greater China, even though its gambling and tourist industry has enjoyed spectacular growth over the last few years.[1] When Macao decided to open up the gambling rights, the Hong Kong SAR did consider the economic consequences of Macao's booming gambling and tourist industry, but never wanted to follow the suit. To Hong Kong, Macao's booming gambling industry could be a win-win situation for the both places.[2]

Historically, Hong Kong and Macao were ruled and molded into quite different societies by their colonial masters. The British rule in Hong Kong left a legacy of a relatively intact, corruption-free, and well-performed civil service system, a strong civil society, rule of law and social order, a robust economy, and independent judiciary, while the Portuguese style of government in Macao gave the impression of maladministration, corruption, and lack of efficiency. In Portuguese Macao, it was commonplace to see abuse of official power, and many civil servants groomed in the colonial era remain ignorant of the concept and practice of accountability.[3] These legacies laid a distinct foundation for the post-colonial development and transformation in the two territories when sovereignty was transferred to China.

Given HKSAR's position in world and regional economy, it is Singapore, not Macao, that has long been a competitor and even threat to the future of Hong Kong as "Asia's World City." In terms of business cultures and legal frameworks Hong Kong and Singapore have shared many similarities, which make them more advantageous in emerging markets and global economy. Hong Kong is a natural gateway into China, while Singapore is busy promoting itself as the regional hub of choice. Both Hong Kong and Singapore have consistently ranked as the world's freest economies. In the *2006 Index of Economic Freedom* prepared by the Heritage Foundation, Hong Kong and Singapore were first and second, respectively. The 2006 index report also praised the two Asian cities' policies on attracting inward foreign investment. Both Hong Kong's and Singapore's investment laws are clear and fair, and they pose few problems for business. "Foreign and domestic businesses are treated equally, there are no production or local content requirements, and nearly all sectors are open to 100 percent foreign ownership," the report explains. The Global Competitiveness Index (GCI) 2005–2006, however, ranked Singapore as Asia's most competitive economy, and the fifth-most competitive economy in the world. In the World Bank report *Doing Business in 2005*, Singapore's economy was ranked third behind New Zealand and the United States in terms of ease of doing business.

Although international rating is just indicative, HKSAR has long felt the heat from Singapore. Recently, Premier Wen Jiabao reminded and encouraged HKSAR officials to study and learn from Singaporean experiences in its economic and social development.[4] Hong Kong's strength is clear but is losing ground to Singapore's competition. Hong Kong remains a model of economic freedom, with its free port, no barriers to trade, simple tax structure, low taxation to starting enterprises, free entry of foreign capital and repatriation of earnings, transparency, and the rule of law. But all these are no longer advantageous over Singapore. After the Asian Financial Crisis, the Singaporean government has readjusted its economic and social policy, which has made it more attractive than Hong Kong to foreign business and trade. Singapore's policy environment and efficient government service have proven to be more attractive to many multinational corporations that have relocated there or chosen Singapore at Hong Kong's expense. Yet HKSAR is still proud of its strength in financial service. For instance, turnover on the Hong Kong stock exchange has increased as more Mainland Chinese enterprises look to raise capital by issuing new shares. As of December 31, 2005, the total amount of funds raised in Hong Kong reportedly stood at $38.6 billion, making it the world's fourth largest fund raising center after New York, London, and Toronto.[5] In 2006 the IPO volume in Hong Kong jumped to the second largest in the world as more international investors expected further increases in fund raising by mainland enterprises. But in a long run, Hong Kong's economic model and social policy will show weakness vis-à-vis the Singaporean model.

Hong Kong's other competitor is Shanghai. This newly rising competitor attracts businesses wanting to get closer to the ground. Shanghai is also fast attracting research and development activities, with its improving infrastructure and investment environment. Hong Kong has largely lost its manufacturing jobs across the border, an exodus before its handover to Chinese rule in 1997. It was further dented by the Asian Financial Crisis and the deadly SARS epidemic. But even as Hong Kong struggles with its *raison d'etre*, and ranked the freest economy in the world for the twelfth year, it begins to feel the heat from Shanghai as its potential to be Asia's Mahattan. HKSAR officials are busy studying the implications of the rise of Shanghai and Hong Kong's future role in the Pearl River Delta (PRD). Hong Kong has no other way but being integrated into PRD, the world's fastest-growing economy to compete with the rising power of the Yangtze River Delta centered around Shanghai.

Under the "one country, two systems" arrangement, Hong Kong has a high degree of autonomy, retaining its strong rule of law and relatively corruption-free civil servant system, which will take years, if not decades, for Shanghai to catch up. HKSAR officials still boast of Hong Kong's know-how, unfettered flow of information and capital, clean and efficient governance with limited interference, simple and low taxes, and global outlook. With these "software" infrastructures, HKSAR is leading the race since Shanghai still lacks transparency, freedom of information, or capital mobility as Hong Kong does. Shanghai is dwarfed by Hong Kong's high-end financial, services, transit, and tourist prowess, which is vital to its economic prosperity and China's economic future.[6] Chinese companies still need Hong Kong's financial market as a window to the world, while overseas firms look to it to tap into the mainland market. Hong Kong is still a top foreign direct investment destination, attracting $34 billion in 2005, much higher than Shanghai's $6.8 billion; and wages in Hong Kong far exceed those in Shanghai. In 2005 Hong Kong was home to 3,800 regional headquarters, a rise of 189 percent over 2004. Shanghai has 124 multinational headquarters, up from 86 in 2004.[7] Hong Kong is now touting itself as the financial and investment center for the Pan-PRD, an area that includes nine neighboring provinces, along with itself and Macao.

Nevertheless, the rapid development of Macao economy in the last decade before the current financial crisis has really turned the heat on Hong Kong in the two-SAR competition. Macao's economy is based largely on tourism, much of it geared toward the gambling industry. In 2002, the Macao SAR government officially ended the monopoly in the gambling industry, and several casino owners from Las Vegas were allowed to enter the market. Since then six casino-operating concessions and subconcessions have been granted to Sociedade de Turismo e Diversões de Macao (STDM), Wynn Resorts, Las Vegas Sands, Galaxy Entertainment Group, the partnership of MGM Mirage and Pansy Ho (daughter of Stanley Ho), and the partnership of Melco and PBL. Today, although casinos operated by the STDM are still crucial in Macao's casino industry, the opening of the Sands Macao, MGM, Galaxy, and other American casinos ushered in a new era.[8] The booming gambling industry has increased the attraction for tourists. Macao has become a very popular place for tourists, especially from the mainland, after the introduction of more new hotels and casinos in recent years. Showcased in the 2005 East Asian Games in Macao, the city proved itself able to offer a good number of festival events every year as well, and that helps to increase its attractiveness. Macao has long been overshadowed by Hong Kong as a main destiny for mainland tourists. Compared with the attractions in Macao, the mainland tourists are now become less satisfied with what Hong Kong can offer to them. As a result, Macao turns out to be a more novel and attractive city than Hong Kong. According to the WTO data, Macao is now ranked twenty-first in the number of tourists and twenty-fourth in terms of tourism receipts, with almost 30.2 million visitors in 2008. That gave a big boost to the city's economic growth. Macao's GDP growth rate was 16.5 percent, 25.3 percent, and 13.2 percent from 2006 to 2008, respectively. It's gross national income per capita in these three years increased from $28,465 in 2006, to $35,533 in 2007, and $39,136 in 2008, which surpassed Hong Kong's by a big margin.[9]

Macao and Hong Kong: One Model, Two Experiences?

The "one country, two systems" model in Hong Kong and Macao have produced two different experiences since their return to the Chinese sovereignty in 1997 and 1999, respectively. The two SARs' experiences of reunification with the motherland constitutes two distinct local transformation processes, and the distinct transformation processes led to different integrative processes with the mainland after the handover. Macao's experience in some way has overshadowed Hong Kong's self-fulfilled sense of superiority over Macua and its long-term ignorance of its closest neighbor.

As a much larger and more salient showcase to the world, the transition and consequence of the "one country, two systems" experiment in Hong Kong after 1997 has more crucial significance than Macao's experience for China and to the prospects of Greater China in the twenty-first century. The "one country, two systems" formula was originally designed for a peaceful reunification of Taiwan with the China mainland. If it was successfully implemented in the Hong Kong experiment, it could generate a "role model" effect for Taiwan. But, for many observers, the HKSAR's experiences of the "one country, two systems" model have not been so smooth in creating effective governance and socioeconomic transformation. In some sense, Hong Kong is dwarfed by Macao's experience under the leadership of Chief Executive (CE) Edmund Ho. The political climate and governance turbulence in HKSAR from 2002 to 2005 was even becoming alarming to Beijing.

In sharp contrast, the metamorphosis in Macao since the handover has been relatively smooth and melodious. Macao has less then a half million population. With a booming gambling industry, Macao has enjoyed a much more stable, prosperous, and harmonious development (more than 20 percent) in the last few years. Macao's success is not just because it has been blessed with economic boom and social stability, it also has a lot to do with a highly popular and effective chief executive, Edmund Ho. In contrast to unpopular HKSAR CE Tung Chee Hwa, Edmund Ho has so far orchestrated a relatively successful play of "one country, two systems" actualization. Nevertheless, we must point out that Macao's successful transition story after 1999 has been undergone in a fairly "traditionalistic" and only partially democratic polity (in which some legislators are still appointed). In this political game informal politics and patron–client networks are practiced in a way that helps to create personalized authoritarian politics similar in the mainland.[10] According to a Macao Foundation–sponsored survey "Macao Quality of Life Report," the confidence level on the "one country, two systems" experience in Macao runs very high, with 51 percent of respondents acknowledging confidence, 35.7 percent half-half, and only 13.3 percent a lack of confidence. Contrary to the similar question asked in Hong Kong, Macao residents have a much higher satisfaction level on political conditions than those in Hong Kong, with 36.9 percent respondents indicating "very satisfied" and "quite satisfied," 38.3 percent "half-half," and only 24.7 "dissatisfied."[11]

However, Macao's story shows its dark side as well. During Edmund Ho's first term in office, there was a major demonstration by unemployed workers on July 2, 2000. Seven years later on May Day 2007, a much larger scale of protest occurred in Macao and it turned to violent confrontation between unemployed workers and police. On the surface, the unemployed workers clashed with the police over MSAR's labor policy, which protestors believed to be biased in favor of big business and foreign laborers. But, more important, the protest revealed much bigger problems than expected—"black holes" in government public spending and scandals with high-ranking officials.[12] Macao's Secretary for Transport and Public Works Ao Man Long (歐文龍) was arrested in 2007 in connection with corruption charges. Mr. Ao was charged with receiving a 167 million patacas bribe from construction companies linked with a list of Macao's well-known constructions projects from the Macao Dome, Galaxy StarWorld Hotel, Macao Shooting Range Field to the Venetian Macao Resort Hotel. He was reported to have ordered his family members and friend to open five offshore companies in the Virgin Isles in the UK (such as Best Choice, Trendfree, Ecoline, Citygrand, and Roselle Corp Limited) as a means to manage his bribes and money laundering activities. Documents seized by the Macao Commission Against Corruption (CCAC) and verified by the Hong Kong High Court and Independent Commission Against Corruption (ICAC) suggested that the ones who actually controlled the companies and bank accounts behind the scene were Ao Man Long and his wife Chan Meng Ieng.[13]

According to Dr. Sonny Lo, a leading expert in Hong Kong and Macao affairs, four major factors have separated Hong Kong and Macao in their post-colonial transformation: colonial legacy, political leadership, state–society relationship, and institutionalization.[14] Historically, the British rule in Hong Kong was quite different from that of the Portuguese style of government in Macao, which led to different experiences of handover. In the final years before the British left Hong Kong, Governor Christopher Patten was determined to combat with Beijing over the pace and scope of his political reforms of Hong Kong's colonial governance system. Patten's fight, though it did not gain too much, succeeded in raising the political expectations of Hong Kong residents and set off waves of popular calls for democratization in the territory. In response to the situation, the central government in Beijing had to reverse the decisions of the last colonial legislature and restarted with a provisional legislative council. On the contrary, a relatively pleasant Sino–Portuguese relationship generated a smooth transfer of power in Macao. The MSAR Provisional Legislative Council (LegCo) did not exclude any democrats whose number remained very small. Nor did new Chief Executive

Edmund Ho view any senior civil servant as harboring pro-Portuguese sentiment. To the newly formed MSAR, the problem was instead a shortage of qualified civil servants due to the slow pace of localization of the civil service during the Portuguese Macao.

Political leadership was another key factor distinguishing HKSAR and MSAR. Although many observers ridiculed Portuguese Macao as the Chinese mainland's "liberated" area, the joint rule involving Portuguese expatriates and local Chinese community leaders nurtured indigenous leadership. HKSAR Chief Executive Tung Chee-hwa's experience in ExCo was brief and his first administration was undermined by an over-ambitious agenda without any reform priority. Unlike Tung, Edmund Ho developed his political skills and administrative experience in Macao's Legislative Assembly before its handover. In the MSAR, Ho adopted a skilful and pragmatic leadership style, which contributed to his efficacy and popularity. Ho was pragmatic and avoided implementing reforms that could upset the masses.[15]

More important, HKSAR presented a more serious challenge to political leadership when its sociopolitical elites are fragmented and even divided into the polarized pro-democracy and pro-Beijing forces. And this is probably the biggest force dragging Tung's feet. The Tung Chee Hwa government was rocked by internal disunity whereas Edmund Ho's leadership was characterized by solidarity. The first Tung administration was affected by his tensions with Anson Chan, who had reservations on such issues as the decision to bid for the 2006 Asian Games. During the second Tung administration, some of his principal officials, who were appointed in July 2002 to strengthen his governance and to curb the influence of senior civil servants, acted controversially. Politically, the Macao public are traditionally more patriotic and pro-Beijing, less politically active or defiant, and more supportive of the government than their counterparts in the HKSAR.[16]

To Hong Kong people, most Macao residents have not yet developed a sense of using democracy as a means to check maladministration. MSAR's governance also dampens the demand for more democratization. While in Hong Kong, most people are no longer politically apathetic and challenge the post-colonial state over all sorts of policies. One explanation for a more assertive Hong Kong society is its problematic political leadership and constitutional reform process. Macao's civil society is still weak. Macao residents are far more interested in materialistic pursuits than the politically assertive Hong Kong residents. The Edmund Ho government's problems since late 2004 have invigorated some public demands for governmental transparency, accountability, and responsiveness, but anti-reform sentiment is still strong.

In terms of SAR–central government relations, there are strains and tensions between officials in Beijing and political elites in Hong Kong. These strains and tensions have developed into the interactive dynamics between the "push" by Hong Kong local activists demanding fuller scope and faster pace democratization and the "pull" of China's huge market forces and Beijing's political–constitutional constraints as empowered by the Basic Law.[17] The HKSAR's simmering governance crisis reached its climax in March 2005 when Chief Executive Chee Hwa Tung was prematurely replaced by Donald Tsang. Despite this sudden leadership change, the root causes of the HKSAR's administrative problems and executive–legislative gridlock remained unresolved, and among them the pace for constitutional reform and universal suffrage top the list. Many felt the high degree of autonomy as guaranteed in the Basic Law had been jeopardized by Beijing's April 2004 pre-emptive interpretation of the Basic Law concerning 2007–2008 local direct elections by universal franchise. This NPC interpretation was followed by another one in May 2005 to limit replacement Chief Executive Donald Tsang's tenure to the remaining twenty five months of Tung's unfinished second term. To protest, the Democrat camp organized a massive 100,000-strong demonstration on July 1, 2005, and used block vote tactics to have Donald Tsang's proposed minor electoral reforms for 2007–2008 rejected in Legco in December of the same year. In Macao, however, everything seems under control and there should be no immediate challenge for the central government in Beijing. Based on recent survey findings, there is no pervasive political apathy in Macao. The people profess a high degree of confidence in the Macao SAR government and show a clearly marked preference for law-abiding and peaceful means to attain whatever systemic changes they may strive for.[18]

In sum, most Hong Kong elites still look down upon Macao. They do not want to see Hong Kong be another Macao, politically and economically. But their Greater Hong Kong mentality has been diluted since the abysmal failure of the Tung Chee Hwa regime. They have to learn more humbly from the lessons of Macao's governance.[19]

Beijing and Two SARs

From Beijing's perspective, both HKSAR and MSAR are non-sovereign entities after the British and Portuguese returned the sovereignty to China, and the central government in Beijing has the supreme authority to make constitutional law for the territories. In order to maintain stability and prosperity of the two SARs, the central government enacted in good faith the Basic Law for the two territories. To guarantee a high degree of autonomy and act in the overall interest of both Hong Kong and the Macao people, Beijing set up the "one country, two systems" formula in conducting its Hong Kong and Macao policy, and will continue to abide by the "one country, two systems" policy and the Basic Law no matter what problem or crisis arises in the two territories. Hong Kong and Macao are neither entirely occidental nor completely oriental and both HKSAR and MSAR are executive-led governments which have developed according to their colonial traditions and social conditions. For Beijing, it would be ideal to keep its direct intervention in Hong Kong and Macao to the minimum so as to uphold "a high degree of autonomy" for the two SARs. Nonetheless, governance crisis in Hong Kong necessitated Beijing's intervention.

As discussed above, Hong Kong people were no longer apathetic to constitutional reforms and universal suffrage after 1997. The civil society has become assertive vis-à-vis the post-colonial political elites and SAR government, and insufficient reforms have exacerbated an unhappy society, whose citizens have been determined to oppose the policies of the post-colonial government. Beijing's reluctance to allow the chief executive directly elected by universal suffrage and a legislature fully directly elected by citizens is viewed by the Democrats as to use procedural legitimacy to prolong the existing structure. On the other side of the debate, legal scholars in Beijing argue that Hong Kong is obliged to maintain its current and executive-oriented structure under the premise that it is part of China and it must do so within the "one country, two systems" framework. Under the current constitutional arrangement, HKSAR does not have the residual power to change its system without the delegation of power from the National People's Congress, which enacted the Basic Law. It is believed that the overwhelming majority of Hong Kong compatriots recognize that identification with the motherland, patriotic love for both the mainland and Hong Kong, close interdependence and commitment to mutually enjoy glory and bear hardship, promote not only the territory's prosperity and stability, but also that of Greater China. This understanding should be accepted and practiced as the basis of the consensus in the society. Within this orientation all of Hong Kong's political and economical activities, political parties, and citizens exist; they too, are proscribed by its limitations. Therefore, it is impractical and without legal merit to reject the power of the central government, thereby laying undue emphasis on Hong Kong's autonomy.[20]

To many observers, political development in the HKSAR is controversial and will be protracted because of the contending views on the pace, scope, and roadmap of the constitutional reforms. On one hand, the Democrats and politically motivated middle-class Democratic reform are a must to maintain the "two systems" and Hong Kong's autonomy. On the other hand, the Hong Kong ruling elites and officials in Beijing see postponed democratization as a necessity to maintain social stability and uphold the political correctness of "one country." The Article 23 episode was a good example of the clash.

The Basic Law Article 23 requires HKSAR government to enact national security laws concerning treason, subversion, and related crimes in its legislature. But the contents and scope of the Article 23 law triggered a society-wide debate about personal freedom and rights and then led to a massive demonstration of more than a half million people against the legislation. The July 1, 2003, demonstration was widely publicized all over the world and created a crisis situation for the Tung Chee Hwa government. To make a turnaround of the situation, Chinese leaders in Beijing were forced by the circumstances to openly support Tung, despite his unpopularity prompted wide-spread outcry for his oust. Beijing had to mobilize the business community and leftwing organizations rally behind Tung Chee Hwa as his legitimacy became much more fragile. In retrospect, many observers believe that the July 1, 2003, demonstration became a watershed for the central government in Beijing to step in more actively in Hong Kong's governance and political reforms. After that, Beijing reorganized the coordination structure in the apparatus of Hong Kong–Macao affairs and strengthened its research and monitoring capacity in Hong Kong.

In comparison, Macao is a completely different ballgame. Beijing did not need to intervene in its domestic affairs explicitly, and the central government's authority and policy was never directly challenged on the street by Macao residents. There has been no such a direct call for more democratic election in Macao. The influential interest groups, such as business chambers, neighborhood associations, and labor unions, are generally pro-Beijing. The central government, through its Liaison Office in Macao, has traditionally participated in the process of reaching compromise among pro-Beijing candidates in the legislative elections, especially in indirect elections that are often uncontested. The Central Government Liaison Office also conducts extensive united front work on interest groups and local communities.

The U.S. Policy toward Two Chinese SARs

The United States has similar interests in Macao and Hong Kong in the areas of protection of American citizens; maintenance of free market economy; respect for civil liberties and human rights; efforts to combat IPR piracy; law enforcement cooperation to prevent transnational crime and anti-terrorism. Based on that, its policy objectives toward the two SARs are largely similar, which include anti-terrorism cooperation, trafficking in persons, narcotics control, anti-money laundering; border and export controls; combating illegal transshipping; protecting American intellectual property rights; human rights; rule of law; and the judiciary. For Macao, it has particular concerns on gambling sector restructuring, money laundering, illegal textile transshipments, and anti-corruption. To the United States, the extent of Macao and Hong Kong's high degree of autonomy also serves as an important indicator of PRC's respect for its international commitments. The U.S Congress, for that purpose, enacted *United States–Hong Kong Policy Act* in 1992 and *U.S.–Macao Policy (Title II of the Malaria Control Act of 2000)*.[21]

Given these similar policy objectives, U.S. interest and its policy toward Hong Kong is much more substantial than those in Macao at least in two areas. First, the United States has much more substantial interest in trade, investment, and business with Hong Kong. In 2006 HKSAR was the world's sixth-largest trading entity and one of the largest financial centers in the world. In 2006, U.S. exports to Hong Kong totaled $17.8 billion, making Hong Kong the United States' fifteenth-largest export market. U.S. direct investment in Hong Kong through 2005 amounted to $37.9 billion. Approximately 1,200 resident American firms operate in Hong Kong. Hong Kong is home to an estimated 60,000 U.S. citizens (including many dual nationals), and more than one million U.S. citizens visit Hong Kong each year.[22] In comparison, U.S. trade with Macao represents a much smaller portion of U.S. total trade even though the United States was Macao's second-largest trading partner after China. In 2003 two-way trade volume was less than $2 billion.[23]

Second, Washington has strong interests in human rights, promoting democratic institutions and democratic values in Hong Kong, ensuring that the people of Hong Kong have a say in the governance of Hong Kong, and supporting steady advances toward universal suffrage.[24] To the United States, the Hong Kong people share many values and interests with Americans, ranging from a society based on rule of law, respect for civil liberties, and human rights. Although Washington believes Hong Kong, after the handover, has remained an open and largely tolerant society, in which both local and foreign non-governmental organizations, businesses, and persons continue to operate freely and the media work with few government-imposed restrictions, its latest Hong Kong Policy Act report expressed concern that "some events over the past ten years present troubling precedents or undermine the high degree of autonomy [of Hong Kong SAR]."[25] The debate about the methods of selecting future chief executives and LegCo will be a key sticking issue in U.S.–Hong Kong policy. In a recent public speech,

James Cunningham, U.S. consul general to Hong Kong, voiced his views on the issue. "I noted some areas where things might have gone better for Hong Kong, notably in the area of developing responsive governance that is rooted in free and fair democratic elections. I also observed there are concerns in some quarters about the preservation of the high degree of autonomy promised in Hong Kong's Basic Law and the 1984 Sino–British Joint Declaration. These are prompted by a widely held perception that Hong Kong's press increasingly practices self-censorship, and by several instances over the years where intervention or interpretation by the Central Government have raised questions in Hong Kong and the international community about Hong Kong's autonomy and competitiveness."[26]

The State Department's U.S.–Macao Policy Report gave a more positive note on the development in Macao. It states that, under Chinese sovereignty, Macao continues to develop in an overall positive direction. Over the past year, the Macao government has stated strong support for the global anti-terrorism campaign, taken decisive steps to open and reposition its economy, reorganized its customs service, and moved further to project its own identity through increased official interaction with the rest of the world. Macao citizens continue to enjoy basic human rights and a unique way of life distinct from China. While Macao's civil society and democratic institutions generally remain weak, the September 2001 Legislative Assembly elections were well run and fair. Pro-democracy groups made a stronger showing than observers expected. The People's Republic of China (PRC) generally has respected its commitments regarding Macao's high degree of autonomy and PRC representatives in Macao generally continue to maintain a low profile except on ceremonial occasions. Macao officials continue to run Macao and make their decisions pursuant to Macao's own identity and interests.[27]

Conclusion: Why Macao Matters Now

Does Macao matter for Hong Kong and Greater China? The answer was no, but not now. With more than a decade of post-colonial transformation experience in Hong Kong and almost eight years in Macao, people have seen true and false, twists and turns, ups and downs in the tale of twin cities. With frustration and disputes in search of better governance and a more harmonious society, the Hong Kong elites began to turn to Macao and they began to look at Macao and its experience after the handover with a different eye. Despite most Hong Kong elites still looking down upon Macao, they now need to learn more humbly from lessons of Macao's governance, as they see a more problematic road ahead.

Notes

1. Zheng Gu, "Macao Gaming: Copying the Las Vegas Style or Creating a Macao Model?," *Asia Pacific Journal of Tourism Research*, vol. 9, no. 1 (March 2004), 89–96.

2. "港府:港澳没恶性竞争,支持一签两地自由行,"《中国评论新闻》, 2007年11月7日, www.chinareviewnews.com.

3. See Fung, Bong Yin, *Macao: a General Introduction* (in Chinese) (Hong Kong: Joint Publishing [H.K.] Co., 1999).

4. "香港发展四方面须改善,"《大公报》, 2007 年11月27日, http://www.takungpao.com:10000/gate/gb/www.takungpao.com:82/inc/print_me.asp?url=/news/07/11/27/LTA-828906.htm&date=07.

5. Mark Lazell, "A Tale of Two Cities," *Asian Times*, June 8, 2006, www.atimes.com/atimes/Asian_Economy/HF08Dk01.html.

6. Xiao Geng, "A Tale of Two Cities: Will Shanghai Overtake HKSAR?" working paper, University of Hong Kong School of Finance and Economics, 2004.

7. Marianne Bray, "A tale of two Chinese cities: Shanghai–Hong Kong debate may pivot on economic development," CNN website, edition.cnn.com/2006/WORLD/asiapcf/03/28/eyeonchina.cities/index.html.

8. See "Vegas vs. Macao, who will win?" in *BusinessWeek* Online (June 8, 2006), www.businessweek.com/investor/content/jun2006/pi20060608_011406.htm; and David Barboza, "Asian Rival Moves Past Las Vegas," in *New York Times* (January 24, 2007), www.nytimes.com/2007/01/24/business/worldbusiness/24macao.html?partner=rssnyt&emc=rss.

9. Hong Kong National Gross Income per capita was $34,833 in 2008. See World Bank, *World Development Indicators 2007*, Washingnton, D.C.: World Bank 2007, and United Nations Development Programme (UNDP), *2007–2008 Human Development Report*, available at hdrstats.undp.org/indicators/5.html.

10. For good discussion, see Eilo Wing-Yat Yu, "Formal and Informal Politics in Macao Special Administrative Region Elections 2004–2005," *Journal of Contemporary China* vol. 16, no. 52 (August 2007), 417–47.

11. *De Ficção Projectos Multimedia*, commissioned for Macao Inter-University Institute (MIUI), *Macao Quality of Life Report (2nd Quarter 2009)*, released on July 9, 2009, www.iium.edu.mo/index.php?option=com_content&task=view&id=833&Itemid=1352.

12. 巩胜利, "2007 全球" 5·1 劳动节 "大扫描——澳警开枪洞穿了什么?"《博讯》特别聚焦, 2007 年 5 月 2 日, boxun.com/hero/2007/gongsl/12_1.shtml.

13. Nikkita Lau, "Driver tells of Ao's shady deals," *Hong Kong Standard*, November 17, 2007, www.thestandard.com.hk/news_detail.asp?pp_cat=11&art_id=57083&sid=16347620&con_type=1&d_str=20071117.

14. Sonny Shiu-Hing Lo, "One Formula, Two Experiences: Political divergence of Hong Kong and Macao since retrocession," *Journal of Contemporary China*, vol. 16, no. 52 (August 2007), 359–87.

15. Sonny Shiu-Hing Lo, "One Formula."

16. Sonny Shiu-Hing Lo, "One Formula."
17. Anthony B. L. Cheung, "The changing political system: executive-led government or 'disabled' governance?," in Lau Siu-kai, ed., *The First Tung Chee-hwa Administration: The First Five Years of the Hong Kong Special Administrative Region* (Hong Kong: Chinese University Press, 2002), 41–68.
18. See *Macao Quality of Life Report (2nd Quarter 2009)*.
19. Sonny Shiu-Hing Lo, "One Formula."
20. See, for example, Rao Geping and Wang Zhenmin, "Hong Kong's 'One Country, Two Systems' Experience under the Basic Law: two perspectives from Chinese legal scholars," *Journal of Contemporary China*, vol. 16, no. 52 (August 2007), 341–58.
21. For full text of *United States–Hong Kong Policy Act* (1992), see hongkong.usconsulate.gov/ushk_pa_1992.html; and for the text of *U.S.–Macao Policy (Title II of the Malaria Control Act of 2000)*, see hongkong.usconsulate.gov/usmo_pa_2000121401.html.
22. U.S State Department Bureau of East Asian and Pacific Affairs, *Hong Kong Policy Act Report* (2007), released on June 30, 2007. For a full text, see www.state.gov/p/eap/rls/rpt/2007/87648.htm.
23. U.S–Macao Policy Act Report, April 1, 2004. Full text: hongkong.usconsulate.gov/usmo_pa_2004040101.html.
24. *Hong Kong Policy Act Report (2007)*.
25. Ibid.
26. James B. Cunningham, "Hong Kong at 10 Years: Prospects for the Future," Center for East Asian Studies, Stanford University, November 12, 2007. The full text can be viewed at hongkong.usconsulate.gov/cg_jc2007111201.html.
27. *U.S.–Macao Policy Act Report*, April 1, 2004, hongkong.usconsulate.gov/usmo_pa_2004040101.html.

CHAPTER SIXTEEN

Macao and Hong Kong in U.S.–China Relations: An American Perspective

Morton Holbrook III

Rather than a single American perspective, there are several perspectives on the role Macao and Hong Kong play in U.S.–China relations. There is the perspective of the U.S. government, as reflected in statements of top U.S. officials and in reports drafted by U.S. government agencies. There is the perspective of the American business community, as seen in the bottom line of trade and investment in the two Special Administrative Regions (SARs) of Macao and Hong Kong. And there is the perspective of other Americans: tourists, sports figures, high rollers, NGOs, and—last but certainly not least, at least not in an academic conference—there is the view of academics. Taken as a whole, these views, while differing in some respects, support a conclusion that, from an American perspective, Macao and Hong Kong play a quietly favorable role outside the sometimes harsh spotlight of U.S.–China relations, with an occasional foray into the main arena of bilateral interests and concerns.

The U.S. Government View: No News is Good News

Looking at the U.S. government perspective, it is hard not to reach the conclusion that the two SARs do not usually play a major role in U.S.–China relations. What do top Chinese and U.S. leaders talk about when they meet? Do they talk about whether Yao Ming will return to the court for the Houston Rockets next year? Do they discuss other good news in U.S.–China relations, such as the growing cultural and educational exchanges, and mutually beneficial trade and investment projects and plans? Well, perhaps briefly, but they are more likely to concentrate on the difficult issues like the financial crisis, the Korean Peninsula, climate change, the bilateral trade balance, Taiwan, and human rights. And what about discussions on how the "one country, two systems" formula is working in Hong Kong and Macao? Evidence suggests that that this subject is not on the top-level agenda.

Let's look at recent statements focused on China by leading U.S. officials. On October 24, 2007, Deputy Secretary of State John Negroponte, then the number two official in the U.S. Department of State, spoke at a National Council on U.S.–China Relations event in New York City.[1] The Deputy Secretary listed the major issues in U.S.–China relations, which he termed challenges and differences. These included terrorism, failing states (Sudan, Burma), economic matters, nonproliferation, Taiwan, human rights, and energy security. Neither Macao nor Hong Kong was mentioned—other than Negroponte's noting that his very first posting in the U.S. Foreign Service had been in Hong Kong.

Similarly, on March 27, 2007, Tom Christensen, then the U.S. deputy assistant secretary of state for East Asian and Pacific Affairs, and the key U.S. official on China policy, made a very detailed statement on U.S.–China relations to the U.S. Congress, addressing the House Subcommittee on Asia, the Pacific, and the Global Environment.[2] Once again, comments on Hong Kong and Macao were conspicuously absent—conspicuously, that is, for those looking for a signal of their role in U.S.–China relations.

This absence of mention is not a cause for concern: in fact, it's likely that at top-level discussions of U.S.–China relations, as a rule of thumb, no news about Hong Kong and Macao is good news! A tempest over U.S. ship visits to Hong Kong confirmed this rule: after months, perhaps years, of being out of the spotlight of bilateral concerns, on November 27, 2007, then-President Bush and Chinese Foreign Minister Yang, in what was likely a discussion of many bilateral and multilateral issues, also touched on cancelled U.S. ship visits to Hong Kong, in what the White House press secretary described, probably accurately, as "one small incident. And in the big picture, in the big scheme of things we have very good relations."[3] So Hong Kong was mentioned—if no news is good news, the corollary is that some news can be bad news.

The U.S. Consul General on Hong Kong: Measured Praise and Criticism

Limited attention by officials in the United States does not signal absence of U.S. government attention and concern. The U.S. government perspective on Hong Kong and Macao is reflected directly and appropriately by the U.S. Consulate General in Hong Kong, which has jurisdiction over both Hong Kong and Macao.

On November 12, 2007, then U.S. Consul General James B. Cunningham, in a talk at Stanford University, presented the U.S. government view on Hong Kong.[4] The consul general noted that, as he had stated previously, in the ten years since the city's return to China in 1997, Hong Kong had "not only survived, but prospered." He said that, looking back over the last ten years, "one country, two systems" had been a success for Hong Kong and for China.

At the same time, Cunningham noted "some areas where things might have gone better for Hong Kong, notably in the area of developing responsive governance that is rooted in free and fair democratic elections." He said that "my government has long supported universal suffrage in Hong Kong, as promised in the Basic Law. We believe it necessary . . . that Hong Kong set out on the path toward governance strengthened by popular elections within a democratic system that meets international standards. The sooner this happens, the better." The consul general also noted concerns about the preservation of the high degree of autonomy promised in Hong Kong's Basic Law, prompted by the "widely held perception that Hong Kong's press increasingly practices self-censorship, and by several instances over the years where intervention or interpretation by the Central Government have raised questions in Hong Kong and the international community about Hong Kong's autonomy and competitiveness."

In conclusion, Cunningham noted that "we remain optimistic about Hong Kong's prospects . . . One country, two systems is working, and I have no doubt it can continue to do so." He also said that the United States had a 'bright vision" for Hong Kong: "We see a Hong Kong that is part of a prosperous, stable and confident China, and which contributes to its country and the world by continuing to be a leading light in economic freedoms, civil liberties, and respect for human rights."

The U.S. Government: Reporters at Large

The consul general's remarks are not the only U.S. government comments on Hong Kong. One cannot accuse the U.S. Department of State and the U.S. government of publishing too few reports on other countries! For all other countries as well as for certain regions of special interest, there is a plethora of required regular, often annual, reports. There are human rights reports, Trafficking in Person Reports, narcotics reports, International Religious Freedom reports, reports on commercial conditions (from the U.S.

Department of Commerce), and reports on intellectual property rights protection (from the U.S. Trade Representative)—just to cite the more prominent reports. Besides supplying employment opportunities for American diplomats, these reports do provide a wealth of information and recommendations—so much that a former U.S. official said that some people regard the United States as a kind of international nanny.

In fact, the U.S. government, and especially the U.S. Congress, has taken special interest in Macao and Hong Kong, and has, until recently required its hard-working diplomats to draft two additional reports, one for each former colony. These are the annual reports on Hong Kong pursuant to the United States–Hong Kong Policy Act (the McConnell Act),[5] through 2006, and, from 1999 through 2004, annual reports on Macao, required by a kind of companion act to the McConnell Act, called the U.S.–Macao Policy Act.

These acts smoothed the way for continued application of U.S. laws in areas such as trade with Hong Kong and Macao after their return to the mainland. The acts also reflected a deep skepticism on the part of some, particularly in the U.S. Congress, about whether China would keep its pledge to allow Hong Kong and Macao considerable autonomy under the policy of one country, two systems. Of course, many in Hong Kong shared that skepticism, particularly in the period after Tiananmen, and departed to live in other countries.

For Hong Kong the period leading up to and immediately following the handover from the United Kingdom to China in July 1997 was its turn to be in the spotlight of U.S.–China relations, and of U.S. concerns, as well as the spotlight of world attention.

So what do the special reports say?

Hong Kong Policy Act Reports: So Far, So Good

The HK Policy Act provided that if the U.S. president determined that Hong Kong was not "sufficiently autonomous" to justify separate treatment under a U.S. law, the president could suspend that law's application to Hong Kong.

As it turned out, no presidential determination has been necessary—you can say that is the bottom line on USG views of Hong Kong under the McConnell Act: no news is good news. The Hong Kong Policy Act reports,[6] prepared annually from 1995 through 2006, (and prepared voluntarily this year) in fact have on the whole given a very positive evaluation of the implementation of "one country, two systems." The most recent report was released on June 30, 2007. Painting a generally favorable portrait, it states that "during the past ten years, Hong Kong has overcome significant economic, social and political challenges to its prosperity, stability, and autonomy."

Further, "Hong Kong continues to maintain its dedication to the rule of law, adherence to free and fair market principles, and respect for fundamental civil rights and human freedoms."

The report also particularly lauds Hong Kong's continued adherence to free market principles: "Hong Kong boasts one of the most open, thriving and prosperous economies in the world. . . . Hong Kong is a duty-free port, with few barriers to trade in goods or services and few restrictions on foreign capital flows and investment." In addition, "The HKSARG continues to maintain a robust regime to protect intellectual property rights, and it continues to encourage respect for intellectual property."

The Policy Act report also emphasizes Hong Kong's continued autonomy on the economic front. "Hong Kong is an independent customs territory and economic entity physically and legally separate from the rest of the PRC, and it continues to participate actively and independently in a range of international organizations and agreements, including the World Trade Organization (WTO), the Asia Pacific Economic Cooperation forum (APEC), and the Financial Action Task Force (FATF)." With reference to the United States, it notes that "more than a dozen U.S.–Hong Kong agreements currently are in force, including a stand-alone Air Services Agreement as well as Extradition, Prisoner Transfer, and Mutual Legal Assistance Agreements that entered into force after Hong Kong's reversion to China."

Like Consul General Cunningham, the report, while generally upbeat, does cite areas of U.S. official concern, noting that "development of democratic institutions remains incomplete," and that there is a growing perception that the Hong Kong press "engages in a degree of self-censorship regarding issues central to the PRC central government." In addition, "there have been several instances in which observers questioned overt interventions by the central government in Hong Kong's political and legal processes."

Human Rights Report and Religious Freedom Report: Qualified Praise

The U.S. government also prepares a separate human rights report annually on Hong Kong, as well as on Macao. The latest report on Hong Kong, released in March 2007,[7] consistent with other U.S. government statements, gives Hong Kong a favorable review, though with qualifications; for example, "The government generally respected the human rights of its citizens, though core issues remain." The core issues included the limitations on residents' ability to change their government, and on the legislature's power to affect policy. On the other hand, the report gives high marks to Hong Kong for freedom of religion, a "fair and efficient" judicial process, freedom of speech and the press, and freedom of assembly, including regular public demonstrations by Falun Gong practitioners.

The U.S. government's International Religious Freedom Report for 2007[8] affirmed that the Hong Kong government's policy "continued to support the generally free practice of religion," citing presence of adherents of Buddhism, Taoism, Christianity, and Islam. Falun Gong was described as "generally free to practice, organize, and conduct nonviolent public demonstrations."

Other Reports: Trafficking in Persons Report; International Narcotics Control Strategy Reports

In contrast with most other U.S. government reports, the most recent U.S. government "Trafficking in Persons Report"[9] describes the Hong Kong SAR in more critical terms as "a transit and destination territory for men and women trafficked for the purpose of commercial sexual exploitation and forced labor." At the same time, the report notes that "estimates of international trafficking victims are modest." In addition, the United States has placed Hong Kong as a "Tier 1" territory, the least serious of three tiers of U.S. government concern (Macao was ranked in Tier 2).

On drugs, the latest report from the U.S. State Department's Bureau of International Narcotics and Law Enforcement Affairs on "Drug and Chemical Control"[10] provides its own succinct and favorable summary: "Hong Kong is not a major transit/transshipment point for illegal drugs destined for the international market because of its efficient law enforcement efforts, the availability of alternate transportation routes, and the development of port facilities elsewhere in southern China." Further, "the Government of the Hong Kong Special Administrative Region (HKSAR) actively combats drug trafficking and abuse through legislation and law enforcement, preventive education and publicity, treatment and rehabilitation, as well as research and external cooperation."

At the same time, a companion report on Money Laundering and Financial Crimes[11] gives both praise and criticism for Hong Kong. On the favorable side, it notes that Hong Hong is "substantially in compliance with the Financial Action Task Force Recommendations on Money Laundering, and has pledged to adhere to the revised FATF forty recommendations." Further, Hong Kong "is a regional leader in anti-money laundering efforts."

On the down side, however, the report asserts that recently "reportedly legitimate Hong Kong business entities and financial institutions have been playing an increasingly important role in the Black Market Peso Exchange (BMPE)," described as "a trade-based money laundering scheme used by Colombian drug cartels to launder illicit drug profits." The report also recommends that Hong Kong take steps to stop the use of "shell" companies set up by solicitors and accountants, with "nominee directors" that conceal the actual ownership of accounts and assets. This concealment is "ideal for the laundering of funds."

U.S. Business: Upbeat on Hong Kong

The U.S. business community, as represented by American Chambers of Commerce in many locations, is generally quite upbeat about business conditions everywhere—and that includes Amcham Hong Kong. At the same time, unlike other Amchams in China (e.g., in Beijing and in Shanghai), Amcham Hong Kong has published no "white paper" setting out areas in the business environment in need of improvement, in the view of the U.S. business community. Of course, lack of a white paper does not mean that Amcham Hong Kong does not have suggestions on how Hong Kong's business environment can be improved. It does, however, seem to reflect a general satisfaction with the business environment in Hong Kong. The latest Amcham journal sets out two issues of concern: limited international school space for expat children, and deterioration of the physical environment in Hong Kong.[12] Important issues to be sure, but not on a scale of the extensive policy discussions put forward by their colleagues in Shanghai and Beijing aimed at prodding Beijing to comply with China's WTO commitments, and highlighting other business issues. In Amcham, Hong Kong's latest annual business confidence survey, 100 percent of respondents had a "good" or "satisfactory" outlook for Hong Kong for 2007.

Meanwhile, Hong Kong continues to be important for U.S. businesses, with 1,280 U.S. company offices, including 889 regional headquarters or offices located in Hong Kong (according to HKSARG figures). The United States is also an important trade and investment partner of Hong Kong. U.S. investment in Hong Kong was measured at $26.6 billion in 2005, in areas such as insurance, trade, and financial institutions. Hong Kong is an important entrepot for Sino–U.S. trade, with about 20 percent ($40 billion) of China's exports to the United States and 11 percent ($7 billion) of China's imports from the United States going through Hong Kong.[13]

Other U.S. Views: The Heritage Foundation and *Wall Street Journal* Index

Elsewhere in the private sector too, many Americans view Hong Kong with favor. The Heritage Foundation and the *Wall Street Journal* jointly publish an annual Index of Economic Freedom, ranking countries and regions according to ten areas of economic interest, such as freedom from government controls and freedom from corruption. Hong Kong is ranked number one in the world on the 2007 Index (the United States ranks fourth), and in fact has ranked number 1 on every index since the rankings were started in 1995—that is, Hong Kong maintained its number one position both before and after the 1997 handover to China.[14] (Note: the index does not evaluate Macao.)

The United States Government and Macao

Macao's turn in the harsh glare of U.S.–China relations came early in 2007, when the spotlight of bilateral attention turned to a private bank, the Banco Delta Asia (BDA), and its relations with both the Macao authorities and with North Korea, which had deposits of about $25 million in the bank. As the six-party talks on the Korean peninsula nuclear issue proceeded, the disposition of those funds was, briefly, an impediment—now resolved—to addressing and resolving the larger issue of nuclear weapons on the Korean Peninsula.[15]

The U.S.–Macao Policy Act of 2000: Thumbs Up

The bottom line on Macao is similar to the McConnell Act reports on Hong Kong: presidential authority to suspend application of U.S. laws has never been invoked. The U.S.–Macao Policy Act[16] mandated U.S. government reports through 2004; the last report was released on April 1, 2004. That final report concluded, "The PRC has respected its commitments regarding Macao's high degree of autonomy," while also noting that "Macao's civil society and democratic infrastructure remain weak."

Human Rights and Religious Freedom Reports on Macao: Yes, But . . .

The U.S. State Department's 2006 report on Human Rights in Macao, released on March 6, 2007, includes much praise and some criticism of Macao.[17] On the favorable side, the report states, "The government generally respected the human rights of its citizens," including specifically freedom of speech, the press, assembly and association, and religion. It also cites favorably the lack of government restrictions on academic freedom and on use of the Internet, and the provision of an independent judiciary, including enforcement of the right to a fair trial.

On the other hand, according to the report, "the Basic Law restricts citizens' ability to change their government," and also "significantly circumscribes the power of the legislative assembly." In addition, Macao "is a transit and destination point for women trafficked for purposes of prostitution." The report also notes that labor unions representing unskilled laborers held a violent demonstration against Macao's chief executive in May 2006, aimed at driving out illegal workers.

The International Religious Freedom Report on Macao released in 2007[18] gives high marks to the Macao SAR, noting the government has "generally respected" the freedom of religion, including prohibiting discrimination on the basis of religious practice. It notes that Buddhism is professed by 79 percent of the population; there are also Roman Catholics (5 percent) and Protestants, "along with a mix of Muslims, Baha'i and other professed faith groups." In addition, "missionaries are active and represent a wide range of faiths." As in Hong Kong, Falun Gong practitioners (estimated at 200) are "active in the region," and, in 2006, "continued their daily exercises in public parks."

Trafficking in Persons Report; Narcotics Control Strategy Report: Mixed Reviews for Macao

The U.S. government's latest "Trafficking in Persons" report[19] places Macao on the "Tier 2 watch list," the second-highest level of official concern. ("Tier 3" is the highest level of concern; tier 3 regions and countries could be subject to certain sanctions, such as withholding certain types of U.S. government assistance.) The report states that "Macao is a destination territory for the trafficking of women and girls . . . for the purpose of commercial sexual exploitation." At the same time, though "Macao does not meet with the minimum standards for the elimination of trafficking, it is making significant efforts to do so." In similar fashion, the 2007 U.S. International Narcotics Control Strategy report[20] praises steps Macao has taken to improve its capacity to tackle money laundering, including passage of an anti-money laundering and counterterrorism legislation in 2006. While praising these new laws, the report cites the need for enforcement.

U.S. Business Community: Bullish on Macao

The business community view is reflected in the bottom line: U.S. investment in Macao has expanded significantly since the gambling industry opened up to outside investment in 2002. U.S. investment in Macao totaled $575 million as of 2005, an increase of over 300-fold since 2001.[21] The United States is also a leading trading partner of Macao, with two-way trade totaling $277 million in 2006. A U.S. representative noted that "Macao, China has long maintained an open trade and investment regime, and continues to demonstrate a commitment to free-market principles." Policies based on these principles have "generated a higher standard of living for (Macao's) citizens, as GDP per capita has increased by 70 percent from 2001 to 2005.

Is Macao a "sure bet" to become the Las Vegas of China, as a *Reuter*'s article stated in 2007?[22] For sure, it is already a magnet for U.S. investment, as reflected in the Venetian Macao, the MGM, the Wynn Macao, and other U.S.-invested establishments. To be sure, these investors have complaints about Macao's business and regulatory environment, which they believe is more geared to the days when Macao was a sleepy Portuguese enclave (in contrast to Hong Kong, an economic powerhouse in colonial days as well as today). But the bottom line is U.S. investment continued to grow in Macao until the financial crisis hit the United States, and even now remains an important element in the Macao economy, despite a slowdown or halt to some construction projects.

Other Views of Hong Kong and Macao

U.S. perspectives on Macao and Hong Kong extend far beyond the areas set out above. In health, in the environment, in education—as well as in visiting sports teams and gambling tourism—Americans visit Macao and Hong Kong, engage in discussions and activities, and generally take full advantage of the hospitable environments in both former colonies.

The Academic View

Since I am now retired from the U.S. government, it's a pleasure to set out my own view. My first thought is that Macao and Hong Kong are unique: there are no really useful comparisons to be made with other "similar" areas—there are no areas meriting the term "similar." The differences with other small enclaves, like Singapore (Singapore is not tethered to another country), or with Berlin in Cold War days (HK and Macao are not surrounded by a hostile power), are immediately evident. A second thought is from the American tradition, the thought that a house divided cannot stand. This doesn't seem to apply either: rather than being divided in some irreconcilable way from the Mainland, Macao and Hong Kong are becoming more integrated, economically, with China. Which is more accurate, one country, two systems, or two countries, one economic system? You can see it both ways.

My final thought is that the two SARS are truly unique, and on the whole very successful. Clearly part of that success is due to their links to the growing Mainland economy; part is also due to what must be called a policy success by Beijing, which has, by and large, allowed the capable people of Macao and Hong Kong to govern themselves, and to maintain their existing systems and way of life, as promised. China has not done so because of a theoretical interest in matters such as universal suffrage (in Hong Kong), free speech, or freedom of religion; the approach has simply been realistic and practical: Adherence to the concept of "one country, two systems" helped stem a mass exodus or an economic depression in the 1990s, as well as provide a possible model applicable to Taiwan. More recently, it has assisted China (as well as Macao and Hong Kong themselves) with economic development, and it has not resulted in any significant threat to Beijing's interests arising from the two former colonies.

So from this American's perspective, Macao and Hong Kong are unique, if qualified success stories—with credit due to Macao and Hong Kong's own post-colonial leadership, to Beijing for basically keeping its word, and also to the rising prosperity in the entire Pearl River Delta area. And political and economic support from the U.S. government and from private U.S. citizens, though not the key to the success of the SARs, has played a positive role. To be sure, these success stories are more evident on the economic side, and the citizens of Hong Kong, in particular, continue to debate with vigor the pace of universal suffrage, and whether Beijing intrudes too much into SAR politics.

Update as of January 2010

The Obama administration has in many respects continued the policies of the Bush administration toward China, with an even greater emphasis on cooperation to resolve bilateral issues and to address multilateral problems. As previously, the "issues" of Hong Kong and Macao are conspicuous by their absence in public reports of top-level discussions and events. The Joint Statement both countries endorsed during President Obama's November 2009 visit to China[23] is notable for its scope, covering every significant area of both cooperation and potential conflict in the bilateral relationship; it makes no reference to Hong Kong and Macao, or to the "one country, two systems" formula. One could argue, of course, that from Beijing's point of view, these are internal matters, to which China would not want to refer in a joint statement. True enough, but if there were pressing U.S. concerns regarding Hong Kong or Macao, these likely would have been reflected in some manner by the United States before or during the president's visit in briefings or other policy statements by top U.S. officials.

A review of such policy statements, including Secretary of State Hillary Clinton's speech on China to the Asia Society on February 13, 2009,[24] Secretary Clinton's press conference in Washington, D.C., on March 11, 2009 (following a meeting with Chinese foreign minister Yang Jiechi),[25] and Deputy Secretary of State James Steinberg's September 2009 speech on China policy,[26] reveals . . . nothing: no mention of Hong Kong and Macao among the many subjects for discussion between the United States and China. Similarly, the issue of U.S. ship visits to Hong Kong, which flaired briefly in 2007 (as noted above) proved to be short lived; for example, the U.S. Consulate in Hong Kong enthusiastically reported the December 28, 2009, visit of a guided-missile cruiser *USS Lake Erie*, quoting the commanding officer as stating, "Our sailors love coming here, and in doing so, we enhance cooperation and understanding which is increasingly vital in today's world."[27]

In similar fashion, a review of required U.S. government reports as of January 2009 does not reflect significant changes in official views since December 2007. Concerning Hong Kong, for example, the Country Report on Terrorism on China for 2008 (released April 30, 2009) states, "Hong Kong's position as a major transit point for cargo, finances and people and its open trade and financial regime made it a potential site for money laundering and terrorist financing activities. The high level of cooperation and successful implementation of the Container Security Intiative (CSI) by Hong Kong Customs officials received continued praise from visiting USG delegations, which described it as a model for CSI implementation."[28]

Also on Hong Kong, the Heritage Foundation in 2009 again gave it top marks: "Hong Kong's economic Freedom score is 90, making its economy the freest in the 2009 Index. Its score is 0.3 better than last year, reflecting minor improvements in fiscal freedom and business freedom."[29]

As before, U.S. government views have been reflected in comments by the chief U.S. official on the scene, the U.S. Consul General in Hong Kong. Joseph Donovan, who succeeded James Cunningham as consul general, gave laudatory comments on Hong Kong, noting its "well-deserved reputation as a vibrant and dynamic, open society." Further, Hong Kong's commitment to free markets, its free press, its independent judiciary, and its respect for individual and human rights, make Hong Kong's continued success important to the United States."[30]

At the same time, like his predecessor, Donovan took note of the on-going debate in Hong Kong on the pace of universal suffrage: "Although later than many in Hong Kong hoped, Hong Kong now has the opportunity to grant universal suffrage for the election of the Chief Executive in 2017 and the Legco in 2020. We hope that all parties will work together to find an effective path to universal suffrage that can be supported by the broad majority of people in Hong Kong."

Notes

1. Remarks by Deputy Secretary Negroponte on U.S.–China Relations. October 24, 2007. New York, www.state.gov
2. Thomas J. Christensen, Deputy Assistant Secretary for East Asian and Pacific Affairs. Statement before the House Committee on Foreign Affairs, Subcommittee on Asia, the Pacific, and the Global Environment. Washington, D.C., March 27, 2007.
3. Dana Perino, White House Press Secretary, Press Conference on November 29, 2007. www.whitehouse.gov.
4. "Hong Kong at Ten Years: Prospects for the Future." James B. Cunningham, Consul General of the United States of America. Center for East Asian Studies, Stanford University, November 12, 2007. hongkong.usconsulate.gov/cg.
5. United States Hong Kong Policy Act of 1992, Public Law 102–383, as amended.
6. The Hong Kong Policy Act Report. Released by the Bureau of East Asian and Pacific Affairs, U.S. Department of State, June 30, 2007. hongkong.usconsulate.gov.
7. U.S. Department of State, Country Reports on Human Rights Practices—2006. Hong Kong. hongkong.usconsulate.gov.
8. U.S. Department of State. International Religious Freedom Report—2007. Hong Kong. hongkong.usconsulate.gov.
9. U.S. Department of State. Trafficking in Persons Report (2007). Hong Kong. hongkong.usconsulate.gov.
10. U.S. Department of State. International Narcotics Control Strategy Report—2007. Vol. I: Drug and Chemical Control. Hong Kong. hongkong.usconsulate.gov.
11. U.S. Department of State. International Narcotics Control Strategy Report—2007. Vol. II: Money Laundering and Financial Crimes. hongkong.usconsulate.gov.
12. American Chamber of Commerce, Hong Kong. www.amcham.org.hk.
13. U.S. Department of Commerce. www.usdoc.gov.
14. Government of the Hong Kong Special Administrative Region, Trade and Industry Department: The United States and Hong Kong Administrative Region: Some Important Facts. (2007). www.tid.gov.hk.
15. White House press briefing by Press Secretary Dana Perino, April 10, 2007. www.whitehouse.gov.
16. The U.S.–Macao Policy Act. hongkong.usconsulate.gov.

17. U.S. Department of State, Country Reports on Human Rights Practices—2006. Macao. hongkong.usconsulate.gov.

18. U.S. Department of State. International Religious Freedomn Report—2007. Macao hongkong.usconsulate.gov.

19. U.S. Department of State. Trafficking in Persons Report (2007). Macao. hongkong.usconsulate.gov.

20. U.S. Department of State. International Narcotics Control Strategy Report—2007. Vol. I: Drug and Chemical Control. Macao. hongkong.usconsulate.gov.

21. U.S. Mission to the United Nations in Geneva, statement by the United States, April 30, 2007. hongkong.usconsulate.gov.

22. Jonathan Landreth, "Macao a sure bet to become the Las Vegas of China," *Reuters*, November 30, 2007.

23. U.S.–China Joint Statement, November 17, 2009, http://beijing.usembassy-china.org.cn/111709.html.

24. Secretary Clinton at the Asia Society, New York, February 13, 2009. U.S.–Asia Relations: Indispensable to our Future, www.state.gov/secretary/rm/2009a/02/117333.htm.

25. Secretary Clinton press conference after meeting with Chinese Foreign Minister Yang Jiechi, March 11, 2009, www.state.gov/secretary/rm/2009a/03/120284.htm.

26. James B. Steinberg, Deputy Secretary of State, Keynote Address at the Center for a New American Security, Washington, D.C., September 24, 2009, www.state.gov/s/d/2009/129686.htm.

27. See hongkong.usconsulate.gov/pas_pr_2009122901.html.

28. hongkong.usconsulate.gov/ushk_state_2009043001.html.

29. www.heritage.org/Index/Country/HongKong.

30. hongkong.usconsulate.gov/cg_jd2008111901.html.

Index

Note to index: An *f* following a page number denotes a figure on that page; a *t* following a page number denotes a table on that page.

About the Contributors

Liu Bolong is professor in the Department of Government and Public Administration, University of Macao. He also serves as head of the Department of Government and Public Administration, and director for the Research Center for Contemporary China Studies in the University of Macao. He has written and edited books on China public policies, evaluation of China's agricultural policies, administrative reforms in Macao and external relations of Macao. He has also contributed many articles on Macao public administration and reforms, comparison between Hong Kong and Macao in political development. His current research interests include policy studies in Mainland China, Hong Kong, and Macao; Macao public administrative reforms; and Macao's external relations with the United States, Europe and Mainland China.

Ming K. Chan is the coordinator of the Hong Kong Documentary Archives at the Hoover Institution, and the holder of a PhD in East Asian history from Stanford University. As archive coordinator, he is collecting materials from Hong Kong and Macao as well as preparing historical dictionaries of Hong Kong and Macao. A former member of the Department of History at the University of Hong Kong, where he was twice voted "best teacher" by the Students' Union, he is the author or editor of ten books, including *Crisis and Transformation in China's Hong Kong* (2002), *The Challenge of Hong Kong's Reintegration with China* (1997), and *Precarious Balance: Hong Kong between China and Britain: 1842–1992* (1994).

T. J. Cheng, PhD, graduated from the English department at Inner Mongolia Normal University, and holds an MA in world economy and politics from the Chinese Academy of Social Sciences. He also holds an MA and PhD in sociology from the State University of New York, and is professor in the Department of Sociology, FSH, University of Macao. Research interests include social transformation in rural society, the household registration (*Hukou*) system, ethnic minorities, the sociology of gambling, youth indicator system, and new immigrants in Macao. His publications include *China's Hukou System*, and several coauthored books, such as *Macao Youth Indicator System*, *Chinese New Immigrants in Macao*, *Introduction to Sociology of Gambling*, and *Cultural Revolution in Inner Mongolia*.

Yufan Hao is professor of political science and dean of Faculty of Social Sciences and Humanities at University of Macao. He obtained his MA and PhD from the Johns Hopkins University School of Advanced International Studies in 1984 and 1989 respectively. He was a McArthur Fellow at Harvard University Center for International Affairs 1988–1989, and a senior visiting professor to Beijing Normal University, Peking University, Tsinghua University, Renmin University of China, and an honorary *jianzhi* professor at Fudan University, Shanghai University of International Studies and Beijing Foreign Affair University. He has published widely on Chinese politics, Chinese foreign relations, U.S.-China relations, and international relations in such journals as *Asian Survey*, *Asian Perspective*, *Journal of Democracy*, *Journal of Contemporary China*, the *China Quarterly*, and so on. His latest books include *Challenges to Chinese Foreign Policy: Diplomacy, Globalization and the Next World Power* (2009); *30 Years of Development in Chinese Social Sciences and Humanities* (2008); *Chinese Foreign Policy Making: Societal Forces in Chinese American Policy Making* (coedited, 2005); *Bush's Dilemma: Experts on the Possible Trend of American Foreign Policy* (2005); *Power of the Moment: American and the World after 9/11* (coauthored, 2002), and *White House China Decision* (2002). He is a regular contributor to *China Newsweek*, *Global Times*, and *Nanfeng Chuang* in China, and is chief editor of the series "Focusing Sino-American Relations" under the auspices of the Xinhua Press in Beijing.

Harry Harding is dean of the Frank Batten School of Leadership and Public Policy at the University of Virginia. His previous positions include faculty appointments at Swarthmore College (1970–1971) and Stanford University (1971–1983), senior fellow in the Foreign Policy Studies Program at the Brookings Institution (1983–1994), dean of the Elliott School of International Affairs at The George Washington University (1995–2005), director of research and analysis at Eurasia Group (2005–2007), university professor of international affairs at George Washington University (2005–2009), and visiting professor of politics and public administration at the University of Hong Kong (2009). A specialist on Asia, his major publications include *The India-China Relationship: What the United States Needs to Know* (coedited with Francine Frankel, 2004); *A Fragile Relationship: The United States and China Since 1972* (1992), *Sino-American Relations, 1945–1955: A Joint Reassessment of a Critical Debate* (coedited with Yuan Ming, 1989), *China's Second Revolution: Reform After Mao* (1987), *China's Foreign Relations in the 1980s* (editor, 1984), and *Organizing China: The Problem of Bureaucracy, 1949–1976* (1981).

Morton Holbrook III is professor at United International College (UIC) in Zhuhai, China. Holbrook was a career U.S. diplomat for thirty-two years prior to coming to UIC in 2007, with assignments to the U.S. Embassy in Beijing, the U.S. Consulate in Shenyang, the former U.S. Embassy in Taipei, and the Office of Chinese Affairs in the State Department in Washington, DC. Other diplomatic assignments included the U.S. Embassy in Tokyo, the U.S. Embassy in Manila, and the U.S. Mission to the Organization for Economic Cooperation and Development (OECD) in Paris. Mr. Holbrook also previously practiced law in Washington, DC, and served as an attorney adviser in the U.S. State Department's Legal Adviser's Office.

Keelian Huang has been serving as a visiting research fellow at the University of Macao since 2008, while working as a project consultant for the Centro de Estudos Estrategicos para o Desesvolvimento Sustentaavel [CEEDS]. He has focused on mid- and long-term development strategy of the MSAR. Currently, he is also working on revising his papers written since the 1960s on China's modernization process, with special references to "one country, two systems" and the emergence of the so-called Chinese paradigm.

Zhang Lili is a special expert with the Ministry of Foreign Affairs of the People's Republic of China (appointed by department-level officials), as well as board member of China Association of Asia-Africa Development and Communications and the Association of National History of China, and an academic board member of China Foreign Affairs University. Lili served as dean of the Department of Diplomacy (2004–2007), and is an editing committee member for the book series "Diplomacy." He is an adviser for MA candidates majoring in contemporary Chinese foreign affairs and in diplomacy, and chief research fellow at the China Academy of Social Sciences for

"Forum on Strategy and Peace in East Asia," as well as guest professor at the Beijing Municipal Institute of Socialist Studies.

Sixin Sheng is a PhD candidate at the School of Organization and Management, University of New South Wales in Sydney. Having a strong belief in interdisciplinary approaches, he is mainly interested in organization studies, covering topics about comparative political economy, corporate governance, and organizational decision-making. Sixin has published in the *Copenhagen Journal of Asian Studies*, *Journal of Social Theory*, *Chinese Journal of Sociology*, and *Asian Journal of Social Science*. As the first translator, he has translated a sociological book from English to Chinese. He has also coedited a special memorial issue on Tan Kah Kee for Tan Kah Kee Foundation. In addition, his commentaries on current affairs have appeared on *Lianhe Zaobao*, a Singapore-based Chinese newspaper.

Zhang Shuguang, PhD, is distinguished visiting professor at Shanghai International Studies University, Shanghai, China, and professor of American international relations at the University of Maryland, College Park. Professor Zhang is also the author of *Deterrence and Strategic Culture: Chinese-American Confrontations, 1949–58* (1992), *Mao's Military Romanticism: China and the Korean War, 1950–53* (1994), and *Economic Cold War: America's Embargo against China and The Sino-Soviet Alliance, 1949–1963* (2001). He coedited with Jian Chen the book *Chinese Communist Foreign Policy and the Cold War in Asia, 1944–1950: Documentary Evidence* (1996). In 1990–1991, Zhang was an Olin Foundation postdoctoral fellow in international security at Yale University. He received a senior Norwegian Nobel Institute fellowship in international studies for the spring of 1995.

Iong Hoi Sun is PhD candidate of international relations at the University of Macao. Her research focuses on Macao and international organizations.

Paul A. Van Dyke is associate professor of history at the University of Macao, and author of *The Canton Trade: Life and Enterprise on the China Coast, 1700–1845* (2005). He has spent many years researching different aspects of life, trade, and societies in the Pearl River Delta, and has published numerous articles on those subjects. He is presently writing new histories of the Chinese merchant families.

Jianwei Wang received his BA and MA in international politics from Fudan University in Shanghai and his PhD in political science from the University of Michigan. He is the Eugene Katz Letter and Science Distinguished Professor at the Department of Political Science, University of Wisconsin–Stevens Point. Concurrently he is associate fellow of Asian society, guest professor at Fudan University, and senior associate of Shanghai Association of American Studies and Shanghai Center for RimPac Strategic and International Studies. His teaching and research interests focus on Asia politics and security affairs, Chinese politics and foreign policy, Sino-American relations, Sino-Japanese relations, UN peacekeeping operations, and American politics and foreign policy. He has published extensively in these areas, including a major work on U.S.-China relations: *Limited Adversaries: Sino-American Mutual Images in the Post-Cold War Era.*

C. X. George Wei is professor and chair of the Department of History at the University of Macao, and "guest professor" of the Institute of History Research of the Shanghai Academy of Social Science, Shanghai, China. He earned PhD in history from Washington University, St. Louis, Missouri, and also taught at Susquehanna University, Pennsylvania; Walla Walla College, Washington; and the University of Toledo, Ohio. He is coeditor of *Challenges to Chinese Foreign Policy* (2009), *Exploring Nationalisms of China: Themes and Conflicts* (2002), and *Chinese Nationalism in Perspective: Historical and Recent Cases* (2001), as well as author of *Sino-American Economic Relations, 1944–1949* (1997) and numerous articles both in English and Chinese.

Hu Weixing is associate professor of political science at the University of Hong Kong. He received his undergraduate degree in international politics from Peking University, an MA in international relations from the Johns Hopkins University SAIS, and a PhD in political science from University of Maryland, College Park. Dr. Hu was a John M. Olin Fellow in National Security Studies at Harvard University in 1991–1992 and an IGCC Postdoctoral Fellow at University of California, San Diego, in 1992–1993. Dr. Hu has taught and held research positions at University of California, San Diego, Monterey Institute of International Studies, the University of Detroit, University of Georgia, the Brookings Institution, and the Uppsala University in Sweden. His teaching and research interests include East Asian international relations, China's foreign relations, Asian regionalism and institution building, and cross-strait relations. He has published widely on Chinese foreign policy, international security, East Asian regionalism, and cross-strait relations. His latest book (coauthored) is *Building a Neighborly Community: Post–Cold War China, Japan, and Southeast Asia* (2007).

Wang Wuyi holds a PhD in economics and is professor of economics at Macao Polytechnic Institute. He is an internationally known gaming economist, and productive researcher and publisher.

Ding Xinghao is president of Shanghai Institute of American Studies. He is concurrently director of Institute of International Economy and Trade, Shanghai University of Foreign Trade. Professor Ding has had extensive interactions with U.S. foreign policy communities through various exchange programs over the years, including visiting scholarships at the Brookings Institution in 1981; the School of Advanced International Studies (SAIS) of Johns Hopkins University from 1984 to 1985; the Institute of International Studies of University of California, Berkeley, in 1988; the Institute of East Asian Studies of University of California at Berkeley in 1990; and the Brookings Institution again in 1991. His writings on American domestic and foreign policies, Sino-U.S. relations, U.S. relations with the former Soviet Union, and the China–U.S.–Japan triangle have been published both in China and abroad.

Hou Ying is a doctoral candidate in international relations at the University of Macao. She obtained her bachelor's degree in French language and literature from Nanjing University in 2001 and a master's degree in international relations from Fudan University in 2004. She has published articles on international relations theory, Chinese foreign relations, and China's information industry as well as Macao–U.S. and Macao–European Union relations. Her dissertation focuses on the role of media as a societal force on Chinese foreign policy-making.

www.ingramcontent.com/pod-product-compliance
Ingram Content Group UK Ltd.
Pitfield, Milton Keynes, MK11 3LW, UK
UKHW012035150926
475560UK00001B/16

9 780739 143674